Decolonizing Knowledge

Decolonizing Knowledge

Looking Back, Moving Forward

Edited by Radha D'Souza and Sunera Thobani

BLOOMSBURY ACADEMIC
NEW YORK • LONDON • OXFORD • NEW DELHI • SYDNEY

BLOOMSBURY ACADEMIC

Bloomsbury Publishing Inc, 1385 Broadway, New York, NY 10018, USA
Bloomsbury Publishing Plc, 50 Bedford Square, London, WC1B 3DP, UK
Bloomsbury Publishing Ireland, 29 Earlsfort Terrace, Dublin 2, D02 AY28, Ireland

BLOOMSBURY, BLOOMSBURY ACADEMIC and the Diana logo are trademarks of
Bloomsbury Publishing Plc

First published in the United States of America 2025

Copyright © 2025 Radha D'Souza and Sunera Thobani

Each chapter © Contributors

For legal purposes the Preface on p. x and the acknowledgement paragraphs on pp. xi–xii constitute an extension of this copyright page.

Cover design by Daniel Benneworth-Gray
Cover image: Sankofa bird symbol

All rights reserved. No part of this publication may be: i) reproduced or transmitted in any form, electronic or mechanical, including photocopying, recording or by means of any information storage or retrieval system without prior permission in writing from the publishers; or ii) used or reproduced in any way for the training, development or operation of artificial intelligence (AI) technologies, including generative AI technologies. The rights holders expressly reserve this publication from the text and data mining exception as per Article 4(3) of the Digital Single Market Directive (EU) 2019/790.

Bloomsbury Publishing Inc does not have any control over, or responsibility for, any third-party websites referred to or in this book. All internet addresses given in this book were correct at the time of going to press. The author and publisher regret any inconvenience caused if addresses have changed or sites have ceased to exist, but can accept no responsibility for any such changes.

A catalogue record for this book is available from the British Library.

A catalog record for this book is available from the Library of Congress.

ISBN: PB: 979-8-7651-2545-8
HB: 979-8-7651-2546-5
ePDF: 979-8-7651-2548-9
eBook: 979-8-7651-2547-2

Typeset by Deanta Global Publishing Services, Chennai, India
Printed and bound in Great Britain

For product safety related questions contact productsafety@bloomsbury.com.

To find out more about our authors and books visit www.bloomsbury.com
and sign up for our newsletters.

In memory of Aziz Choudry

Contents

Notes on contributors		viii
Preface		x
1	Introduction *Radha D'Souza and Sunera Thobani*	1
2	Decolonizing knowledge: Science, scientists and science education *Radha D'Souza*	27
3	Decolonization, feminist politics and the 'Muslim woman's question': Reading Fanon in the context of the Afghan and Gaza wars *Sunera Thobani*	55
4	On ethnographic refusal: Indigeneity, 'voice' and colonial citizenship *Audra Simpson*	81
5	Fire: The decolonial pedagogy of subversion in Césaire and Djonga *Angelica de Freitas e Silva*	101
6	Class and struggle: Cabral, Rodney and the complexities of culture in Africa *David Austin*	125
7	The politics and place of Rajani Palme Dutt *Tanroop Sandhu*	137
8	Labour super-exploitation, Black liberation and communist thought *Andrew Higginbottom*	163
9	Before intersectionality: Difference, exploitation and emancipation in Ruy Mauro Marini, Walter Rodney and Andaiye *Amanda Latimer*	189
10	From statehood to democratic confederalism: Decolonization and Abdullah Öcalan's solution to the Kurdish question *Behnam Amini*	213
11	Reflecting on coloniality of power, colonial violence and decolonization through the University of Rojava *Jan Yasin Sunca*	235
Index		259

Notes on contributors

Behnam Amini is a PhD candidate in the Graduate Programme of Social and Political Thought at York University, Toronto, Canada. His research interests include democratic theory, colonialism and decolonization, critical race theory, the Kurdish question, state theory and Iranian modern politics and history.

David Austin teaches in the Humanities, Philosophy, and Religion Department at John Abbott College and in the McGill Institute for the Study of Canada. His writing engages the work of C. L. R. James, Frantz Fanon, Sylvia Wynter, Hannah Arendt, Walter Rodney and Linton Kwesi Johnson in relation to politics, poetry and social movements. A former youth worker and community organizer, he has also produced radio documentaries for the Canadian Broadcasting Corporation's Ideas on C. L. R. James and Frantz Fanon.

Radha D'Souza is Professor of Law, Development and Conflict Studies at the University of Westminster. She is a lawyer, social justice activist, writer and critic. Her inter and transdisciplinary research straddles legal studies, development studies, history, comparative philosophy, resource conflicts and geography from Third World perspectives.

Angelica de Freitas e Silva's research interests include climate justice, global and social justice, decolonial approaches, social movements and resource conflicts in the Global South. She has a background as a construction lawyer in Brazil and held the post of Senior Lecturer at the University of Westminster Business School from 2016 to 2022. She is currently Project Manager and International Fundraising Consultant at AIC, a Brazilian civil society organization for third-sector sustainability.

Andrew Higginbottom is a retired associate professor at Kingston University, London. He gives online classes on the three volumes of Marx's *Capital* and is active in solidarity with movements fighting imperialism.

Amanda Latimer is Senior Lecturer in Politics at Kingston University, UK, and a doctoral candidate in social anthropology at York University, Canada. Her research examines workers' opposition to the neoliberal crisis of work and free trade agreements in Brazil.

Tanroop Sandhu is a PhD candidate studying the interconnections between British and Indian communism in the interwar period. Tanroop holds a BA in History and an MA in the Tri-University History Programme from the University of Waterloo.

Audra Simpson is Professor at Columbia University and a political anthropologist whose work is focused on contextualizing the force and consequences of governance through time, space and bodies. Her research and writing is rooted within Indigenous polities in the United States and Canada and crosses the fields of anthropology, Indigenous studies, American and Canadian studies and gender and sexuality studies as well as politics.

Jan Yasin Sunca teaches at the Department of Political Science at Université libre de Bruxelles. He is a co-founder and current main advisor of the Faculty of Political Science at the University of Rojava, where he teaches international relations. His work intersects international historical sociology, revolutionary politics, radical and decolonial political theory, and conflict analysis/transformation with a geographical focus on West Asia and Central America.

Sunera Thobani is Distinguished Professor in the Department of Asian Studies at the University of British Columbia and Fellow of the Royal Society of Canada. Her scholarship focuses on critical race, postcolonial, diasporic and feminist theory and practice, colonialism, globalization, citizenship and migration, Muslim women, media and the war on terror, and South Asian women's and sexuality studies.

Preface

The idea for this book emerged from the *Third World in Theory* reading group that the Law, Development and Conflict Research Group (LDC) at the University of Westminster (chaired by D'Souza) organized in 2019. The reading group, which aims to understand the theoretical lenses through which the Third World is understood, has organized thematic reading groups on and off since 2009 and, in 2019, decided to focus on 'decolonization' as the theme. Since the #RhodesMustFall campaign in 2015, the question of why the curriculum was so white became a pressing issue. For many Black, Asian and Ethnic Minority (BAME) academics in the UK who, for decades, had taught about decolonizing thought and practice, had sensitized students to the pain of colonialism in old and new forms and had introduced them to the nuances of contemporary racism, the students' demands were an affirmation of their work.

The atmosphere in UK universities began to feel different, however, when one university after another began to 'mainstream' decolonization in their curriculum. It felt strange to hear vice chancellors, higher education bodies and others in authority canvassing for 'decolonization'. Mainstreaming decolonization took the form of revising reading lists for a more 'inclusive' curriculum. It was a puzzling moment for many BAME teachers when they too, like the others, were invited to develop 'inclusive' curriculum (which they had been doing for decades) even as non-BAME colleagues assumed leadership roles in teaching and learning committees to mainstream the decolonization agenda. Before long 'decolonization' became a part of the 'diversity and inclusion' agendas of UK universities. The LDC Research Group responded to these developments in the UK academia by asking a very basic question: what does decolonization mean?

The LDC Research Group decided to do a little studying themselves by reconvening the *Third World in Theory* reading group to revisit how previous generations of anti-colonial thinkers understood and conceptualized 'decolonization'. As the group revisited Fanon, Césaire, Sankara, Mariátegui and other anti-colonial thinkers, it became apparent that the influential anti-colonial thinkers of the twentieth century were direct participants in the anti-colonial struggles that were around them. For them, decolonization was about addressing the theoretical questions that the anti-colonial movements threw up; it was about understanding the nature of the colonial beast, how it walked and talked and behaved, an understanding that would inform their political interventions. What kind of theoretical and practical problems were teachers being invited to address by the universities in the decolonization that was unfolding before us? There was a sense that it was important to look back to move forward.

In early 2022, Thobani was invited to join as co-editor for the book to include North American debates on decolonization and the university. The inclusion of North American perspectives expanded discussion of the complexities of decolonization in the settler societies of North America, across Euro-America more generally, and in the Third World. This also raised vital questions about the nature of US imperialism and its support for particular nationalist movements in the war on terror. The editors consider it important to flag the different perspectives in these sites.

In the first section of the Introduction, D'Souza takes a global and internationalist approach to decolonization, while in the second section Thobani addresses the complexities of 'theorizing decolonization', how this term is now taken up in Western universities and the uses to which the term is put to work in its newfound institutional success. The chapters of this book straddle multiple theoretical and ideological approaches, from Critical Race Theory and decolonization thought to more conventional readings of Third World Marxist approaches. The chapters highlight how the very meaning of terms like 'revolution' is understood in different sites.

Westminster Law School's support for this project has been critical to its success. Besides hospitality, the Law School provided generous funding to engage publishing services. We are especially grateful to Jayashree Anand and Prathima Rajan from Sanam Solutions for their patience with the project and for working under pressure in its final phase. We could not have delivered the book on time without their support. Angelica de Freitas e Silva, as coordinator of the LDC Research Group, did many of those unseen tasks that must be done to keep a year-long reading group going. We are thankful for Angelica's commitment and the energy she brought to LDC's work. Thanks are due to Leuphana Institute of Advanced Studies in Leuphana University of Lüneburg, where D'Souza was Senior Research Fellow, for funding her travel to attend the American Studies Association conference in November 2023 where the editors organized a panel for the book project.

We thank all the contributors to this book. There are many who attended the study group but did/could not contribute to this volume for various reasons.

We value their contributions to the discussions and thank them for this. Some contributors were not part of the study group or the subsequent workshops. We thank them too for their contributions. Thanks to Jan Yasin Sunca, who stepped in at short notice to fill in for other comrades. David Austin's and Audra Simpson's chapters are republished from previous publications; we thank them both for their generosity. We also thank Firoze Manji, Daraja Press and the editors of *Junctures* for granting us permission to republish the two articles. Last but not least, our thanks to Amy Martin and Hali Han from Bloomsbury; not only did they welcome this project but they have been immeasurably helpful in navigating the publication process smoothly and speedily. Our deep gratitude to both and to the rest of the Bloomsbury team.

Although decolonizing curriculum and academia was the point of departure and inspiration for this volume, the contributors go beyond academia in their chapters. We hope the volume will contribute to forwarding the decolonization agenda in theory and practice as colonialism and imperialism continue to pillage and plunder natures and communities around the world.

1

Introduction

Radha D'Souza and Sunera Thobani

Education, society and knowledge:
The global context for decolonization
Radha D'Souza

In 2015, South African students stirred up academia around the world when they rallied around the slogan '#RhodesMustFall'. Their protests highlighted institutional racism in universities, the continued legacies of apartheid in their curriculum long after the Bantu Education Act of 1953 and the 'rainbow constitution' of 1991. In the South African context, the '#RhodesMustFall' campaign quickly expanded to the '#FeesMustFall' campaign to become one of the most important student protest movements of the decade. The #FeesMustFall campaign was a natural extension in a social and historical context where structural poverty in society and structural racism in universities were inseparably entwined. Like in South Africa, in India too, student protests by Dalit and Adivasi students and marginalized nationalities like the Kashmiris and Manipuris for example, across campuses from 2016 to 2018, explicitly linked the neoliberalization of education to wider historical, and socio-economic deprivations (Vijayan 2016; Gupta and Chattarji 2019; Thapliyal 2021).

Echoes of the '#RhodesMustFall' campaign reverberated in the august campuses of Oxford University in the UK and universities elsewhere in the Anglo-American world. In the UK too fees had trebled since 2012. The Liberal Democrats, who had long advocated a return to free university education, dropped their promise after they joined the Conservative Party in a coalition government from 2010 to 2015. Indeed, in the 2017 general elections, university tuition fees was an important issue. However, the #RhodesMustFall campaign in the UK did not expand into UK's own '#FeesMustFall' campaign in a comparable way. This, notwithstanding the fact that racialized students in UK universities also face societal marginalization and structural economic deprivation (Kenway and Palmer 2007).

In the United States too, student debt rose to levels never seen before, rising from US$ 15,000 per student in academic year 2010–11 to US$ 22,700 in 2020–21. In the United States, neoliberal reforms and cuts to higher education funding by the states resulted in student debt skyrocketing to US$ 1.6 trillion, roughly the size of Brazilian or Australian economies. Standing at 7.2 per cent of the GDP, student debt became a national *economic* problem about 'household debt' in the state's ledger books and a political football in federal/state and Democrat/Republican politics. African American students carried a disproportionate 30 per cent of the debts (Koeze and Russell 2022). The federal government introduced the loan 'forgiveness' scheme, which the Republican states challenged successfully in *Biden v Nebraska* (Oladipo 2023). Outside the campuses, police violence against African Americans continued to rise and George Floyd's anguished cry 'I can't breathe' became the slogan for a resurgent Black Lives Matter movement. There were no parallel calls for an American variant of the '#loansmustfall' movement, such as debt forgiveness as extensions of affirmative action policies in education, for example, that joined with the movements against police repression. The UK and US stories are likely to resonate with other Anglo-American states where higher education remains deeply entangled in societal racism, racialized poverty and limited visibility of racialized students.

Problematic categorizations like 'minority–majority' based on numbers (Mamdani 2020) to explain these differences conceal the hiatus between the racialized political economies in the Anglo-American capitalist centres and the struggles by students over education, compared to the South African, Indian and other students in the Third World, where the nexus between race/ethnicity and political economy is more apparent in the neocolonial contexts of their countries. This hiatus, in turn, informs the different trajectories of decolonization in theories and practices in the education sector and the wider society in the two contexts.

Over the decades, at least since the 1970s, 1980s and 1990s, critical research, teaching and learning about race, racism and race relations has made its way into Anglo-American institutions of higher education, establishing itself within specialist institutes and departments. By 2005, public universities in Philadelphia, New York and New Jersey and elsewhere had introduced mandatory teaching of Black histories (Morgan 2024). The introduction of critical race and ethnic studies in the North American universities, in turn, was a spin-off from student protests inspired by Black and indigenous movements in society such as the Black Panther Party, the anti-Vietnam War protests, the Civil Rights movements and the indigenous struggles for self-determination, land and dignity (Morgan 2024). In the UK too, marginalization of Black, Asian and ethnic minority communities, who later came to be known as BAME, spilt over in a spate of race riots in the 1970s, 1980s and 1990s and inspired academics to introduce critical research, teaching and learning about race and ethnic relations in society (Henriques and Abushouk 2018). There were differences in the approaches and orientations within Anglo-American contexts.

In the UK, race and ethnic studies found incubating spaces within the broader field of 'Cultural Studies' in institutions such as the Centre for Contemporary Cultural Studies, Birmingham University. The birth of so-called cultural Marxism associated with the New Left in the post-war era became influential within 'Cultural Studies' as a disciplinary field. Consequently, critical race and ethnic studies, nurtured within the wider Cultural Studies and New Left approaches in the UK context, brought with it an emphasis on Marxism, race and class intersections, and social justice, including economic and racial justice. In North America, in contrast, race and ethnic studies were rooted in North American histories of slavery, indigenous land confiscations and migrations. There, race and ethnic studies tended to pivot to identity issues and identity politics. Whatever their points of departures, Anglo-American knowledge exchanges fed off each other in ways that need not concern us here.

What does concern us here is that the focus of structural critique of race and ethnicity and its linkages to political economy within Anglo-American academia remained inward looking, that is, focused on racism and racial oppression *within* the capitalist Anglo-American states. Their critique turned on capitalism and the production of racialized social relations, in other words on racialized capitalism (Robinson and Kelley 2000; Jenkins and Leroy 2021). This inward focus on identity and the embeddedness of race and ethnicity within the structures of state and capitalism naturally led to calls for equality and non-discrimination within the legal and constitutional frameworks of Anglo-American states. As Angela Harris notes, '[In] the middle between assimilation and expulsion, color blindness and color hierarchy, stand proponents of a "multicultural America", one that seeks justice through recognition and redistribution along racial lines, yet also affirms solidarity in diversity. Whether such a society is possible remains to be seen' (Harris 2000).

This middle ground of 'multiculturalism' in the mainstream, the outcome of denial and the assertion of racial identities under capitalist political economies sought what may, as a shorthand, be called 'deracialization' of society *within* the constitutional order. In the Anglo-American context, unnoticed, the South African moment elided 'deracialization' into 'decolonization'.

It was different in the Third World. In the Third World, 'decolonization' had always been a popular emotive idea that had powered some of the most transformative national liberation struggles, especially during and after the First World War. Decolonization was inextricably entwined with ideas of self-rule, self-governance and self-determination. In the Third World, decolonization of society, political-economy and education *preceded* identitarian theories and politics. Decolonization focused *outwards* against Anglo-American colonialism and imperialism, that is, the external aspect of capitalism (D'Souza 2012). It was the 'divide and rule' policies under colonial governance, anti-colonial leaders argued, that sowed seeds of racial, religious and national discord between people (D'Souza 2020). Therefore, there was nothing essentialist or inevitable about racial and ethnic differences. If the imperialists had arbitrarily, and for political expediency, cobbled together diverse nations, religions, peoples, races and ethnicities under a centralized colonial state structure, anti-colonial movements sought to build a broad-based unity of diverse races, ethnicities, religions and nationalities against colonial rule (D'Souza 2013, 2020).

In the so-called New World Order established after the end of Second World War, the Newly Independent States (NIS) emerged as a political force on the international stage turning their energies to decolonize structures of global economic and political power which remained in the hands of imperialist states. Internationally, decolonization within the United Nations, whether that be within economic organizations such as the Economic and Social Council (ECOSOC) or cultural ones like the UNESCO, provided new opportunities for Third World intellectuals to decolonize structures of power and knowledge. These moments were just that: opportunities. Within the ECOSOC, the attempts to decolonize the NIS came to be articulated in economics as Dependency theories, Unequal Trade theories and in politics as reformulations of sovereignty to include natural resources and self-governance for indigenous peoples. These efforts led to demands for the New International Economic Order (NIEO), recognition of the principle of sovereignty over natural resources and greater autonomy for indigenous peoples within nation states. On the cultural front, the push for 'de-Europeanization' of history nearly unravelled UNESCO's *History of*

Mankind project with NIS challenging 'Eurocentric' histories. By the time the *History of Mankind* project entered its sixth volume, it had imploded, and the critique of the Eurocentric 'history of mankind' had splintered into Afrocentric and Asiacentric histories of peoples (Betts 2015).

NIS saw political independence as the first step to economic and cultural independence. For many Third World academics, political independence of their country from old colonial rule was an opportunity to decolonize education in the service of their peoples (see D'Souza's chapter in this volume). The ink had barely dried on their independence agreements, and the thinkers and practitioners of decolonization were already warning their people about new avatars of imperialism after the Second World War. Political leaders like Allende, Sukarno, Lumumba and a galaxy of others voiced concerns about the limits to their political independence and the continued economic and military domination of imperial powers. Kwame Nkrumah coined the phrase 'neocolonialism' to describe a new type of colonialism that had emerged after the end of the Second World War (Nkrumah 1968). Even as academics in the Third World were figuring out ways to decolonize curriculum and education in their newly independent countries, one by one the heroes of anti-colonial struggles, including Allende, Sukarno and Lumumba, were 'taken out' by Western powers, notably the Central Intelligence Agency (CIA) of the United States. In state after Third World state, the hard-fought independence was rolled back either by military force or by neutralizing political leaders or under economic duress.

Neocolonialism produced new tensions within the UN and its organs and agencies and new demands to extend and apply decolonization to economic and legal practices in the international constitutional order under the UN Charter. In the early years, decolonization in the Third World was always about independence from imperialism and colonialism in whatever form. Externally, decolonization was about dismantling international structures of economic, political and military power and ideological power of colonial knowledge. Internally, within the formally independent states, decolonization was about strengthening the alliances between diverse racial, religious, ethnic and national groups forged during the anti-colonial struggles to build a new society. These alliances relied on a range of ideological orientations – the Chinese four class alliance or the Indonesian *Pancasila* or the Indian 'unity-in-diversity' or the Tanzanian *Ujamaa*. This is not to overlook or understate the impact of the colonial divide-and-rule politics in many parts of the world that manipulated identitarian differences and resulted in violent partitions, balkanization and civil conflicts. If anything, those conflicts highlighted to the NIS the perils of identitarian politics and its dangers for the decolonization project at hand. With the liquidation of the leadership of the anti-colonial struggles after formal independence, imperial powers after the end of Second World War installed leaders, often forcibly through military coups, that were more favourable to the new imperial power alliances such as the G7 or NATO. With independence rolled back, nascent efforts to decolonize education too was rolled back (see D'Souza's chapter in this volume).

Instead, throughout the 1970s, 1980s and 1990s bilateral and multilateral aid policies in the imperial centres, together with influential private organizations like Ford and Fulbright foundations, targeted education in the Third World as a key developmental goal (Altbach 1971). Justified as necessary to combat communism, these educational policies aimed at effacing the very idea of education as a vehicle for decolonization in the NIS. With the rise of neoliberalism, influential thinkers, especially in the United States, advocated the uses of 'soft-power' in the neoliberalization of the Third World, the major component of which was education (Nye 2004).

In a global context where imperial powers took concerted political, economic and cultural steps to recolonize education and to devalue its anti-colonial histories, theories and practices, the influence of theoretical and pedagogical orientations of critical race and ethnicity studies introduced in the Anglo-American universities had very different effects within the politico-cultural ecologies of the Third World. As Arif Dirlik ([1998] 2018) points out, new opportunities opened up for a new generation of Third World intellectuals within Anglo-American universities under the bilateral and multilateral educational aid and 'soft-power' policies of imperial states. The new generation of Third World academics, arriving in the Anglo-American academia during the 1970s, 1980 and 1990s, came to see their own societies through the theoretical prisms developed in the Anglo-American universities at the time. Those lenses developed in very different economic, political, historical and cultural contexts distorted questions of race, ethnicity and nationality in the Third World (Dirlik [1998] 2018). In the ethnically and racially diverse Third World, extending identitarian theoretical frameworks developed in Anglo-American contexts had the effect of disengaging knowledge of those issues from the histories of the freedom struggles and the numerous political experiments that followed to build on the anti-imperialist alliances forged during the anti-colonial struggles (D'Souza 2020). More importantly, it had the effect of disengaging those questions from the unities in diversities that characterized pre-colonial societies

(D'Souza 2014, 2018a). The ideological inspirations for such experiments drawing on their own ancient and recent pasts such as Indonesia's *Pancasila* or India's 'unity in diversity', or China's four class alliance, or Tanzania's *Ujamaa* or the *Bandung* and Non-alignment ideals came to be rolled back and devalued. Instead, new geographies of knowledge emerged where theories developed in Ango-American contexts became the lens through which the Third World came to be understood (Raju 2006; D'Souza 2018a). Third World academics found themselves under '"methodological and notional" siege' in the words of Ranjan Ghosh (2006: 25) writing about Indian academics working in India.

The identitarian theories and politics that percolated to the Third World turned research, teaching and learning about race, ethnicity and nationality away from global imperialism and the nascent attempts to decolonize education. Instead, mimicking their counterparts in the Anglo-American states, Third World academics too turned their attention *inwards* to their own states and national constitutional orders and to ideas of human rights, equality and non-discrimination instead of the earlier decolonization, self-determination, self-rule, self-governance and, one may add, self-rediscovery as a component of decolonization after political independence (Rakowski 1993; Ghosh 2006; Raju 2006; D'Souza 2014; Vijayan 2016; Baquer et al. [1979] 2019; Uberoi 2019). This, at a time when the Third World states were themselves beleaguered by the international economic policies and debts imposed by international economic organizations such as the World Bank and the International Monetary Fund and the militarism of Anglo-American powers throughout the so-called Cold War.

Before long, many states in the Third World were rife with conflicts between diverse racial, ethnic and nationality groups, each making claims against their states for human rights, equality and non-discrimination within the Third World state's post-independence constitutional frameworks. Even as external pressures to open up the economy to transnational corporations, liberalize the economy and dismantle nascent public sector enterprises increased the vulnerabilities of Third World states, internal demands for human, minority and nationality rights also increased. With the establishment of the National Endowment for Democracy in the United States in the 1970s supported by other Anglo-American and European powers, 'democracy promotion' became the official foreign policy instrument of imperial powers. Democracy promotion opened the international relations spaces to manipulation of the civil/sectarian conflicts to further pressurize Third World states (D'Souza 2018b). The pressures included military interventions in the name of 'humanitarian intervention' and geopolitical insecurity ostensibly caused by 'failed states' (Bricmont 2007; Mamdani 2009; Clancy 2011; Davidson 2012; D'Souza 2020). Decolonization as an ideal and a national goal vanished from politics and from educational institutions. In the Third World, decolonization elided with 'deracialization' (used as a shorthand here for a wide variety of identitarian conflicts) within a liberal constitutional framework.

Notwithstanding the different, indeed opposite, political and historical trajectories of developments in Anglo-American and Third World societies, the convergence of theories and practices of decolonization and deracialization rendered both concepts opaque. Regardless, history has ways of resurfacing at critical moments. The differences in the trajectories of the development of theories and concepts of racial and ethnic discrimination in the Anglo-American centres of capitalism and the (neo)colonial Third World played out very differently in the way politics and economics of race, ethnicity and colonial histories intersected in the South African, Indian and the Anglo-American contexts.

These differences led some of us to ask a basic question: what does 'decolonization' mean?

As the word buzzed within campuses, as many Anglo-American educational institutions sought to 'mainstream' the idea of 'decolonization' by integrating it into educational policies, we were troubled by the fact that decolonization had become the justification for fundamentalist Far Right authoritarian regimes in some Third World states to suppress, in the name of nation-building, claims by religious, racial and ethnic minorities for greater autonomy and freedom (Menon 2022; Singh 2023). Was the 'decolonization' happening in the Anglo-American universities the same as the 'decolonization' happening in universities in countries like India, Pakistan, Iran, Malaysia or Afghanistan? We found ourselves asking: is the current movement to decolonize curriculum and education in Anglo-American universities the same as the decolonization that once inspired anti-colonial struggles? What is the relationship of decolonization of education in the Anglo-American universities and decolonization from imperial domination globally? What is the connection between decolonization in the Anglo-American context and decolonization in the Third World context, and what ought to be that connection? Are capitalism and imperialism one and the same thing? If not, what are the differences and commonalities? This project was born from comparing notes and experiences, from conversations and observations during that moment when deracialization elided into decolonization in Anglo-American academia. These conversations produced a sense that to move forward it is important to look back at the road travelled.

The 'Third World in Theory' reading group that was organized by the Law, Development and Conflict Research Group (LDC) at University of Westminster and chaired by D'Souza decided to do a little studying themselves by returning to anti-colonial thinkers of previous generations. How did earlier generations of anti-colonial thinkers conceptualize decolonization? How do their thoughts on decolonization feed into contemporary ideas of decolonization, if at all? What are their legacies if there are any? Decolonizing academia presupposes engagement with theories as well as histories that inform the critique of colonialism and imperialism. How can academics and activists extend, adapt, update and modify the insights of anti-colonial thinkers of the past so that struggles against continued injustices of contemporary colonialism and imperialism in their new avatars can be renewed and rejuvenated?

As the group revisited canonical texts, Fanon, Cesaire, Sankara, Mariátegui and many others, many differences between decolonizing then and now became apparent. For a start, many aspects of the thoughts and works of the earlier generations were erased from memory. One big difference that stood out was that the anti-colonial thinkers of the past were direct participants in the anti-imperialist struggles that were everywhere around them. Another big difference was that for thinkers of the past decolonizing education was part of a wider political project to decolonize society. Furthermore, for them, society could be decolonized only by ending imperial domination as an objective reality in the world globally. Decolonization for the earlier generations of thinkers was about addressing the theoretical questions that the anti-colonial movements threw up; it was about understanding the nature of the colonial beast, how it walked and talked and behaved, an understanding that would inform their political interventions. What kind of theoretical and practical problems were teachers being invited to address within Anglo-American universities in the decolonization that was unfolding before us? And how did those questions relate to the wider movements against militarism, economic domination, civil wars and widespread poverty in the Third World? Do the initiatives to decolonize curriculum and universities underway in the Anglo-American universities have anything to do at all with the movements against imperialism and neocolonialism in the Third World? Indeed, were they even obliged to address or, at the least, factor in questions of neocolonialism and imperialism?

Framing the agenda as decolonizing curriculum and universities misdirects the remedial actions and political responses. It confines the problem to existing educational institutions, including existing disciplinary silos, and presents the solution as inclusion of diverse teaching materials and equal career opportunities for academics of colour. It misses the fact that decolonizing curriculum presupposes decolonizing *knowledge itself*, which is a larger epistemological programme, and more importantly, an epistemological programme that must, necessarily, be anchored to wider societal decolonization. It is about understanding the role that knowledge plays in the intimate interrelationships between the Anglo-American centres of capitalism and Third World neocolonialism. When we speak of epistemology and structures of knowledge, we mean 'modern' structures of knowledge and epistemology. Modernist knowledge systems in turn are an integral and inalienable part of capitalist–colonial modernity. Any epistemological programme to decolonize cannot remain indifferent to the structural and institutional contexts which form the conditions for decolonizing knowledge (D'Souza 2009).

There are increasing numbers of scholars who offer critical analyses of structures of modernist knowledge (Quijano 2007; Mignolo 2009; Grosfoguel 2013; Oladipo 2023). These critiques open important pathways to deconstruct modernist knowledge as a system and a condition for capitalist modernity. Their limitation however is that they 'reverse the gaze', a phrase that emerged in the 1990s and has become embedded in the methodologies and epistemologies of critique today. It is important to recognize that the gaze and reverse-gaze, while standing in opposition, nevertheless share the same epistemological underpinnings and semiotic structures of modernist knowledge (D'Souza 2021). 'Reversing the gaze' may be possible discursively, but without establishing the material preconditions for decolonized knowledge, decolonization at the discursive level could veer off in many political directions and appropriated for purposes that the discourse did not intend. Decolonizing knowledge requires much more than a deconstruction of modernist epistemologies. It was precisely the material conditions for decolonized knowledge that weighed heavily in the minds of the anti-colonial thinkers and their writings. What conditions then must be established so that knowledge can be decolonized in the service of human and non-human beings?

Institutionalizing 'decolonization/decoloniality': Context, issues, challenges
Sunera Thobani

Decolonization remains the most pressing of challenges in the twenty-first century. Certainly, the term itself is complex and contested. While 'decolonization' is commonly reduced to the transfer of legal and institutional power from colonial rulers to 'indigenously based formally sovereign, nation-states', decolonization has also been conceived of as 'a movement for moral justice and political solidarity against imperialism . . . [an] anti-imperialist political movement . . . an emancipatory ideology . . . to liberate the nation and humanity itself' (Duara 2003: 2). These latter iterations inspired the praxis of anti-colonial revolutionaries who envisioned the term to refer not only to 'national' sovereignty and self-determination for colonized peoples but also to the end of Western domination and the transcendence of the 'nation state', nationalism and capitalism through a 'new humanism' forged by the struggles, historical consciousness, knowledges, experiences and dignity of the wretched of the earth (Fanon 1963).

'Decolonization' is a term that presently enjoys unprecedented popularity in the Western university, where it is often conflated with the term 'decoloniality'. The manner in which both terms have been taken up in the institution – as in public debates and the politics of social movements – makes their meanings difficult to decipher, for these are neither transparent nor readily comprehensible. Within the university's administrative structure, 'decoloniality/decolonization' is taken up to expand the institution's techniques of inclusion and equity, which, as past experience has demonstrated, function to forestall the transformative objectives of anti-racism and anti-colonial politics, scholarship and movements. In public discussion, the terms 'decoloniality' and 'inclusion' are taken as public good in and of themselves within liberal multicultural quarters while coming under fierce attack from conservative factions and ultra-right political movements. In some social movements, these terms are advanced with little self-reflexivity as inherently progressive, often reduced to slogans and sentimentalized expressions of solidarity.

Although 'decoloniality' implies a relation to 'coloniality', the institutional absorption of the former does not engage with the meaning of the latter as defined by the anti-colonial thinkers who coined the term. This absorption thus elides the revolutionary politics these terms encode. 'Coloniality', building on the third worldist concept of decolonization, was advanced in the context of the Indigenous and anti-colonial politics of South/Latin American movements (Maldonado-Torres 2007; Quijano 2007; Mignolo 2011). Coloniality, as Quijano (2007) defined the term, refers to a mode of power that emerged in the European conquest of the Americas and has since shaped the global field. By fusing modernity and rationality in the process of colonizing most of the world's population, coloniality became a condition that was not reducible to direct European rule of the colonies. This modality of power remained ongoing in the post-independence period to reproduce Western domination through control over the planet's resources by a Euro-American minority and its ruling classes. Quijano's (2007) point is that even as direct colonial rule was confronted by anti-colonial movements during the mid-twentieth century, this form of control morphed into imperialist domination. The structure of colonial rationality that shapes this form of power remains ongoing through the codification of 'race', 'ethnicity' and 'nation' within which operate class relations. As Maldonado-Torres (2007: 243) argues, '[Coloniality] is maintained alive in books, in the criteria for academic performance, in cultural patterns, in common sense, in the self-image of peoples, in aspirations of self and so many other aspects of our modern experience. In a way, as modern subjects, we breathe coloniality all the time and every day'. Clearly, the institutional turn to the decolonial cannot be read as having any affinity whatsoever to the deep critique of the modality of power that shapes the racial-capitalism of the present. This section interrogates the contested meanings of decolonization/decoloniality and the conditions and struggles that have led to the enthusiastic adoption of these terms by the Western university – and beyond – in what I refer to as the institutional turn to the decolonial.

The institutional adoption of the terms 'decolonization' and 'decoloniality' occurred during the 'war on terror', which followed the 9/11 attacks that revealed the consequences of US foreign policy in the Middle East. The global war brought to the fore continuities between the US Empire, neoliberal globalization and earlier histories of colonialism; it also ignited anti-war and anti-Islamophobia movements which drew attention to these continuities in their public mobilizations and political debates (Asad 2003; Mamdani 2005). The global war also led anti-racist movements, including Black Lives Matter, to link the anti-Black racism and police violence that were the ongoing legacies of transatlantic slavery to the war's militarization and securitization (including police use of armoured vehicles used earlier in Iraq in the Ferguson Uprising, and the use of surveillance technologies in both the Afghan War and the United States to profile 'Muslim' Black and Brown bodies, see Thompson 2014). Indigenous activists also linked the war to settler colonialism by drawing connections between the massacres of the 'Indian Wars' in the United States and those in the Afghan War (Kanji 2021), as well as in the state's depiction of water protectors and land rights activists as 'terrorists' (Levin 2017). Recognition that the wars of the US Empire across the Third World, including the Middle East and South Asia, were rooted in long-standing forms of colonial violence was a theme common across these movements; all had their corelates in faculty and student scholarship and politics, albeit in marginalized spaces within the university.

Moreover, the war on terror drew attention to the imbrication of the university in the military-industrial complex and the diligence with which it served economic and state interests. The public sector funding cuts of the 1990s had restructured the institution so that it had become overly reliant on private donors who increasingly intervened in its inner workings, as well as on the lucrative market for international students who were central to the economy's growth strategy. These changes spurred the university's corporatization and centralization of its administrative power, processes now further strengthened by the institution's deeper integration into the military–corporate nexus advanced through the global war.

The destabilizing effects of the growing international momentum of anti-war and anti-racism movements – outside and inside the university – with their demands for an end to militarization and state violence, and for a more just order, began to elicit greater state and institutional attention by the second decade of the global war. This is the immediate context for the university's turn to 'the decolonial', but where these movements demanded an end to imperialist wars and to racist state violence, the university set about making changes to the curriculum and extending the diversification of the faculty, staff and student body. Every discipline, particularly in the social sciences and humanities, was now under pressure to take the lead in meeting these 'decolonial' needs of the moment.

Not surprisingly, publications critical of Western knowledge traditions found an unusually warm reception in the mainstream of the academic disciplines. In *Colonialism and Modern Social Theory*, for example, Bhambra and Holmwood (2021) argued that 'classical' modern social theory was Eurocentric and had, for the main, ignored the phenomenon of colonialism. Linking modernity to processes of Westernization, the authors made their case by revisiting the core ideas of canonical thinkers in the social sciences and humanities, from Hobbes, Hegel and Tocqueville to Marx, Weber and Durkheim. Bhambra and Holmwood (2021) illustrated their critique of social theory by drawing attention to the groundbreaking work of W. E. B. Du Bois, the African American sociologist, whose work on race and the construction of Blackness made significant contributions to the study of US state and nation formation, and to the development of sociology itself. As Bhambra and Holmwood (2021) pointedly noted, Du Bois's work was virtually unacknowledged in the field.

Although Bhambra and Holmwood's (2021) book focused on the discipline of sociology, its reception in the university brought to the fore long-standing debates about the persistence of Eurocentric frameworks in social–political theory, including that of the 'progressive' Frankfurt school (Bhambra 2021). Rejecting the idea that 'adding' colonialism to the mix of topics taken up by social theory would solve the problem of eurocentrism, Bhambra and Holmwood (2021) argued instead for interrogation of the 'five fictions' they identified as shaping this tradition's conceptual framework: (1) the state of nature and stages of social development; (2) the progressive nature of modern subjectivity; (3) the nation state; (4) class and the construct of 'formally' free labour; and (5) sociological reason.

Such critiques of the social sciences and the humanities soon became prolific, as did their robust arguments in support of decolonizing Western knowledge traditions (Joseph-Salisbury et al. 2020; Khoo 2021; Meghji 2021; Reiter 2021). In their review of the numerous critiques of political theory's implication in imperialist ideologies and practices, for example, Getachew and Mantena (2021: 360) noted that 'One potent rubric that draws together these various lines of revision is a shared interest in diagnosing the Eurocentric character of the field and offering remedies for its overcoming'. Such 'remedies' however, were rarely anchored in anti-colonial and anti-racist movement politics as had been the case in the mid-twentieth-century anti-colonial critiques of Eurocentrism. What was also notable about many of these new critiques was their lack of substantive engagement with the anti-colonial and anti-racist traditions well established in the interdisciplinary fields of Indigenous Studies, Critical Race Theory – including within the Black, Asian-American, LatinX and related sub-fields broadly conceived under the rubric of 'Ethnic Studies' – or even with Decolonization Studies, Cultural Studies and Postcolonial Studies, among other theoretical traditions that rose out of the revolutionary political upheavals and radical movements of the late 1960s/1970s.

The anti-colonial/anti-racist theoretical traditions thrown up by the movements of the 1960s were driven by contestation of the Eurocentrism and whiteness of the social sciences, of their investment in the political-economic order and of their 'race-blind' methodological approaches that reproduced global racial hierarchies. These theoretical advances were grounded in and built upon the intellectual traditions developed by the anti-colonial thinkers of the Third World revolution; they were also shaped by the political experience of the movements that followed: opposition to the Vietnam War, apartheid, US Empire abroad and its settler colonial, and anti-Black/Asian racisms in North America. Demands for reigning in corporate power, democratizing the state and institutions and ending imperialist militarization characterized these movements. The linkages they made between their fight for racial justice and their opposition to the post–Second World War political order that continued to subjugate the Third World to US-dominated Western imperialism kept alive the internationalism of the earlier anti-colonial movements.

The point to note is that recent scholarly critiques of the Eurocentrism of the academic disciplines are not, of course, as novel a phenomenon as one might be led to believe by the institutional turn to the decolonial. Take the example of Du Bois that was used in *Colonialism and Modern Social Theory*. Du Bois (1903) is certainly overlooked in the mainstream of academic disciplines, particularly jarringly so in the case of sociology, given his affiliation with the discipline. Yet Du Bois's (1903) work is foundational to Critical Race Studies, to Black/African American Studies, to the subfield of Black Sociology and to political critiques of the US Empire. Thus, even as recent texts critiquing Eurocentrism speak to the politics of the present and to the omissions in the disciplines they address, they stand – whether explicitly acknowledged or not – on the shoulders of much longer and deeper traditions of anti-colonial and anti-racist thought grounded in political opposition to the racial-capitalist order. These long-standing critiques, initially cultivated within movement politics as described above, were also advanced within the university where they struggled in marginalized spaces to transform the institution itself by interrogating its very purpose. Like their Third Worldist antecedents, the 1960s/1970s theoretical advances in the new interdisciplinary fields also began with exposing the violence enfolded into Western epistemological frameworks as these continued to organize the dehumanization of colonized peoples, the erasure of their cosmologies and contesting traditions of knowledge, and of their forms of being in the world.

Significantly, the Third Worldist critiques of Western power and knowledge advanced a collective revolutionary consciousness as they exposed the hypocrisy of the West's civilizing mission and its pretentions to democracy and the rule of law. This anti-colonial critique was also 'a mode of self-critique meant to diagnose and break the collective enthrallment with the West', as was pointed out by Getachew and Mantena (2021: 361). Fanon (1963), for example, rejected the cultural essentialization of 'nativism' as vociferously as he did the exalting of the West by native elites. Warning against the pitfalls of nationalism and the dangers of self-serving native elites derailing revolutionary change, Fanon nevertheless defended the Algerian national struggle while remaining staunchly committed to Third World internationalism. Building on Fanon's critique of the colonized's internalization of race and Western ideologies, 'decolonizing the mind' remained a significant objective of the post-1960s struggles against neocolonialism, racism and apartheid (Rodney 1972; wa Thiongo 1986; Biko 1987). And as was the case with the earlier solidarities that shaped the Third World resistance, post-independence radical intellectuals recognized that building cross-racial/national and cross-continental alliances remained vital to the possibility of collectively 'turning away' from Europe and its murderous modernity (Fanon 1963). One would be hard-pressed to find such critiques of the neoliberal order or contestation of its racial demonization of contemporary revolutionary movements in the recent institutional turn to the decolonial.

The insurgent movements of the 1960s, with which radical scholar-activists were also affiliated, were met with repression and state violence on and off campus. Eventually however, the university yielded space to the new interdisciplinary fields thrown up by these movements. The epistemological traditions advanced by activist scholars, including Indigenous and women of colour faculty within the academy, continued to remain grounded in wider movements that struggled also for the transformation of the institution itself (Davis 1981; Moraga and Anzaldua 1981; LaDuke 2002). These 'new' interdisciplines, including Indigenous Studies and Critical Race Studies, advanced critiques of settler colonialism, US Empire, race, migration within the emergent neoliberalism. It was from within these traditions that settler colonialism was linked to ongoing Indigenous dispossession and genocide; neoliberal restructuring to racial capitalism and imperialist wars; the dismantling of the welfare state to the structural adjustment in the 'independent' Third World; and the restructuring of the international labour force to repressive border control policies, particularly their gendered, sexual and racialized dimensions. Cultural Studies turned the focus of attention to racism, policing, mass media and the racial-cultural practices of power that became dominant under Thatcherism and neoliberalism in general (Hall et al. 1981), even as Postcolonial Studies tracked how colonial discourses were internalized and reproduced in the nationalist politics and governance practices of the post-independence state and nation (Chatterjee 1993; Spivak 1999).

In the case of the United States, as Ferguson (2012) has argued, the university's 'administrative power' worked to domesticate these interdisciplinary fields and their concerns through processes of institutionalization that fostered severing their ties to the political objectives of the movements from which they had originated. Underscoring instead the politics of 'difference', the university offered 'recognition' to particular minoritized communities in its managerial approach to these interdisciplinary fields, harnessing them in the service of state and economy (Ferguson 2012). The institutional incorporation of these interdisciplines thus became a means to restabilize the larger socio-economic order (Ferguson 2012). Ferguson's critique of 'the will to institutionality', as Lewis (2014: 819) argued, revealed this to be 'a will that orients the subject's agency towards the institutions that grant visibility, legitimacy and a sense of permanence only at the cost of regulation, discipline and normalization'.

If the new interdisciplines were transformed into institutional sites for containment of transformative politics, the university's diversity policies tapped into the state-sponsored multiculturalist discourses which tokenized particular forms of 'inclusion' to deepen the university's whiteness and Eurocentrism (Smith 2010; Thobani 2022). Sara Ahmed (2012) followed the workings of such equity/diversity initiatives through the administrative structure in the UK and Australian university. Finding that women of colour faculty and administrators were treated as 'natural' equity champions and embodiments of 'diversity', she delineated the ways in which they were drawn into undertaking the university's equity work. Ahmed (2012) argued that the anti-racism policies thus developed were actually rendered 'non-performative' in their adoption by the university; that is, these policies did not accomplish the change that they proclaimed – anti-racist transformation. Ahmed's (2012) point was that the institution treated its adoption of these policies as 'doing' the work of anti-racism. These institutional practices were, however, highly effective in rebranding the university as 'inclusive' even as it contained and commodified minority difference (Ahmed 2012). These institutional moves to containment in the university did not go unchallenged, but they were fortified by the institutional turn to the decolonial (Thobani 2022).

The 9/11 attacks on the US and the ensuing war on terror hastened the crisis of neoliberalism that had been brewing during the 1980/90s, and soon enough, the war – waged on domestic and international levels – resulted in the reinvigoration of the movements discussed at the beginning of this section. The combined effects of these movements was to place anti-colonial and anti-imperialist politics once again on the national and global agenda, setting the stage for the institutional turn to the 'decolonial'. As I have been arguing, the institutional adoption of 'decolonization' and 'decoloniality' seeks to transform the meanings and effects of these terms as the university attempts to redefine the political contestations of the movements from which they have originated in a moment particularly perilous to the US Empire in decline.

It is in the context of the growing momentum of anti-colonial/racism and anti-war movements that the 'decolonization' critiques – coming from 'within' the established academic disciplines – have been met with an enthusiastic response by/in the university. As noted earlier, the revisionist projects associated with this institutional turn to the decolonial pay little attention to the revolutionary critiques of Western knowledge traditions developed by earlier anti-colonial movements or heed their radical demands for a fundamental transformation of the political economy of contemporary racial-capitalism and its violent political order. As Getachew and Mantena (2021: 361) have noted of the institutionalization of such 'internal' critiques within specific academic disciplines, 'we lose track of what arguably was the primary context and aspiration of anticolonial argument: an attempt to reconstruct viable political futures in the aftermath of European domination'. Equally important, romanticizing the Third World revolution by defining it as unsullied by internal asymmetrical relations of power – including race, gender, class, religion, sexuality and nation – is to fail to understand what was revolutionary about the movements that forged that historic moment laden with immense possibilities.

The present institutionalization of 'decoloniality' in the university functions to obscure, if not actually counter, contemporary struggles to advance revolutionary transformation of the existing 'order of things'. Yet there are limits to the institutional turn to containment as demonstrated by the pro-Palestinian movements that are now irrupting on campuses across North America and Europe in support of the resistance in Gaza. On the frontlines of opposing the might of the US Empire and its prodigy, the Zionist Israeli state, the Palestinian resistance confirms yet again that attending to history, learning from past experience and directly confronting the violence of the settler colonial state remains indispensable to revolutionary transformation. The vision of justice, of building a humane world, which inspires this resistance and its allied movements was one that also inspired the anti-colonial and anti-racist movements of the past.

Recall, revisit, relearn: Introduction to the chapters

This volume aims to mark a moment in the present debates around decolonization which have appeared within Euro-American academia. The contributors to this volume reflect on where the current moment sits within the struggles for decolonization, which have a much longer historical trajectory and wider global outreach. The aims for this volume are to recollect, revisit, relearn; they stem from the understanding of the centrality of history, indeed its formative role, in how we got to where we are and how we can respond to the challenges of the present to move into just futures. History needs to be recalled, especially during moments of crises, to adapt, modify and change knowledges inherited from the past, that is, revisit history so that it becomes possible to develop the knowledge base necessary to address the challenges that the future presents, that is, relearn.

The chapters in this volume focus on the ideas of decolonization espoused by thinkers of the past, including those less known or forgotten. D'Souza's opening chapter recollects the works of JPS Uberoi, an Indian sociologist, who, together with his contemporaries, articulated a vision for what decolonizing curriculum and education should look like in independent India and, to undertake the task, founded the Centre for European Studies in Delhi University, where he taught. Drawing on non-dualist philosophical traditions in the subcontinent, he argued that the central problem with the structure of modernist knowledge is that it delinks and disconnects knowledge from values/ethics on the one hand and practice/actions including political practices on the other. As neocolonialism and later neoliberalism won out, the Centre was wound down, and the 'soft-power' of Anglo-American universities made new inroads into Indian universities in new ways. In Chapter 3, Thobani highlights the role of violence in colonial relations by turning to the ideas of Frantz Fanon, the iconic anti-colonial revolutionary and theorist of decolonization. Situating his analysis of Algerian/Muslim women's role in the revolution within his larger anti-colonial framework, she discusses key insights to be gleaned from his reading of the women's embodied practice of un/veiling as reflection of their revolutionary praxis. Comparing Fanon's analysis to the feminist fetishization of the veil in the war on terror, she discusses how racial-gender politics are deployed to dehumanize Muslim women in the Afghan War and in the genocide in Gaza.

In Chapter 4, Simpson takes the notion of 'refusal' to be an alternative to 'recognition' politics in settler colonial society. Derived from Haudenosaunee history and contemporary politics, 'refusal' here is a political practice through time as well as an ethnographic imperative for writing ethnography that tends to the silences and expressed gaps in communication that honour the will of interlocuters and communities to draw a boundary around what is written about them and, thus, to generate other possibilities for interpretation.

The popular Brazilian rapper Djonga's lyrics reminds de Silva of Amie Césaire's poetry, as she discusses in Chapter 5. Djonga may never have heard of Césaire, but his words, coming from the depths of the favelas where he grew up as a racialized impoverished young man, echo the anti-colonial sentiments of Césaire's poetry. His lyrics are the curriculum for society that teaches thousands of marginalized people about racism and discrimination. In Chapter 6, Austin poses the question of how anti-colonial revolutionaries in the Caribbean imagined their relationship to Africans on the continent. Austin revisits how Walter Rodney and Amílcar Cabral approached the contradictions between the experiences and struggles of Africans in Africa and of the descendants of Africans in the Caribbean, the two faces of colonialism as it were in two different locations. Misreading that relationship between the two ends of colonialism in Africa and Caribbean could well lead to disillusionment with the decolonizing project, Austin reminds us, by recalling C. L. R. James, the iconic Caribbean intellectual in the UK.

In Chapter 7, Sandhu recalls the work of Rajini Palme Dutt, a mixed-race British national born of Swedish and Indian parents; Dutt lived and worked in the UK but is largely forgotten there today. Palme Dutt's anti-imperialist approach prompted him to study British imperialism in India closely, and he became well known in India as a champion of the struggle against British imperialism in the subcontinent. Sandhu also recollects the questions about Dutt's identity as a mixed-race activist that dogged his anti-imperialist political work. Dutt's problems remain with diaspora activists whose revolutionary political views are undermined through the question of 'authenticity'. The politics of these diasporic subjects are also undermined in their countries of migration where their right to 'belong' is constantly challenged. Chapter 8 focuses on political groups who intervened in anti-colonial struggles but may be overlooked by future generations. Higginbottom traces the concept of super-exploitation that was to have profound influence on Latin American dependency theories such as those of Roy Mauro Marini of Brazil back to the interventions of African American thinkers in the Communist International or the COMINTERN. With socialism and communism downgraded by later-day liberal internationalism, the strand of African-American thought that engaged with the communist movements also becomes marginalized. Higginbottom unearths this history.

Latimer recalls Walter Rodney in Chapter 9 to study his approaches to addressing the contradictions between descendants of slaves and indentured labour, one group with African roots and the other with Indian roots, but both consigned to work in plantations in Guyana. Latimer highlights the problems for decolonization arising from the segmented labour force by bringing in Andaiye and the women's question. In Chapter 10, Amini recalls young Abdullah Öcalan's ideas of Kurdish self-determination, a concept that occupies a prime position in the conceptual repertoire of decolonization, and the reformulation of the concept as 'democratic confederalism' by the later Öcalan. The young Öcalan, one of the founders of the Kurdish Workers Party (the PKK) in the early 1970s, understood, like many other anti-colonial thinkers of the past, decolonization and self-determination as independent statehood for the Kurdish nation. The later Ocalan breaks with the idea of equating decolonization with statehood and, instead, anchors it to 'democratic confederalism'.

The closing chapter, a postscript by Sunca, describes the challenges of running Rojava University, an educational institution established after the Rojava revolution of 2012 with the aim of decolonizing education in practice to build a social order based on Ocalan's theory of democratic confederalism.

The chapters in this volume make clear that the thinkers, whose works they address, formulated their ideas of decolonization in response to the problems that anti-colonial struggles encountered. These thinkers remind us of the need to study colonialism and neocolonialism in all their specificities but without losing sight of the overarching framework of the ways in which colonialism and imperialism structure different societies in different ways. The challenge today is to learn from their ideas to contest the shifting formation of colonial power and imperialism in the present.

References

Ahmed, Sara (2012), *On Being Included: Racism and Diversity in Institutional Life*, Durham: Duke University Press.

Altbach, Philip G. (1971), 'Education and Neocolonialism: The Educators Speak - I', *Teachers College Record*, 72 (4): 533–58.

Asad, Talal (2003), *Formations of the Secular: Christianity, Islam, Modernity*, Stanford, CA: Stanford University Press.

Baquer, Ali, Nandy, Ashis, Uberoi, J. P. S., Mohan Ram, H. Y. and Reynolds, Norman ([1979] 2019), 'A Social Lesson for Science', in Khalid Tyabji (ed.), *Mind and Society: From Indian Studies to General Sociology*, 18–26, New Delhi: Oxford University Press.

Betts, Paul (2015), 'Humanity's New Heritage: UNESCO and the Rewriting of World History', *Past & Present*, 228: 249–85.

Bhambra, Gurminder and Holmwood, John (2021), *Colonialism and Modern Social Theory*, Cambridge: Polity Press.

Bhambra, Gurminder K. (2021), 'Decolonizing Critical Theory? Epistemological Justice, Progress, Reparations', *Critical Times*, 4 (1): 73–89.

Biko, Steve (1987), *I Write What I Like*, Portsmouth, NH.: Hienemann.

Bricmont, Jean (2007), *Humanitarian Imperialism: Using Human Rights to Sell War*, New Delhi: Aakar Books.

Chatterjee, Partha (1993), *The Nation and Its Fragments*, Princeton: Princeton University Press.

Clancy, Mary-Alice C. (2011), 'Democracy and Security Special Issue: Foreign Intervention in Ethnic and Ethnonational Conflicts', *Democracy and Security* 7 (2): 85–98. https://doi.org/10.1080/17419166.2011.572771.

Davis, Angela (1981), *Women, Race and Class. Penguin*, New York: Random House.

D'Souza, Radha. (2009), 'The Prison Houses of Knowledge: Activist Scholarship and Revolution in the Era of "Globalisation"', *McGill Journal of Education*, 44 (1): 1–20.

D'Souza, Radha (2012), 'Imperial Agendas, Global Solidarities and Socio-legal Scholarship on the Third World: Methodological Reflections', *Osgoode Hall Law Journal*, 49 (3): 6–43.

D'Souza, Radha (2013), 'Imperialism and Self-determination: Revisiting the Nexus in Lenin', *Economic and Political Weekly*, 48 (15): 60–9.

D'Souza, Radha (2014), 'What Can Activist Scholars Learn from Rumi', *Philosophy East and West*, 64 (1): 1–24.

D'Souza, Radha (2018a), 'The Conceptual World of the Ghadarites', *Socialist Studies (Special Issue)* 13 (2): 15–37.

D'Souza, Radha (2018b), *What's Wrong with Rights?: Social Movements, Law and Liberal Imaginations*, London: Pluto Press.

D'Souza, Radha (2020), 'Wars Beyond the Armed Forces: Colonialism and Militarisation of Ethno-national Conflicts in Contemporary South Asia', in Jude Lal Fernando (ed.), *Resistance to Empire and Militarization: Reclaiming the Sacred*, 25–44, Sheffield: Equinox Publishing.

D'Souza, Radha (2021), 'Transcending Disciplinary Fetishisms: Marxism, Neocolonialism, and International Law', in Paul O'Connell and Umut Ozsu (eds), *Elgar Handbook on Law and Marxism*, 335–55, Cheltenham: Edward Elgar Publishing Limited.

Davidson, Joanna (2012), 'Humanitarian Intervention as Liberal Imperialism: A Force for Good?' *POLIS Journal*, 7 (Summer): 128–64.

Dirlik, Arif [1998] (2018), *The Postcolonial Aura: Third World Criticism in the Age of Global Capitalism*, New York, London: Routledge.

Du Bois, William Edward Burghadt (1903), *The Souls of Black Folks: Essays and Sketches*, Chicago, IL: AC McClurg and Company.

Duara, Prasanjit (2003), *Decolonization: Perspectives from Then and Now*, London and New York: Routledge.

Fanon, Frantz (1963), *The Wretched of the Earth*, New York: Grove Weidenfeld.

Ferguson, Roderick A. (2012), *The Reorder of Things: The University and Its Pedagogies of Minority Difference*, Minneapolis: University of Minnesota Press.

Getachew, Adom and Mantena, Karuna (2021), 'Anticolonialism and the Decolonization of Political Theory', *Critical Times*, 4 (3): 359–88.

Ghosh, Ranjan (2006), 'Institutionalised Theory, (In)fusion, Desivad', *Oxford Literary Review*, 28 (1): 25–36.

Grosfoguel, Ramón (2013), 'The Structure of Knowledge in Westernized Universities Epistemic Racism/Sexism and the Four Genocides/Epistemicides of the Long 16th Century', *Human Architecture: Journal of the Sociology of Self-Knowledge*, XI (1): 73–90.

Gupta, Suman and Chattarji, Subarno (2019), 'Protests, Repression, Restructuring: Contemplating Indian Higher Education in 2018', *Postcolonial Studies*, 22 (1): 117–30. https://doi.org/10.1080/13688790.2019.1568175.

Hall, Stuart, Critcher, Chas, Jeffercon, Tony, Clarke, John and Roberts, Brian (1981), *Policing the Crisis: Mugging, the State and Law and Order*, London: MacMillan Press.

Harris, Angela P. (2000), 'Equality Trouble: Sameness and Difference in Twentieth-Century Race Law', *California Law Review*, 88 (6): 1923–2015. https://doi.org/10.2307/3481212.

Henriques, Anuradha and Abushouk, Lina (2018), 'Decolonising Oxford: The Student Movement from Stuart Hall to Skin Deep', in Jason Arday and Heidi Safia Mirza (eds), *Dismantling Race in Higher Education: Racism, Whiteness and Decolonising the Academy*, 297–309, Cham: Springer International Publishing.

Jenkins, Destin and Leroy, Justin, eds. (2021), *Histories of Racial Capitalism*, New York: Columbia University Press.

Joseph-Salisbury, Remi, Ashe, Stephen, Alexander, Claire and Campion, Caris (2020), *Race and Ethnicity in British Sociology*, British Sociological Association, Belmont, Durham: BSA Publications, Ltd.

Kanji, Azeezah (2021), 'War of Terror: Legal Colonialism Reincarnated', *Al Jazeera*. https://www.aljazeera.com/opinions/2021/9/18/war-of-terror-legal-colonialism

Kenway, Peter and Palmer, Guy (2007), 'Poverty Among Ethnic Groups: How and Why Does It Differ?' New Policy Institute: Rowntree Foundation. Available at https://www.jrf.org.uk/sites/default/files/migrated/migrated/files/2042-ethnicity-relative-poverty.pdf (Accessed: 01 May 2024).

Khoo, Su-Ming (2021), 'On Decolonial Revisions of Modern Social Theory', *International Sociological Reviews*, 36 (5): 704–19.

Koeze, Ella and Russel, Karl (2022), 'The Toll of Student Debt in the U.S.', *The New York Times*, 26 August. Available at: https://www.nytimes.com/interactive/2022/08/26/your-money/student-loan-forgiveness-debt.html (Accessed: 30 May 2024).

LaDuke, Winona (2002), *The Winona LaDuke Reader*, Penticton, BC: Theytus Books.

Levin, Sam (2017), 'Revealed: FBI Terrorism Taskforce Investigating Standing Rock Activists', *The Guardian*, 10 February. Available at https://www.theguardian.com/us-news/2017/feb/10/standing-rock-fbi-investigation-dakota-access (Accessed: 10 June 2024).

Lewis, Tyson J. (2014), 'Review', *Signs: Journal of Women in Culture and Society*, 39 (3): 817–21.

Maldonado-Torres, Nelson (2007), 'On the Coloniality of Being', *Cultural Studies*, 21 (2–3): 240–70.

Mamdani, Mahmood (2005), *Good Muslim Bad Muslim: America, the Cold War and the Roots of Terror*, New York: Penguin Random House.

Mamdani, Mahmood (2009), *Saviours and Survivors: Darfur, Politics, and the War on Terror*, New York: Pantheon Books.

Mamdani, Mahmood (2020), *Neither Settler nor Native: The Making and Unmaking of Permanent Minorities*, Cambridge, MA and London: Harvard University Press.

Meghji, Ali (2021), 'What Can the Sociology of Race Learn from the Histories of Anti-colonialism?' *Ethnicities*, 21 (4): 769–82.

Menon, Annapurna (2022), 'Debunking Hindutva Appropriation of Decolonial Thought', *Interfere: Journal for Critical Thought and Radical Politics*, 3 (3): 36–57.

Mignolo, Walter D. (2009), 'Coloniality: The Darker Side of Modernity', in Sabine Breitwisser (ed.), *Modernologies. Contemporary Artists Researching Modernity and Modernism. Catalog of the Exhibit at the Museum of Modern Art*, 39–49, Barcelona: Museum of Modern Art.

Mignolo, Walter D. (2011), *The Darker Side of Western Modernity*, Durham: Duke University Press.

Moraga, Cherrie and Anzaldua, Gloria, eds. (1981), *This Bridge Called My Back*, Boston: Kitchen Press.

Morgan, Hani (2024), 'Ethnic Studies Programs in America: Exploring the Past to Understand Today's Debates', *Policy Futures in Education*, 1–23. https://doi.org/10.1177/14782103241229528.

Nkrumah, Kwame (1968), *Neo-colonialism: The Last Stage of Imperialism*, London: Heinemann Educational.

Nye, Joseph S., Jr. (2004), *Soft Power: The Means to Success in World Politics*, New York: Public Affairs.

Oladipo, Gloria (2023), 'US Progressives Call for Urgent Actions after Court Blocks Student Debt Relief', *The Guardian*, 30 June. Available at https://www.theguardian.com/money/2023/jun/30/biden-federal-student-loan-forgiveness-democrats-supreme-court-decision (Accessed on 30 May 2024).

Quijano, Aníbal (2007), 'Coloniality and Modernity/Rationality', *Cultural Studies*, 21 (2–3): 168–78.

Raju, Saraswati (2006), 'Production of Knowledge: Looking for "Theory" in "Familiar" Places?' *Geoforum*, 37: 155–8.

Rakowski, Cathy A. (1993), 'The Ugly Scholar: Neocolonialism and Ethical Issues in International Research', *The American Sociologist*, 24 (3): 69–86. https://doi.org/10.1007/BF02691920.

Reiter, Bernd (2021), *Decolonizing the Social Sciences and the Humanities: An Anti-Elitist Manifesto*, New York: Routledge.

Robinson, Cedric J. and Kelley, Robin D. G. (2000), *Black Marxism: The Making of the Black Radical Tradition*, Chapel Hill, NC: The University of North Carolina Press.

Rodney, Walter (1972), *How Europe Underdeveloped Africa*. London: Bogle-L'Ouverture.

Singh, Aditi (2023), '"Decolonizing" the NCERT Social Science Textbooks: Hinduization of History and Issues of Gender and Caste', in Chanwahn Kim and Misu Kim (eds), *Great Transition in India: Issues and Debates*, 33–56, Singapore: World Scientific Publishing Co Pte Lte.

Smith, Malinda (2010), 'Gender, Whiteness and the "Other Others" in the Academy', in Sherene Razack, Malinda Smith and Sunera Thobani (eds), *States of Race: Critical Race Feminism for the Twenty-first Century*, 37–58, Toronto: Between the Lines.

Spivak, Gayatri (1999), *A Critique of Postcolonial Reason*, Harvard: Harvard University Press.

Thapliyal, Nisha (2021), '(No) Right to Protest? Student Activism at Public Universities in India in the Modi Era', in Judith Bessant, Analicia Mejia Mesinas and Sarah Pickard (eds), *When Students Protest: Universities in the Global South*, 89–151, Lanham; Boulder; New York; London: Rowman & Littlefield.

Thobani, Sunera, ed. (2022), *Coloniality and Racial (In)Justice in the Academy*, Toronto: University Press.

Thompson, Mark (2014), 'Why Ferguson Looks So Much Like Iraq', *Time*, 14 August. Available at: https://time.com/3111455/ferguson-missouri-michael-brown-iraq/ (Accessed: 15 June 2024).

Uberoi, J. P. S. (2019), 'The Sciences and the Arts in the University', in Khalid Tyabji (ed.), *Mind and Society: From Indian Studies to General Sociology*, 27–31, New Delhi: Oxford University Press.

Vijayan, P. K. (2016), 'Privatising Minds: New Educational Policies in India', in Suman Gupta, Jernej Habjan and Hrvoje Tutek (eds), *Academic Labour, Unemployment and Global Higher Education: Neoliberal Policies of Funding and Management*, 57–78. London, UK: Palgrave Macmillan.

Wa Thiong'o, Ngugi (1986), *Decolonizing the Mind: The Politics of Language in African Literature*, Nairobi: East African Educational Publishers.

2

Decolonizing knowledge

Science, scientists and science education

Radha D'Souza

If half the scientists in the world are servants of the military, which does violence to man, and the other half are servants of industry, which does violence to nature, then the love of man and nature obliges us to seek to rescue most of science from scientists and set it in a new and different philosophical and practical direction – nonviolent and non-dualist. *(Jit Pal Singh Uberoi [1982] 2019: 16)*

Introduction

Decolonizing education, the academia and universities presupposes decolonizing modernist *knowledge* as a comprehensive system. In this chapter, I consider the significance of the writings of Jit Pal Uberoi (more popularly, J. P. S. Uberoi) whose work provides a deeper interrogation of the very structures of modernist knowledge as a comprehensive system of thought. Typically, decolonizing approaches focus on social sciences and humanities. The disciplinary lenses through which decolonizing is understood obscure the ways in which the sciences structure contemporary systems of knowledge and the extraordinary violence that the fragmented disciplinary knowledges unleash upon natures and peoples everywhere. I begin by recalling Uberoi's writings on science and knowledge, more specifically his text *The European Modernity: Science, Truth and Method*, published in 2002. In the section titled 'J. P. S. Uberoi's critique of European modernity', I discuss his ideas on science, knowledge and the structure of modernist thought, his non-dualist approaches to knowledge, his critique of the hiatus between knowledge, values and actions in modernist knowledge and the systemic violence that the hiatus inscribes in the very architecture of modernist knowledge. Uberoi was an important voice in the debates to decolonize education and curriculum in India that took place after Independence. Uberoi's critique and his pointers to the routes out of the knowledge traps of European modernity are important to revisit in the contemporary context.

In the section titled 'Science and scientists as knowledge producers', I map the architecture of knowledge in the sciences, natural and social, and the violence entailed in it. I do this by examining the wider ramifications of the disciplinary separation of the natural sciences from humanities by reflecting on the events of Hiroshima–Nagasaki. In the section on 'States and corporations as the primary users of knowledge', I examine modernist institutions that actualize the theories as violent practices. States and corporations form two most important institutional conditions for capitalist modernity. I reflect on the wider social ramifications of the two types of modernist organizations that operate as 'legal persons' with independent personhood. These two modernist institutions with personhood are the most important political actors and users of modernist knowledge. In the final section, 'Unity of knowledge, values and action', I summarize the debates on science policy in India after independence to highlight different ways in which decolonization in education was understood. The purpose is to better appreciate Uberoi's pointers to what a programme for decolonizing knowledge entails. In the concluding section, I consider the return of decolonization to the agendas of academia and beyond in recent times, notably the advocacy for 'inclusion' of marginalized groups in science education, to underscore the significance of Uberoi's critique in a renewed movement for decolonization. It is important for the critique to turn its attention to modern Europe's knowledge systems and heed Uberoi's call for a sociologically, historically and contextually grounded non-dualist critique that helps to unify knowledge, values and actions to transcend the extraordinary violence unleashed by European modernity on natures and cultures since its inception to the present times.

J. P. S. Uberoi's critique of European modernity

Uberoi's critique of European modernity as a knowledge system may be broken down into three strands for analytical purposes. The first strand concerns his critique of the dualist structure of modern European thought in science and culture. The second strand concerns his exposition of what non-dualist knowledge means, and lastly his non-dualist approach to decolonizing European science and culture.

Uberoi begins *European Modernity* with the question: what is it about European modernist thought that produced what he calls 'endo-cannibalistic and exo-cannibalistic' (2002: 77) events such as the Holocaust and the nuclear bombing of Hiroshima–Nagasaki? Both events were carried out by countries considered politically opposed: Germany and the United States, one 'totalitarian', the other a 'democracy'; one a national event, the other international; one a war against an ethnic group within a state, the other a war between states. For Uberoi (2002: xi), 'the implosion of Auschwitz and the explosion of Hiroshima ... formed one civilizational event' (1945) and states everywhere have a 'bimodal distribution of existence, the one manifest in peace and the other in war'. The bimodal existence permits changing gear from one to the other mode of existence. A single semiological theory must be found to explain *both* modes of existence that also permits changing gear from one to the other (Uberoi 2002: xii).

For Uberoi, three epistemological dualisms form the axes of modern European science and culture: body/mind, fact/value, theory/practice. Together, these formative epistemological dualisms produce a 'master system of classification' of the arts and sciences that is institutionalized in modern universities as distinct disciplines and subdisciplines.

> It is a system of knowledge that is unified in principle and suspended horizontally between the two poles of fact (the sciences) and values (the arts). It is also stretched vertically between the two poles of theory (theoretical disciplines of the university) and practice (practico-technical arts and crafts, including industrial arts). Underlying or behind both of these oppositions is the ultimate dualism of truth and reality, *vertitas* and *realitas*, the subject and the object or of mind and the world. (Uberoi [2011] 2019: 42)

The axes of fact/value and theory/practice mark out 'the four quarters of modern Western civilization to be occupied by the new science, technology, philosophy, politics, economics or ethics' (Uberoi [2011] 2019: 39). Their unity in principle but discreteness along dualist poles in the structure of thought means disciplinary knowledge can be combined and manipulated in any number of ways using proximity/distance and conflict/collaboration methods (Uberoi [1982] 2019a). Disciplines of the mind, that is, science and philosophy are proximate to the theory axis, whereas technology and politics, economics and ethics sit beside each other on the praxis axis in theory/practice dualism. Science and technology are concerned with facts, whereas philosophy, politics, economics and ethics are concerned with values and social purpose and are distant from science and technology. This is the 'elementary structure of modern, positivist regime as a system, which produced the inner organization of modern western science, on the one hand, and its relations with the whole of the European modernity, on the other hand' (Uberoi 2002: 39).

The three epistemological dualisms (body/mind, fact/value, theory/practice) organized around the disciplinary poles of science/humanities in academia and the world outside, in turn, rest on the ontological dualism of truth and reality and the cosmological dualism of nature and humans (Uberoi 1978: 16). Together these dualisms establish a structure of knowledge that is all encompassing. The dualism that characterizes the structure of European science as well as its culture was achieved when the separation of science, religion and politics or of faith, knowledge and action was formally severed by establishing three distinct institutions of civil society, the church and the state (Uberoi 2002: 77).

However, the unity *and* diversity of the natural and social worlds and the separation and difference of the identities of human beings and their worlds are not possible within a segregated institutional order. The epistemological, ontological and cosmological are 'inseparable aspects of one and the same regime of thought and life that we call civilization or culture' (Uberoi 1978: 16).

> The latter position [difference] would inevitably lead us either (a) to a philosophy of absolute atomism by the infinite regression of dualism (Russell), variety at the cost of unity; or (b) to the opposite mistakes of the so-called new 'systems' view of the world, unity at the cost of variety, which perhaps correctly emphasises the autonomy, self-regulation and self-organisation and coherence of systems, but forgets their rules of transformation and metamorphoses. (Uberoi [1982] 2019a: 14–15)

Armed with the divide between theory and practice, fact and value, body and mind, European civilization established institutions that were internally divided but externally united against the 'non-elite and the non-expert' (Uberoi 2002: 78). European modernity, which began around *c.* 1500 ended in 1945 when science, industry, bureaucracy and politics reached the ultimate in 'endo-cannibalism as well as exo-cannibalism' (Uberoi 2002: 77). 'What had been at first sight simply oppositions and contradictions to be perhaps exploited, resolved, mediated or transcended had been turned by infinite regress into the nightmare of pure dissociation, self-deception and self-alienation by the end' (Uberoi 2002: 78).

Turning to the next strand, non-dualism, what is it about dualist structure of thought that has put human beings on a path that is so destructive of natures, societies and human beings? Uberoi (2002: vii) argues that the real problem with what he calls 'duopoly' of knowledge is that it severs the unity of knowledge, values and action, such that the heart and the mind are unable to communicate. The dualism of power (enabled by European sciences) and culture (European modernity) produces knowledge that is inherently divided internally but unified against society and the world at large (Uberoi 2002: viii). Consequently, the inwardly divided structure of knowledge produces outward violence in the world against natures, societies and peoples/individuals.

> The dissolution of the unity of man's estate as a vision and a perspective to be realized in thought (truth) and somehow made concrete in life (method) led to the dissociation as well as the independence of its parts. Gloriously released from irksome mutual discipline under the ordered whole, the truth and the reality, thought and life, the inner and outer, the truth of the mind and the reality of the senses, simply flew apart, like God and the world, and renounced all necessary connection with each other. (Uberoi 2002: 40)

Modern science is powerless to influence ethical actions in politics or economics and vice versa. The consequence of the mutual independence of modern science and culture is 'the mindless praxis of amoral technicism' that is hived off from the spirit of philosophy, a move that renders their mutual relationship 'arbitrary and extrinsic to the special merits and respective categories of each separate domain' (Uberoi 2002: 41). The result is, as Rajani Kothari (1988) notes, the more we know the less we are able to address the conditions of our existence.

What is important to note here is that elite decision-makers know the truth, but it is taught to the non-elite, 'only if it was applicable to the good, let us suppose, of Enlightenment democracy or socialism but not necessarily because it was truth. Similarly *untruths* are tolerated and encouraged if they serve extrinsic value in politics and ethics, e.g. in promoting social stability and cohesion' (Uberoi 2002: 41). The essence of decolonizing knowledge is to transcend epistemological dualisms of body/mind, fact/value and theory/practice, the ontological dualism of human beings and their world; and the cosmological dualism of nature and culture. The universe is characterized by unity in diversity. Epistemological dualism is unable to grasp the unity *and* diversity *at the same time* as part of the *same* unified reality.

Non-dualist approaches to knowledge must work to unify the self (inner world), the world (social world) and the cosmos (natural world) in the very internal structures of knowledge. Non-dualism for knowledge workers is about restoring the unity of the sciences, natural and social, and arts and humanities in the academia and working towards dismantling European modernity's 'duopoly' of knowledge between power/culture, truth/method, theory/practice and elite/non-elite that characterize European systems of knowledge and informs practices in every walk of modern life. To do this, knowledge workers must seek to establish 'self-rule' and 'self-determination' from the positivist elites and their institutions, the pervasive military–industrial–academic complexes, for example. Non-dualist scholarship is produced from a dialectical relationship of theory and practice, the scholar and the worker, and directed at understanding human purpose, human destiny and human ethics to better locate herself in the wider world and the universe.

In an insightful comment in the *Grundrisse*, Marx ([1973] 1993: 276) notes that the forcible eviction of people/communities from land/nature, or what he calls primitive accumulation, a violent social transformation that kick-started the process of transforming commodity production into capitalism as a commodity producing social system, produced, as its consequence, all sorts of dualisms in capitalist societies. If the birth of dualist knowledge was marked by extreme violence against non-elites at the dawn of early modern European capitalism, the events of 1945 mark modern European civilization as the hand that could, potentially, bring human life on this planet to extinction.

It is possible to ask whether Uberoi's critique of European modernity is yet another variation of the Eurocentrism critique that is popular in academia. In criticizing the dualist structure of modern European knowledge, does Uberoi fall into another type of European/non-European dualism that runs counter to the very non-dualism that he canvasses? This question brings us to the third strand in Uberoi's critique.

Typically, the Eurocentrism, orientalism and postcolonialism critique of European modernity adopts the 'West versus Rest' format of argumentation. The 'West versus Rest' format of critique, in turn, is a reaction to capitalist modernity's mission to 'civilize', 'develop' and 'progress' the world. The civilized/uncivilized dualism considers Western knowledge to be superior and non-Western knowledge as 'unscientific' and belonging to the domain of faith and belief, that is, not knowledge, properly speaking, that is useful for this world (Uberoi 1978: 14). Although the 'West versus Rest' may appear in the first instance to challenge the dualism by bringing to light what the modernist epistemology obscures, it falls into the same dualist structure of thought by reversing the 'gaze' as it were or negating categories of thought, such as scientific/unscientific, civilized/uncivilized, in modernist knowledge by adopting the format of 'not this, not that'. Consequently, the critique remains within the same dualist structure of thought without transcendence. In contrast, Uberoi's non-dualist approach seeks to transcend the 'West versus Rest' format of critique.

First, Uberoi argues that European modernity may have originated in Europe, but it is no longer confined to Europe. European modernity has spread around the world today due to colonialism and imperialism. Many in the colonial and neocolonial worlds enthusiastically embrace(d) European modernity together with its propensity for violence in their own countries, against their own people. Third World leaders and intellectuals become cheerleaders for European modernity despite its demonstrable failure (Uberoi 2002: viii).

The 'West versus Rest' format of argumentation leaves Indian intellectuals in a sorry position where either they must cede intellectual autonomy or 'self-rule', as Uberoi (2002) calls it, to the theories and methods produced in Western universities or sit back and moan and complain about everything that is wrong with Western knowledge without offering a solution as the Eurocentrism critique does. For Uberoi, the 'West versus Rest' format of critique absolves Third World intellectuals. 'We are its [the Enlightenment project's] appointed trained missionaries supported in the colonies with regular metropolitan home leave from time to time, its loyal soldiers and subalterns fighting against Oriental despotism, feudalism or medieval superstition and antique obscurantism, or else [. . .], hired coolie labour or babus in its ethnic or local data collection branch' (Uberoi 2002: viii). Decolonizing knowledge is, first and foremost, about Third World intellectuals, wherever they may be located around the world, taking responsibility for their own thoughts and actions in the perpetuation and transformation of European modernity into global modernity (Uberoi 2002: vii–viii).

According to Uberoi (2002), the problem with European modernity is not that it arose in a certain geographical area or that the Enlightenment thinkers belonged to certain racial, religious or ethnic groups. The new systems of knowledge emerging in Europe were a contested process. Alongside the better-known Enlightenment thinkers, for example, Bacon, Locke, Newton, there was another parallel intellectual tradition that opposed the emergent, new systems of knowledge. Uberoi calls such thinkers the 'European underground'. Underground, because the thinkers who were critical of European modernity were pushed underground and made invisible by the way dualist power and culture was institutionalized within and outside academia. A non-dualist approach to European modernity must include both types of Europeans: those who nurtured and grew it and those who were critical of the new knowledge system that was emerging.

Instead of taking essentialist approaches that treats all European knowledge as problematic, Uberoi focuses attention on European modernity as a specific moment in European history made possible by a constellation of factors. Beginning with the Renaissance and continuing through the Reformation and the Counter-reformation, from the fifteenth to seventeenth centuries, the coming together of European merchants, intellectuals and sections of the aristocracy, made it possible to bring about a comprehensive transformation in the structure of thought that can be recognized as European modernity (Uberoi 1978). It is the specific structure of thought occurring at a particular moment in European history that is problematic. Modern science and its independence from modern culture, therefore, is the problem. 'I would rather say that modern Western science at some time took the wrong direction in the intrinsic sense; and that its findings, theories and techniques in all its various branches are largely untrue, misleading and senseless for mankind as a whole' (Uberoi 1978: 15).

The constellation of factors that produced the wrong turn in human history are important to understand and address. Indians, and by extension Third World scholars, must study closely the constellation of factors, its history, sociology and anthropology and the science and culture that has sustained European modernity for over five centuries but brought human beings and their worlds to an existential abyss. Why did European science take such a terrible turn? What was it about European culture that allowed such a turn? Why was European culture unable to arrest it? And how can the world overcome the consequences of that fatal wrong turn. Decolonizing knowledge is first and foremost about an explanatory critique of European modernity. To undertake the task, Uberoi set up a programme of European Studies in Delhi University where he taught (K. Tyabji 2019).

Epistemologically, Uberoi (1978: 16) transcends the dualist structures of knowledge of European modernity by adopting semiotics as his methodological approach or what he calls 'semiology of civilization'. Semiology, for Uberoi (1978: 22), is characterized by four key terms: wholeness, structure, symbols and dialectics. In examining the structure of European modernist thought semiologically, Uberoi (1978) takes four key aspects of the structure of human cognition as his point of departure: the concept of symmetry, the relationship of mind and matter, the relationship of self and the other, and understandings of unity and difference. On each one of these cognitive aspects of human thought, Uberoi (1978) examines the challenges and contestations of the 'European underground' during the course of Europe's modern history. Thus, Newton's dualistic theory of optics and Goethe's non-dualist theory of optics are considered side by side. Why and how then did Newton's optics become mainstream and Goethe is not even recognized as a scientist?

Uberoi's inspiration for his semiological method is Panini, the ancient South Asian grammarian (dated around 600–400 BCE). Modern natural science, 'fathered' by Bacon, Locke, Newton and their progeny in thought and mind, establishes observed facts first followed by their causes and effects or their sequences and correlations, determinants and conditions, which also are precise, discrete and observable in the external world. There is no place in this scientific method for the observer and her human mind. In contrast,

> Semiological science ... would be occupied with the truth, order and sense of the universe or of some selected segment of it, viewed as a system of signs and relations, an individual sign being treated as both a fact and a value, objective and subjective at one and the same time. The semiological ideal is always to achieve statements like the rules of grammar and syntax or like the laws of utterance and discourse, i.e. statements of the interrelations of a body or forms and signs which help to make each element and all combinations and patterns of elements intelligible, communicable, effective and meaningful for both the participant and the observer. Thus, a semiological science will try and interrelate the phenomenon under investigation and its conditions as two parts of a still larger whole which includes them both as well as the participant–observer, while bearing in mind the necessary qualification that wholeness here consists not so much of comprehensive all-inclusiveness *but of the habit of seeing all things in the round.* (Uberoi 1978: 19: italics added)

Uberoi's semiological method offers a non-dualist way out of the 'West versus Rest' without diluting the critique of European modernity. Indeed, it deepens and widens that critique and opens up pathways to transcending European modernity in thought and actions. The next two sections highlight the urgent need to advance Uberoi's mission of non-dualist critique of European modernity in thought and in action.

Science and scientists as knowledge producers

Two events mark the inaugural moment of the so-called New World Order after the end of the Second World War: the Holocaust and Hiroshima–Nagasaki. Both events were made possible by the coming together of scientific knowledge, political actions and prevailing normative standards, ethics and values, intrinsically divided knowledges that were mobilized extrinsically. The scientists whose knowledge produced the nuclear bombs believed their work would contribute to the defeat of fascism, a 'public good' and therefore ethical. Once the war was over, they believed liberal democracy, deferring to popular will (the core assumptions in liberal theories), would put away the dreadful weapons forever (Born 1965; D'Souza 2010). Instead, liberal democracy morphed into an ever-expanding military–industrial–academic complex, a reality acknowledged by none other than President Eisenhower of the United States as early as 1961 (Edgerton 2005; Kone 2013). 'If I knew they were going to do this, I would have become a shoemaker', Albert Einstein, whose revolution in quantum physics made the nuclear weapons possible, is reported to have said after the Hiroshima–Nagasaki explosions (D'Souza 2010: 479). Seventy-five years after the first nuclear explosion, scientists continue to produce ever more deadly weapons.

Why do scientists as knowledge workers continue to work so hard to enhance the destructiveness of already-deadly weapons when they know how states have used them against people, for over a century now, if we take the First World War as the beginning of modern warfare? Most of their science-based inventions are used on people of the Third World, often desperately poor, facts about which are reported almost daily in newspapers. For example, we know from newspapers as well as academic research that depleted uranium, a weaker form of natural uranium used in the Hiroshima bombings was used as recently as 1991 in the Balkans, and 2003 in Iraq, and in the Afghan wars, and produced long-term health and environmental impacts for people. These effects are now recognized in medical sciences as a condition known as the Gulf War Syndrome (Bertell 2006; Briner 2010; Considine 2013; *Tasnim New Agency* 2020). At a personal level, most scientists working in university research laboratories are, most likely, ordinary, decent people and good citizens. How do they relate their everyday goodness at home with the destructiveness of their everyday jobs, if at all? Such questions reveal an internal schizophrenia within the scientist as a knowledge worker and as a human being with conscience. A few of them move away from the destructive knowledge production to save their individual conscience (or soul if you prefer). When they do that, they cease to be scientific workers. Most continue to do their jobs as scientists producing knowledge that is destructive and live with the schizophrenia, a reality exemplified by the life and works of Noam Chomsky.

Noam Chomsky is perhaps America's best-known dissident intellectual. A committed philosophical and political anarchist, Chomsky has been at the forefront of opposition to every American war since the Vietnam War, an outspoken critic of the media's role in contemporary propaganda and a champion for global justice. Chomsky worked at the Massachusetts Institute of Technology (MIT), where he began his academic career in linguistics in 1955 and remains a professor emeritus (Knight 2016). The MIT built its reputation as the premier site for defence research during the interwar years when it emerged as a leading contractor for the Department of Defence of the US state. It remains a core component of America's gigantic military–industrial complex (Leslie 1993; Moran 2020). Chomsky's research was funded largely by the Department of Defence (Knight 2016; Moran 2020). There are two questions that arise from Chomsky's professional and political life.

Why did MIT hire and retain Chomsky despite his political activism against the very Department of Defence that paid his salary (Knight 2016)? Why did Chomsky continue to work for the MIT even when he knew about its close links to the Pentagon and America's sprawling military–industrial–academic complex within which it was located (Knight 2016)? Chomsky is reported to view his life 'as a "sort of schizophrenic existence"', made possible by a fortunate glitch in his brain which causes it to function 'like separate buffers in a computer' (as quoted in Knight 2016: 3). It is precisely this bifurcation of the brain into a 'science' compartment and a 'humanities' compartment that the scientists who had worked on the weapons that made Hiroshima–Nagasaki possible became worried about when they saw the extraordinary expansion of the military–industrial complex within which universities became a core component.

The foundations of the post–Second World War world were established by the science of cybernetics or the science of communications and the command–communication–control (3C) technologies based on the science. The nature of warfare was transformed by 3C technologies from wars dominated by naval warfare reliant on artillery and ammunition before the First World War to aerial warfare based on communications between humans and machines that

3C technologies made possible (Edgerton 2005; D'Souza 2010). Nobert Wiener, who established the field of cybernetics and gave it its name, is rightly considered the father of the information age (Conway and Siegel 2005). Wiener's science of cybernetics established principles of communication between humans, humans and non-humans, and humans and machines (Wiener [1948] 1961). Wiener too was employed by MIT and was involved in research on machine learning, a field of research that Chomsky later joined in the same Research Laboratory of the Electronics department where Wiener had worked (Conway and Siegel 2005: 167–8). The father of the information age remains an uncelebrated figure. He never received the Nobel Peace Prize for his epoch changing work and is largely forgotten in MIT. Why, one might ask?

Wiener could see the social ramifications of his scientific discoveries. Wiener became an ardent campaigner against wars and against uses of technology for destructive purposes. He refused to be involved in research funded by the Department of Defence. He was among the earliest scientists to speak out categorically against disciplinary tunnel visions in knowledge that compartmentalized scientific knowledge from knowledge of ethics (humanities) and society (social sciences) (Wiener 1964, [1950] 1989). Wiener belonged to a generation of wartime scientists alongside Einstein, Max Born, Robert Oppenheimer (the physicist who oversaw the development of the nuclear bombs used in Hiroshima–Nagasaki) and others who became outspoken critics of state interference in scientific research, and many among them were targets of investigation by the US intelligence agencies for anti-national activities (Conway and Seigel 2005; D'Souza 2010). In 1969, fifty top MIT scientists were sufficiently concerned about government interference in scientific research to issue a statement which became the founding document for the Union of Concerned Scientists the following year (Union of Concerned Scientists 1968). The Union canvassed for a unified science that bridges the nature/culture divide.

The nature/culture divide is institutionalized as science and humanities in academia and constitutes the basic structure of modernist knowledge. The divide compartmentalizes science and the ethical uses of scientific knowledge into two distinct disciplinary fields such that one side of the brain has no idea what the other side does. Arguably, this disciplinary split permeates the minds of the knowledge workers as exemplified by Chomsky's 'schizophrenic' mind which did not ask why, in the first place, was one branch of linguistics moved from humanities, where it engaged in the study of languages in human communities, to the sciences that extended the knowledge to machines, military sciences at that (Knight 2007). In theory, there ought not to be any need for a specialist organization for ethics of the sciences like the Union of Concerned Scientists. In theory, all scientists ought to be 'concerned' knowledge workers who are conscious about the potential consequences of their work in the wider world.

On their part, knowledge workers in humanities responded to the crisis among scientists by examining the social context for science. Beginning by questioning claims of value neutrality of science and the philosophical foundations of science, Science Technology and Society (STS) studies congealed as a subfield in humanities by the 1970s (Rohracher 2015). Human relations to machines, Wiener's generation had insisted, must be inseparable from ethics and social impacts, including state interferences (Wiener 1964; Union of Concerned Scientists 1968; Wiener [1950] 1989). Knowledge workers in humanities brought with them constructivist and hermeneutical approaches to knowledge and anthropological and ethnographical methods to STS studies. These theoretical orientations and research methods, popular in humanities, took the science and technologies of the natural scientists as a given. Scientific knowledge and the technology derived from it became a natural order of society at a given historical conjuncture. For example, Bruno Latour (2005), the well-known anthropologist of science, effaces the distinction between machines and humans in his influential Actor Network Theory (ANT).

Far from tunnelling knowledge at the humanities end as the war-time scientists tried to do at the science end to bring down the nature/culture divide, STS further congealed and solidified the divide by shifting attention to the scientists and their ways of working or by extending concepts in the sciences to humanities (e.g. the concepts and theories of 'networks' in biology and mathematics to social analysis). Haraway (1991) extends constructivist approaches to human–machine relations to women and feminism. In the process, she redefines the meaning of nature and women's place in it as understood in many cultures. The science that is designed by scientists to destroy human lives around the world offers new opportunities for feminist socialism in the Euro-American 'West' (Haraway 1991). STS studies made this possible by objectifying the sciences and their methods and delinking it from the producers and users of that knowledge. Humanities became bystanders and commentators on the impacts of the sciences on societies and cultures (Bauman 1987).

The nature/culture divide, on which the edifice of European modernist knowledge stands, does two things. It invisibilizes human beings, their sufferings and pains by delinking scientific work from its social context (Uberoi 1978: 18).

It expunges human values, human purpose, human ethics and human destiny from scientific work. Knowledge workers in the sciences continue to uncover evermore truths about nature, for example, searching for natural resources in Mars, Moon and elsewhere, conquering space, inventing superior robotic warfare technologies and much more without asking what past discoveries, such as theories of nuclear fission, atoms, particle physics or artificial intelligence, have done for humanity. Humanities, which started out by challenging the value neutrality of sciences very briefly in the aftermath of the world wars, takes the dehumanized knowledge of the sciences as given, inevitable even, that could be understood anthropologically, ethnographically and sociologically without in anyway transforming or challenging the practices of the scientists or the states that use their knowledge, as discussed later in this chapter.

For their part, knowledge workers in the humanities invisibilize the very idea of Truth. Truth as a socially constructed idea, is no longer related to cosmological (nature) or ontological (human life) realities. Instead 'facts', the brick and mortar of the sciences, stand in for Truth; they become a way of understanding Truth (D'Souza 2013). This way of understanding facts as Truth opens up possibilities of evermore epistemological manipulations of facts that are delinked from the human condition, human bonds to nature, people and places, and human relations to the generations, past, present and future. Within the institutional contexts for knowledge production, that is, the universities, knowledge workers, whether scientists or humanities scholars, are not required by their institutions, the state and private funders to consider who will use their knowledge and for what purposes. Nor do they have any control over how their knowledge will be used (Werskey 2007). Indeed, the primary users of knowledge are not even human any longer. European modernity created new types of 'persons' – the 'legal person', the states and corporations – that subsume the scientists and their work.

States and corporations as the primary users of knowledge

The First World War, known to be the first industrial warfare, marked a rupture from earlier wars. Industrial warfare brought together scientific knowledge and industrial methods of investments, production and management and transformed state and society. The First World War introduced the concept of Total War, techniques of mobilizing entire societies for wars (Edgerton 2005; D'Souza 2019,

2020). The industrial methods and scales of organizing and conducting wars included not only high-end scientific and technological innovations like the atomic bomb (considered earlier) but also low-end scientific innovations like chemical and biological warfare. Chemical warfare was made possible by what is called the second industrial revolution based on advancements in chemistry and its applications initially in agriculture (war on nature) in the late nineteenth century and later in the military (war on people) in the early twentieth century.

In the first phase, natural dyes came to be replaced with synthetic dyes to meet the expanding demands of the textile industry, a transformation that pushed thousands of farmers in the colonies into penury (economic violence). The First World War pushed industrial countries like Britain, Germany and France to support synthetic substitutes to natural materials to reduce dependence on imports from enemy states. For example, Britain depended on Germany for 88 per cent of her dye stuff needed for army uniforms (Visvanathan 1985: 5), and Germany depended on Chile, which was under blockade, for saltpetre used both as fertilizer and as gunpowder (Born 1965: 194).

The second industrial revolution produced 'industrial research', a new type of research in which science became instrumentalized for technology, which, in turn, aided large-scale commercial manufacturing as well as the war industries (Born 1965; Visvanathan 1985). As Nasir Tyabji (1997) points out, the second industrial revolution altered the relationship between science and technology. Applied sciences became the drivers for technical development and economic growth (Meyer-Thurow 1982; N. Tyabji 1997). The problems for science were set not by the need to explain natural phenomena but rather by the need to expand industrial production. States and corporations together led the second industrial revolution, by extrinsically mobilizing knowledge produced in discrete disciplines to expand and intensify their production for war and commerce (N. Tyabji 1997). Interdisciplinary studies, popular within academia in recent times, arose from the need to extrinsically mobilize disciplinary knowledges for wartime goals and continues to be sustained by the military-industrial–academic complexes (Fuller 2017). The second industrial revolution industrialized invention and in Georg Meyer-Thurow's (1982: 363) words 'the consulting scientist and the scientific entrepreneur were replaced by the salaried industrial research worker'.

The demands of investments in research, derivation of technology from pure sciences and their adaptation for large-scale commercial uses led to the integration of universities, corporations and nation states, a unity institutionalized in the industrial research laboratories as much as in the military–industrial complexes. Industrial research laboratories that came to be established everywhere during the First World War continued after the world wars ended to become a feature of the post–Second World War order. The large capital investments necessary for industrial research also led to mergers of enterprises into large transnational corporations. For example, none of the three large German corporations, Bayer, BASF and Hoechst, could individually support the research for commercial manufacture of synthetic indigo and later saltpetre. The three merged to form the first scientific cartel IG Farben (Beer 1959), a corporation that was to play a pivotal role in the Holocaust in Germany. Other science cartels such as ICI in Britain and Dupont in the United States followed (Beer 1959; Hippler 2017).

Although Germany bore the opprobrium for large-scale chemical warfare in 1915, Britain and France had led the development of chemical weapons, incorporating them into their armed forces by 1914 (Spiers 2010: 29). The real expansion of chemical warfare took place during the interwar years. Faced with the need to demobilize after the First World War, chemical and biological weapons provided a 'cost effective' way of dealing with the anti-colonial movements that swept across European Empires during that period. For example, Winston Churchill favoured use of chemical weapons against 'uncivilized tribes', 'recalcitrant Arabs' and the Afghans in the Third Afghan War (Spiers 2010: 70–1).

By the time Adolf Hitler's 'Final Solution' against European Jews became official German state policy in 1942 at the Wansee Conference (Halebsky 2014: 246), the scientists were well entrenched within the corporations, the corporations embedded within capitalist states and together, the integration of the three had produced a new type of state, the 'warfare state', in the capitalist world that flourished after the end of the Second World War (Edgerton 2005; D'Souza 2019). The manufacture of Zyklon-B by IG Farben (science), the lifting of restrictions on its use by the regulatory bodies (law), the administrative mobilization of furnace manufacturers (economic production), transport authorities (infrastructure) and the SS (ideology), all worked seamlessly as one 'efficient' machinery (DuBois and Johnson 1952; Hayes 1995; Allen 2002; Jeffreys 2008; Baar 2015). Stephen Halebsky (2014: 240) argues that there are important similarities in the high level of organization involved in the Holocaust and the organization of the corporations in their 'relationship to labour; the involvement of professionals, scientists and engineers; the use of secrecy and deception' that produce 'a collective effect whereby these practices combine to weaken potential countervailing forces'. Max Born (1965: 195, 196), the other star among the galaxy of physicists in the first half of the twentieth century, noted 'chemical warfare was a decisive moral defeat for humanity' because 'poison which had been considered an instrument of cowardly murder from time immemorial' was 'sanctioned as a weapon of war'. The Holocaust took the use of this new weapon of chemical warfare to another level of premeditated mass murder, thanks to the 'efficient' machinery of states, corporations and scientists, integrated in a seamless military–industrial–knowledge complex.

Zygmunt Bauman (1989) begins his seminal work on the Holocaust by noting that sociological studies of the Holocaust were more or less absent and that the extensive scholarly literature on the Holocaust were written either by historians or by theologians. Without a sociological account, studies of the Holocaust limit our understanding, reducing it to a one-off event that either occurred in the past (history) or a moral evil that must be condemned (theology). As a one-off event, there are no lessons to be learnt from the Holocaust, and as moral evil, nothing more than condemnation is possible. In either case no lessons can be learnt from the event. Moreover, sociology's own stance on the status of morality is 'awkward and ambiguous' (Bauman 1989: 169). 'Indeed the very idea of the sociological approach to the study of morality has become synonymical with the strategy of, so to speak, sociological reduction; one which proceeds on the assumption that moral phenomena in their totality can be exhaustively explained in terms of non-moral institutions which lend them their building forces' (Bauman 1989: 170). For Bauman (1989: 170), the Holocaust undermines the three stratagems sociology deploys to sustain the idea of 'society as a factory of morality': first, by 'presenting the events as truly unique' and therefore irrelevant for a 'general *theory* of morality' (1989: 175); or second, by dissolving it into a wider 'regular and normal by-product or limitation of a morality producing system' (1989: 175); or lastly, by refusing 'to admit the evidence into the discursive universe of the discipline' and proceeding as if the event had not taken place (1989: 176). Sociology's 'awkward and ambiguous' stance about the status of ethics is important not least because of the field's preeminent place as knowledge producer for political actions, state and corporate policies and as the mediator between science and humanities (Porter 1995). Max Born notes:

> The devaluation of ethics is due to the length and complication of the path between a human action and its final effect. Most workmen know only their special tiny manipulation in a special section of the production process and

hardly ever see the complete product. Naturally they do not feel responsible for this product, or for its use. Whether this use is good or bad, harmless or harmful is completely beyond their field of vision. The most horrid result of this separation of action and effect was the annihilation of millions of human beings during the Nazi regime in Germany; the Eichmann type of killers pleaded not guilty because they 'did their job' and had nothing to do with its ultimate purpose. (Born 1965: 52)

It is states and corporations, as the archetypal social institutions of European modernity, however, that have the capacities to lengthen and complicate the 'path between a human action and its final effect' and mobilize the knowledge produced for purposes that lie beyond the vision of the knowledge producers (Born 1965: 52).

The physical and psychic distance between the act and its consequences is the crux that makes the rupture between knowledge, Truth and values/ethics complete. The rupture between knowledge, Truth and values/ethics in modernist knowledge delinks the producers of knowledge from its users. For Uberoi (2002: x–xi), it is this rupture between knowledge, Truth and ethical actions that constitutes the essence of European modernity. The essence of decolonizing knowledge must therefore turn to unifying knowledge, Truth and ethical actions as the primary aim. Far from decolonizing knowledge, the New World Order after 1945 altered the very meaning of decolonization as the Indian experience demonstrates.

Independence and the two roads for Indian science

On the eve of independence in 1947, a small group of Indian scientists were already well entrenched in the Anglo-American scientific circuits, especially those engaged in nuclear science. By the 1920s, scientists like Meghnad Saha, Satyendra Nath Bose and C. V. Raman, Indians working under the colonial British state, were already making significant contributions to the scientific developments underway in theoretical physics, mathematics and chemistry. (In 1930, physicist C. V. Raman became the first Asian to be awarded the Nobel Prize for contributions to any scientific field (Anderson 2010; Phalkey 2013)). This small group began efforts to institutionalize nuclear science in British India (Anderson 2010; Phalkey 2013). After independence, the dominant scientific elite, well entrenched in the Western scientific community, argued for the continuation of state-led Big Science and Britain's colonial science policies.

This strand mimics Western sciences with remarkable continuity and remains resilient as the mainstream science in post-independence India.

From its very inception, British science policy in India developed under the shadow of the anti-colonial movements that were underway in the country. As Britain's involvement in the world wars deepened, the anti-colonial movements too intensified (D'Souza 2018). Cooperation between the 'white' Anglo-American Allies on nuclear science to the exclusion of British India created trust deficits among Indian scientists. For example, India's rare earth deposits in thorium and beryl were considered crucial for the three Anglo-American Allies – the United Kingdom, the United States and Canada – who signed the 1943 Declaration of Trust agreement to maintain monopoly over fissile materials like uranium and rare earth but excluded British India from the agreement even when the minerals were located in India and Indian scientists were contributing to developments in nuclear sciences and establishing scientific institutions in the country. Indian scientists were also excluded from international conferences, and British India was excluded from interstate discussions on nuclear science, even though they were part of the network of scientists and the British Empire. In contrast, the former USSR invited Indian scientists to their conferences (Anderson 2010: 183). Against the backdrop of the anti-colonial struggles underway, the exclusion of Indian scientists and British India by the Western Allies prompted more contextual understandings of science as discussed in the paragraphs that follow.

Debates over science policy came to the fore after independence by which time Hiroshima–Nagasaki troubled scientists around the world. Those debates centred around the meaning of decolonizing science policy (Abraham 1997; Sur 2002; Anderson 2010; Arnold 2013; Phalkey 2013). For example, Meghnad Saha, one of the world's most prominent nuclear scientists at the time and a modernizer committed to Western state-led science, opposed mimicking the West and its institutions arguing India did not have the social infrastructure, the educational institutions, the technicians, engineers, industrial and manufacturing capacities and other social conditions necessary to sustain Big Science. Without these conditions, Big Science, including nuclear weapons and energy, would paralyse India's independence if not reverse it (Sur 2002). As early as 1935 Meghnad Saha founded the National Institute of Science and its journal *Science and Culture*. The group around *Science and Culture* became an influential voice that sought to promote modern science with context sensitivity and social justice. Decolonizing science for the post-independence circle of scientists around *Science and Culture* was about adapting European modernity to Indian conditions.

With independence also came the search for India's place in the world and in history, inviting questions about whose nation, what kind of nation and what kind of science? If the European Enlightenment provided the philosophical underpinnings for science and modernist knowledge, what are the philosophical underpinnings for Indian science? Is there such a thing as *Indian* science? British scholars had classified Indian philosophy as a field that produced knowledge of the soul and Western philosophy as inherently oriented towards material progress. Indian thinkers challenged the spiritual/material dualism in modern philosophy (Raina 2012). Debiprasad Chattopadhyay's (1959) seminal work *Lokayata*, for example, laboriously set out the materialist traditions in Indian philosophy. The neo-Gandhians challenged the very idea of Western science, arguing that the knowledge system was inherently violent (Nandy 1988), a position that is sometimes seen as a negation of science altogether (Raina 2012). Others plugged into the global search that was underway after the Holocaust and Hiroshima–Nagasaki for a global intellectual history of humankind under the institutional umbrella of the UNESCO. The British biochemist Joseph Needham's seminal work on science in ancient China (Needham n.d.) and the Indian philosopher Debiprasad Chattopadhyay's three volumes of *Science and Technology in Ancient India*, published in 1986, 1991 and 1996, respectively, explored non-European pre-colonial science. Physicists like Capra (1983) turned to Buddhist philosophy for a new basis for science. The British scientist Julian Huxley, who became the first director general of UNESCO, hoped the organization would provide an international institutional umbrella for a just, humane and nonviolent science (Dronamraju 1993).

Necessarily generalizing, UNESCO's attempts understood decolonizing science as 'diversity and inclusion'. Interpreting decolonization as 'diversity and inclusion', far from facilitating 'self-rule' of the scientist and self-determination of nations, following Uberoi, deepened and reified the structures of knowledge of European modernity. Although ostensibly driven by the desire for decolonization, the 'diversity and inclusion' approach remained within the dualist architecture of European modernity, its science and culture and the separation of knowledge from values and action. Not surprisingly, decolonizing knowledge soon merged into state-led nation-building, corporations-led economic development and adaption of Western knowledges to non-Western contexts. Modernization missions in the Third World (Phalkey and Lam 2016) and systematization of military–industrial complexes in the imperial centres put universities at its front and centre (Leslie 1993).

In 1945, under the umbrella of UNESCO, the 'diversity and inclusion' mission was led by scientists. By the 1970s, even the early UNESCO-inspired efforts at 'diversity and inclusion' of knowledges were rolled back. If a milestone is needed to mark the moment, the UN Conference on the Human Environment in 1972 is that moment. Thereafter, European science and culture returned safely to international organizations to become loyal servants of 'legal persons', the states and transnational corporations, with renewed legitimacy granted by the 'diversity and inclusion' mission of international organizations like the UNESCO. In India too, the European Studies programme established by Uberoi was wound up, thus ending a creative moment in efforts to decolonize knowledge (K. Tyabji 2019). Whither decolonizing knowledge and knowledge institutions?

Unity of knowledge, values and action

In contrast to the decolonizing mission after 1945, which was led by scientists, it is both interesting and significant that the decolonizing mission that has returned to Western and Third World universities alike is spearheaded by humanities scholars. Contemporary approaches to decolonizing knowledge sit within the 'West versus Rest' critique in theory and 'diversity and inclusion' goals in practices. At the theory end, indigenous critique focuses on the continued uses of colonial, theoretical and methodological lenses in research and education (Smith 1999). Decolonizing knowledge is frequently framed as 'epistemic injustice' (Mitova 2020; Mukunda 2014; Santos 2014). Both approaches veer towards a new type of essentialism in which everything European is necessarily colonial. In practice, indigenous critique retains the 'tradition versus modern' approaches of the past. The 'epistemic justice' approach revives 'diversity and inclusion' solutions of the early UNESCO era. 'Diversity and inclusion' sounds aspirational at best and rhetorical at worst. Either way, the theory/practice dualism characteristic of the modern knowledge system and culture remains intact. The divide is sharper in science education structured as it is by the fact/value, nature/culture dualism.

Decolonizing science education focuses on making science more sensitive to indigenous values and cultures, more useful socially to indigenous communities, and more participatory, methodologically (Keane, Khupe and Seehawer 2017; Nhemachena, Hlabangane and Matowanyika 2020). Notwithstanding the efforts to 'join up the disciplines' extrinsically, the 'West versus Rest' framework retains the disciplinary divisions between science and humanities and the intrinsic divisions between knowledge, values and actions. Instead, science education seeks to incorporate knowledges of the 'rest' within the intrinsic dualist frameworks (for computing science, see Birhane and Guest 2020; for law, Dhanda and Parashar 2009; for mathematics, Raju 2011, 2017). Whatever its aspirations, decolonizing science curriculum ends up trying to better educate ethnic minority students and those from (neo)colonial nations in modern sciences (Ramani 2011; Chilisa 2017: 29; Kochan 2018; Koopman 2018; Bristol Conversations in Education 2021; Gandolfi 2021). In between, there are a wide range of approaches and discourses about decolonizing knowledge, education, curriculum and universities (Bhambra, Gebrial and Nişancıoğlu 2018; Choudry and Vally 2020).

These efforts reify the idea that modern science can be fitted into another kind of political, cultural or educational system to mitigate its effects, for example welfare capitalism or socialism or more diverse and inclusive educational institutions. This idea is false. In Uberoi's ([1982] 2019a: 12–13) words: 'It appears that the new capitalism of the West produced, just as the old capitalism had done, not any internal perversity of science, but only some external obstacles to the fullness of advance and practical application.'

By pushing the European 'underground' and the anti-colonial critics of modernity in the Third World to the margins, the 'West versus Rest' critique deflects attention from the central challenges to decolonizing knowledge. Why decolonize knowledge? Why decolonize anything? If the purpose is to end the violence against people around the world, it must be asked, as Uberoi (2002: ix–x) does, what is it about European modernist thinking that has brought natures and cultures around the world, in the West *and* the rest of the world, to the brink of extinction? If European modernity became possible because of the coming together of European merchants, intellectuals and a section of the aristocracy during its birth, what are the constellation of forces that keep the modernist knowledge system alive despite its absolute and abject destructiveness over five centuries? Besides, as Uberoi ([1982] 2019b: 35) points out, at the practice end, participatory research and student participation, which so preoccupies contemporary engagement with decolonizing science education, 'cannot solve the deeper problem of colonized self-estrangement in our intellectual culture'.

Attempts to humanize the sciences makes little sense when the scientists as key knowledge workers are alienated from their work and have no control over how the knowledge they produce is used and who uses it. The Union of Concerned Scientists has continued to work even as the war machines of the military–industrial–academia complexes refine their capacities to create 'war ecologies' to unleash even more violence on (neo)colonial subjects. It matters little whether the scientist as knowledge worker is Black, Brown, yellow or white; man, woman or LGBTQ+; from Western or Third World universities. What is at stake is the autonomy of the scientists from states and corporations, who are the key social actors with capacities to organize knowledge production on industrial scales and use it, as the Holocaust demonstrated. The experiences of decolonizing knowledge and society in the Third World show how quickly 'self-rule' and 'self-determination' can be rolled back when the knowledge systems and institutional structures remain 'bimodal' with their capacities to switch from war to peace modes of existence and vice versa. Therefore, the reasons for the failures of past attempts to decolonize need close interrogation.

Being simultaneously outsiders, as non-Europeans, and insiders as recipients of European education, Third World intellectuals and scholars of colour are in a better vantage position to undertake the task of answering the central question of our times. At the present conjuncture, it becomes imperative that the new mission to decolonize knowledge examines the failed attempts to 'renew the medium, message and code of the modernity project' and its inability to 'renew the conditions of its existence' and develops explanatory critiques that illuminate the ontological, semiological and sociocultural necessity for 'renewal of the self at all levels: philosophical, social, and personal' (Uberoi [1982] 2019c) so that human life and nature can be salvaged, and repeated Holocaust and Hiroshima - Nagasaki do not become a condition of existence for the elite as it has today. It is imperative that the mission to decolonize knowledge establishes the intrinsic unity of knowledge, values and actions that leads to the renewal of ourselves as human beings and individuals, and as society, if we are to regenerate the conditions necessary for human life to be possible. As Uberoi ([1982] 2019c: 10) notes: 'Swaraj, or the freedom and sovereignty of self-rule and self-reform, will be achieved through a simultaneous re-examination of the foundations of science, art or culture and politics, their divisions and interrelations with philosophy, or it will not be achieved at all in the world of thought.'

References

Abraham, Itty (1997), 'Science and Secrecy in Making of Postcolonial State', *Economic and Political Weekly*, 32 (33/34): 2136–46.

Allen, Michael T. (2002), 'The Devil in the Details: The Gas Chambers of Birkenau, October 1941', *Holocaust and Genocide Studies*, 16 (2): 189–216. https://doi.org:10.1093/hgs/16.2.189.

Anderson, Robert S. (2010), *Nucleus and Nation : Scientists, International Networks, and Power in India*, Chicago: University of Chicago Press.

Arnold, David (2013), 'Nehruvian Science and Postcolonial India', *Isis*, 104 (2): 360–70. https://doi.org:10.1086/670954.

Baar, Annika Van (2015), 'Corporate Involvement in the Holocaust and Other Nazi Crimes', in Judith Van Erp, Wim Huismanand and Gudrun Vande Walle (eds), *The Routledge Handbook of White-Collar and Corporate Crime in Europe*, 133–50, London: Routledge.

Bauman, Zygmunt (1987), *Legislators and Interpreters: On Modernity, Post-Modernity and Intellectuals*, Cambridge: Polity Press.

Bauman, Zygmunt (1989), *Modernity and the Holocaust*, Cambridge: Polity Press.

Beer, John J (1959), *The Emergence of the German Dye Industry*, Urbana: University of Illinois Press.

Bertell, Rosalie (2006), 'Depleted Uranium: All the Questions about Du and Gulf War Syndrome Are Not Yet Answered', *International Journal of Health Services*, 36 (3): 503–20. https://doi.org:10.2190/13jl-9lhm-fmr4-0v7b.

Bhambra, Gurminder K., Gebrial, Dalia and Nişancıoğlu, Kerem, eds. (2018), *Decolonising the University*, London: Pluto Press.

Birhane, Abeba and Guest, Olivia (2020), 'Towards Decolonising Computational Sciences'. Available at https://arxiv.org/2009.14258 (Accessed: 21 March 2022).

Born, Max (1965), *My Life and My Views*, New York: Charles Scribner's Sons.

Briner, Wayne (2010), 'The Toxicity of Depleted Uranium', *International Journal of Environmental Research and Public Health*, 7 (1): 303–13.

Bristol Conversations in Education (2021), 'Decolonising Education for Sustainable Futures' (UNESCO Chair seminar series). Available at https://www.bristol.ac.uk/education/events/2021/bce10-24feb.html (Accessed: 21 March 2022).

Capra, Fritjof (1983), *The Turning Point: Science, Society And the Rising Culture*, London: Flamingo.

Chattopadhyaya, Debiprasad (1959), *Lokayata: A Study in Ancient Indian Materialism*, Bombay: People's Publishing House.

Chattopadhyaya, Debiprasad (1986), *History of Science and Technology in Ancient India* Vol. 1, Calcutta: Firma KLM.

Chattopadhyaya, Debiprasad (1991), *History of Science and Technology in Ancient India* Vol. 2, Calcutta: Firma KLM.

Chattopadhyaya, Debiprasad (1996), *History of Science and Technology in Ancient India* Vol. 3, Calcutta: Firma KLM.

Chilisa, Bagale (2017), 'Decolonising Transdisciplinary Research Approaches: An African Perspective for Enhancing Knowledge Integration in Sustainability Science', *Sustainability Science,* 12 (5): 813–27. https://doi.org:10.1007/s11625-017-0461-1.

Choudry, Aziz and Vally, Salim, eds. (2020), *University and Social Justice: Struggles Across the Globe*, London: Pluto Press.

Considine, Craig (2013), 'U.S. Depleted Uranium as Malicious as Syrian Chemical Weapons', *HuffPost*. Available at https://www.huffpost.com/entry/us-depleted-uranium-as-ma_b_3812888 (Accessed: 21 March 2022).

Conway, Flo and Siegel, Jim (2005), *In Search of Norbert Wiener The Father of Cybernetics*, Cambridge, MA: Basic Books.

D'Souza, Radha (2010), 'When Unreason Masquerades as Reason: Can Law Regulate Trade and Networked Communication Ethically?' in George Cheny, Steven May and Debashish Munshi (eds), *Handbook of Communication Ethics,* 475–93, New York; Oxon: International Communication Association Routledge/Lawrence Erlbaum.

D'Souza, Radha (2013), 'Review Essay: Justice and Governance in Dystopia', *Journal of Critical Realism*, 12 (4): 518–37.

D'Souza, Radha (2018), 'The October Revolution and the Anti-colonial Movements in South Asia', *Economic & Political Weekly (Special Articles)* 52 (43): 46–58.

D'Souza, Radha (2019), 'The Surveillance State: A Composition in Four Movements', in Aziz Choudry (ed.), *Activists and the Surveillance State: Learning from Repression,* 23–52, London: Pluto Press.

D'Souza, Radha (2020), 'Wars Beyond the Armed Forces: Colonialism and Militarisation of Ethno-national Conflicts in Contemporary South Asia', in Jude Lal Fernando (ed.), *Resistance to Empire and Militarization: Reclaiming the Sacred*, 25–44, Sheffield: Equinox Publishing.

Dhanda, Amita and Parashar, Archana, eds. (2009), *Decolonisation of Legal Knowledge*, Abingdon: Routledge.

Dronamraju, Krishna R. (1993), *If I Am to be Remembered: Correspondence of Julian Huxley*, Singapore: World Scientific Publishing Company.

DuBois, Josiah E. and Johnson, Edward (1952), *The Devil's Chemists: 24 Conspirators of the International Farben Cartel Who Manufacture Wars*, Boston: Beacon Press.

Edgerton, David (2005), *Warfare State: Britain, 1920–1970*, Cambridge: Cambridge University Press.

Fuller, Steve (2017), 'The Military - Industrial Route to Interdisciplinarity', in Robert Frodeman, Juliet T. Klein and Roberto C. S. Pacheco (eds), *The Oxford Handbook of Interdisciplinarity,* Second edn, 53–67, Oxford: Oxford University Press.

Gandolfi, Haira E. (2021), 'Decolonising the science curriculum in England: Bringing decolonial science and technology studies to secondary education', *The Curriculum Journal*, 32 (1): 510–32. https://doi.org/10.1002/curj.97.

Halebsky, Stephen (2014), 'Corporate Practices and Harmful Consequences: Learning from the Holocaust', *Humanity & Sciences*, 38 (3): 237–67.

Haraway, Donna J. (1991), *Simians, Cyborgs, and Women: The Reinvention of Nature*, New York: Routledge.

Hayes, Peter (1995), 'Profits and Persecution: Corporate Involvement in the Holocaust', in James S. Pacy and Alan P. Wertheimer (eds), *Perspectives on the Holocaust: Essays in Honor of Raul Hilberg*, 51–85, New York: Routledge.

Hippler, Thomas (2017), *Governing from the Skies: A Global History of Aerial Bombing*, New York: Verso Books.

Jeffreys, Diarmuid (2008), *Hell's Cartel: IG Farben and the Making of Hitler's War Machine*, London: Bloomsbury.

Keane, Moyra, Khupe, Constance and Seehawer, Maren (2017), 'Decolonising Methodology: Who Benefits from Indigenous Knowledge Research?' *Educational Research for Social Change*, 6: 12–24.

Knight, Chris (2007), 'Noam Chomsky: Politics or Science?'. Available at http://www.chrisknight.co.uk/noam-chomsky-politics-or-science/ (Accessed: 10 March 2022).

Knight, Chris (2016), *Decoding Chomsky: Science and Revolutionary Politics*, New Haven/ London: Yale University Press.

Kochan, Jeff (2018), 'Decolonising Science in Canada: A Work in Progress', *Social Epistemology Review and Reply Collective*, 7 (11): 42–7.

Kone, Aminata M. (2013), 'The Military-Industrial Complex in the United States: Evolution and Expansion from World War II to the War on Terror', *Inquiries Journal*, 5 (8): 1–6. Available at http://www.inquiriesjournal.com/articles/749/the-military-industrial-complex-in-the-united-states-evolution-and-expansion-from-world-war-ii-to-the-war-on-terror (Accessed: 30 March 2022).

Koopman, Oscar (2018), 'Towards Decolonising Teaching Strategies: How to "Domesticate" and "Infuse" Western Science with Indigenous Knowledge', *Journal of Education (University of KwaZulu-Natal)*, 74: 102–15.

Kothari, Rajni (1988), *Rethinking Development: In Search of Humane Alternatives*, Delhi: Ajanta.

Latour, Bruno (2005), *Reassembling the Social: An Introduction to Actor-Network-Theory*, Oxford: Oxford University Press.

Leslie, Stuart W. (1993), *The Cold War and American Science: The Military-Industrial-Academic Complex at MIT and Standford*, New York: Columbia University Press.

Marx, Karl ([1973] 1993), *Grundrisse: Foundations of the Critique of Political Economy (Rough Draft)*, London: Penguin Books.

Meyer-Thurow, Georg (1982), 'The Industrialization of Invention: A Case Study from the German Chemical Industry', *Isis*, 73 (3): 363–81.

Mitova, Veli (2020), 'Decolonising Knowledge Here and Now', *Philosophical Papers*, 49 (2): 191–212. https://doi.org:10.1080/05568641.2020.1779606.

Moran, Patrick (2020), 'War Criminals Fit Right in at MIT'. Available at https://thetech.com/2020/05/27/mcraven-military-connection-mit (Accessed: 30 March 2022)

Mukunda, N. (2014), '*Atomic State: Big Science in Twentieth-Century India* by Jahnavi Phalkey', *Current Science,* 107 (11): 1897–99.

Nandy, Ashis, ed. (1988), *Science, Hegemony and Violence: A Requiem for Modernity*, Oxford, New Delhi: Oxford University Press.

Needham, Joseph (n.d.), Needham Research Institute. Available at https://www.nri.cam.ac.uk/science.html (Accessed: 05 December 2021).

Nhemachena, Artwell, Hlabangane, Nokuthula and Matowanyika, Joseph Z. Z., eds. (2020), *Decolonising Science, Technology, Engineering and Mathematics (STEM) in an Age of Technocolonialism Recentring African Indigenous Knowledge and Belief Systems*, Cameroon: Langaa RPCIG.

Phalkey, Jahnavi (2013), *Atomic State: Big Science in Twentieth Century India*, Ranikhet, India: Permanent Black.

Phalkey, Jahnavi and Lam, Tong (2016), 'Science of Giants: China and India in the Twentieth Century', *BJHS Themes* 1: 1–11. https://doi.org:10.1017/bjt.2016.12.

Porter, Theodore M. (1995), *Trust in Numbers: The Pursuit of Objectivity in Science and Public Life*, Princeton: Princeton University Press.

Raina, Dhruv (2012), 'Decolonisation and the Entangled Histories of Science and Philosophy in India', *Polish Sociological Review* 178: 187–201.

Raju, Chandrakant K. (2011), 'Teaching Mathematics With A Different Philosophy–I Formal Mathematics As Biased Metaphysics', *Science and Culture,* 77 (7/8): 274–9.

Raju, Chandrakant K. (2017), 'Black Thoughts Matter: Decolonized Math, Academic Censorship, and the "Pythagorean" Proposition', *Journal of Black Studies,* 48 (3): 256–78. https://doi.org:10.1177/0021934716688311.

Ramani, Srinivasan (2011), 'Decolonising Knowledge Systems', *Economic and Political Weekly,* 46 (30): 17–19.

Rohracher, Harald (2015), 'Science and Technology Studies, History of', in James D. Wright (ed.), *International Encyclopedia of the Social & Behavioral Sciences,* Second edn, 200–5, Oxford: Elsevier.

Santos, Boaventura de Sousa (2014), *Epistemologies of the South: Justice Against Epistemicide*, Boulder: Paradigm Publishers.

Smith, Linda T. (1999), *Decolonizing Methodologies: Research and indigenous Peoples*, Dunedin: University of Otago Press.

Spiers, Edward M. (2010), *A History of Chemical and Biological Weapons*, London: Reaktion Books Ltd.

Sur, Abha (2002), 'Scientism and Social Justice: Meghnad Saha's Critique of the State of Science in India', *Historical Studies in the Physical and Biological Sciences,* 33 (1): 87–105. https://doi.org:10.1525/hsps.2002.33.1.87.

Tasnim News Agency (2020). 'Iraq to Sue US over Use of Depleted Uranium Weapons: Official'. Available at https://www.tasnimnews.com/en/news/2020/12/15/2410735/

iraq-to-sue-us-over-use-of-depleted-uranium-weapons-official (Accessed: 30 March 2022).

Tyabji, Khalid (2019), 'Foreword', in Jit Pal S. Uberoi and Khalid Tyabji (eds), *Mind and Society: From Indian Studies to General Sociology*, 11–17, New Delhi: Oxford University Press.

Tyabji, Nasir (1997), 'Technology and Dialectics', *Economic and Political Weekly*, XXXII (13): 651–62.

Uberoi, Jit Pal S. (1978), *Science and Culture*, Bombay; Calcutta; Madras: Oxford University Press.

Uberoi, Jit Pal S. (2002), *The European Modernity: Science, Truth and Method*, New Delhi: Oxford University Press.

Uberoi, Jit Pal S. ([1982] 2019a), 'Right, Left and Centre in the Sciences of Nature', in Jit Pal S. Uberoi and Khalid Tyabji (eds), *Mind and Society: From Indian Studies to General Sociology*, 11–17, New Delhi: Oxford University Press.

Uberoi, Jit Pal S. ([1982] 2019b), 'The Student Question', in Jit Pal S. Uberoi and Khalid Tyabji (eds), *Mind and Society: From Indian Studies to General Sociology*, 32–9, New Delhi: Oxford University Press.

Uberoi, Jit Pal S. ([1982] 2019c), 'Swaraj in Ideas of God, Man and Nature', in Jit Pal S. Uberoi and Khalid Tyabji (eds), *Mind and Society: From Indian Studies to General Sociology*, 8–10, New Delhi: Oxford University Press.

Uberoi, Jit Pal S. ([2011] 2019), 'Mind and the World in Modern European Sociology', in Jit Pal S. Uberoi and Khalid Tyabji (eds), *Mind and Society: From Indian Studies to General Sociology*, 41–62, New Delhi: Oxford University Press.

Union of Concerned Scientists (1968), 'Founding Document: 1968 MIT Faculty Statement'. Available at https://www.ucsusa.org/about/history/founding-document-1968-mit-faculty-statement (Accessed:30 March 2022)

Visvanathan, Shiv (1985), *Organizing For Science: The Making of an Industrial Research Laboratory*, Delhi: Oxford University Press.

Werskey, Gary (2007), 'The Marxist Critique of Capitalist Science: A History in Three Movements?' *Science as Culture*, 16 (4): 397–461.

Wiener, Norbert ([1948] 1961), *Cybernetics: Or Control and Communication in the Animal and the Machine*, Cambridge, MA: The MIT Press.

Wiener, Norbert (1964), *God and Golem, Inc.: A Comment on Certain Points where Cybernetics Impinges on Religion*, Cambridge, MA: The M.I.T Press.

Wiener, Norbert ([1950] 1989), *The Human Use of Human Beings: Cybernetics and Society*, London: Free Association Books.

3

Decolonization, feminist politics and the 'Muslim woman's question'

Reading Fanon in the context of the Afghan and Gaza wars

Sunera Thobani

Introduction

The gender–racial politics of the 'war on terror' (2001) came to the fore as soon as the US-led alliance reframed opposition to US foreign policy into an attack on Western civilization. Reinstating the colonial binary between a civilized, equality-oriented West and a 'fanatical' Islamic culture characterized by innate hatred of women, the veil was fetishized to signify Islamic 'terror' and 'misogyny'.[1] The Afghan War thus advanced the racial–gendered dehumanization of Afghan/Muslim women as objects of oppression and of Afghan/Muslim men as irredeemable misogynists (Abu Lughod 2002; Thobani 2002; Al-Saji 2010). Images of veiled Afghan women became pervasive across Western media and public culture as the trope of the oppressed 'Muslim woman' gained traction to mobilize public support for the occupation of Afghanistan. The veil also energized feminists across North America and Europe to make common cause with their states to 'save' Afghan women from Islamic culture and Muslim men.

The veil, however, did not surface as an explicit issue in Israeli/Western state discourse or feminist politics in the Gaza War in 2023. Despite the Islamophobic construction of Hamas, the Palestinian Islamist organization, as 'barbaric'; of the racial dehumanization of Palestinians as 'human animals', 'savage terrorists' and 'children of darkness'; and the presence of the veil in mainstream and social media, the absence of an overt fixation with the veil was striking.

In this chapter, I revisit Fanon's (1959) groundbreaking *Algeria Unveiled*, published in the throes of the Third World revolution, to think through the dynamics of racial–gender politics in the colonial–imperialist wars of the present. The relation between colonialism, race and gender was defined as co-constitutive by Fanon (1986); it was instantiated through violence, epistemic domination and psychic alienation. Explicating this relation was central to the development of his intellectual thought and revolutionary praxis. The anti-colonial movements of the mid-twentieth century had galvanized women across the colonial world; Algeria was no exception. Fanon studied the women's participation in the armed struggle and what their changing relation to the veil revealed about the racial–gender dimensions of colonial violence.

Rejecting the orientalist construct of the veil that shaped the policies of the French Occupation, Fanon (1959) focused on the women's embodied relation to un/veiling to argue that this reflected their evolving revolutionary consciousness in the anti-colonial struggle. Fanon's (1959) de-orientalizing approach to the veil is striking given his lack of engagement with Islam, the tradition with which Western discourses linked the veil, or with the 'Muslim-ness' of Algerian society. His silence on the anti-colonial history of the Islamic tradition across the Maghreb during the late nineteenth and early twentieth centuries, particularly the activities of the Sufi orders, points to his lack of familiarity with its political evolution (Slisli 2008; Thobani 2020; Blaine 2022).

Fanon's (1963) theorization of violence and Third World revolution was, of course, very much of his times. Moreover, the histories and politics of the Algerian revolution, the US-led occupation of Afghanistan in the war on terror and the Zionist/US war in Gaza speak not only to different modalities of colonialism, historical conjunctures and material conditions, they also differ in scope, scale, duration, objective and consequence (Fanon 1963; Said 1979b; Johnson 2002; Khalidi 2004; Mamdani 2004; Khalidi 2020). All three, however, share similarities that cannot be overlooked: all three have been subjected to Western occupation and have been embroiled in Western wars shaped by anti-Islam discourses of racial barbarity, fanatical 'terror' and 'cultural barbarism'.

In an earlier work, I demonstrated how anti-Islam discourses that link this tradition to violence became a structuring feature of the formation of the West at significant junctures: from the Crusades and the emergence of the modern state through colonialism to the post–Second World War international order and the war on terror (Thobani 2020). I also showed how a submerged element in the Orientalism that Said (1979a) identified as central to the making of the West,

Islamophobia, was transformed into the defining expression of this colonial discourse by the war on terror (Thobani 2020). Although Islam did not feature large in Fanon's thought, I demonstrate here that the depth of his understanding of race and colonialism led him to recognize how central the fetishization of the veil was to colonial policies in Algeria. No doubt contemporary racial–gender configurations of power, like the activism of women, are more complex than Fanon might have anticipated, but the racial–gender dynamics of the colonial violence he studied are no less pronounced in contemporary global politics. Fanon's (1959) insights regarding these dynamics, rooted in anti-colonial praxis, have much to offer present struggles for decolonization, not least because the revolutionary upheavals of his times shape the conflicts of the present.

Fanon's biography is well known; it needs little recounting here. Born in the French colony of Martinique, he fought with the Allied Forces in the Second World War, where, disillusioned with the racism he experienced, he trained as a psychiatrist in France and went on to work in a French hospital, *Blida-Joinville*, in Algeria. Acutely attuned to the global structure of race by his experiences in the Caribbean and France, Fanon's psychiatric practice shaped the development of his political–philosophical concerns, which soon led him to join the Algerian resistance (Macey 2012). Fanon's anti-colonial thought was centred on the violence that produced race and the colonial order. Violence was indispensable to territorial control, economic exploitation and political subjugation, he argued (Fanon 1963); violence was also waged at the psycho-social and cultural level to destroy the historical consciousness and psychic integrity of subjugated peoples (Fanon 1986). Fanon's theorization of colonialism, racial subjectivity and revolutionary consciousness situated him at the forefront of the Third World struggles that reshaped global politics after the mid-twentieth century.

Yet Fanon's theories of violence, race and gender were not without controversy (Bhabha 1986; Gordon, Sharpley-Whiting and White 1996; Gibson 1999; Cornell 2001; Alessandrini 2016). *Black Skin White Masks*, in which Fanon (1986) explored racial alienation and colonial subjectivity, remains favoured by those working on the psychology of oppression, but Fanon's theories of violence and critiques of nationalism, colonial as well as anti-colonial, presented in *The Wretched of the Earth* received a frostier reception (Bhabha 1986; Alessandrini 2016). This work nevertheless became foundational to anti-racist and anti-colonial studies and politics. Influential feminist critics, however, considered his treatment of women of colour and female sexual desire as little more than sexist denigration, emblematic of his phallocentrism, male chauvinism and/or Black nationalism (Faulkner 1996; Helie-Lucas 1999; Conway 2007), despite his well-known critiques of Negritude, masculinity and nationalism.

In the section that follows, I begin with a reading of *Algeria Unveiled* by attending to its content as well as methodological approach in the context of Fanon's anti-colonial framework. Demonstrating how Fanon's (1959) historicized and grounded approach to Algerian women's practice of veiling and unveiling led him to understand these as reflection of their agency, I highlight how Fanon identified the development of the women's revolutionary consciousness as a transformative force in the larger Third World revolution. The second section of my chapter addresses dominant feminist responses to *Algeria Unveiled* to show how their decontextualizing fixation on the veil contributed to their definition of his work as anti-woman. I also discuss more nuanced readings of Fanon from marginalized feminist traditions, which argued for the salience of his insights against their dismissal by Western and Westernizing feminists.

In the final section, I turn to the fetishization of the veil in the Afghan War and the overt silence on this sartorial object in the Gaza War. Exploring this seeming paradox, my contention is that the Western state and feminist essentialization of Afghan women (victims of 'Islamic' terror) and of Palestinian women (supporters of 'Islamic' terror) denies both communities of women political – and *politicized* – subjectivity. The dehumanization of Palestinian women, however, is such that the gendered dimension of the Gaza genocide met with state and feminist silence. Acknowledgement of this gendered dimension, I argue, requires, even if only implicitly, recognition of the humanity of Palestinian women. Dehumanizing as the fetishization of the veil was in the Afghan War, recognition of the veil entailed some recognition of Afghan women's gendered – albeit racially and culturally degraded – humanity. Such recognition was dispensed with in the Gaza War as its genocidal objective demands the complete dehumanization of Palestinians. Read alongside Israeli/Western state attempts to erase Palestinian history, presence and political claims, feminist silence renders Palestinian women non-existent within feminist politics. Feminists have yet to contend with such alignments of feminist politics with the violence of Western states at the global level.

Rereading *Algeria Unveiled*

Fanon's essay was informed by his astute insight into the racial–gender politics of colonialism: French control of Algeria depended on the destruction of the very structure of Algerian society and gaining control of Algerian women was key to the realization of this objective. This led him to describe the Occupation's 'precise political doctrine' in the following terms: 'If we want to destroy the structure of Algerian society, its capacity for resistance, we must first of all conquer the women; we must go and find them behind the veil, where they hide themselves and in the houses where the men keep them out of sight' (Fanon 1959: 37–8). Identifying the French attempt to 'get' to the women as 'the theme of action' (Fanon 1959: 38), Fanon studied how this unfolded in the psychic-embodied effects of Algerian women's practice of veiling and unveiling. Given his unfamiliarity with Islam, the hermeneutic power of Fanon's essay is all the more remarkable.

Noting how clothing – women's and men's – functions as visual marker of 'difference' to an outsider, Fanon (1959: 37) distinguished the visibility of the veil as an item of clothing from its construction as symbolic object and 'bone of contention in a grandiose battle of which the occupation forces were to mobilize their most powerful and most varied resources'. Colonial administrators, working with the 'scientific coloration' and 'sociological discoveries' of European experts, determined that 'outside appearances are paramount' in Arab society and that, underneath the external patrilineal surface of Algerian society, lay a strong matrilineal order, Fanon (1959: 37) explains. The destruction of this order required contending with the veil, deemed representative of the people's 'originality' and 'forms of existence likely to evoke a national reality directly or indirectly' (Fanon 1959: 37). This became an overriding colonial objective which involved the social and charitable agencies that 'descended on the Arab quarters' (Fanon 1959: 38). Once colonial authorities 'won over' the women, they anticipated 'the rest' of Algerian society would follow (Fanon 1959: 37). Reordering gender relations in Algerian society was, therefore, vital to the interests of the French state; failure to subjugate Algerian women endangered the stability of the Occupation. At a later date, Edward Said (1979a) would identify this Western fixation with gender as an organizing principle of the Orientalist discourse that feminized the 'Orient' as static and despotic while constituting Europe as masculine and modernizing.

In response to French pressure to unveil the women, Algerian society would 'display a surprising force of inertia', which Fanon (1959: 38) read as refusal to subjugation. French 'indignation' and 'lamentations' shaped the 'sadistic and perverse' everyday encounters as they constantly berated Algerian men for the 'degraded condition' of Algerian women (1959: 38). If Algerian women were interpellated to 'play a functional, capital role in the transformation of their lot' (Fanon 1959: 38), Algerian men, particularly from professional classes, faced a double bind: humiliation (for delivering Algerian women to the French) or derision (branded misogynist for their reluctance).

The Algerian unwillingness to deliver themselves to colonial power was attributed to Islam by the French (Islam's 'hold' over its 'prey') (Fanon 1959: 41), but, attuned to the politics of desire, Fanon turned his attention to the sexual desire that infused the colonial fixation with the veil. Analysing the dream material of his French patients, Fanon identified the 'romantic exoticism, tinged with sensuality' that animated the colonial drive to get to Algerian women. His French patients' obsession with uncovering Algerian women's 'hidden' beauty, whose seductive power they believed to be unparalleled, fetishized the veil. Analysing the compulsion to make this woman 'available for adventure', Fanon linked these sexual phantasies to the rapes of Algerian women by French troops. The production of this sexualized phantasm of 'the Algerian woman' was subsequently documented by Malek Alloula (1986) in his study of the French photographers whose staged and eroticized images of semi-clad veiled Algerian women were displayed in postcards that became popular across French society. This sexual obsession was also pointed out by Marnia Lazreg (1994: 3) in the 'colonial gendered double standard' of highlighting Algerian women's 'cultural victimization' while commodifying their sexuality by transforming '[D]ancers and daughters of recalcitrant opponents of colonialism' into 'prostitutes'.

In Fanon's (1959: 42) view, the Algerian resistance to unveiling revealed the attempt to assert a 'distinct identity', a 'concern with keeping intact a few shreds of national existence'.[2] This refusal, Fanon (1959: 47) argued, revealed 'one of the laws of the psychology of colonization': the 'plans of the occupier' come to 'determine the centers of resistance around which a people's will to survive becomes organized'. Previously a 'dead element of the Algerian cultural stock', the French obsession with the veil gave this object 'new life' (Fanon 1959: 47). What was once an 'undifferentiated element in a homogenous whole acquires a taboo character', such that women's attitude towards the veil would 'be constantly related' to their attitude towards the Occupation (Fanon 1959: 47). Holding on to the veil dealt 'a spectacular setback' to the Occupation and signalled the women's 'keeping up the atmosphere of an armed truce' with the colonizers (Fanon 1959: 47). In short, Algerian women's refusal to unveil signified their refusal to submit to the power of the Occupation.[3]

This reluctance to unveil changed dramatically with the advance of the armed struggle as women responded in unexpectedly large numbers to the leadership's strategy for recruitment into the resistance. Quickly becoming 'active' and 'essential elements' in the armed struggle, women on its frontlines faced the threat of torture, rape and murder from the French authorities (Fanon 1959: 49). This development was 'a wholly revolutionary step', Fanon (1959: 49) observed, for the women made themselves anew by expressing their revolutionary consciousness in their political, and politicized, agency.

The transformation of the women was both corporeal and psychic. Previously 'accustomed to confinement', Fanon (1959: 49) observed that they 'did not have the normal mobility before a limitless horizon of avenues, of unfolded sidewalks, of people dodged or bumped into'. Here, Fanon came close to undercutting his own radical reading of the veil by describing it as 'imprisoning'. Yet he believed the women 'instinctively' took to their new role, given that such unveiled mobility was not their 'bringing to light a character known and frequented a thousand times in imagination or stories'; instead, the women's unveiling signified 'an authentic birth in a pure state without preliminary instruction' (Fanon 1959: 50).

Fanon was clearly unfamiliar with the complex heterogeneity in the lives and experience of Algerian women (Lazreg 1994): my reading of Fanon suggests he identified the women's act of unveiling as an 'authentic birth' because it arose from a conscious decision to unveil in order to advance the armed struggle, not in pursuit of an abstract idea of 'freedom'. Fanon's (1963, 1986) anti-colonial framework theorized revolutionary consciousness as grounded in revolutionary praxis; this led him away from the Orientalist conflation of unveiling with an amorphous, ahistoric idea of 'freedom'. Women's experience of unveiled mobility was physically disorientating, a shift from (veiled) comfort to unaccustomed public encounter with a fracturing gaze, but Fanon (1959: 50) describes this act of unveiling as 'an intense dramatization, a continuity between the woman and the revolutionary'. His highlighting of 'continuity' between 'woman' and 'revolutionary' indicates that Fanon read the act of unveiling as 'authentic birth' because the act marks the moment of organic transformation in the subjectivity of the woman. By her consciously determined revolutionary action, the woman moves into revolutionary subjecthood. Where Fanon is often read as 'speaking' for a homogenized 'Algerian woman' (Lazreg 1994), his essay demonstrates an attempt to study a concrete, embodied experience.

Once the French authorities discovered women had joined the resistance, the revolutionaries turned to the veil to protect themselves from detection and continue their war. But this shift was no reversion to an older 'cultural' practice, Fanon argued, for, having been

> [re]moved and reassumed again and again, the veil has been manipulated, transformed into a technique of camouflage, into a means of struggle. The virtually taboo character assumed by the veil in the colonial situation disappeared almost entirely in the course of the liberating struggle. Even Algerian women not actively integrated into the struggle formed the habit of abandoning the veil. (Fanon 1959: 61)

His point is colonialism had rendered veiling outmoded as a 'cultural' practice, indeed colonialism had rendered that 'culture' itself 'outmoded' (Fanon 1959). Hence the veil, even when readopted, had already been 'stripped once and for all of its exclusively traditional dimension' (Fanon 1959: 63). What Fanon (1959: 63) called 'the historic dynamism of the veil' was evident in its redefinition in the revolutionary sentiment he identified as organically reworking the people's cultural norms and expressions.[4]

Notwithstanding his limited engagement with Algerian society, a valuable insight to be gleaned from Fanon's (1959: 41–2) analysis is that organic shifts in a society's given practices and forms of acculturation require re-evaluation of its 'deepest values, its most stable values' as part of the process of change itself. The revolution, like the decision of the women to unveil, demanded such re-evaluation, including renegotiation of gender roles within family and society which had already changed with colonial dispossession. The Algerian family and society changed yet again, but now as organic phenomenon that exceeded the explicit objectives of the revolution.

Fanon's analysis of such transformation of Algerian society underscored the gendered nature of the revolution itself. As he noted, 'In reality, the effervescence and the revolutionary spirit have been kept alive by the women in the home. For her war is not a war of men' (Fanon 1959: 66). Where the phantasm of the 'the Algerian woman' transformed colonized women into absent presence in the French obsession with unveiling, into 'Fatimas' and 'Muslim natives' (Lazreg 1994), Algerian women, in their role as revolutionary agents, made themselves wilfully present in their decision to fight for the collective social. Where the French sought to recruit the women – by shame, compulsion or persuasion – in the destruction of their culture and society, the women's decision to unveil, and then to veil again, advanced – on their terms – their struggle for their own and collective Algerian liberation.

As Fanon (1959: 66) came to understand, it was the women who exposed and condemned the gendered violence of the war: 'The Algerian woman is at the heart of the combat. Arrested, tortured, raped, shut down, she testifies to the violence of the occupier and his inhumanity. As a nurse, a liaison agent, a fighter, she bears witness to the depth and density of the struggle.' Moreover, where French policy aimed to turn Algerian women against Algerian men and society, the women's revolutionary praxis transformed their own as well as Algerian men's being: 'The militant man discovers the militant woman, and jointly they create new dimensions for Algerian society' (Fanon 1959: 63). The transformation in the women's consciousness brings the possibility of building a new world into the political horizon.

Colonialism was a global phenomenon, and as theorized in Fanon's (1963) larger political framework, the anti-colonial revolution was likewise internationalist in scope and affiliations. The revolution given momentum by Algerian women was part of this internationalist resistance, given that the political strategies and epistemological advances of the Algerian struggle made it the 'vanguard' of the global revolution (Byrne 2016). Fanon's intellectual-political work approached anti-colonialism as an intercontinental revolution that was mobilizing 'a collective subjectivity of the Third World' against the Euro-American order (Bose 2019). Remaking their own subjectivity in their own particular location, Algerian women revolutionaries also advanced this Third World intercontinental revolutionary consciousness.

Fanon's insights into the anti-colonial revolution cannot be severed from his methodological approach. His essay situated the veil in its historical context and material conditions. Attending to the specificity of gender in the colonial condition and engaging with women's lived experiences in the context of his overall anti-colonial framework, Fanon (1959) was able to glimpse the extent of the transformative power embodied by the women. In his psychiatric practice, Fanon attended to his patients' – including women's – own accounts of their embodied experience to develop his own understanding of the traumatic effects of colonial violence. As such, he was privy to the collective as well as individual phantasies, desires and pathologies that shaped the driving impetus for the French Occupation *and* for the opposition it faced. These experiences, which he read in light of his own experience of being racialized, led to Fanon's (1986) insistence that 'sociogeny' stands alongside phylogeny and ontogeny in his critique of the Eurocentric psychoanalytic tradition. Stressing the relevance of history and context, Fanon rejected the political as well as psychoanalytic representation of the European male subject as standing in for 'Man', the 'universal' Subject.

Despite the acumen of Fanon's reading of the transformative potential of Algerian women's activism, the expectations he had of the political moment they helped forge was to prove overly optimistic. For the counterrevolution that Fanon (1963) also warned of rapidly took hold, thwarting the possibilities for change thrown up by the women's activism.

Feminists respond to *Algeria Unveiled*

Fanon's analysis of the women's participation in the Algerian war, Lazreg (1994: 120) argues, 'does not shed light on the FLN's ambivalence towards women', nor did it undertake 'a historical analysis of the ways in which colonial domination affected women as women', although she also notes that he 'was right, even if only rhetorically so, to affirm that "revolutionary war is not a war of men"'. This ambiguity runs through Lazreg's (1994: 120) reading as she notes that the veil was an urban issue, that women 'could move in and out of identities' and argues that although Fanon's views on the 'dialectics of the body and the world are important', he reduced women's participation in the struggle to the question of the veil and hence shared the colonial fascination with its mystique as well as with the women's 'bodily transfiguration'. Nevertheless, Lazreg (1994: 121) concludes, '[No] matter how problematic Fanon's explanation of women's motivations as well as engagement in the war on decolonization was, it did not question the revolutionary spirit that animated them'. While Lazreg is right to point to the limitations of Fanon's understanding of Algerian history and gendered society, she reads *Algeria Unveiled* outside the context of his larger anti-colonial framework, reduces his psychoanalytic analysis to 'remarks' and does not address his reading of the veil's centrality in the policies of the Occupation.

Despite such notable exceptions, hegemonic feminist readings of *Algeria Unveiled* were not friendly. Marie Helie-Lucas (1999) argued that Fanon grossly exaggerated Algerian women's agency in the revolution. Algerian women were oppressed by the movement's male leadership and their compatriots, she argues, as she describes the women as 'brainwashed' into complying with 'female tasks', covering up male 'misbehavior', and baulking at criticizing the nation or state (Helie-Lucas 1999). In her account, Algerian women remained bound to 'tradition' while men enjoyed 'access to modernity' (Helie-Lucas

1999). Curiously, she resuscitated the idea of colonial benevolence by claiming that whereas 'French officials had insisted that Algerian women should be freed from the oppression of the veil. . . . Fanon praised the revolutionary virtue of the veil' (Helie-Lucas 1999: 275). Had her criticism of Fanon's essay not enjoyed success among feminists (Helie-Lucas was a founder and executive coordinator of the transnational network, *Women Living Under Muslim Laws*), it would hardly merit attention. No doubt Algerian women struggled against the sexism of the male leadership and revolutionaries. But Helie-Lucas (1999) dismissed the women's agency by representing them as 'brain-washed'. Her claim that French officials 'insisted' on Algerian women's 'freedom' from the 'oppression' of the veil reveals more about her Orientalist leanings than about Algerian women's agency or Fanon's analysis of the veil. Nigel Gibson (1999: 18) noted that Helie-Lucas 'falls into the trap of equating Fanon with the politics of the post-colonial regime', given her attribution of responsibility to Fanon for the post-independence reversals of the gains made by women during the revolution. More significant from my perspective, Helie-Lucas reinstituted the ahistoric and orientalizing *European* approach to the veil as *the* Algerian feminist position on the veil.

Rita Faulkner (1996: 847–8) advanced a similarly dismissive argument claiming Fanon considered the French view on the veil as 'a purported colonial plot', depicted Algeria 'as a veiled woman' and defined unveiling 'as tantamount to rape'. Fanon's nuanced critique of the veil's fetishization, tradition and modernity, violence of the colonial state as well as the dangers of nationalism seemed to have escaped her notice. Gibson's assessment of Helie-Lucas is as applicable to Faulkner's reading of Fanon, who she claims defined Algerian women as liberated, their equality secured. Reducing Algerian women to the position of hapless victims, Faulkner too ejected them from 'feminist' history, agency and politics.

A more nuanced approach to *Algeria Unveiled* was taken by Anne McClintock (1999), who noted Fanon's rejection of the centralized state, militarization and the metaphor of nation as family, as well as his critique of nationalism. Describing Fanon as exemplary for his attention to gender, she noted also he made no 'easy relation of identity between the psychodynamics of the unconscious and the psychodynamics of political life' (McClintock 1999: 284). Fanon recognized the 'traitorous agency' the French offered to Algerian women, she stressed, primarily as means to control Algerian men and society. Despite acknowledging these contributions, McClintock (1999: 291) argued that Fanon ultimately negated Algerian women's agency because he did not recognize 'feminist grievance' before the national uprising; nor did he think Algerian women's agency was learned from other women. By positing Algerian women's agency as learned 'instinctively', at the 'invitation' of men, Fanon turned this into a 'passive offspring of male agency', thus foreclosing it even as he 'brilliantly raises this as a question' (McClintock 1999: 291).

McClintock (1999: 292) further argued that the Algerian woman revolutionary functioned as 'phallic substitute' in Fanon's analysis, a 'masculinized rapist' who carried 'the men's pistols, guns and grenades beneath her skirts' to 'penetrate a little further into the flesh of the revolution'. A masculine 'dread', an alarm that arming Algerian women 'might entail a fatal unmanning of the Algerian man', was at work in Fanon's essay (McClintock 1999: 292). It is notable that McClintock reads this allegedly castrating effect of Algerian women's agency on Algerian men, not on the Occupation forces that were targeted by the women. She concludes Fanon was unable to countenance the women's agency *outside* the constraints of national agency (McClintock 1999).

McClintock overlooks Fanon's observation of the transformative effects of the women's praxis on the consciousness of Algerian men and society more broadly. His observation that *the* revolutionaries – female as well as male – experienced psychic, political and *social* radicalization in the struggle was not addressed by her. Where Algerian women's participation recognized the revolution as a collective struggle, McClintock (1999) elevated gender over the racial-colonial divide to represent as unbridgeable the gender divide between Algerian women and men. This argument may have been more persuasive had McClintock accounted for Fanon's (1959, 1986) critique of the psychically fracturing effects of racial-colonial violence on Algerian men (indeed on Black and Brown men), which incited the desire to 'mimic' white masculinity.

Overlooking this crucial aspect of Fanon's analysis of racial-colonial masculinity, McClintock's (1999) claim of a 'male dread' projects onto Fanon, and Algerian men, the psychic conundrums of European men whose 'civilizing' masculinity relied on mastering women. At best, McClintock's criticism is misplaced, given Fanon's analysis of the visceral 'unmanning' effects of colonial subjugation on the Black/Algerian male, emasculated by the colonizing-racializing practices of the white Man and Woman, even the white Child, not by the colonized Algerian female. Colonized women might have such an effect on colonized men, as Fanon (1986) recognized (see his reading of Mayotte Capecia), but only to the extent they allied themselves with the power of white men and/or 'mimicked' white women. Resorting to an ahistoric universalizing conception of masculinity, McClintock obscures the historically specific experience of colonized males and forecloses the possibility of their capacity to learn from, or find inspiration in, colonized women's revolutionary praxis.

Liam Decker (1990–1991) similarly argued that Fanon overlooked the oppression of women in Muslim society and the 'phallocentrism' with which they had to contend, along with colonialism. He uses Kristeva's psychoanalytic concept of the 'veiled Phallic Mother' to argue for alliance between Algerian women and Western feminists once the former's 'different' subjectivity is accounted for (Decker 1990–1991). Overlooking Fanon's critique of the role of the Eurocentric psychoanalytical tradition in advancing colonial violence, Decker deployed ahistoric concepts from this very tradition (albeit in its feminist variant) in an attempt to reconcile the 'difference' between Algerian women and feminist politics as essentially Western.

Illustrative of a larger trend in feminist approaches to Fanon, the readings discussed in the preceding paragraphs do not attend to his critique of the role of French/Western women in the domestication and unveiling of Algerian/colonized women. Instead, all assume *a priori* a common interest among 'women' across the racial–colonial divide. If an abstract male dread is invoked to disappear the revolutionary consciousness Fanon (1959) discerns in the activism of Algerian women, an equally abstract cross-national/cultural women's solidarity is posited as liberatory for colonized women. In the process, the conflicting racial–colonial interests that divide colonized women and Western women is elided. These feminist methodological approaches would be reproduced in the war on terror, as I discuss in the next section.

A receptive reading of *Algeria Unveiled* came from Tracy Denean Sharpley-Whiting (1999: 338), who argued Fanon saw Algerian women as struggling to free themselves from colonial domination and the 'time-honored traditions of silence, invisibility and sequestration' as they transformed the 'value systems' of the Algerian family. Rejecting the contention that Fanon considered Algerian women the 'symbolic repository of group identity, or body through which traditions passed', Sharpley-Whiting (1999: 338) argued that Fanon's analysis of the changes in the revolutionary woman's personality as she 'discovered the exalting realm of responsibility' was crucial to his understanding of her agency. Fanon's point was that the women took responsibility for themselves and their own actions in defiance of 'traditional Islamist laws' that were 'challenged, overturned, during the course of the revolutionary struggle' (Sharpley-Whiting

1999: 338). And while Fanon (1959) ascribed responsibility to the state for protection of the women's rights and wellbeing, not only in the constitution but also in the workplace and parliament, he argued that Algerian women's right to exist as autonomous beings relied on their coming to this realization themselves. Moreover, Fanon believed the revolutionary transformation undergone by the women would be difficult to reverse:

> This woman, who . . . would carry grenades or submachine gun chargers, this woman who tomorrow would be outraged, violated, tortured, *could not* put herself back into her former state of mind and relive her behaviour of the past; this woman who was writing the heroic pages of Algerian history was, in doing so, bursting the bounds of the narrow world in which she had lived . . . and was at the same time participating in the destruction of colonialism and in the birth of a new woman. . . . The woman-for-marriage progressively disappeared, and gave way to the woman-for-action. . . . The man's words were no longer law. The women were no longer silent. . . . The woman ceased to be a complement for man. *She literally forged a new place for herself by her sheer strength.* (Fanon 1959: 347)

The post-independence reversal of the gains of the revolution closed off this space for change opened by the women revolutionaries.

More pointedly, Sharpley-Whiting (1999: 342) emphasized Fanon's exposure of the hypocrisy of 'colonial feminists', their unequal 'intra-gender power' and the benefits *they* derived from the colonial construct of 'archaic tradition' as the *cause* of Algerian women's oppression; these feminists aided 'the expropriation of resources, raw materials and labor' to the detriment of Algerian society and cultural identity. Fanon recognized the radical possibilities thrown open in moments of revolutionary upheaval, and, unlike Western feminists, he did not believe Algerian/Muslim women to be incapable of recognizing and advancing these possibilities. Drucilla Cornell (2001) likewise read *Algeria Unveiled* as a 'tribute to the courage and fearlessness' of the women and underscored the point that Fanon considered the women's voluntary act of unveiling as an act of political self-identification that reclaimed national identity and rejected the colonial condition.

The feminist responses to Fanon's essay discussed in this section are representative; they illustrate a range of *feminist* reading practices and methodological approaches, many of which resurfaced in feminist interventions in the war on terror. Dominant among these practices were, unfortunately, de-historicization, abstraction and universalization of the Western subject, Man and Woman. These particular approaches, and their fixation with the veil, helped shape the feminist politics of the early twenty-first century (Thobani 2020).

Terror, war, occupation: Contemporary feminist politics

The 'precise political doctrine' of the French Occupation described by Fanon – that is, destruction of the structure of Algerian society and derailment of native resistance through control of Algerian women – was reinvoked in the war on terror. The US-led alliance reframed 9/11 from an attack on US foreign policy in the Middle East to an attack on Western civilization by 'Islamic terrorism' and, by tying this 'terror' to gender oppression in the figure of the veiled Afghan woman, renewed the political charge of the veil in global politics. The launch of the occupation of Afghanistan as the means to destroy 'Islamic' terror and 'liberate' Afghan women fused imperialist violence with gender politics; the 'liberation' of Afghan women was thus transformed from a feminist demand of Afghan women into a rallying cry for the occupation of Afghanistan (Abu-Lughod 2002; Thobani 2002). Shunting aside the histories of Afghan women – their struggles against British colonialism, their response to the nationalist/reformist linking of unveiling to Westernization and modernization, their opposition to the Soviet Occupation as well as their struggles with the Taliban's reimposition of the veil (Kolhatkar 2002; Dossa 2014; Kohari 2022) – the US-led alliance fetishized the veil into a symbol of 'Islamic barbarism'. As was the case in Algeria, this overdetermination of the veil essentialized Afghan, and by extension Muslim, women into passive victims of Afghan men and Islamic culture. Drawing on the political language and values of Western feminism, especially its privileging of individualism, free choice and gender equality, US-led states integrated these feminist tropes into their militarized alliance.

Feminist intellectuals and organizations, for the main, furthered the reach of this 'precise political doctrine' of Western imperialism by grounding it in feminist theory. Their integration of the tropes of cultural barbarism, imprisoning *burqa*s and woman-hating Muslim men into feminist politics aligned these with the interests of the imperialist state. Feminist activists and networks, including that co-founded by Helie-Lucas in 1984, enjoyed newfound popularity as they called for the imposition of Western gender norms and individual rights onto the Muslim world (Narain 2023).

Interrogating this renewed obsession with the veil and its 'repetitive representational logic', al-Saji (2010: 876) noted how this worked to 'de-subjectify' Muslim women. As al-Saji (2010: 877) argued, 'western representations of veiled Muslim women are not simply *about* Muslim women themselves. Rather than *representing* Muslim women, these images fulfil a different function: they provide the foil or negative mirror in which western constructions of identity and gender can be *positively* reflected'.

Alongside international human rights networks, feminists developed reconstruction projects and lobbied Western states and agencies to provide opportunities for education, employment and political participation to Afghan women. These networks 'partnered' with Afghan women to integrate them into the institutions set up by Western agencies under the aegis of the Occupation, while Western feminist politicians soon developed 'feminist foreign policy' for their states (UN Women 2022). As had been the case in Algeria, Afghan women were 'invited' to participate in the Occupation's institutions and governance systems that advanced US/Western interests, an invitation that remains ongoing even now (USAID 2022). As had also been the case in Algeria, immense resources were invested in projects seeking to transform Afghan women into an active force in the cultural and socio-economic subjugation of their communities. Given Afghanistan's strategic location and its rich mineral deposits, the integration of Afghan women in service of US imperialist domination was organized through extending Western discourses of women's and human rights as the global norm.

The possibility of Afghan women having the capacity to advance the anti-imperialist interests of their own societies in the context of their own political, cultural and social histories was rendered illegible in international feminist politics (Kolhatkar 2002; Kohari 2022). Instead, exaltation of Western gender values reinstated what Fanon (1959) described as the 'sadistic and perverse' interactions of the colonial condition, now between Western and Afghan/Muslim men, between Western feminists and Afghan/Muslim women. Despite the violence of the war reaching 'the inner recesses of life' (Dossa 2014: 7) as Afghan women bore 'the brunt of the harm and suffering' of the war and its displacements (Dossa 2014: 10), the narrative of US benevolence has persisted. The war's immense death toll, including women and children, was dismissed by Occupation forces as 'collateral damage' to compound the devastations of the Afghan population (Thobani 2020). Such violence was also rendered irrelevant in the feminist politics that decried the withdrawal of US forces (2020) as Western betrayal of Afghan women.

If racial–gender politics were integral to the Afghan War, this was no less the case with the Gaza War, which I read as yet another front in the war on terror. The Israeli/US War on Gaza, which followed the Hamas attack on 7 October 2023, accelerated the Zionist project of ethnic cleansing of the Palestinian nation that began with the 1948 Naqba (Said 1979b; Khalidi 2020; Massad 2024; Shehadeh 2024). Dispossessing Palestinians from most of their territories over the decades that followed, Israel imposed a blockade on Gaza in 2007 upon the election of Hamas, the Islamist–Palestinian resistance organization. With the backing of Western states, Israel subsequently launched serial wars on the Gaza strip to isolate, punish and eventually destroy its people. With Palestinians pushed to subsistence-level existence in Gaza and subjected to increasing settler encroachment in the West Bank, their resistance against the occupation took a dramatic turn with the breakout of Hamas, along with other Palestinian factions, from the 'open-air prison' that was Gaza (October 7, 2023). Armed and protected by the United States, the United Kingdom and Germany, Israel launched its deadliest war to date on Palestinians, devastating the population and destroying most of the infrastructure in Gaza in a matter of months.

Reproducing the discourse of the war on terror, the Gaza War was waged as an existential Israeli/Western fight against Hamas and its purported 'Islamic barbarity'. Yet there was marked silence on the veil in the political framing of this war, despite the veil's extensive visibility in mainstream and social media images of Palestinian women under siege. If 'winning' over the veiled Afghan woman was a key objective in the Afghan War, why the silence on the veil in the Gaza War? If there had been widespread Western feminist mobilization to 'save' Afghan women, why the feminist (non)-engagement with the violence done to Palestinian women? What does such silence reveal about the contemporary articulation of racial–gender politics to colonial–imperialist violence?

The relation of Palestinian women to the veil is complex and varied; it has also been spatially and temporally specific. As in Algeria, the veil was Orientalized to signify the gender oppression of all Arab women in earlier colonial discourses (Farah 2002). Palestinian women's embodied experiences in the present reveal the practice to be an expression of resistance to Israeli Occupation, a means to protect women's safety and modesty in conditions of Occupation, an assertion of national and anti-colonial identity and a symbol of personal piety (Farah 2002; Shalhoub-Kevorkian 2010).

Palestinian women have been 'frontliners' in the resistance against Israeli violence, argues Shalhoub-Kevorkian (2010). Their everyday reproductive labour is essential to their families' survival in conditions of conflict, war and dispossession, this daily determination to 'fight with whatever resources they can muster . . . reflect the hidden energies within women who are confronting political violence' (Shalhoub-Kevorkian 2010: 1–2). Moreover, women's work within the home is grounded in their memories which keep alive their relationship to their land and defy Israeli attempts to erase their presence. Despite Palestinian women's situated resistance being 'an inescapably analytical feminist location' as Shalhoub-Kevorkian argues (2010: 3), these women have been rendered 'faceless, voiceless and a-historical subjects who lack agency and who are in need of "modernization" to raise them from their "uncivilized" state' (Shalhoub-Kevorkian 2010: 2). The humanity of Palestinians is denied in Zionist politics by their designation as 'present-absentees', 'security threats' and 'demographic threats' (Shalhoub-Kevorkian 2010). The war on Gaza has taken such dehumanization of Palestinians, including women, to unprecedented levels, not only in Israeli policies but also in the policies of the United States, United Kingdom and Germany.

The salience of racial–gender politics to the Gaza War was immediately evident. Israeli forces relentlessly bombed the sites with heavy concentrations of women and children – homes, refugee shelters, schools, universities, hospitals, bakeries, mosques, churches and camps. The death and destruction were legitimized through the classic racial–colonial tropes of a civilized Israeli society with its 'disciplined' army fighting 'savages' and 'terrorists' even as Palestinian women, who had the power to inspire, sustain and pass on the anti-colonial resistance to future generations, were slaughtered alongside their children. As the United Nations noted, 70 per cent of those killed were women and children (Albanese 2024).

The war's racial–gender politics were further evident in the workings of the well-oiled Israeli propaganda machine, which immediately disseminated stories alleging widespread use of rape, mutilation and sexual violence against Israeli women by Hamas, and of its butchering and burning alive of Israeli babies. These narratives were repeated endlessly by Western politicians and in mainstream media, even as they were constantly revealed to be fabrications (Middle East Eye Staff 2024; Plitnick 2024; Scahill, Grim and Boguslaw 2024). Projecting utter depravity and barbarity onto Hamas, these sensational reports shaped the political construction of Palestinians as 'human animals', 'savages', 'monsters', 'children of darkness', who deserved the violence they were said to have invited. These narratives simultaneously humanized the Israeli women who supported the genocide, and whose protection was represented as rationale for the genocidal war.

Racial–gender politics were also evident in the actions of the Israeli soldiers who stole Palestinian women's underwear and lingerie and recorded themselves 'playing' with these (Hindawi-Wyatt 2024). Dozens of such videos were posted online. 'In one video, an Israeli soldier sits in an armchair in a room in Gaza grinning, with a gun in one hand and dangling white satin underwear from the other over the open mouth of a comrade lying on a sofa', Reuters reported (Shirbon and Grzanka 2024). Such publicly sexualized violation of Palestinian/Muslim women reveals the implicit working of the discourse of the veil. The pleasures these clothing items, and the recorded images, generate for the soldiers reveals the violence that permeates such display; the pleasure/violence constitutes a symbolic and sexualizing 'unveiling' of Palestinian women. The images' erasure of the physical presence of the women reduces them to the clothing items on display and transforms them into sexual phantasms. This process of transforming the actual Palestinian women to whom these items belong into sexualized phantasies obliterates their humanity *as women*. Reading this symbolic and deadly unveiling alongside the Israeli sexual fixation on Hamas's 'rape strategy' reveals how Palestinian women's gendered dehumanization functions alongside the exaltation of Israeli women as the 'real' sexual victims, thus humanizing the latter as worthy of state defence. The racial–gender politics at work here legitimizes the genocide of Palestinians, including the absent-present Palestinian woman, as vital to the protection of the gendered humanity of Israeli women.

Such erasure of Palestinian women *moved beyond* the racial–gendered discourse of earlier phases of the war on terror; the eradication of Palestinian women was put in service of the humanization of the Israeli woman as the 'worthy' gendered victim. Whereas the dehumanization of Afghan women in the early phase of the global war took the form of their racialized construction as passive objects without agency through the discourse of the veil, this discourse was dispensed with in the case of Palestinian women in this latest phase of the war, denying any recognition of their humanity *as women*. Even the most perfunctory recognition of gendered oppression demands a measure of acknowledgement of the women's humanity, degraded as this might be in racial and gendered terms. The degendering of Palestinian women intersected with their Islamophobic-racialized dehumanization to deny them recognition of *any* shared humanity.

The explicit dispensing with the discourse of the veil to advance the physical extermination of Palestinian women, and through them, the Palestinian people, came not only from Israeli/Western states; it was shared in Western feminist silence. The marked lack of Western feminist concern for Palestinian women worked in tandem with the lack of feminist denunciation of Israeli women and politicians who publicly called for, and worked towards, the extermination of Palestinian women. As Israeli woman politicians, soldiers and public figures actively and systematically 'disappeared' Palestinian women from the legal-political field to expand the legitimacy of the Israeli settler state, feminist silence 'disappeared' Palestinian women from feminist politics. Israeli/Western states redeemed Israeli women's humanity through the essentialization and projection of sexual violence to signify the depravity of Hamas/Palestinian men, feminist silence dehumanized Palestinian women into degendered obliteration.

The genocide in Gaza demonstrates the depth of the saturation of colonial violence with racial–gender, not to mention sexual, politics. State and feminist discourses exalting Western gender norms in the Afghan War helped direct attention – through the figure of the Afghan woman – *away* from the violence of Western states and *towards* Afghan/Muslim men. One needs to account for the acceptance of the discourse of the veil by urbanized, Westernized Afghan women, many of whom supported the US-led imposition of Western gender norms onto their society, in order to study the contemporary effectiveness of the fetishization of the veil by Western states. Among Afghan feminist organizations, the Revolutionary Afghan Women's Association (RAWA) was most vocal in its rejection of the US drive to unveil Afghan women as the means to protect their 'rights' under conditions of US-led occupation. In contrast, the Afghan Women's Network called for demilitarization of the conflict in their opposition to the US-led war. But such anti-Occupation politics did not become the dominant position in the 'feminist' activism of Afghan women, anti-colonial opposition remained a marginalized position unable to break through the power of the discourse of the veil. And despite the indiscriminate killing of large numbers of Afghan women and children by Occupation forces, the discourse of the veil continues even now to shape the representation of 'the Afghan woman' in geopolitics as the victim of 'Islamic' barbarism and the 'terror' of Muslim men.

In the case of the Gaza War, the absence of feminist opposition to the Israeli Occupation and its genocidal war ejected Palestinian women from the terrain of feminist politics. Palestinian women's long-standing rejection of Zionist/Western discourses of humanitarianism and of Western feminist saviour narratives continues to ground their anti-colonial politics. Western feminist silence on the gendered nature of the Palestinian genocide signals feminist complicity with the Zionist/Western state. Such collusion is evident in the feminist turning away from Palestinian women on the grounds of race, of colonialism and of violence.

Conclusion

The driving force of Fanon's intellectual and political praxis was decolonization, a struggle in which he argued Algerian women's activism was indispensable. In his analysis of the veil, he came to understand that the object of oppression becomes the subject of resistance and, in the process, provokes a radical shift in consciousness that is collective as well as individual. His analysis of the veil opened this up to humanizing readings and to its potential to galvanize anti-colonial politics. Fanon (1986) lived viscerally his critique of colonialism: he argued for nothing short of international revolutionary transformation in which ending colonial rule was a necessary first, certainly not the last, step. He also argued that ending colonial violence demanded a much deeper transformation of consciousness, a transformation that would be countered in the racial–gender politics of colonial powers, which included the fetishization of the veil. These insights, developed in the throes of the mid-twentieth-century revolutionary upheaval, have much to offer contemporary anti-colonial struggles to think through hegemonic racial–gender politics and their relation to imperialist wars.

Fanon's critique of the nativist-nationalist elite and of its resuscitation and fossilization of archaic practices as 'authentic', 'traditional' Algerian/Muslim 'culture' as the means to neutralize the revolutionary spirit that inspired Algerian women in the Third World revolution remains as pertinent now as then. The essentialization of 'Islamic culture' as static and barbaric, of 'the Muslim Woman' as abject gendered object and of 'the Muslim Man' as virulent misogynist that was contested by Fanon has acquired new purchase in the wars of the present. The utter dehumanization of Palestinian women in Gaza points to a new phase in these racial–gender politics of colonial violence.

The feminist refusal to centre, or learn from the lessons of colonized women's activism in earlier anti-colonial and anti-racist movements, reinforces fossilized colonial constructs that attempt to erase the revolutionary subjectivity and agency of colonized/Muslim women. Influential feminist networks continue to contribute to the deradicalization or outright destruction of these women's ground-up resistance to Western imperialism and racial–colonial domination. The parallels between the 'precise political doctrine' of the French Occupation described by Fanon (1959), the US-led Western bid to 'liberate' the Afghan Muslim woman in the global war, and the Israeli genocide in Gaza are inescapable. Yet *les damnes de la terre* continue the resistance left unfinished in the Third World revolution. Fanon's theories of decolonization bring into sharp focus the racial–colonial violence folded into contemporary formations of racial–gender and feminist politics as these are deployed to restabilize the power of an imploding US Empire.

Active in the resistance, Fanon was writing for the revolution as he highlighted the ways in which Algerian women were advancing its movement. Yet Muslim women's anti-colonial resistance is presently rendered illegible in the terms set by hegemonic feminist politics. Whether the forms of struggle developed by these women meet the standards of feminist agency as determined by feminists who see in the figure of the Muslim woman only her oppression by 'Islamic culture' is beside the point. For the liberation of Muslim women, then as now, relies not on their 'mimicking' of Western women; it relies on the success of the anti-colonial revolution that is the condition for transcending the violence that shapes the present international order.

Notes

1 The Western fetishization of the 'Islamic veil' conflates the different forms of body, head and/or face coverings used by Muslim women across time and space.
2 The unveiling of the few Algerian women 'saved' and celebrated by the French was accomplished through 'maximum psychological attention to the veil' (Fanon 1959: 42). The women included domestic workers, sex workers and women living in poverty; their public unveiling by French settlers is described by Fanon (1959: 42) as 'penetration' and 'rape of Algerian society'.
3 Examples of the veil's dynamism can be found in its use by Iranian women in the Islamic Revolution to signify their rejection of Western imperialism, by Egyptian women in opposition to neoliberal consumerism in Egypt, and by Turkish women to assert their right to public space and political representation (Gole 1997; Cooke 2001; Ahmed 2011).
4 Fanon's insights regarding this transformation in gender relations cannot be lightly dismissed, for as he argued:

There is thus a historic dynamism of the veil that is very concretely perceptible in the development of colonization in Algeria. In the beginning the veil was a mechanism of resistance, but its value for the social group remained very strong. The veil was worn because tradition demanded a rigid separation of the sexes, but also because the occupier was *bent on unveiling Algeria*. In a second phase, the mutation occurs under special circumstances. The veil was abandoned in the course of revolutionary action. What had been used to block the psychological or political offensives of the occupier became a means, an instrument. The veil helped the Algerian women to meet the new problems created by the struggle. The colonialists are incapable of grasping the motivations of the colonized. It is the necessities of combat that give rise in Algerian society to new attitudes, to new modes of action, to new ways. (Fanon 1959: 63–4)

References

Abu-Lughod, Leila (2002), 'Do Muslim Women Really Need Saving? Anthropological Reflections on Cultural Relativism and Its Others', *American Anthropologist*, 104 (3): 783–90.

Ahmed, Leila (2011), *A Quiet Revolution: The Veil's Resurgence from the Middle East to America*, New Haven: Yale University Press.

Albanese, Francesca (2024), 'Anatomy of a Genocide: Report of the Special Rapporteur on the Situation of Human Rights in the Palestinian Territories Occupied since 1967', *United Nations Human Rights Council Advance Report*, 25 March.

Alessandrini, Anthony C. (2016), *Frantz Fanon and the Future of Cultural Politics*, Lanham, MD: Lexington Books.

Alloula, Malek (1986), *The Colonial Harem*, Minneapolis: University of Minnesota Press.

Al-Saji, Alia (2010), 'The Racialization of Muslim Veils: A Philosophical Analysis', *Philosophy and Social Criticism*, 36 (8): 875–902.

Bhabha, Homi (1986), 'Foreword: Remembering Fanon', in *Black Skin White Masks*, vii–xxv, London: Pluto Press.

Blaine, Mahdi (2022), 'Frantz Fanon Unveiled', *Africa as a Country*. Available at https://africasacountry.com/2022/10/frantz-fanon-unveiled (Accessed: 10 June 2024).

Bose, Anuja (2019), 'Frantz Fanon and the Politicization of the Third World as a Collective Subject', *Interventions*, 21 (5): 671–89.

Byrne, Jeffrey J. (2016), *Mecca of Revolutions: Algeria, Decolonization and the Third World Order*, Oxford: Oxford University Press.

Conway, Liam (2007) 'The 'Veil' – Symbol of Liberation or Oppression?' *Workers Liberty*, 13 April. Available at https://www.workersliberty.org/story/2017-07-26/veil-symbol-liberation-or-oppression (Accessed: 10 June 2024).

Cooke, Miriam (2001), *Women Claim Islam: Creating Islamic Feminism Through Literature*, New York: Routledge.

Cornell, Drucilla (2001), 'The Secret Behind the Veil: A Reinterpretation of *Algeria Unveiled*', *Philosophia Africana*, 4 (2): 27–35.

Decker, Jeffrey Loius (1990–1991) 'Terrorism (Un) Veiled: Frantz Fanon and the Women of Algiers', *Cultural Critique*, 17: 177–95.

Dossa, Parin (2014), *Afghanistan Remembers: Gendered Narrations of Violence and Culinary Practices*, Toronto: University of Toronto Press.

Fanon, Frantz (1959), 'Algeria Unveiled', in *A Dying Colonialism*, 35–67, New York: Grove Press.

Fanon, Frantz (1963), *The Wretched of the Earth*, New York: Grove Press.

Fanon, Frantz (1986), *Black Skin, White Masks*, London: Pluto Press.

Farah, Randa (2002), 'To Veil Or Not To Veil is Not The Question: Palestinian Refugee Women's Voices on Other Matters', *Development*, 45 (1): 93–8.

Faulkner, Rita (1996), 'Asia Djebar, Frantz Fanon, Women, Veils and Land', *World Literature Today*, 70 (4): 847–55.

Gibson, Nigel, ed. (1999), *Rethinking Fanon: The Continuing Debate*, New York: Humanity Books, Wiley-Blackwell.

Gole, Nilufer (1997), *The Forbidden Modern: Civilization and Veiling*, Ann Arbour: University of Michigan Press.

Gordon, Lewis, Sharpley-Whiting, T. Denean and White, Renee T., eds. (1996), *Fanon: A Critical Reader*, Oxford: Wiley-Blackwell.

Helie-Lucas, Marie A. (1999), 'Women, Nationalism and Religion in the Algerian Liberation Struggle', in Nigel Gibson (ed.), *Rethinking Fanon: The Continuing Debate*, 271–82, New York: Humanity Books.

Hindawi-Wyatt, S. (2024), 'What Israeli Soldiers' Display of Palestinian Women's Lingerie Reveals about the Zionist Psyche', *Middle East Eye*, 14 March.

Johnson, Chalmers (2002), *Blowback: The Costs and Consequences of American Empire*, The Empire Project, New York: Holt Paperbacks.

Khalidi, Rashid (2004), *Resurrecting Empire: Western Footprints and America's Perilous Path in the Middle East*, Boston: Beacon Press.

Khalidi, Rashid (2020), *The Hundred Year's War on Palestine: A History of Settler Colonialism and Resistance, 1917–2017*, New York: Picador.

Kohari, Alizeh (2022), 'The Afghan Revolutionary Who Took on the Soviets and Patriarchy', *Al Jazeera*. Available at https://www.aljazeera.com/features/2022/3/1/the-afghan-revolutionary-who-took-on-the-soviets-and-patriarchy (Accessed: 10 June 2024).

Kolhatkar, Sonali (2002), 'The Impact of U.S. Intervention on Afghan Women's Rights', *Berkeley Women's Law Journal*, 17: 12–30.

Lazreg, Marnia (1994), *The Eloquence of Silence: Algerian Women in Question*, London: Routledge.
Macey, David (2012), *Frantz Fanon: A Biography*, New York: Verso Books.
Mamdani, Mahmood (2004), *Good Muslim, Bad Muslim: America, the Cold War and the Roots of Terror*, New York: Pantheon Books.
Massad, Joseph (2024), 'How Israel's Genocide in Gaza Became a Showdown between the West and the Global South', *Middle East Eye*, February.
McClintock, Anne (1999), 'Fanon and Gender Agency', in Nigel Gibson (ed.), *Rethinking Fanon: The Continuing Debate*, 283–93, New York: Humanity Books.
Middle East Eye Staff (2024), 'Journalism Professors Urge "Independent Review" of *New York Times* 7 October Report of Sexual Violence Report', *Middle East Eye*, 30 April. Available at https://www.middleeasteye.net/news/-journalism-professors-new-york-times-independent-review-7-oct-report (Accessed: 10 June 2024).
Narain, Vrinda (2023), 'The Taliban's War on Women in Afghanistan must be Formally Recognized as Gender Apartheid', *Women Living under Muslim Laws*. Available at https://www.wluml.org/2023/08/14/the-talibans-war-on-women-in-afghanistan-must-be-formally-recognized-as-gender-apartheid/ (Accessed: 28 June 2024).
Plitnick, Mitchell (2024), 'Dehumanization and Misinformation in Service of Genocide', *Mondoweiss*, 9 February.
Said, Edward (1979a), *Orientalism*, New York: Vintage Books.
Said, Edward (1979b), *A Question of Palestine*, New York: Vintage, Random House.
Scahill, Jeremy, Grim, Ryan and Boguslaw, Daniel (2024), 'Between the Hammer and the Anvil: The Story behind the New York Times October 7 Expose', *The Intercept*, 28 February. https://theintercept.com/2024/02/28/new-york-times-anat-schwartz-october-7/ (Accessed 10 June 2024).
Shalhoub-Kevorkian, Nadera (2010), *Militarization and Violence Against Women in Conflict Zones in the Middle East*, Cambridge: Cambridge University Press.
Sharpley-Whiting, Tracy Denean (1999), 'Fanon's Feminist Consciousness and Algerian Women's Liberation: Colonialism, Nationalism, and Fundamentalism' in Nigel Gibson (ed.), *Rethinking Fanon: The Continuing Debate* 329–53, New York: Humanity Books.
Shehadeh, Raja (2024), 'After Six Months of War, I Fear We May Lose Palestine Completely', *The Guardian*, 9 April.
Shirbon, Estelle and Grzanka, Pola (2024), 'Israeli Soldiers Play with Gaza Women's Underwear in Online Posts', *Reuters*. Available at https://www.reuters.com/world/middle-east/israeli-soldiers-play-with-gaza-womens-underwear-online-posts-2024-03-28/ (Accessed: 28 June 2024)
Slisli, Fouzi (2008), 'Islam: The Elephant in *Fanon's Wretched of the Earth*', *Critique: Critical Middle Eastern Studies*, 17 (1): 97–108.
Thobani, Sunera (2002), 'War Frenzy', *Meridiens*, 2 (2): 289–97.

Thobani, Sunera (2020), *Contesting Islam, Constructing Race and Sexuality: The Inordinate Desire of the West*, London: Bloomsbury Academic.

UN Women (2022), 'Feminist Foreign Policies: An Introduction'. https://www.unwomen.org/en/digital-library/publications/2022/09/brief-feminist-foreign-policies (Accessed: 10 June 2024).

USAID (2022), 'United States Announces $30 Million Commitment to Advance Women's and Girls' Rights in Afghanistan'. Available at https://www.usaid.gov/news-information/press-releases/aug-12-2022-united-states-announces-30-million-commitment-advance-women-girls-rights-afghanistan (Accessed: 28 June 2024).

4

On ethnographic refusal

Indigeneity, 'voice' and colonial citizenship

Audra Simpson

Anthropological need

To speak of Indigeneity is to speak of colonialism and anthropology, as these are means through which Indigenous people have been known and sometimes are still known. In different moments, anthropology has imagined itself to be a voice, and in some disciplinary iterations, the voice of the colonized (Paine 1990; Said 1989). This modern interlocutionary role was not self-ascribed by anthropologists, nor was it without a serious material and ideational context; it accorded with the imperatives of Empire and in this, specific technologies of rule that sought to obtain space and resources, to define and know the difference that it constructed in those spaces and to then govern those within (Asad 1973; Deloria 1988; Said [1974] 1994). Knowing and representing the 'voices' within those places required more than military might, it required the methods and modalities of knowing, in particular: categorization, ethnological comparison, linguistic translation and ethnography.

These techniques of knowing were predicated upon a profound need, as the distributions in power and possibility that made Empire also made for the heuristic and documentary requirements of a metropolitan and administrative readership, hence the required accounts of the difference that 'culture' stood in for in these 'new' places (Cohn 1987; Pratt 1992; Thomas 1994; Wolfe 1999). These accounts were required for governance, but also so that those in the metropole might know themselves in a manner that accorded to the global processes underway. Like 'race' in other contexts, 'culture' was (and still is in some quarters) the conceptual and necessarily essentialized space that stood in for complicated bodily and exchange-based relationships that enabled and marked colonial situations in Empire: warfare, commerce, sex, trade, missionization. 'Culture' described the difference that was found in these places and marked the ontological endgame of each exchange: a difference that had been contained into neat, ethnically defined territorial spaces that now needed to be made sense of, to be ordered, ranked, to be governed, to be possessed (Pels and Salemink 1999).[1] This is a form of politics that is more than representational, as this was a governmental and disciplinary possession of bodies *and* territories, and in this were included existent forms of philosophy, history and social life that Empire sought to speak of and speak for.

In this chapter, I will argue that the techniques of representation and analysis that avail themselves to us when the processes sketched out above have been accounted for make for a form of representation that may move away from 'difference' and attendant containment as a unit of analysis. I am interested in the way that cultural analysis may look when difference is *not* the unit of analysis, when culture is disaggregated into narratives rather than wholes, when proximity to the territory that one is engaging in is as immediate as the self and what this then does to questions of 'voice'. I will argue that in such a context of anthropological accounting – an accounting I started to do in the preceding paragraphs but will do more robustly in the ones that follow – 'voice' is coupled with sovereignty that is evident at the level of interlocution, at the level of method and at the level of textualization. Within Indigenous contexts, contexts that are never properly 'post-colonial', the sovereignty of the people we speak of, when speaking for themselves, interrupt anthropological portraits of timelessness, procedure and function that dominate representations of their past and, sometimes, their present.

As an anthropologist, I always found such portraits of Indigenous peoples to be strange in light of the deeply resistant, self-governing and relentlessly critical people that I belong to and work with. When I started to do my work on a topic that simply matters to the Mohawks of Kahnawake – the question of who we are and who we shall be for the future – I found that anthropological histories on the Iroquois[2] and analytics used for cultural analysis were exceedingly ritualistic and procedural, and so much so that they privileged particular communities and peoples in ways that stressed harmony and timelessness even where there was utter opposition to and struggle against the state. Again, this is more than a representational problem or a superficially representational problem. The people that I work with and belong to do care deeply about ceremony and tradition, but hinged those concerns to nationhood, citizenship, rights, justice, proper ways of being in the world, the best way to be in relation to one another, political recognition, invigorating the Mohawk language – they did not talk about the usual anthropological fare that dominated the prodigious amount of research upon them. They clearly had and have critiques of state power, hegemony, history and even one another that made them appear anomalous against the literature written upon them.

And so it was that I asked questions about the questions that mattered to us and had to write in certain ways, as these matterings sometimes were more our business than others, but clearly had import for much larger questions, questions concerning just forms of dominion, or sovereignty or citizenship. I want to reflect upon the dissonance between the representations that were produced by writing away from and to dominant forms of knowing and commitment to what people say (imperfectly glossed here as 'voice'). I do so in order to ask what the form of knowledge might look like when such histories as the one sketched out above are accounted for in disciplinary form and analysis. And further to that, I consider what analysis will look like, or sound like, when the goals and aspirations of those we talk to inform the methods and the shape of our theorizing and analysis.

Particular ways of knowing

Unlike anthropologies of the past, accounting for Empire and colonialism and doing so in the context of 'settler societies' (code for proximal-to, or once 'Indigenous') is now becoming more acceptable. This is owing to political currents, critiques and philosophical trends outside of and within anthropology that have embedded the discipline within the history of colonialism, have highlighted ethics and form, and pluralized the places and peoples that are now considered viable for ethnographic analysis. Although more acceptable than in the past, anthropological analyses of indigeneity may still occupy the 'salvage' and 'documentary' slot for analysis, an elaboration of object that results from the endurance of categories that emerged in moments of colonial contact, many of which still reign supreme. In those moments, people left their own spaces of self-definition and became 'Indigenous'. And 'Indigenous' is a category that did not explicitly state or theorize the shared experience of having their lands alienated from them or that they would be understood in particular ways. This shared condition might be an innocent tale of differential access to power, of differing translations of events, were there a level field of interpretation within which to assert those different translations, as well as an agreed-upon vocabulary for comparison. No situation such as the one we all inherit and live within is 'innocent' of a violence of form, if not content, in narrating a history or a present for ourselves. But like the law and its political formations that took things from them, there are disciplinary forms that must be contended with by Indigenous peoples. Anthropology and the 'law' (both, necessarily, reified in this iteration) mark two such spaces of knowing and contention with serious implications for Indigenous peoples in the present.[3]

Aileen Moreton-Robinson (2000) links this form of differential access to power and historical knowing to an a *priori* privilege, one that is gendered and racialized by the relationships mentioned earlier (warfare, commerce, sex, trade, missionization) in the exchange-based histories that became reified and thus possessive, relationships that dialectically shaped those engagements as well as colonial possibilities in the *present*. As an example, Moreton-Robinson cites Captain Cook's account of the people he first encountered in what is now Australia. It was 'stated that the Indigenous people of Australia had no form of land tenure because they were uncivilized, which meant the land belonged to no-one and was available for possession under the doctrine of terra *nullius*' (Moreton-Robinson 2004). The legal doctrine of terra *nullius*, an 'empty land', held sway in Australia until the High Court overturned it in 1992 with the Mabo decision and offers stark testimony to the differential power of one account over another in defining not only difference but establishing presence, by establishing the terms of even being seen: a historical perceptibility that empowered possibilities of self- and territorial possession in the present (Russell 2005). We see in this example how historical perceptibility is used, and is still used, to *claim*, to define capacities for self-rule, to apportion social and political possibilities and to, in effect, empower and disempower Indigenous peoples in the present. Such categorical forms of recognition and mis-recognition are indebted to deep philosophical histories of seeing and knowing; tied to legal fiat, they may enable disproportionately empowered political forms (such as Empire or particular nation states such as the United States, Canada and Australia) to come into being in a very short time, as without that category of knowing and its concomitant force land could not be wrested from those that belong to it, and those to whom it rightfully belongs.

And so it is that concepts have teeth and teeth that bite through time. By legally acknowledging the presence of Indigenous peoples in Australia, Mabo enabled Indigenous peoples there to finally claim legal title to their ancestral territories. But they could only do so after 215 years of settler occupation that coincided with 215 years of their continued presence in their own lands. These historical and legal effacements of Indigeneity are predicated upon accounts such as Cook's – accounts that became histories which dialectically informed theories, which then emboldened the laws of nation states. The traffic between theory and event moved colonies into nation states. This trafficking disabled future claims of Indigenous occupation and ownership of territory because, in part, their own voices were imperceptible, or unknowable, or unimportant, or were sieved through analytics that interpreted their aspirations in ways that were not their own (Andersen and Hokowhitu 2007).

These effective effacements rested upon ways of knowing that imbricated the ethnological, ethnographic and cartographic with social and political theory (Ryan 1994; Brealey 1995; Harris 2002) and enabled the justification (Pagden 1982) of dispossession.

Cook's thinking was very much of a piece with that of political theorists such as John Locke, who argued most persuasively, it seems, that the origins of property rest only in that which has been mixed with labour, and, thus, that which does not *appear* to have been mixed with labour is alienable. A panoptic view of labour here is essential as only certain forms of labour, those which are perceptible to certain viewers, will matter. But of equal import for Indigenous peoples is the conflation of property with a larger economy of social and political rank and value – 'and amongst those who are *counted the civilized part of mankind* (italics added), who have made and multiplied positive laws to determine property ... is by the labour that removes it out of that common state nature left it in made his property who takes pains about it' (Locke 2003).

This fragment from Locke's text *Of Property* enunciates the hierarchies of social value and accordant rights that were tied to the understanding of people and a social ranking within humanity. Thus, property could be defined only as that which was mixed with labour and belonged to those who perceived it, in contradistinction to the living histories of Indigenous peoples in those places (Moreton-Robinson 2000).

Cultural form is critical here, recognizing and apportioning out rights, and is broken down and sieved into different hierarchies of value and accordant analytics – in their contemporary forms, those of 'structure', 'practice' and 'meaning'. We must be mindful, however, that in its theoretical and analytic guises 'culture' is defined in anthropological terms most consistently by its proximal relationship to difference. And that difference was to be defined against the sameness and omniscience of a stable ontological core, an unquestioned 'self' that defined that difference and thence 'culture' for a readership, one that corresponded to a metropole and to a colony, a self and an other to define oneself proximally against (Cooper and Stoler 1997).

Territories of the familiar

It is in this brief context of anthropological need and political history that I will now talk about forms of analysis after such an accounting – in particular, ethnographies of the familiar, ethnographies of refusal and the making of claims and the staking of limits. The discursive appeal to the language of territory is deliberate, although the territory that I wish to talk about is the space of method, critique and construction in *contemporary* ethnographies of Native North America and, in particular, my own ethnography of Mohawk nationhood and citizenship across the borders of the United States and Canada. In a sharp move away from the ethnohistorical salvage paradigm that evacuates theory from the space of 'native North American anthropology', and in particular, the prodigious anthropology 'of' the Iroquois, of whom the Mohawk is a member nation, I will talk about refusal.

It was theorized by the early American anthropologist and Indian advocate Lewis Henry Morgan that, in fact, the Iroquois, a once-significant military power in what is now the Northeastern United States, were (in his moments of reckoning) of such a 'civilized' state that they were, in fact, ceasing to be different and thus most worthy of the trappings of civilization: education and agriculture. This was of a piece with his political advocacy, itself an outgrowth of his 'play' as an Indian and later his scientific observations and analysis of Indian culture, also an outgrowth of earlier play (Deloria 1998). Morgan was highly critical of the government of his time and wrote at least two well-intentioned and bold articles that some have argued were an unusual and early form of advocacy in anthropology (Sanjek 2004). However, his explicit writings on Indian 'advancement' were tied to a racialized social hierarchy that placed African Americans at the bottom of the social order (Baker 1998: 45), as well as expressing the belief in the inevitability of Iroquois decline. Morgan advocated for Iroquois advancement not only because he believed them to be 'ready' for and 'worthy' of such a change in their legal and political status but also because their 'absorption' into the white race was inevitable and most virtuous. Their readiness for absorption was owing to their 'civilized state' (*contra* the Aboriginal example cited by Moreton-Robinson earlier), which was tied to the perceived death of Iroquois culture – the death really, of difference – the remnants of which needed to be recorded and documented *at the same time* as he advocated for a more citizenship-worthy social status for them (Bieder 1986). Thus, with the assistance of Ely S Parker, a condoled Seneca chief, he produced the highly referenced documentary ethnography, *The League of the Haudenosaunee*, which detailed the social and governmental structure of the Iroquois Confederacy – a paradigmatic text of reconstructed and salvage ethnography (Morgan [1851] 1996). The *League* prompted many studies in its wake, and prompted as well a subfield of specialization in North American anthropology called 'Iroquois Studies'. Focusing almost exclusively upon the history of the Five and then Six Nations, Iroquois Studies quite literally took off where Morgan left off, and as such is a documentary form. Although generated within a North American anthropology informed by international currents and translations in social and cultural theory, there is no theory evident in the key texts of this subfield beyond that of Sapir, and the anthropological and historical project it embodies may be characterized as one that seeks to authenticate cultural forms rather than analyse them. This is interesting, for many reasons, but perhaps most importantly for the discussion at hand is the largely agreed-upon fact that the Six Nations are among the most strident and vociferous critics of British and French settlement and also among the most insistently and stridently sovereign Indians in North America (Johnston 1986; Woo 2003).

These sovereign articulations do not accord with the anthropologies of timeless, procedural 'tradition' that form the bulk of knowledge on the Iroquois. And so it is within this particular tradition, embedded within the structures of anthropological need discussed earlier, that I now want to turn to a very simple thing: the living (and their nationhood) within settled places. As well, I want to turn to questions of ethics and the normative work of representing and analysing the form of their nationhood within those spaces. If we are to do analyses of such political forms, we must consider not if sovereignty matters – that should be evident enough (the salvage/ethno-historical blind spot of many aside) and central enough – but ask, does it matter at the level of method and representation? And if so, how does that mattering manifest? Indeed, sovereignty matters, as a methodological issue in and of itself, but such mattering also engenders other ethnographic forms, namely, refusal. And this form of refusal is not to operationalize nor to genuflect to recent formulations of alternative methodology such as 'radical indigenism' – something that is neither radical nor indigenous but rather, in the name of 'tradition', structuring yet another expectation of a culturally 'pure' indigenous subject (Simpson 2007). Rather, it is my proposition that to think about 'sovereignty' – a construct which is always a bestowal and as such is deeply imperfect but critical for these moments in Indigenous/SettlerState relations – is to think very seriously about needs and, basically, involves a calculus ethnography of what you need to know and what I refuse to write in.

Histories of being refused: The Indian Act in Canada

I was stimulated to frame my project on Mohawk nationhood and citizenship by the complete disjuncture between what was written about my own people and the things that mattered the most to us. I was interested in the unambiguous, sometimes virulent and violent boundaries that were being drawn within the reservation community of Kahnawake over the question of 'membership'. At the time I started to think about my research, the elected government of the community had already devised, with some participation from the membership, a 1984 code which would require a 50 per cent blood quantum for membership in the community. This membership code itself was stimulated by several factors, most recently an international human rights decision that made Canada amend its Indian Act and reinstate onto a federal registry previously disenfranchised Indian women and children (Bill C-31). Aimed at redressing the patrilineal bias in the Indian Act, Bill C-31 was passed into effect in 1984. With this legislation, Indian women who lost their status upon marriage to non-Indian men (or non-status Indian men) were put back on the federal registration list of Indians in Canada (Cassidy and Bish 1989). It was now up to each reserve to devise membership codes that were of their own making and to then admit (or deny) membership to these women and their children in their own local registries.

Bill C-31 followed on the heels of a decade-long battle that saw non-status Indian women go head to head with their reserve, or band council governments, the state and, finally, international authorities. The women had unsuccessfully petitioned their band council governments to let them return, to raise their children and exercise their rights as Indians. The band council governments upheld the Indian Act and challenged the women to bring their case to the courts. The women then organized into political action groups, Equal Rights for Indian Women and the Native Women's Association of Canada, which then brought the Canadian government to court for the inherent gender bias in the Indian Act. They lost their case. It was only when they brought the case to the United Nations that Canada was forced to amend the Indian Act and remove the bias of determining membership in Indian bands along the father's line. Perceived as a victory for Indian women (and perhaps for all women, as there was some coalition-building between women's organizations at the time), Bill C-31 was intended to mend the fabric of Indian societies torn apart by unjust legislation. In practice, however, matters were much different.

Kahnawake had already assimilated some tenets of the Indian Act into the social fabric of the community. The means for defining kinship and determining community belonging, the traditional means for determining descent – through the mother's clan – was supplanted by the Indian Act and its European model of patrilineal descent as detailed above. Kahnawake had formally accepted the Indian Act in the community in 1890; however, as a reserve on Crown land, the community had been subject to elements of the act as early as 1850. In 1850, however, Indian status was transferable to both male and female non-Indian spouses of Indians. Therefore, non-Indian men or women could hold land, operate businesses and claim tax exemption on the reserve. Unwilling to accept the possibility of white men holding land in the community, Kahnawake contested this aspect of the act and brought it to the courts so that the act would be changed.

As detailed above, as a result of the Indian Act matrilineal descent and property holding was transferred to the father's line. This was an unambiguously raced and gendered injustice that Indian women, disenfranchised from their Indian status across Canada, fought against. But the complex of factors – Canada's bestowal of a right to reserves to determine membership after 100 years of living under Indian Act rules for recognition; Canada's reinstatement of the women on a federal registry – led, in part, to the development of a blood quantum code in Kahnawake, a code that was in defiance of Canadian norms for political recognition but appeared to be 'objective' and gender-neutral. The membership code was contested and defended by, it seemed, everyone within the community and sometimes all at once. Bill C-31 appeared as a most recent imposition (read by some as being told who was an Indian, *again*), and this iteration of the code reflected a century of colonial impositions, along with a desire for scientific rigour and objectivity. No one was completely happy with the code but everyone agreed that 'something had to be done' and that membership was the number one issue facing the community. In such a context, there were not only boundaries being constructed and deconstructed daily, but there was also a heightened awareness and deep and generalized concern over what would be the means for determining who we were – and who was not eligible to be recognized by us as being who we are.

In such a context, I knew that there were limits to what I could ask – and then what I could say – within the scope of my project on Mohawk nationhood, and those limits extended beyond any statement on ethical forms of research that either the American Anthropological Association or the Social Sciences and Humanities Research Council of Canada (two professional and research-regulating bodies for anthropologists in Canada and the United States) required. And so it was that I wrote an ethnography that pivoted upon refusal(s). I was interested in the larger picture, in the discursive, material and moral territory that was simultaneously historical and contemporary (this 'national' space) and the ways in which *Kahnawakero: non*, the 'people of Kahnawake', had *refused* the authority of the state at almost every turn. The ways in which their formation of the initial membership code (now replaced by a lineage code and board of elders to implement the code and determine cases) was refused; the ways in which their interactions with border guards at the international boundary line were predicated upon a refusal; how refusal worked in everyday encounters to enunciate repeatedly to ourselves and to outsiders that 'this is who we are, this who you are, these are my rights'. There was no place in the existing literature for these articulations, nor was there a neat placement for them within postcolonial studies or analysis – there was not a doubleness to their consciousness, a still-colonial but striving to be 'post-colonial consciousness' that denied the modern self that Fanon, Bhabha and Giddens speak of and from (Fanon 1967; Giddens 1991; Bhabha 1994). There seemed rather to be a tripleness, a quadrupleness, to consciousness and an endless play, and it went something like this: 'I am me, I am what you think I am and I am who this person to the right of me thinks I am and you are all full of shit and then maybe I will tell you to your face.' There was a definite core that seemed to reveal itself at the point of refusal and that refusal was arrived at, of course, at the very limit of the discourse.

Anthropology in such a context is, I think, sometimes really funny. Others would say uncomfortable. But contemporary fieldwork with Iroquois peoples involves being pushed and pushing back, a kind of discursive wrestling. There are *multiple* sovereignties at work, all of which have worked to protect, to limit, to entrench what was already in place, an exercise of political will that generated an exception, in Agamben's (2005) theorization, to the liability of the subject. To speak of limits in such a way makes some liberal thinkers uncomfortable, and may, to them, seem dangerous. When access to information, to knowledge, to the intellectual commons is controlled by the people who generate that information, it can be seen as a violation of shared standards of justice and truth. However, in the context that I have worked and still work within, history rears its head at every turn and did so through the bodily presence of white women (with Indian status), through the bodily presence of the children that they had with Indian men. These are the inheritors of colonial rules of recognition and were rendered, in some dark moments, as colonial residues and reminders. Their juridical identities spoke *not* of Eastern Woodlands Fever, a historical and contemporary transgression and erotic fantasy which a cultural analyst with the vim, vigour and verve of Spike Lee should dwell upon, but rather of something less sexy: Iroquois citizenships (a clan system) strangulated and arrested by the Indian Act.

The Indian Act of 1868 recognized the union between an Indian man and a white woman as one that maintained his legal recognition as an Indian, and would transfer the same recognition to the woman in the eyes of the state. The union of an Indian woman and white man, on the other hand, would deny her legal recognition as an Indian, her status under the Indian Act, and that of her children in the eyes of the state and, sometimes, the community. These bizarre logics of recognition and residues of history structured and still structure (in part) the bodies and persons and personalities and cousins and friends and enemies that comprise my version of Kahnawake. The punctuating, juridical bestowals of settler colonialism were read, like a text, with the status designations inscribed upon each one of us – 'C-31, status, non-status' – co-existing with traditional Iroquois modalities of recognition: 'clan, no-clan'. Thus, historical and juridical moments were carried by us, upon our very bodies – historical moments which settled upon the body, read as rights. I saw, unfolding before me in a fleshy, Hegelian *present*, the processes of settlement and its contracting and expanding forms of recognition – in the form of the people before me who spoke endlessly, it seemed, of how we shall determine who we are and who is *not* who we are. They did so while simultaneously refusing these logics.

'No one seems to know': Doing history and ethnography in the familiar

This question of recognition has surfaced repeatedly through time, and, although completely originating in Canadian settlement and the Indian Act, its contemporary guises are most local. In the beginning of my own research on this subject, the Mohawk Council of Kahnawake placed a notice in the weekly newspaper, *The Eastern Door*. It read: 'The following members of the community are housing non-natives', with the name of the community member, their band number (number on the local Indian registry) and the name of their non-Indian guest. The concern over non-Indians in Kahnawake, I would later learn through archival research, extended back to the earliest correspondence between the Indian Agent and Ottawa. Readable now in Record Group 10, letters from the Agent documented Kahnawake's 'sensitivity' to outsiders:

> To the half breed Canadians of the village. We wish to have a final decision to know if Delormier, Giasson, Deblois, Meloche and others are masters in our Reserve. There are eight of us who write (Indians) and if you do not leave the village look out for your heads, your buildings, your cattle and take warning of what we now tell you. (Reid 2004)

This was a warning to 'half-breeds' and whites living within Kahnawake in 1878, a time of great scarcity (of firewood and land). This warning, publicly posted to the 'half breeds' and 'whites', all of whom owned disproportionate amounts of property on the reserve, enunciated a still earlier anxiety over distribution of resources and power and the wrongful recognition of certain whites as Indians in the eyes of the state.

Thus, the notice in *The Eastern Door* was not without a context, and the context is the material and semiotic history from which Mohawk speak and by which they are simultaneously informed: land loss; scarcity of firewood; the one year that white men could legally obtain Indian status and buy and sell land; more encroachment; the earlier 'settling' of New York State and loss of the Mohawk Valley; the end of the Indian Wars; the Riel Rebellion in Canada; the ascendancy and decline of the British in North America. I do not wish to say that managing these historical vicissitudes ethnographically and in the present is unusual for those who wish to understand sovereignty as central to the lives, and the territorial integrity and the dignity of people that we work with. But in my brief discussion of the ways in which I came to understand my project, this concern over membership is part of the anthropological and *colonial* accounting that must happen for ethnography to make sense. Recall that the Indian Act, a specific body of law that recognizes Indians in a wardship status in Canada, created the categories of person and rights that served to sever Indian women from their communities upon marriage to white men. It did the reverse to Indian men – white women *gained* Indian status upon their marriage into an Indian community. This created the conditions for blood quantum and the contestation (and accordance) of it that I examined as part of my research. How does one write about this or analyse what is so clearly offensive to the anthropological sensibilities of access, of replicable results, in some ways of 'fairness', and reconcile all this with the plight of those who are struggling every day to maintain what little they have left? And when they are struggling so clearly with the languages and analytics of a foreign culture that occupies their semantic and material space, and naturalizes this occupation through history-writing and the very analytics that are used to know them?

The work of understanding these issues of membership, political recognition, sovereignty and autonomy within communities requires a historical sensibility (and reckoning) that is deeply horizontal as well as vertical. While there was a hearty oral archive of the structuring logics of exclusion – of how people got to get 'here', how they married each other when they did – there was co-terminously the logic of the present that I saw and lived and suffered through and enjoyed (and still do), of tolerance and exceptions and affections – what I call in other places 'feeling citizenships' that are structured in the present space of intra-community recognition, affection and care, outside of the logics of colonial and imperial rule (re: the Indian Act or blood quantum). And here I give such an example of these alternative logics from someone I interviewed, but also of a refusal, or a denial within the space of ethnography:

Q: Tell me what you think our ideal form of citizenship is . . . are citizenship and membership the same thing?
A: From my understanding, and whomever I ask, I get these grey, cloudy answers in return, so I am not quite sure. I am a citizen of Kahnawake but I am not a member of Kahnawake. I am not on this mysterious list that no-one seems to have any information about. So although I dearly love Kahnawake, there are many positions I will never be able to hold until this membership issue is cleared up, so I don't know much about it, other than, I don't think it to be fair – there are those who leave the community, as I said, we all come back to Kahnawake, but there are those who leave for twenty-five years and they come

back and they're a member, and they will have all these opportunities that I won't, even though I've never left. I don't think that's fair.

But I think there's a distinction – one could be a citizen without being a member.

Q: Interesting, and that citizenship is based on . . . let me push you on that then, how is that different, explain it to me?

A: Citizenship is, as I said, you live there, you grew up there, that is the life that you know – that is who you are. Membership is more of a legislative enactment designed to keep people from obtaining the various benefits that Aboriginals can receive. So I am a citizen, I live there, that is who I am, yet I cannot be a member because of these laws, which I feel is unfair. If I had been there my whole life I should have the same opportunity to run for Council that anyone else can. Yet I cannot.

Q: Do you think that's because of public sentiment, the Indian Act, is that because o . . .

A: I don't know what you know, or what others know – this is an area that I can't get straight answers from, no-one seems to know . . .

We discussed further:

Q: What do you think the legacy of C-31 is in Kahnawake?

A: I think I really don't know much about this. There's this generation of people, myself included, who were young during that time, and we had no recollection of that time or even of these laws – as I said, I inquire, but nobody seems to know; I don't seem to get answers from anybody . . .

Q: But you ask people?

A: I ask people – the same thing with this traditional government movement that is happening in Kahnawake, people speak of traditional government, they speak of Bill C-31 and no one seems to know anything about it.

Q: In your personal experience, how did you come to understand C-31?

A: With what I do understand with it, I think from my mother. From what I understand, she tends to avoid speaking of this; I believe she was one of the C-31 people, but I don't know for sure.

Q: To get it [her status] back?

A: To get back on, she married my father who was a Canadian, she was taken off this list, she got back on with C-31 – and all the details I do not know.

Q: 'Cause it's unpleasant?

A: She doesn't speak of it and, as I say, I inquire, but I receive no answers, people seem to side-step it or give these very vague summaries – it's almost like it is a taboo subject.

Q: Would you like to see it discussed more openly, or to find stuff out or be able to ...
A: I would like to, out of curiosity, know a bit more about it – but if I don't, I will live my life and for the most part I don't think it will really bother me other than not being able to be on this list, I guess. (Simpson 2003)

'No one seems to know' was laced through much of my informant's discussion of C-31, and of his own predicament – which I knew he spoke of indirectly, because I knew his predicament. And I also knew everyone knew, because everyone knows everyone's 'predicament'. This was the collective 'limit' – that of knowledge and thus who we could or would not claim. So it was very interesting to me that he would tell me that 'he did not know' and 'no one seems to know' – to me these utterances meant, 'I know you know, and you know that I know I know ... so let's just not get into this'. Or, 'let's just not say'. So I did not say, and so I did not 'get into it' with him, and I won't get into it with my readers. What I am quiet about is his predicament and my predicament and the actual stuff (the math, the clans, the mess, the misrecognitions, the confusion and the clarity) – the calculus of our predicaments. And although I pushed him, hoping that there might be something explicit said from the space of his exclusion – or more explicit than he gave me – it was enough that he said what he said. 'Enough' is certainly enough. 'Enough', I realized, was when I reached the limit of my own return and our collective arrival. Can I do this and still come home; what am I revealing here and why? Where will this get us? Who benefits from this and why? And 'enough' was when they shut down (or told me to turn off the recorder), or told me outright funny things like 'nobody seems to know' – when everybody *does* know and talks about it *all the time*. Dominion then had to be exercised over these representations, and that was determined when enough was said. The ethnographic limit, then, was reached not just when it would cause harm (or extreme discomfort) – the limit was arrived at when the representation would bite all of us and compromise the *representational* territory that we have gained for ourselves in the past 100 years, in small but deeply influential ways, with a cadre of scholars from Kahnawake whose work has reached beyond the boundaries of the community (Alfred, G. R. 1995; Alfred, T. 1999, 2005; Simpson 2001).

At the start of this chapter, I discussed the anthropological relationship to Empire, one that was encouraged by a need to describe the difference that was found in new places. This need precipitated certain cultural forms and modes of analysis. In this process, people became differentiated, their spaces and places possessed. 'Culture' served a purpose of describing the difference (always against a norm of sameness) that was encountered in those places. Describing difference also involved the analysis of difference, one that had (and still has) serious implications for Indigenous peoples, especially in their attempts to write their own histories, to claim their own intellectual and material space and to exercise dominion over it.

The work of Indigenous scholars rests upon Empire as well, and through the vocabularies and analytics it put into play. They might, however, work from different historical vantage points and locations within the space that Empire has claimed for some peoples. In this, theirs might be the centuries of warfare, exchange, alliance-making, diplomacy, petitioning, letter-writing and, most recently, armed resistance to the settler societies that have claimed and now claim North America as their own. I argued that this may produce different forms of analysis and thereby produce some of the anthropological limits that are discussed in this paper. Rather than stops, or impediments to knowing, those limits may be expansive in what they do not tell us. I reached my own limit when the data would not contribute to our sovereignty or complicate the deeply simplified, atrophied representations of Iroquois and other Indigenous peoples that they have been mired within anthropologically.

The people I interviewed do *know* the different forms of recognition that are at play, the simultaneities of consciousness that are in work in any colonial encounter (including those with me) in the exercising of rights – and that knowledge translates into the 'feeling side' of recognition, one that is not juridical, is home-grown and is dignified by local history and knowledge. What is theoretically generative about these refusals? They *account* for the history detailed above; they tell us something about the way we cradle or embed our representations and notions of sovereignty and nationhood; and they critique and move us away from statist forms of recognition. In listening and shutting off the tape recorder, in situating each subject within their own shifting historical context of the present, these refusals speak volumes, because they tell us when to stop. Whether or not we wish to share that is a matter of ethnography that can both *refuse* and also take up *refusal* in generative ways.

Acknowledgements

This chapter has profited from comments made at the American Anthropological Association Meetings (San Jose, 2006), the 'Indigenous Movements and their

Intellectuals' Symposium (Tufts University, 2007) and the Indigenous Peoples and Governance Colloque (Saskatoon, 2007). I am grateful to the editorial interventions of Annemarie Jutel, Brendan Hokowhitu and Jessica Cattelino. During the final revisions of this chapter, Gail Guthrie-Valaskakis passed on. She was a scholar of great equanimity, strength and intellectual elegance, and I dedicate this chapter to her memory.

Notes

1 Pels and Salemink (1999) trace the anthropological 'culture' concept back to the eighteenth century, to Johann Gottfried Herder's notion of a nation that is necessarily differentiated from others, and possessing a history that was generated internally and shaped by language. They argue that '[b]y assimilating the quantitative aggregate of "population" to an identity of type, he laid the ground work for the scientific conception of race and culture' (Pels and Salemink 1999).
2 'Iroquois' is a French transliteration of *Haudenosaunee,* or 'People of the Longhouse'. The Iroquois form a confederacy of six Indigenous nations – Mohawk, Oneida, Onondaga, Cayuga, Seneca and Tuscarora – that extended their dominion across what is now the Northeastern United States. They now reside on fifteen reservations and unrecognizsed/traditional communities and cities across the borders of the United States and Canada. The Mohawks of Kahnawake are *a* single nation, a reservation community located in what is now Southern Quebec (Canada).
3 For an examination of the dialectic between anthropological theory and the formation of racial categories (focusing on African Americans) and the law in the United States, see Baker (1998).

References

Agamben, Giorgio (2005), *State of Exception*, Chicago: University of Chicago Press.
Alfred, Gerald R. (1995), *Heeding the Voices of our Ancestors: Kahnawake Mohawk Politics and the Rise of Native Nationalism*, Toronto: Oxford University Press.
Alfred, Taiaiake (1999), *Peace, Power and Righteousness: An Indigenous Manifesto*, Toronto: Oxford University Press.
Alfred, Taiaiake (2005), *Wasáse: Indigenous Pathways of Action and Freedom*, Peterborough: Broadview Press.

Andersen, Chris and Hokowhitu, Brendan (2007), 'Whiteness: Naivety, Void and Control', *Junctures*, 8: 39–49.

Asad, Talal (1973), *Anthropology & the Colonial Encounter*, London: Ithaca Press.

Baker, Lee (1998), *From Savage to Negro: Anthropology and the Construction of Race, 1896–1954*, Berkeley: University of California Press.

Bhabha, Homi K. (1994), *The Location of Culture*, London: Routledge.

Bieder, Robert E. (1986), *Science Encounters the Indian, 1820–1880: The Early Years of American Ethnology*, Norman: University of Oklahoma Press.

Brealey, Ken G. (1995), 'Mapping Them "Out": Euro-Canadian Cartography and the Appropriation of Nuxalk and Ts'ilhqhot'in First Nations' Territories, 1793-1916', *The Canadian Geographer*, 39 (2): 140–56.

Cassidy, Frank and Bish, Robert L. (1989), *Indian Government: Its Meaning in Practice*, Lantzville, BC: Oolichan Books.

Cohn, Bernard (1987), *An Anthropologist among the Historians and Other Essays*, Delhi: Oxford University Press.

Cooper, Frederick and Stoler, Ann L. (1997), 'Between Metropole and Colony: Rethinking a Research Agenda', in Frederick Cooper and Ann L. Stoler (eds), *Tensions of Empire: Colonial Cultures in a Bourgeois World*, 1–56, Berkeley: University of California Press.

Deloria, Philip J. (1998), *Playing Indian*, New Haven: Yale University Press.

Deloria, Vine (1988), *Custer Died for Your Sins: An Indian Manifesto*, Norman: University of Oklahoma Press.

Fanon, Frantz (1967), *Black Skin: White Masks*, New York: Grove Press.

Giddens, Anthony (1991), *Modernity and Self Identity: Self and Society in the Late Modern Age*, Stanford: Stanford University Press.

Harris, Cole R. (2002), *Making Native Space: Colonialism, Resistance, and Reserves in British Columbia*, Vancouver: UBC Press.

Johnston, Darlene (1986), 'The Quest of the Six Nations Confederacy for Self Determination', *University of Toronto Faculty of Law Journal*, 44 (1): 1–32.

Locke, John (2003), *Two Treatises of Government and a Letter Concerning Toleration*, ed. Ian Shapiro, New Haven: Yale University Press.

Moreton-Robinson, Aileen (2000), *Talkin' up to the White Woman: Indigenous Women and Feminism*, Queensland: University of Queensland Press.

Moreton-Robinson, Aileen (2004), 'Whiteness, Epistemology and Indigenous Representation', in Aileen Moreton-Robinson (ed.), *Whitening Race: Essays in Social and Cultural Criticism*, 75–88, Canberra: Aboriginal Studies Press.

Morgan, Lewis H. ([1851] 1996), *League of the Iroquois*, Secaucus, N.J.: Carol Publishing Group.

Pagden, Anthony (1982), *The Fall of Natural Man: The American Indian and the Origins of Comparative Ethnology*, Cambridge: Cambridge University Press.

Paine, Robert (1990), 'Our Authorial Authority', *Culture*, 9: (2): 35–47.

Pels and Salemink (1999), 'Introduction: Locating the Colonial Subjects of Anthropology', in Peter Pels and Oscar Salemink (eds), *Colonial Subjects: Essays on the Practical History of Anthropology*, 19, Ann Arbor: University of Michigan Press.

Pratt, Mary L. (1992), *Imperial Eyes: Travel Writing and Transculturation*, London: Routledge.

Reid, G. F. (2004), *Kahnawà:ke: Factionalism, Traditionalism, and Nationalism in a Mohawk Community*, Lincoln: University of Nebraska Press.

Russell, Peter H. (2005), *Recognizing Aboriginal Title:The Mabo Case and Indigenous Resistance to English-Settler Colonialism*, Toronto: University of Toronto Press.

Ryan, Simon (1994), 'Inscribing the Emptiness: Cartography, Exploration and the Construction of Australia', in Chris Tiffin and Alan Lawson (eds), *DeScribing Empire: Post-Colonialism and Textuality*, 115–30, London: Routledge.

Said, Edward W. (1989), 'Representing the Colonized: Anthropology's Interlocuters', *Critical Inquiry*. 15 (Winter): 205–25.

Said, Edward W. ([1978] 1994), *Orientalism*, New York: Vintage Books.

Sanjek, Roger (2004), 'Going Public: Responsibilities and Strategies in the Aftermath of Ethnography', *Human Organization*, 63 (4): 444–56.

Simpson, Audra (2001), 'Paths Toward a Mohawk Nation: Narratives of Citizenship and Nationhood in Kahnawake', in Duncan Ivison, Paul Patton and Will Sanders (eds), *Political Theory and the Rights of Indigenous Peoples*, 113–36, Cambridge: Cambridge University Press.

Simpson, Audra (2003), 'To the Reserve and Back Again: Kahnawake Mohawk Narratives of Self, Home and Nation', PhD dissertation, McGill University.

Simpson, Audra (2007), 'On the Logic of Discernment', *American Quarterly*, 59 (2): 479–91.

Thomas, Nicholas (1994), *Colonialism's Culture: Anthropology, Travel, and Government*, Princeton: Princeton University Press.

Wolfe, Patrick (1999), *Settler Colonialism and the Transformation of Anthropology: The Politics and Poetics of an Ethnographic Event*, London: Cassell.

Woo, Grace L. X. (2003), 'Canada's Forgotten Founders: The Modern Significance of the Haudenosaunee (Iroquois) Application for Membership in the League of Nations', *Law, Social Justice and Global Development Journal*, 1. Available at http://www2.warwick.ac.uk/fac/ soc/law/elj/lgd/2003_1/woo/ (Accessed: 31 July 2007).

5

Fire

The decolonial pedagogy of subversion in Césaire and Djonga

Angelica de Freitas e Silva

The spark

Each generation must, out of relative obscurity, discover its mission, fulfil it, or betray it.

(Frantz Fanon 1990: 166)

The sentence *fogo nos racistas!* (fire on the racists!) has become one of the anthems of the anti-racism struggle in Brazil. The iconic sentence is the chorus verse of the 2017 single *Olho de Tigre* (Tiger Eye) (PineappleStormTV 2017a) by the rapper Djonga, born in 1994. The song intones sharp verses against racism and fascism in Brazil with lyrical rage informing the author's awareness of his singular identity as a dark-skinned young Black man from a favela; of his role within the collective; his Black pride; and the call for contemporary Black youth to be ready to dismantle the 'whites' castle'[1] (PineappleStormTV 2017a). Cultural manifestations such as 'fire on the racists!' inform the legitimacy of the claims of a nation and have revolutionary power (Fanon 1990: 167). Consequently, cultural suppression and annihilation are some of the constitutive elements of the present-day global configuration of power, the remains of colonialism that Aníbal Quijano (1992) calls coloniality of power. Cultural expressions that resist the suppressions of colonial hegemony are fundamental mechanisms to trigger collective change. Anti-hegemonic cultural manifestations have been historically suppressed and even criminalized because they represent political threats. In the face of increasing ultra-conservative movements aiming at the destruction of decolonial achievements globally, and especially in the Third World, 'flowers grow from the dump'.² This chapter analyses the pedagogical power of anti-hegemonic cultural manifestations such as rap music, proposing that cultural movements are educational and serve as means of social change. The chapter concludes by observing how Brazilian rap music can be a 'miraculous weapon' (Césaire 1946) against ultra-conservative setbacks in the country's sociopolitical arenas. The proposed analysis of the works of Fanon, Quijano, bell hooks and Lélia Gonzalez help to understand the pedagogical power of rap in the works of Brazilian rappers Djonga, Racionais and Emicida for libertarian citizen rebellion. Rap music teaches, politicizes and enables imaginaries of social change because it brings historical subjects into existence.

This chapter is divided into four parts. This first part, 'The spark', refers to the power of culture to trigger social change. The second part, 'Coloniality and culture', is a return to aspects of decolonial thought that open up the cracks in understanding the place and pedagogical role of rap. The third part, 'Miraculous weapons', is a reflection on how Brazilian rap can be a 'miracle weapon' against ultra-conservative setbacks in the country's social and political areas. The fourth and final part, 'Fire on the racists!', takes a closer look at Djonga's creative work in parallel with Aimé Césaire's anti-colonial writings. The chapter concludes by drawing together the political influence of artistic movements, collective resistance and social change.

Coloniality and culture

> This side of the bridge, first of all, it is a school.
> (Racionais MC's, Da Ponte pra Cá, in Nada Como um Dia Após o Outro Dia 2002)³

Coloniality of power endures through time because it is self-referenced in its own forms of legitimization for domination. From time to time, the same mechanisms of domination are repackaged in new ways for the same old hierarchization of bodies, places and knowledges, aiming at the maintenance of historical oppressions. It is not surprising that at the dawn of the second decade of the twenty-first century, Nazi and fascist groups were growing bigger across the world. For people who experienced colonization, these 'far right' or 'ultra-conservative right' movements constitute elements of the present configuration of power: violence, authoritarianism, white supremacy, conservativeness, capitalism, militarization, scientific scholastic knowledge, employer supremacy, good citizen definitions and role model behaviour. Above all, the control of images, representations and manifestations is structurally necessary for a process that Lélia Gonzalez called 'domestication' (Gonzalez et al. 2021). Colonial domination is total and tends to oversimplify existence by systematic suppression of beliefs, ideas, images, symbols and knowledge that are not conducive to accumulation of capital and, hence, global domination (Fanon 1990: 190). There is no doubt that the control of images and representation have ideological intent. The analysis of cultural expressions in the colonial era requires the acknowledgement of the complex framework of oppression that it entails.

The term 'coloniality of power' was proposed by Aníbal Quijano in 1992 to describe the pattern or matrix of power that consists in the perpetuation of a specific modus of hierarchization of peoples, places and knowledge, naturalizing oppressive realties as the only way to exist in the world. It explains how European culture, behaviour and violence gives access to power (Quijano 1992: 12). This means that the non-powerful could, somehow, change their social and economic status by mimicking the colonial power, thereafter the imperial power and then the financial power. Such mimetic forces are in place in many spheres of individual and communal life, from the self-recognition of each individual and the recognition of social identity to the production of legitimate valid knowledge.

Acknowledging the colonial past and present – the self-identification of our inner and social colonial realities – is an action towards liberation. This action was named by the Brazilian educational philosopher Paulo Freire (2000: 60) as *conscientização* or conscientization (hooks 1994). For Freire (2000: 61), conscientization is a step towards liberation and takes place via dialogue, 'the encounter between people, mediated by the world, in order to name the world'. The dialogical process must aim at the transformation of reality. Cultural manifestations inform and contextualize dialogue, conferring legitimacy to change. The exclamation, 'fire on the racists!' enables dialogue because it challenges colonialities of knowledge and being and aims at social transformation.

The Freirean dialogue involves actors in ethically open intercommunication for conscientization (Freire 2000: 102). This way, the effort at conscientization cannot be restricted to those with 'technical or scientific training of intended specialists' (Freire 2000: 132). Conscientization is then cultural action as the praxis for the oppressed to leave behind the status of objects and to assume the status of historical subjects. The word 'dialogue' allows the alienated, objectified individual to become a subject and, therefore, capable of transforming reality.

For Fanon (1990: 190), the denial of historical subjectivity is made possible by the negation of national reality, by new legal relations introduced by the colonizing power, by the banishment of the natives and their customs to outlying districts by colonial society, by expropriation and by systematic enslaving of men and women. In this sense, cultural manifestations take place concurrently with the struggle for liberation. Cultural identification is, thus, the movement of humanization as against dehumanization.

The process of developing subjective historical awareness is a constant activity of learning. The challenge resides in the fact that this knowledge is to be learnt in the context of the systematic colonial imposition of Eurocentric epistemologies. The vast majority of people do not see themselves represented in the dominant discourse, except as the *Other* forced to conform with the norm. As coloniality of power is power in itself and the means to access power, the colonized peoples experience life as an 'endless catching up' with the imposed hierarchizations (hooks 2014: 6).

The subjective encounter with knowledge, that is, the conversion of the objectified alienated person into a historical subject, requires that people act and reflect upon the reality to be transformed. Such movements take place in school and non-school sites, concurrently, in constant transformation. Cultural manifestations play a crucial role in the dialogical process for conscientization towards liberation. In this sense, literary and artistic movements contain a pedagogical power to establish identification and, hence, dialogue that politicizes those who relate to them. Such power triggers change. The revolutionary power of culture is legitimate and capable of dismantling the 'master's house' to use Audre Lorde's (1978) expression. The subversive, transgressive potential of cultural manifestations to enable subjective awareness towards collective ruptures must be observed in times of obscurantism and social throwbacks. It informs where and when the revolution is already happening.

In *The Wretched of the Earth*, Fanon (1990: 196) writes that culture is not 'put into cold storage during the conflict'. In the chapter 'On National Culture', Fanon (1990: 206–48) addresses the potency of culture for the overthrow of the colonial power; it is like a trigger, *the spark* needed for the transformation, a flame that starts to throw light on the possibility of change.

> Well before the political or fighting phase of the national movement, an attentive spectator can thus feel and see the manifestation of new vigour and feel the approaching conflict. He will note unusual forms of expression and themes

which are fresh and imbued with a power which is no longer that of invocation but rather of the assembling of the people, a summoning together for a precise purpose. Everything works together to awaken the native's sensibility and to make unreal and inacceptable the contemplative attitude, or the acceptance of defeat. The native rebuilds his perceptions because he renews the purpose and dynamism of craftsmen, of dancing and music and of literature and the oral tradition. His world comes to lose his accursed character. *The conditions necessary for the inevitable conflict are brought together.* (Fanon 1990: 196: italics added)

Anti-hegemonic literary and artistic movements talk back to colonial efforts to force historical subjects into colonial objects. By applying other epistemologies and methodologies, anti-hegemonic cultural movements establish dialogue, in the Freirean sense, with the oppressed. Art for conscientization is a social process that first enables humanization and then consciousness and identification of the enemy; and then ignites the possibility of radical overthrow of colonial settings.

Spoken words as 'Miraculous Weapons'

The declining voices in the hands of this Barabbas – where the miracle dies – only prove the urgency of books in the face of the damage that a wise man does. *(Emicida 2021)*[4]

Among the various counter-hegemonic artistic movements across the globe, the ones that come from the Third World – the geopolitical locus of the annunciation of knowledge – have informed important historical transformations. Aimé Césaire's (1946) first collection in book form was *Miraculous Weapons*, and by weapons Césaire meant spoken words (Davis 1997: 70). From the anti-colonial manifestations of the twentieth century to the anti-racist movements such as Black Lives Matter in the early 2020s, Black literature and arts have especially taught, in a universal manner, the specificities and commonalities of the Black struggle due to colonial, imperial and economic violence. Manifestations such as the Négritude movement, the Harlem Renaissance and the hip-hop movement proclaim from local to global, in different historical times of the Black struggle, a whole multidimensional affirmation of complex Black existence, with its pains and delights, informing generations to come.

'Négritude' is a term that refers to an aesthetic, literary, epistemic and political movement of writers, intellectuals and politicians of the francophone African diaspora who, from the 1930s onwards, have addressed Black conscientiousness. The term Négritude was first used by the Martinican poet and statesman Aimé Césaire in an article for the May 1935 issue of the student journal *L'Étudiant Noir* (The Black Student):

> Too bad for those who are content to be Western in defiance of what they call 'racism'. For us, we want to exploit our own values, know our strengths through personal experience, dig into our own racial domain, sure that we are to encounter in depth, the gushing sources of the universal human. So before making the Revolution and in order to make the revolution – the real one – the destructive ground swell and not the shaking of surfaces, one condition is essential: to break the mechanical identification of races, to tear up superficial values, to grasp within us the immediate negro, to plant our négritude like a fine tree until it bears its most genuine fruit. (Césaire 2013)[5]

By asserting Black people as historical subjects, Négritude was constituted as a movement to defy whiteness in all its structures of domination, contributing to the shaping of anti-colonial ideology on a global scale. Francophone intellectuals such as the Nardal Sisters of Martinique (Church 2013), Léopold Senghor, Léon Damas and Aimé Césaire were calling for the development of a Pan-African identity, shifting the representation of Black and Blackness. They organized social reform, published widely and influenced some of the most important politicians, artists and intellectuals of their time (Davis 1997; Church 2013).

The Négritude movement was inspired by the Harlem Renaissance, an aesthetic, artistic and intellectual movement of Black culture in the United States. In the early 1920s, escalating racial violence, massacres and lynching prompted millions of Black people to flee the rule of discrimination in the neocolonial Third World for a new life in the imperial First World of the United States. Attracted by affordable rents, many settled in tenement buildings of the Harlem neighbourhood in New York City. It was the first time in the history of the United States that such a high percentage of Black American artists, intellectuals and activists lived side by side (Wintz and Finkelman 2004). Exponents like the sociologist and activist William Du Bois, visual artist Augusta Savage, jazz musicians Louis Armstrong and Ma Rainey, among various others, were part of the cultural phenomenon of lifting the issue of race and representation beyond a critique of the status quo. The Harlem Renaissance laid the foundations of the

North American Civil Rights Movement and inspired aesthetically, epistemically and politically several other anti-hegemonic movements across the globe, including the Négritude movement. Although the Harlem Renaissance and the Négritude movement have much in common, such as the focus on Black episteme, ontology, aesthetics and history, the latter aimed for the Pan-African liberation as a political challenge of the colonial era, giving a global dimension to the Black struggle and inspiring other decolonial manifestations in the Third World.

In the mid-1970s, the hip-hop movement began in the Afro-Caribbean, African American and Latino neighbourhoods in New York City. As a culture, hip-hop emerged in the United States strongly influenced by the Harlem Renaissance and the Civil Rights Movements (Rabaka 2011), building on Black identity, aesthetics and expression. As a *movement*, hip-hop emphasized the political nature of Black popular culture in general and Black popular music in particular, inspired and educated by the Black Power Movement and the Black Arts Movement. The complexity of being both a culture and a social movement makes the multidimensional organic character of hip-hop a universe for dialogue and conscientization towards liberation. Reiland Rabaka (2013: 271) asserts: 'To invoke hip hop as a "movement", rather than merely a "generation", is to conjure up and consciously conceive of hip hop as the *accumulated politics and aesthetics of each and every African American movement and musical form that preceded it*.'

It is undeniable that the hip-hop movement has had a global impact through time and connects peoples from peripheral countries, from the Moroccan Desert through Sri Lankan voices.[6] This is due to the components of the movement that gave it the possibility of moving beyond the United States in the 1980s and enabling people from all over the world to relate to it, which explains the far-reaching influence of the movement today. Briefly, the hip-hop movement has four basic elements: the master of ceremony or MC singing rap (rhythm and poetry) and singing the lyrics with the flow (emceeing, rapping); the beat, incorporated in the figure of the D.J., the 'mixer' (DJing); the breakdance (b-girling and b-boying); and graffiti, the visual art expression (Weatherford 2019). Broadly speaking, the term 'hip-hop' refers to aesthetically subversive behaviour that is political. As Jeff Chang writes:

> a community cannot have a useful discussion about racial progress without first taking account of the facts of change. . . . My own feeling is that the idea of the Hip-Hop generation brings together time and race, place and polyculturalism,

hot beats and hybridity. It describes the turn from politics to culture, the process of entropy and reconstruction. It captures the collective hopes and nightmares, ambitions and failures of those who would otherwise be described as *post-this or post-that*. (Chang 2011: 2–3)

Although an originally North American movement with constitutive roots in the Harlem Renaissance and the Black Power movements, hip-hop has become a global movement of resistance. As contradictory as any social and cultural movement can be (Rabaka 2011), it presents method and community for survival and living in the colonial era. For this reason, rap music, one of the elements of hip-hop, can be sung in any language, because it brings in the four elements of hip-hop to address local dilemmas, livelihood, neighbourhood and existence.

It is clear that Black movements and the claims of the oppressed will differ, depending on geopolitical and historical factors. In this sense, the Brazilian hip-hop movement(s), for example, although inspired and influenced by the North American movement, has its own approach, aesthetics and impact. Although the history, constitution, action and repression of the Black movements in Brazil are undeniably different from that of the United States, the hip-hop movement has been incorporated by peripheric peoples in Brazil from the 1980s onwards and has become the means of identity and reference as well as the space for political debate. As it happened in the United States, rap music in Brazil gets much more publicity than the hip-hop movement as a whole because of its interaction with the music industry and the sellable products. But apart from that, rap music can reach audiences that may not have any contact with the hip-hop movement as a culture, including struggles beyond Black identity.

Rap is an acronym that stands for rhythm and poetry. The poetic word spoken to the beat forms the songs. Following Paulo Freire, the word is the essence of the dialogue itself, composed of two dimensions – reflection and action. To speak a true word is to name the world to change it (Freire 2000: 61). Rap music is anti-hegemonic. Its epistemic canon of annunciation aims at the liberation of the oppressed. Brazilian rap and the wider hip-hop culture of which it is part, is sometimes criticized for mimicking North American colonial culture. Léopold Senghor, when asked about the contradictions in having chosen the French language to express the claims of the Négritude movement, refers to Aimé Césaire's first collection in book form, *Miraculous Weapons*.

> We have been reproached, particularly on the Anglo-Saxon side, for having chosen French to express the Negro–African. We wanted to be more royalist

than the King. I will answer that we did not choose. And, if we had to choose, maybe we would have chosen French. Not by feeling, I say by reason. But, I repeat, we did not choose. It was our situation as colonized which imposed on us the language of the Colonizer, more precisely the policy of assimilation. All was not bad, moreover, in this policy, which proceeded from the 'immortal principles' of 1789. The misfortune is that these principles of the Revolution were not applied in their entirety, without hypocrisy; the good thing is that they were partially applied, enough for their virtues, including French culture, to bear fruit. Because Négritude is the fruit of the Revolution, by action and reaction. As Jean-Paul Sartre says, we have chosen the weapons of the Colonizer to turn them against him. 'Miraculous weapons', specifies Aimé Césaire.[7] (Senghor 1963: 9)

Following Senghor and Césaire, it can be argued that rap – the vocal expression of hip-hop – is a miraculous weapon. Rap is all about the word – the spoken word.

The strength of cultural movements such as the hip-hop movement and rap as the spoken word, the miraculous weapon, consists in the organic dynamics of change, dazing the colonial methods of control. By discussing the astonishment of the colonizer with the changes of style in pottery making, Fanon explains that artistic manifestations were being influenced by the repercussion of the rising revolution. Changes in style were perceived by the colonialist specialists as *subverting the original traditions and culture* – 'the colonialists who become the defenders of the indigenous style' (Fanon 1990: 175). The same reactions were noticed when new jazz styles such as the be-bop came up in the South of the United States after the Second World War:

> The fact that in their [colonizer] eyes jazz should only be despairing, broken down-nostalgia of an old Negro who is trapped between five glasses of whisky, the curse of his race, and the racial hatred of the white man. As soon as the Negro comes to an understanding of himself, and understands the rest of the world differently, when he gives birth to hope and forces back the racist universe, it is clear that his trumpet sounds more clearly and his voice less hoarsely. (Fanon 1990: 195–6)

In this sense, it is arguable that Brazilian rap has the power to show the light at the end of the tunnel of obscurantism. Rap enables a place for dialogue against the fascist ideology clouding Brazilian politics and society since the parliamentary coup in 2016 and, thereafter, the election of the bizarre conservative figure of Jair Bolsonaro as president in October 2018, and the growing of Bolsonarism as a political ideology. Openly racist, misogynist, militarist, homophobic, afflicted with severe 'mongrel complex'[8] and advocating for the power of milícias,[9] Bolsonaro represents yet another edition of the predictable Brazilian colonial structure serving imperial powers.

As Fanon (1990) suggests, cultural manifestations inform the conditions for the inevitable conflict. Brazilian rap uses the word as the vehicle for reflection and action through dialogue. Faced with the emergence of the institutionalized fascist threat in Brazil, artistic manifestations have responded widely. Rap has played this role since its origins: inspiring and rescuing those deeply depressed in the face of the destruction of historically acquired rights and the trivialization of setbacks. Before turning to Djonga and his work, more specifically to the power of the chorus 'fire on the racists!', it is necessary to set the context by briefly describing the construction of anti-racist imaginary in the hip-hop musical expression – rap – in Brazil since the 1980s. It is impossible to say something about the history and impact of Brazilian hip-hop and rap music without mentioning the Racionais MC's. It is fair to say that the Brazilian rap group comprising Edi Rock, DJ Kld, Ice Blue and Mano Brown permanently marked the country's cultural history from the perspective of the poor, peripheral Black communities. Started in 1988, the group's first single *Pânico na Zona Sul* (Panic in South São Paulo) was released by an independent label, Zimbabwe Records. The single was part of a collection named *Consciência Black* (1988) (Discografias Completas Do Rap Nacional 2017) and sets the tone of the Racionais' message: political, peripheral, anti-racist, historically aware and calling for conscientization. It was in 1992 that Racionais released their groundbreaking first anthem: *Voz Ativa* (Active Voice) (Racionais TV 2017a). The political lyric voice calls for identification for political change:

> We need a leader with popular credibility
> Like Malcom X once was in America
> May he be Black to the bone, one of our own
> And rebuild our pride that was torn apart
> Our brothers are bewildered
> Between pleasure and money, disoriented
> Fighting for pretty much nothing
> Little crumbs and banal things
> Honouring the lie
> The speeches are too uninformed
> Enough of celebrating the disadvantage
> And allowing them to wear out our image

> Current black descendant, my name is Brown
> I'm not troubled and such
> Just rational
> It's the purest truth
> Definitive posture
> The Black youth
> Now have an active voice
>
> Racionais MC's *Voz Ativa* 2017a

Racionais' first studio album, *Raio X do Brasil* (Brazil X-ray) (Racionais MC's 1993), has epic songs such as *Fim de Semana No Parque* (Weekend at the Park) (Racionais TV 2018) and *O Homem na Estrada* (The Man on the Road) (Racionais TV 2017b), narrating situations of racism and police violence in São Paulo's marginalization of poor and Black people. The song 'The Man on the Road' describes the marginalized through the senses – visual, olfactory, tactile and auditory – the epic tragedy of a man who comes out of prison and seeks a new life from then on. The piece is so artistically whole-souled because of its shocking realism, transporting the audience to rage as there is no happy ending. The song was performed by Senator Eduardo Suplicy (PT-SP) on 26 April 2007, during the examination of the proposal to amend the Federal Constitution regarding the reduction of the age for criminal liability from eighteen to sixteen years. In an attempt to convince his peers to vote against the approval of lowering the age of criminal liability, the senator gave a performance at the Constitution and Justice Commission by interpreting the lyrics of the rap song and imitating the sound of gunshots at the end (as in the song). Racionais MC's were educating white male politicians as well; their lyrics were resonating within the walls of parliament.

Rabaka (2013: 43) reminds us that rap essentially 'expand[s] our understanding of human experience by telling stories we might not otherwise hear'. The author emphasizes that 'rap is poetry, and poetry is a textual and, at times, oral form that can lyrically express both love and hate, the sacred and the secular, comedy and tragedy and ecstasy and agony' (Rabaka 2013: 43). The awareness of this subjective identification is the strongest remark of the rapper, Djonga. Among all the anti-Bolsonarism manifestations in the arts and culture in Brazil, Djonga's verse *fogo nos racistas!* (fire on the racists!) has become an anthem of sorts and become popular in the mainstream. Considered an exponent of the new generation of rap in Brazil, Djonga carries on with the tradition of politically sensitive Brazilian rap.

Gustavo Pereira da Silva, aka Djonga, started rapping at the age of twenty-three in the centre of Belo Horizonte. Despite being one of the largest capitals with some of the largest peripheral populations in the country, Belo Horizonte has never been part of the national rap scenario like São Paulo and Rio de Janeiro, which are the centres of media and arts production in Brazil. Without a recording label, from the periphery of music production, and fundamentally focused on his local realities, the rapper from the state of Minas Gerais became 'the king of rap'.

Fire on the racists!

'Art is to disturb', said Djonga smiling, sipping a small glass of cold beer, while being interviewed by the influential Brazilian journalist Pedro Bial. The interview took place remotely because of Covid-19 restrictions, on 17 November 2020. Weeks before that interview, Djonga was headline news in one of the most influential Brazilian TV news channels, *Jornal Nacional*, which announced live on prime-time open TV: 'with a work focused on anti-racism, the rapper from Minas Gerais, Djonga is the only Brazilian representative in an international hip-hop award'. The nomination was for best international artist at the BET Hip Hop Awards 2020, the first Brazilian nomination ever, motivated by the impact and critique of Djonga's fourth album, *Histórias da Minha Área* (Stories From my Area) (2020). The extract given here is from the interview:

> *Bial*: 'BET' stands for Black Entertainment Television, a network of black art that has just completed 40 years. Being nominated to this award, like you were . . . Is this the Oscars of Black art?
>
> *Djonga*: It's like that. . . . From the standpoint of a guy who raps in Brazil it is even more important [the BET Awards nomination] because of the language barrier. . . . Seeing that hip-hop, the hip-hop movement starts there [in the United States], we break through this language barrier and get people there to notice us here and admire our way of making rap, of making music, of making art, of expressing ourselves politically. (Djonga 2020)

It is indeed remarkable that (at the time) a twenty-five-year-old dark-skinned Black man from the favelas of Belo Horizonte was featured on the covers of magazines[10] and in the national news in 2020 as a national achiever. Brazil in

2020 must be viewed in the context of being at the peak of the dismantling of rights by the devastating far-right administration of Bolsonaro, with the legacy of over six hundred thousand deaths because of Covid-19 and violent conservative manifestations, such as street protests, calling for the return of military dictatorship around the country. Cheering Djonga in the national news in such a context could be considered a way to inform the nation that his life and work would be worth knowing because he was about to represent Brazil internationally. The remarkable part is not so much his current international celebrity status but what he says and represents. Djonga's art evidences awareness of his colonial subjectivity and the power to record history while addressing the origins of his joy and pain. He bridges the language gap in a way that informs and establishes him as a protagonist of reactions in the mainstream media.

The 2017 single *Olho de Tigre* (Tiger Eye) (PineappleStormTV 2017a) is an example of the combination of subjective awareness and historical power. With over twenty-six million viewers on Youtube (in November 2023), the video is part of a list of singles from various artists presenting their works related to the hip-hop scene and rap music. Tiger Eye soon became an anti-racist anthem because of its chorus, 'fire on the racists!', carrying lyrical rage against whiteness and powerful affirmation of blackness. Although the single was never recorded in an album, the song is very popular and most sung at concerts. Nevertheless, Djonga has been severely criticized as being too angry and accused of 'reverse racism' and of allegedly inciting violence against white people. The shallowness of the controversy affirms the fact that when addressing colonialities of being, knowledge and power, there must be a controlled reaction to colonial violence. To what extent does the reach and popularity of the chorus 'fire on the racists!' play a decolonial pedagogy role in the mainstream? Historically, Black artistic and cultural movements have been crucial for the elaboration of Black subjectivities, impacting the way young Black people learn about themselves and their history. This is because the education in schools and academia ignores their colonial wounds, imposing an understanding of the world that conflicts with their perceptions and experiences. Black artists and cultural movements subvert Eurocentric pedagogies and enable learning from a broader and more coherent range of factors, overstepping the limits allowed by the dominant discourse. From the beginning of the Négritude movement in the 1930s to the twenty-first century hip-hop scene, addressing colonial violence is in fact about responding to it. Exponents of such movements deliver their message through decolonial subversive pedagogies. Like fire, decolonial learning may lead to unforeseeable consequences, escaping the control of the colonizers. Audre Lorde said that the masters' tools will never dismantle the masters' house (Lorde 2017). Decolonial subversive pedagogies such as rap and the poetry of Négritude have such dismantling power. Djonga's 'fire on the racists' exemplifies the subversive pedagogical power of his songs.

> Tiger Eye
> A white boy asked me to high-five
> I mistook it for a 'heil, Hitler'
> Who has my colour is a thief
> Anyone who has Eric Clapton's colour is a kleptomaniac
> At the time of judgment, god is black and Brazilian
> And to save the country Christ is an ex-military
> Who thinks that women gathered form a whorehouse
> . . . .
> Sensation, sensational
> Sensation, sensational
> Firm it up! Firm it up! Firm it up!
> Fire on the racists!
> (Djonga in PineappleStormTV 2017a)

The first two verses of Djonga's *Tiger Eye* evidence the distrust towards the white boy as a potential Nazi: 'A white boy asked me for a high five / I mistook it for a "heil, Hitler"' (PineappleStormTV 2017a). The approximation of the white boy doing the hand gesture of raising one hand about head high as a greeting or celebration, expecting to slap the flat of his palm against the flat palm of the other person, is perceived by Djonga as a demonstration of white domination. While the white boy invites to 'celebrate together', Djonga interprets his action as the continuous act of racist violence. Referring to the 'friendly' white boy as a Nazi implies the perception of whiteness as violence. This 'Hitler within' has been addressed by Aimé Césaire in the classic anti-colonial essay 'Discourse on Colonialism', first published in 1950. From the reflections of Césaire (2000) and Djonga, the colonizer is brutalized to a point of savagery to justify colonization, applying their own violence against themselves. Hitler and Hitlerism are not exceptions of European powers, but instead, their very nature:

> Yes, it would be worthwhile to study clinically, in detail, the steps taken by Hitler and Hitlerism and to reveal to the very distinguished, very humanistic, very

Christian bourgeois of the twentieth century that without his being aware of it, he has a Hitler inside him, that Hitler *inhabits* him, that Hitler is his *demon*, that if he rails against him, he is being inconsistent and that, at bottom, what he cannot forgive Hitler for is not *the crime* in itself, the *crime against man*, it is not *the humiliation of man as such*, it is the crime against the white man, the humiliation of the white man, and the fact that he applied to Europe colonialist procedures which until then had been reserved exclusively for the Arabs of Algeria, the 'coolies' of India, and the 'niggers' of Africa. (Césaire 1955: 36)

Both Djonga and Césaire address a supposed 'innocence' of the white man, as in the cheerful high-five gesture of the white boy or the Western *humanist* saviours and their universal human rights (Césaire 1955: 37). The two mentioned works (the song '*Tiger Eye*' and the essay 'Discourse on Colonialism') have in common the description of the racist's condition: 'no one colonizes innocently' (Césaire 1955: 35).

Throughout their artistic lives, Césaire and Djonga had to handle the backlash to their lyrical anger against repeated dehumanization as a consequence of racist colonial oppression. In this sense, calling white people 'Nazi' or 'Hitler' seemed to be more problematic than racism. Both poets, in different historical times, were accused of victimization of the Black race, of dramatically exaggerating to make a point; it was argued that their method of voicing their revolt would replace one evil with another. In the 1951 essay *Black Orpheus*, Jean-Paul Sartre refers to the Négritude movement as 'anti-racism racism'. Sartre's controversial analysis views Négritude as an antithetical stage in a historical Hegelian dialectic to be superseded eventually by a synthesis (Davis 1997: 53, 188). Césaire discussed the question in the 1966 essay 'Discours sur l'art africain' (Discourse on African Art):

This notion of négritude, some have wondered if it was not racism. I believe the texts speak for themselves. It is enough to read them, and any reader in good faith will realize that if négritude involves taking root in a particular soil, négritude is also transcendence and expansion into the universal. . . . The appearance of négritude literature and négritude poetry produced such a shock only because they disturbed the image that the white man had of the black man, that they marked with his qualities, with his faults, therefore with his charge as a man; in the world of abstractions and stereotypes that the white man had hitherto unilaterally made up about him. (Césaire 1973: 103)

The white boy's beckoning is a sign of pacification to which Djonga responds with historical memory. The rapper informs awareness of a constitutive subjective element of the 'peaceful' white boy: the certainty that white superiority comes at the expense of oppression. The acknowledgement and historical imprint of the violence that structures whiteness is received by whites as the retribution of such violence. In the song *Junho de 1994* (June of 1994), in the second track of his second album *O Menino Que Queria Ser Deus* (The Boy Who Wanted to Be God), the rapper responds to the hate suffered:

> Had to hear that I was wrong for telling you
> That your people remind me of Hitler
> They carry slavery traditions
> And they can't stand to see a black leader
>
> (Djonga 2018)

As Césaire writes, the shock caused by the angry artistic manifestation resides in the disruption of the sub-ontological difference created by the hierarchization of races. The victims of this structure of oppressions are negated, in the sense that talking to the colonizer would mean speaking the colonizer's language but, in this language, the racialized are denied any humanity and, therefore, cannot speak. Nonetheless, the truth of historical facts is blurred by ontological suppression and epistemic annihilation, aligned with institutional physical violence. This led to a constant search, on the part of the offended whites, for apologies and explanations for such anger. In 1966, Césaire was obliged to inform that the 'reader in good faith' comprehends that Négritude aims at the allocation of words into epistemic existence from local to universal. In a similar fashion, in 2020 Djonga had to explain the meaning of his anthem 'fire on the racists' at the interview with Pedro Bial.

> *Bial*: One of your anthems, a diverse one, but with a catchphrase like a slogan, is 'fire on the racists!'. When you shout 'fire on the racists!', where does poetry end and what might be called an 'incitation of violence' begin?
>
> *Djonga*: I don't know. I don't know where Djonga starts nor where Gustavo ends. How would I know where poetry is, whether what I'm saying is true? That guy who says he's not angry . . . that there aren't times when he wants to retaliate against the violence he's suffering . . . That guy is lying. Everyone suffers it [violence]. Sometimes you express it in action, sometimes in words – that's a fact. When I said that, I was saying that. It's simple. When I say 'fire on the racists!', I'm saying: fire on the racists! It's very difficult for me to control the

reactions and know to what extent what I was talking about was an artistic yell or a real yell. I would be a hypocrite if I said otherwise. In a world where those guys set us on fire in the past, it's very sad to know that just by saying this in a song, somehow assuming that . . . Because I've never set anyone on fire, you know? In a world where those guys [the police] go to the favela and put bullets in the head of a 14- 13-year-old kid, or even younger, who hasn't done anything! In this world, it's strange for people to get annoyed sometimes with the things that, next to all of that, are very small things. (Djonga 2020)

The rapper puts in perspective the negative reactions against his lyrical rage. The suggestion of incitation of violence is, again, a way to create an aura of criminal offence around a young Black man. In Brazilian criminal law, Articles 286 and 287 of the Criminal Code 1940 deal with incitement to crime and advocacy for crime or criminal, respectively. Although Pedro Bial did not use the word 'crime' as typified in the Criminal Code, he used the word 'violence', which could be one of the many ways to describe it as a crime in mainstream media. The technical distinction between inciting crime (which is a crime) or inciting violence depends on the interpretation of the audience, and mainstream media knows that. Djonga, however, meets the description of the historically built criminal, the standard suspect exhaustively used in police journalism (Reis 2019), despite being a Brazilian international celebrity. Through racist stereotypes, mainstream media explores the antipathy based on a flawed and inflexible generalization that is addressed to an entire group or to an individual simply because he is part of that group (Techio, Torres and Sousa 2020). It is not an argumentative stretch to consider that when the journalist asks Djonga whether his anthem is an 'incitement', the accustomed audience hears the suggestion of a crime related to a young Black man. Social psychology informs that police violence is more acceptable when addressed to members of minority groups.[11] Ergo, the rapper's reaction to structural racism is framed as an offense, instead of as information. As Césaire said, Negritude is a literary and cultural movement of combat and shock against racism and colonialism. The poet of Negritude hates racism and colonialism because these are 'barriers that prevent communication from being established' (Césaire 1973: 104).

Independent of the audience's approval, Césaire and Djonga answer with the same bored, almost tired inflection: '*les textes sont là*' (the texts speak for themselves) (Césaire 1973: 103) and '*quando eu disse aquilo ali, eu estava dizendo aquilo ali*' (when I said that, I was saying that) (Djonga 2020). As if their own acknowledgement of their subjectivity or of the violence they suffer should be explained over and over until words lose their punch. The reactions against anti-racist manifestations could discourage the youth. Notwithstanding, the identification with the struggle is the very call for resistance.

In the cypher[12] song *Favela Vive 3* (Favela Lives 3), the question of violence against Black and peripheral youth is not treated as scientific data or as unfortunate misinformation of the news. The track is an emotional song that sends shivers down the spine of those who live the sad Brazilian reality that violence is the main cause of death among young people, and that 77 per cent of victims of homicide in Brazil are Black (Ipea – Atlas da Violência 2023: 27; 49). *Favela Vive 3* is the third song of the *Favela Vive* series, which the rappers, DK from the project ADL, Choice MC, Djonga, Menor do Chapa and Negra Li denounce as real stories. An accompanying music video for the song was shot in the favelas in Belo Horizonte and Rio de Janeiro. The first verse, by DK, speaks about the assassination of the fourteen-year-old Marcos Vinicius da Silva by representatives of the power of the state of Rio de Janeiro. The teenager was killed on 20 June 2018 with a shot in the stomach inside the Ciep Operário Vicente Mariano elementary school. Marcos Vinicius was killed wearing the school uniform, inside the school where he studied, in the favela Complexo da Maré, north of Rio. He was hit by a bullet during an operation by the Civil Police in conjunction with the Army. The rapper DK urges revolt:

> If you don't stop, my tram will come and stop you
> If you don't embrace it, it will embrace you
> Bro, the po-pos chicken out to go up the favela at night
> They always schedule an operation when the doors of the daycare centre are full
> Another angry mother, an unanswered question
> How did the cop not see his school uniform?
> Vinicius is hit with the backpack on his back
> How am I going to shout that the favela lives now?
>
> (Além da Loucura ADL 2018)

The action of the police inside the favelas of Rio de Janeiro has strong public appeal in the most conservative areas of society. Not coincidentally, this demographic is the same that sustains and encourages Bolsonarism at the same time that it preaches the total liberation of the economy for foreign markets, the censorship of artistic manifestations and the return of military dictatorship. Disguised as protectors of the moral and the anti-corrupt, the conservative aisle of Brazilian society has historically occupied places of political power, with representatives from the local politics to the national congress. Supported by the industrial barons, the agribusiness' kings, the neo-Pentecostal leaders and the arms industrialists, Brazilian colonial politics has been denounced.

Djonga invites other young Black men to think collectively about how they are targeted by the multiple forms of violence: victimization, police violence and racial stereotypes. The message, however, reaches more audiences than the ones immediately related to his lyric voice. It is a collective call for concern:

> I know, I know . . .
> Yeah, it looks like we only get beaten up
> But put yourself in my place, and suppose that
> In the twenty-first century, every twenty-three minutes a young Black man dies
> And you're black like me, little Black boy, oh
> Wouldn't you be worried?
> I know well what you are thinking:
> 'I am sure he was no saint, must be a tramp'
> But the minor was coming back from work
> They said the shot was just hasty
> Overall, I miss the friends who passed away
> P.J.F.[13] for the brothers who are locked

(Djonga in Além da Loucura ADL 2018)

It is imperative that the youth in Brazil react against the conservative forces that aim at the maintenance of the colonial era. Although Bolsonaro and his sui generis ultraliberal fascism did not remain in the executive after the end of his presidential mandate, Bolsonarism as an ideology remains. Out of such obscurity, the present generations, whether called the hip-hop or the decolonial generation, have been driven to get conscientization of their mission in order to fulfil it, as Fanon says. In this sense, shouting 'fire on the racists!' has the power to unveil colonialities through the awareness of historical subjectivity.

E firma, firma! Fogo nos racistas! (So firm it up! Firm it up! Fire on the racists!) PineappleStormTV (2017a).

Notes

1 The verse says: 'This castle will crumble / they are weak / they'll cry even if it doesn't hurt.' Original in Portuguese: *Esse castelo vai ruir / eles são fracos / vão chorar até se não doer.*

2 This is a reference to the emblematic rap song *Vida Loka parte I*, by Racionais MC's. The author, Mano Brown, encourages the peripheric young Black man to be faithful. The verse says: 'Faith in God that he is just / Hey brother, never forget / On guard, warrior / Raise your head, bro / Wherever you are / Whatever happens / Be faithful / Because even in the dump / Flowers are born' (Racionais MC's – Topic 2015).

3 Author's translation. Original in Portuguese: *da ponte pra cá, antes de tudo, é uma escola*.

4 Author's translation. Original in Portuguese: *as voz em declive nas mãos desse Barrabás – onde o milagre jaz – só provam a urgência de livros perante o estrago que um sábio faz*.

5 Author's translation. Original in French : *Tant pis pour ceux qui se contentent d'être des Occide par mépris de ce qu'ils appellent du 'racisme'. Pour nous, nous voulons exploiter nos propres valeurs, connaître nos forces par personnelle expérience, creuser notre propre domaine racial, sûrs que nous sommes de rencontrer en profondeur, les sources jaillissantes de l'humain universel. Ainsi donc avant de faire la Révolution et pour faire la révolution – la vraie –, la lame de fond destructrice et non l'ébranlement des surfaces, une condition est essentielle : rompre la mécanique identification des races, déchirer les superficielles valeurs, saisir en nous le nègre immédiat, planter notre négritude comme un bel arbre jusqu'à ce qu'il porte ses fruits les plus authentiques* (Césaire 2013).

6 'Bad Girls' is a song by British recording artist M. I. A. for her fourth studio album, Matangi (2013). An accompanying music video for the song was shot in Ouarzazate, Morocco, in solidarity with the women to drive the movement; it premiered on 3 February 2012 (Noisey 2012).

7 Original in French: *On nous a reproché, singulièrement du côté anglo-saxon, d'avoir choisi le français pour exprimer le Négro-africain. On a voulu être plus royaliste que le Roi. Je répondrai que nous n'avons pas choisi. Et, s'il avait fallu choisir, peut-être aurions-nous choisi le français. Non par sentiment, je dis par raison. Mais, je le répète, nous n'avons pas choisi. C'est notre situation de colonisés qui nous imposait la langue du Colonisateur, plus précisément la politique de l'assimilation. Tout n'était pas mauvais, au demeurant, dans cette politique, qui procédait des 'immortels principes' de 1789. Le malheur est qu'ils ne furent pas, ces principes de la Révolution, appliqués intégralement, sans hypocrisie; le bonheur est qu'ils furent partiellement appliqués, assez pour que leurs vertus, dont la culture française, portassent leurs fruits. Car la Négritude est fruit de la Révolution, par action et réaction. Comme le dit Jean-Paul Sartre, nous avons choisi les armes du Colonisateur pour les retourner contre lui. 'Les armes miraculeuses », précise Aimé Césaire'* (Senghor 1963: 9).

8   Literal translation of the Brazilian expression *complexo de vira-lata*. Mongrel complex or alternatively 'Mutt complex' (Portuguese: *complexo de vira-lata*, literal meaning: 'street dog complex' or 'mutt complex') is an expression used to refer to a collective inferiority complex reportedly felt by many Brazilians when comparing Brazil and its culture to that of other parts of the world, primarily the Global North (such as Europe or North America), as the reference to a 'mongrel' carries negative connotations attributed by Brazilians to the racist perception of most Brazilians being racially mixed as well as lacking in desirable cultural refinement.
9   In speeches and other manifestations, Bolsonaro has repeatedly praised militias and death squads (Franco 2018).
10 *Rolling Stone* magazine headline: Rapper Djonga is the highlight of the North American Billboard: 'Moment of reflection' (Antunes 2020).
11 This bias can be explained by the fact that when groups are classified as lacking uniquely human characteristics, that is, they are dehumanized or infra-humanized, they are perceived as more dangerous, savage, incapable of feeling social and moral emotions (guilt, empathy, shame, etc.). Therefore, aggressions and violent actions directed at them are justified (Techio, Torres and Sousa 2020: 287).
12 A cypher is a gathering of rappers, beatboxers and/or breakers in a circle, extemporaneously making music together. In recent years, the cypher has also grown to include the crowd and spectators who are integral to maintaining the energy of a given cypher.
13 P. J. F. stands for 'peace, justice and freedom', literal translation of P. J. L. 'paz, justiça e liberdade'.

References

Além da Loucura ADL (2018), *Favela Vive 3 - ADL, Choice, Djonga, Menor Do Chapa and Negra Li* (Prod. Índio & Mortão). Available at https://www.youtube.com/watch?v=avbOUVHr0QI"https://www.youtube.com/watch?v=avbOUVHr0QI (Accessed: 24 June 2024)

Antunes, Pedro (2020), 'Rapper Djonga é Destaque Da Billboard Norte-Americana: "Momento de Reflexão"*Rolling Stone Brasil online, Notícias*, 22 May. Available at https://rollingstone.uol.com.br/noticia/rapper-djonga-e-destaque-da-billboard-norte-americana-momento-de-reflexao/"https://rollingstone.uol.com.br/noticia/rapper-djonga-e-destaque-da-billboard-norte-americana-momento-de-reflexao/ (Accessed: 23 March 2022)

Atlas Da Violência (2023), *Ipea – Atlas Da Violencia v.2.7*. Available at https://www.ipea.gov.br/atlasviolencia/publicacoes (Accessed: 22 March 2022).

Césaire, Aimé (1946), *Les armes miraculeuses*, Paris: Gallimard

Césaire, Aimé (1955), *Discours sur le colonialisme*, Paris: Éditions Présence Africaine

Césaire, Aimé (1973), 'Discours sur l'art africain (1966)', *Études littéraires*, 6 (1): 99–109. https://doi.org/10.7202/500270ar.

Césaire, Aimé (2000), 'Discourse on Colonialism. Translated by Joan Pinkham', New York: Montly Review Press. Available at: https://files.libcom.org/files/zz_aime_cesaire_robin_d.g._kelley_discourse_on_colbook4me.org_.pdf (Accessed: 24 June 2024).

Césaire, Aimé (2013), 'Nègreries: Conscience raciale et révolution sociale', *Les Temps Modernes,* 676 (5): 249–51. https://doi.org/10.3917/ltm.676.0249.

Chang, Jeff (2011), *Can't Stop Won't Stop: A History of the Hip-Hop Generation*, New Edition, London: Ebury Digital

Church, Emily Musil (2013), 'In Search of Seven Sisters: A Biography of the Nardal Sisters of Martinique', *Callaloo,* 36 (2): 375–90.

Davis, Gregson (1997), *Aimé Césaire*, Duke University, NC: Cambridge University Press.

Discografias Completas Do Rap Nacional (2017), *Coletânea "Consciência Black" Vol. 1 Disco Completo [1989]*. Available at https://www.youtube.com/watch?v=4khNAOIb5gA"https://www.youtube.com/watch?v=4khNAOIb5gA (Accessed: 24 June 2024).

Djonga (2018), *Djonga – JUNHO DE 94 (Clipe Oficial)*, Available at https://www.youtube.com/watch?v=hTUEjPmX0tE"https://www.youtube.com/watch?v=hTUEjPmX0tE (Accessed: 24 June 2024).

Djonga (2020), Interviewed by Pedro Bial, '*Conversa con Bial*', Globo TV. Available at https://globoplay.globo.com/v/9032651/ (Accessed: 24 June 2024)

Emicida (2021), *Emicida – Principia – Ao Vivo Part. Pastor Henrique Vieira #AmarEloAoVivo*. Available at https://www.youtube.com/watch?v=h8gotN_Na28 (Accessed: 24 June 2024).

Fanon, Frantz (1990), *The Wretched of the Earth*, Harmondsworth: Penguin.

Franco, Bernardo Mello. "Em Discursos, Bolsonaro Já Exaltou Milícias e Grupos de Extermínio. O Globo, 14 October 2018. Available online at https://blogs.oglobo.globo.com/bernardo-mello-franco/post/em-discursos-bolsonaro-ja-exaltou-milicias-e-grupos-de-exterminio.html (Accessed 23 March 2022)

Freire, Paulo (2000), *Pedagogy of the Oppressed*, 30th Anniversary Edition, New York: Continuum

Gonzalez, Lélia, Barros, Bruna, Feva, Oliveira, Jess and Reis, Luciana (2021), 'Racism and Sexism in Brazilian Culture', *Women's Studies Quarterly,* 49 (1): 371–94. https://doi.org/10.1353/wsq.2021.0027.

hooks, bell (1994), *Teaching to Transgress: Education as the Practice of Freedom*, 1st edn, New York: Routledge.

hooks, bell (2014), *Black Looks: Race and Representation*, 2nd edn, New York: Routledge. https://doi.org/10.4324/9781315743226.

Lorde, Audre (2017), *The Master's Tools Will Never Dismantle the Master's House*, London: Penguin.

M.I.A. (2013), *M.I.A. -Matangi (Audio)*. Available at https://www.youtube.com/watch?v=mTOADPPywq8 (Accessed: 24 June 2024).

Noisey (2012), *M.I.A. – 'Bad Girls' (Official Video)*. https://www.youtube.com/watch?v=2uYs0gJD-LE"https://www.youtube.com/watch?v=2uYs0gJD-LE (Accessed: 14 March 2022).

Reis, Ana Carolina Soares (2019), 'O espelho da Branca de Neve: como a mulher negra é retratada no telejornalismo policial', Postgraduate dissertation. Escola de Estudos Latino-americanos sobre a Cultura e Comunicação: Universidade de São Paulo.

PineappleStormTV (2017a), *Perfil #22 – Djonga – Olho de Tigre (Prod. Malive/Slim)*. https://www.youtube.com/watch?v=0D84LFKiGbo"https://www.youtube.com/watch?v=0D84LFKiGbo (Accessed: 30 November 2023).

Quijano, Aníbal (1992), 'Colonialidad y Modernidad/Racionalidad', *Perú Indígena*, 13 (29): 11–20.

Rabaka, Reiland (2011), *Hip Hop's Inheritance: From the Harlem Renaissance to the Hip Hop Feminist Movement*, Lanham, MD: Lexington Books.

Rabaka, Reiland (2013), *The Hip Hop Movement: From R&B and the Civil Rights Movement to Rap and the Hip Hop Generation* Lanham, MD: Lexington Books.

Racionais MC's (1993), *Raio X do Brasil*. https://open.spotify.com/intl-pt/album/2QMZRtm35gtG3ZJs0yl9EM?si=lmuJ9J9RR_Sx7HXouBM5zA (Accessed: 24 March 2022).

Racionais MC's – Topic (2015), *Vida Loka, Pt. 1*. https://www.youtube.com/watch?v=LiwDa5rCmYc"https://www.youtube.com/watch?v=LiwDa5rCmYc (Accessed: 14 March 2022).

Racionais TV (2017a), *Racionais – Escolha o seu Caminho – Voz Ativa*. https://www.youtube.com/watch?v=C1F7Y2rUHM4 (Accessed: 14 March 2022).

Racionais TV (2017b), Racionais – *Raio X Do Brasil – Homem Na Estrada*. https://www.youtube.com/watch?v=SkHS9r1haXE"https://www.youtube.com/watch?v=SkHS9r1haXE (Accessed: 15 March 2022).

Racionais TV (2018), *Racionais – Coletânea 2013 – Fim de Semana No Parque*. https://www.youtube.com/watch?v=oSxnR7cERpI"https://www.youtube.com/watch?v=oSxnR7cERpI (Accessed: 15 March 2022).

Senghor, Léopold Sédar (1963), 'Négritude et Civilisation de l'Universel', *Presence Africaine*, 2: 8–13.

Techio, Elza Maria, Torres, Ana Raquel Rosas and Sousa, Yuri Sá Oliveira (2020), 'Violência e ações coletivas no Brasil: reflexões para a intervenção psicossocial',

Inclusão Social, 13 (2). Available at http://revista.ibict.br/inclusao/article/view/5531 (Accessed: 25 June 2024).

Weatherford, Carole Boston (2019), *The Roots of Rap: 16 Bars on the 4 Pillars of Hip-Hop*. Illustrated edn, New York, NY: Little Bee Books.

Wintz, C.D. and Finkelman, P. (Eds.). (2004), *Encyclopedia of the Harlem Renaissance*, 1st edn, Routledge. https://doi.org/10.4324/9780203319307

6

Class and struggle

Cabral, Rodney and the complexities of culture in Africa

David Austin

They say that the countryside has turned verdant, a most beautiful colour, because it is the colour of hope. *(Amílcar Cabral (1946))*

Sometime in the late 1990s, I had a series of discussions with a friend from Senegal that helped to crystallize for me some of the challenges related to Caribbean political-intellectuals who wrote and thought about African politics. At the time, I had inherited the recordings of several lectures by C. L. R. James that had been delivered in Montreal in the late 1960s. The lectures covered a range of topics, including one presentation titled 'Policy and Program for Developing Countries'. In the lecture, James described the dismal social and political state in Africa – corruption, poor governance, illiteracy – and then, drawing on his deep knowledge of European history, acknowledged the inevitability of military coups in much the same way that they had historically occurred in Europe during Cromwell's Revolution in Britain and during the French Revolution. Then, drawing on Lenin's analysis of Russia in 1920–1, James (1967) called for a literacy campaign in African societies as, he argued, those who are illiterate are 'outside of politics'. He also called upon African politicians to 'change those governments which they inherited from former colonial powers' and introduce cooperative systems that would 'involve the population in the development of the economic and social life of the country' (James 1967). That James did not suggest how his ideas would be carried through does not detract from his analysis as, in the final prognosis, he called for a process that would actively engage Africans in politics or, more appropriately, would allow Africans to actively engage in the political process. As I read James's account, it was difficult to ignore the sense of despair that undergirded his reasoning. While his pragmatic approach made sense on one level, I was left with the sense that he saw the African continent as existing outside the boundaries of modern history and, despite his hopes for change, hopelessly sinking into a political abyss. And while his analysis reflected his understanding of current trends in African politics, it lacked the nuance and depth of understanding of the deep structures of African cultures and societies that had characterized his work in other areas. In other words, unlike so much of his other work, and despite his understanding of conventional African politicians – many of whom he had been associated in London in the 1930s – when it came to the African continent, James was writing from the outside.

I shared James's lecture with Ameth Lo, who at the time had recently moved to Montreal and was an active member of the Group for Research and Initiative for the Liberation of Africa (GRILA). And while I dithered and attempted to make sense, and even justify James' analysis – despite my unease – Ameth's response was swift, clear and to the point – in a manner that was reminiscent of Amílcar Cabral. Ameth simply pointed out that James's limited understanding of the African continent – the nuances of its diverse politics, cultural dynamics and social structures – had prevented him from developing a full appreciation of the challenges confronting the continent and the prospects for social change within it. As I would later conclude after listening to Ameth, James was applying Western, and West Indian, sensibilities to a continent and terrain that he could not possibly have understood from his limited contact with Africa and despite – or perhaps as a result of – his close contact with African leaders such as Kwame Nkrumah, Jomo Kenyatta, Namdi Azikiwe, among others.

In retrospect, Ameth helped to save me from what, in his own way, V. Y. Mudimbe has described as the African diaspora's invention of Africa. While Mudimbe was speaking about a different kind of invention to that of James, the end result was the same: James's invention or imagining ultimately hovered above the lived experience of the majority of Africans, so-called ordinary people for whom in other contexts James had often described in terms of their ability to do the extraordinary.

James was part of a long history of Caribbean engagement with the African continent that loosely fits under the broad banner of Pan-Africanism. In the nineteenth and early twentieth centuries, African emancipation was the central preoccupation of West Indian Pan-Africanists such as Edward Wilmot Blyden, Henry Sylvester Williams and Marcus Garvey. The African continent was a beacon of hope, the figurative motherland, and Caribbean Pan-Africanists believed that their freedom was intricately tied to the fate of the African continent.

But the 'West Indian road to Africa', to borrow a term from James, was not without its share of controversy. Not only did West Indians often 'invent' Africa, creating an imaginary continent, replete with often romanticized notions of ancient African societies and kingdoms on the one hand and an image of contemporary Africa as a dark continent in decline from this illustrious past on the other; implicit, and often explicit, in this reasoning was the idea that 'scattered Ethiopians' of the Americas would rescue Africa and restore it to its former glory (Mudimbe 1988: 98–134). Seen as a component part of the West Indian's recovery from the legacy of slavery and the colonial degradation, this idealized perception of Africa is understandable. The road to Caribbean rehabilitation passed through Africa, and, if West Indians were to humanize their own existence, the continent itself would have to be rehabilitated, even if this meant reimagining it in ways that were not in keeping with the lived experience of continental Africans.

By the 1930s, however, a new and highly politicized Caribbean conception of Africa emerged as exiled West Indians and Africans came into close contact with one another in European metropolitan centres.[1] It was while in exile that a second wave of West Indians 'rediscovered' the continent, as they sought to reclaim their humanity in the face of colonialism at home and racism abroad. In the process, West Indian paternalism partially gave way to genuine collaboration and solidarity among West Indians and Africans. In London in the 1930s, West Indians George Padmore and James of Trinidad, Amy Ashwood Garvey of Jamaica and Ras Makonnen (formerly George T. N. Griffith) of British Guyana agitated for African liberation alongside several future African leaders, including Nnamdi Azikiwe of Nigeria, I. T. A. Wallace Johnson of Sierra Leone, Jomo Kenyatta of Kenya and later Kwame Nkrumah of the Gold Coast (later Ghana). Their work in exile culminated in the Fifth Pan-African Congress in Manchester in 1945, laying the foundation for the independence of Ghana and other colonial territories on the continent. During this same period in Paris, Aimé Césaire and Suzanne Lacascade of Martinique, Léon Damas of French Guyana and Léopold Senghor of Senegal, among others, established the literary–philosophical Negritude movement. Along with the emergence of the journal *Présence Africaine* and a publishing house of the same name founded by Alioune Diop, Negritude inspired a cultural renaissance in

Africa and the Caribbean as France's colonies agitated for independence and self-determination.

In the 1960s, the focus of the Caribbean exiles shifted from Africa to the Caribbean as a new generation of West Indians, in part inspired by independence and liberation movements in Ghana and other parts of Africa, set about transforming the Caribbean. Building on the foundation of their predecessors, they embraced a combination of Caribbean nationalism, Third World internationalism and socialism. These exiles played a crucial role in the emergence of the Caribbean New Left, which began, in a sense, with the 'Rodney Riots' in Jamaica following Walter Rodney's expulsion from that country after his participation in the Montreal Congress of Black Writers and culminated with the rise and subsequent fall of the Grenada Revolution (1979–83) (Meeks 1996: 1–2; Austin 2010).

But Africa remained central to the work of West Indians such as Frantz Fanon and later Rodney and many other Caribbean political-intellectuals of the post–Second World War period, and continued to inform those who were now primarily concerned with the Caribbean. But of the Caribbean women and men that attempted to engage the African continent, it was Rodney, even more than Fanon, who developed a complex understanding of African societies and attempted to understand those societies on their own terms, not through the lens of modernist notions of progress.

In *A History of Upper the Guinea Coast: 1545 to 1800*, Walter Rodney examines trade and social relations between primarily Portuguese merchants and West Africans. As we learn from him in *Walter Rodney Speaks: The Making of an African Intellectual*, the book represents an effort to bring to bear a kind of proto-class analysis of the history of slavery and colonization in Africa (Rodney 1990: 27). *A History of Upper Guinea Coast* is centred on the sociology and economic history of the West African coast prior to and during the slave trade, and the impact of the trade on African societies. And in this painstakingly researched study, Rodney provides the reader with insight into the inner workings and dynamics of West African societies during this period. In the process, he raises similar issues to those raised by Amílcar Cabral in relation to twentieth-century Guinea-Bissau under Portuguese rule. In many ways, Cabral's analysis of Guinea-Bissau makes explicit in the twentieth-century context what Rodney projects in his analysis of sixteenth- to eighteenth-century West African history.

Walter Rodney was a close associate of James. He read James's classic work on the Haitian Revolution as a university student in Jamaica and participated in a study group with C. L. R. and Selma James as he pursued a PhD in history in London. These study sessions at the James's home included a number of Caribbean nationals, several of whom would go on to play active political roles in the post-independence Caribbean. From Rodney's account, the study group had a tremendous impact on him. Grappling with his own ideas and approach to history, and finding nothing 'in the English political scene that was helpful', Rodney (1990: 27) found the study group indispensable to his political development. 'Getting together in London and meeting over a period of two to three years on a fairly regular basis', says Rodney (1990: 27), 'afforded me the opportunity... to acquire a knowledge of Marxism, a more precise understanding of the Russian Revolution and of historical formulation'. 'One thing is certain about C. L. R. James', adds Rodney (1990: 28-9): 'he has mastered a whole range of theory and historical data and analysis. This explains why he was very good at focusing in [on the subject matter]' and 'as many people know, C. L. R. had that habit of really incisively dismissing bourgeois foolishness. And I think that his wife, Selma James, in her own right had a complementary if different style that tended in that same direction' (Rodney 1990: 29). For Rodney, both C. L. R. and Selma James 'exemplify the power of Marxist thought. That's what one got – a sense that a bourgeois argument could never really stand a chance against a Marxist argument, provided one was clear about it' (Rodney 1990: 29). But despite his admiration for the Jameses, it was Rodney who made a unique contribution to our understanding of Marxist theory and class struggle during this period, and not by drawing on European history, but by turning to a troubled part of the history of the African continent.

In 1970, a revised version of Rodney's PhD thesis was published as *A History of the Upper Guinea Coast*. The book is the least known of his major publications, and it is fair to say that it has been generally ignored by Rodney scholars, particularly American scholars, according to Rodney (1990: 27); although, perhaps for different reasons, Pan-Africanists have also tended to shy away from it. *A History of the Upper Guinea Coast* is unique for its nuanced description of the relationship between Africans and Europeans during the period of the European slave trade of Africans. It also illustrates the role of Africans in the slave trade, as Rodney distinguishes between the aims and aspirations of the African ruling class, on the one hand, and those of the majority population, on the other. Somewhat empirical in its approach, the book outlines the way in which the African elite were both used and manipulated by Europeans during the slave trade, and the way in which African elites also consciously manipulated their European counterparts in order to profit from the enslavement of other Africans. Rodney never loses sight of the fact that it was Europeans who orchestrated and were the primary beneficiaries of the slave trade. But, referring to the existence of social classes in the Upper Guinea Coast and the phenomenon of slavery, Rodney (1980: 117) informs us: 'the kings were just as likely to rob their own people as to attack their neighbors'. He also suggests, 'it could scarcely have been simple coincidence that the Djolas and the Balantas, who produced the least slaves either by raiding or by preying upon each other, were the very tribes with an amorphous state structure, from which a well-defined ruling class was absent' (Rodney 1980). Rodney (1980) also suggests that 'Tribal divisions were not, then, the most important'. 'When the line of demarcation is clearly drawn between the agents and the victims of slaving as it was carried on among the littoral peoples', he adds, 'that line coincides with the distinction between the privileged and the unprivileged in the society as a whole' (Rodney 1980). 'The Atlantic slave trade was deliberately selective in its impact on the society of the Upper Guinea Coast', according to Rodney (1980), 'with the ruling class protecting itself, while helping the Europeans to exploit the common people. This is of course the widespread pattern of modern neocolonialism'.

Several major points stand out in Rodney's arguments, points that illustrate his unique traits as a historian and Pan-African figure. First, Rodney had no qualms about implicating African rulers in the Atlantic slave trade, a critique that he would later extend to contemporary African and Caribbean rulers. Yet he did so without absolving Europe of its pivotal role in the trade of Africans and without overlooking the fact that those who most benefited from the trade were Europeans and white North Americans. Hence his mention of neocolonialism, which suggests that the book was animated by political and economic developments in 'postcolonial' Africa. Second, in identifying class differences in Africa, Rodney was able to separate the 'common' people from the elite, who acted in accordance with their own interests as opposed to those of the entire population. This too is an analysis that he would draw upon in his assessments of contemporary African and Caribbean developments in his later work. Third, in reflecting on class in Africa during the early days of the slave trade, Rodney contributed to our understanding of class struggle and capitalism. Perhaps more than anyone else, C. L. R. James understood the central role that slave labour played in the emergence of global capitalism. As James remarked in *The Black Jacobins: Toussaint L'Ouverture and the San Domingo Revolution*, slave plantations in the Caribbean housed the first factories of global capitalism.

These factories carried out the complicated process of turning raw sugar cane into sugar and, situated on the North Plain of Haiti, they were the jewel of colonial trade (James [1938] 1980: 47–8). For James ([1938] 1980: 86, 2009: 54), the concentrated presence of large numbers of slaves labouring in these proto-capitalist factories was closer to the modern proletariat than its counterparts anywhere in the world at the time. This point has yet to be fully appreciated.

African slave labour was central to inaugurating the modern capitalist era. This was the most economically advanced (and socially backward) system in the world. And James argued that Black slaves were being socialized in the production process in a manner that, as Marx argued, would lead to the overthrow of the system that dominated workers as they developed class-consciousness. Despite the fact that Marx was not thinking about Black or African labourers when he described the working-class, the Haitian Revolution not only struck a blow against slavery but was also important because it struck at the heart of French and European capital and capitalist production. In reflecting on class struggle and the slave trade in West Africa, Rodney provides insight into a process that would lead to among the first acts of resistance to the enslavement of Africans and, thus, among the first acts of resistance against what would become capitalism. In the process, Rodney, like James, challenges us to shift our understanding of capitalist development and the primacy of labour from Europe to Africa, laying the seeds for his later work in *How Europe Underdeveloped Africa*.

Rodney's description of the Djola and Balanta is reminiscent of the writing of Amílcar Cabral. While Rodney's analysis was informed by historical research, Cabral was an agronomist by training who surveyed the rural areas of Guinea-Bissau and, in the process, drew conclusions about the social structures of diverse African ethnic groups within the region. His intimate and very detailed understanding of the territory of Guinea-Bissau, coupled with his penetrating insights, brought him to conclusions that complement Rodney's: 'In societies with a horizontal structure, like the Balanta society . . . the distribution of cultural levels is more or less uniform, variations being linked solely to individual characteristics and to age groups. In the societies with a vertical structure', Cabral (1970) informs, 'like that of the Fula . . . there are important variations from the top to the bottom of the social pyramid. This shows . . . the close connections between the cultural factor and the economic factor, and also explains the differences in the overall or sectoral behavior of these two ethnic groups towards the liberation movement' (Cabral 1970: 144). Moreover, the 'class character is still more noticeable in the behavior of privileged groups in the rural environment, notably where ethnic groups with a vertical structure are concerned, where nevertheless the influences of assimilation or cultural alienation are nil, or virtually nil'.

This is the case of the Fula ruling class, for example. 'Under colonial domination', adds Cabral, 'the political authority of this class (traditional chiefs, noble families, religious leaders) is purely nominal, and the mass of the people are aware of the fact that the real authority lies with and is wielded by the colonial administrators. However, the ruling class retains in essence its cultural authority over the mass of the people in the group, with very important political implications' (Cabral 1970: 145). The colonial authorities, knowing this reality, 'install chiefs whom it trusts and who are more or less accepted by the population, gives them various material privileges including education for their eldest children, creates chiefdoms where they did not exist, establishes and develops cordial relations with religious leaders' (Cabral 1970: 145–6). This system, we are told, 'by means of the repressive organs of colonial administration . . . ensures the economic and social privileges of the ruling class in relation to the mass of the people', though 'this does not remove the possibility that, among these ruling classes, there may be individuals or groups of individuals who join the liberation movement' (Cabral 1970: 146).

Cabral's ideas resonate not only with Rodney's but also with the work of Mahmood Mamdani. In *Citizen and Subject: Contemporary Africa and the Legacy of Colonialism*, Mamdani (1996: 294) argues that until the problems of the urban–rural dilemma – the dichotomy between urban civil rule and rural or customary law – is resolved, factionalism will continue to prevail and political governance will remain, at the very least, a major challenge and, at its worse, continue to manifest itself in bloodletting and inter-ethnic conflicts. The similarities between Cabral and Mamdani rest less in their overall analyses and more in the fact that they both point to the dilemma that the hierarchical and centralized urban rule and customary law have posed for the African continent. For Mamdani (2018: 301), in order to get beyond the present state of political despair in Africa, the nature of rule in both the rural and urban regions must be simultaneously transformed and democratized, creating the conditions for the active participation of both citizens in the city and subjects under customary rule in the country while attempting to reconcile the differences in these forms of social organization.

Perhaps like no other African political leader, Cabral spoke frankly and openly about class and the dangers of the ruling elite betraying the aspirations of their people. (It is perhaps time that we reconsider the word 'betrayal' in this context. Betrayal implies that common interests have been compromised, when in actual fact what both Rodney and Cabral suggest is that the interests of the ruling elite are often closer to those of the colonizers than they are to their subjects.) Like Rodney and Fanon, Cabral understood the importance of class differentiation in the shaping of African societies and was fully conscious of the role these differences could play in postcolonial Africa. But unlike Fanon's modernism, and like Rodney, Cabral's analysis was rooted in an understanding of the peculiar features of Guinea-Bissau which he then, as great theorists do, generalized in his analysis of Africa, but without overgeneralizing.

It is remarkable that Cabral's analytical contributions are not more widely acknowledged and studied in greater detail. He was certainly one of the last century's brilliant political minds and theorists who lent clarity to the complex interplay of forces that define the African continent. Cabral was one of the major influences on Walter Rodney's thought, and it is not surprising that, through different means, they would come to similar conclusions about the nature of class struggle in Africa. In writing about the Atlantic slave trade at this early stage in his political life, Rodney was conscious of the prevailing socio-economic climate in Africa and the Caribbean and used history as a means of contextualizing and assessing contemporary events in much the same way that Cabral arrived at theoretical–political conclusions through his intimate understanding of the social and economic structure of Guinea-Bissauan society. Both challenged the dominant narrative of Marxism and the primacy of European (white) labour, a history that has historically omitted the centrality of slavery and Black labour and the significance of colonialism to the formation of capitalism. Both, in their own ways, point to the importance of conducting assiduous research – one as a historian and the other as an agronomist and revolutionary leader and theorist. For them, theory is not abstract, but drawn from social relations and specific historical contexts; this is what makes ideas potentially universal and part of the universal human experience – provided we don't attempt to impose purported universals upon particular human experiences.

Of course, culture and history are not only experienced through class but also through gender and various kinds of human experiences, and clearly women did not experience class differentiation, slavery or colonialism in precisely the same way that men did. These are obvious omissions in Cabral and Rodney's work. With this in mind, there is much that we can learn from their analyses as we attempt to disentangle the contemporary dynamics of struggle on the African continent, its diaspora and in other social and political contexts around the world.

Note

1 For an analysis of the role of exiled intellectuals and politicos in anti-colonial struggles and on C. L. R. James in particular, see Said (1993: 336, 1996: 47–64) and Schwartz (2003). For references to Caribbean exiles in Canada, see Austin (2007, 2009), Roberts (2005), and Buhle (2006).

References

Austin, David (2007), 'All Roads Led to Montreal: Black Power, the Caribbean, and the Black Radical Tradition in Canada', *Journal of African American History*, 92 (4): 516–39.

Austin, David (2009), 'In Search of a Caribbean Identity: C. L. R. James and the Promise of the Caribbean', in David Austin (ed.), *You Don't Play with Revolution: The Montreal Lectures of C. L. R. James*, Oakland, CA: AK Press.

Austin, David (2010), 'Vanguards and Masses: Global Lessons from the Grenada Revolution', in Aziz Choudry and Dip Kapoor (eds), *Learning from the Ground Up: Global Perspectives on Social Movements and Knowledge Production*, 173–89, New York: Palgrave Macmillan.

Buhle, Paul (2006), *Tim Hector: A Caribbean Radical's Story*, Jackson: The Press of University of Mississippi.

Cabral, Amilcar (1970), 'National Liberation and Culture', in *Unity and Struggle*, 169–84, London: Heinemann Educational Books Ltd.

James, C. L. R. (1967), *Policy and Program for Developing Countries*, Montreal: unpublished.

James, C. L. R. ([1938] 1980), *The Black Jacobins: Toussaint L'Ouverture and the San Domingo Revolution*, London: Allison & Busby.

James, C. L. R. (2009), 'The Haitian Revolution in the Making of the Modern World', in David Austin (ed.), *You Don't Play with Revolution: The Montreal Lectures of C. L. R. James*, Edinburgh/Oakland: AK Press.

Mamdani, Mahmood (1996), *Citizen and Subject: Contemporary Africa and the Legacy of Late Colonialism*, Princeton: Princeton University Press.

Meeks, Brian (1996), *Radical Caribbean: From Black Power to Abu Bakr*, Kingston, Jamaica: The Press of the University of the West Indies.

Mudimbe, V. Y. (1988), *The Invention of Africa: Gnosis, Philosophy, and the Order of Knowledge*, Bloomington and Indianapolis: Indiana University Press.
Roberts, Alfie (2005), *A View for Freedom: Alfie Roberts Speaks on the Caribbean, Cricket, Montreal, and C. L. R. James*, Montreal: Alfie Roberts Institute.
Rodney, Walter (1980), *A History of the Upper Guinea Coast, 1545–800*, New York: Monthly Review Press.
Rodney, Walter (1990), *Walter Rodney Speaks: The Making of an African Intellectual*, Trenton, NJ: African World Press.
Said, Edward (1993), *Culture and Imperialism*, New York: Vintage Books.
Said, Edward (1996), *Representations of the Intellectual*, New York: Vintage Books.
Schwartz, Bill, ed. (2003), *West Indians in Britain*, Manchester: Manchester University Press.

7

The politics and place of Rajani Palme Dutt

Tanroop Sandhu

Looking backwards is a way of looking forwards. *(Rajani Palme Dutt (1966))*

Introduction

When he died in 1974 at the age of seventy-eight, Rajani Palme Dutt (fondly referred to as RPD by his communist colleagues) had been more than five decades into a long and storied political career. Born to a Bengali father and a Swedish mother in Cambridge, he was a student radical, conscientious objector during the First World War, a leading intellectual light of the Communist Party of Great Britain (CPGB) and a formative influence on the Communist movement in India. His works spanned a variety of topics – fascism, anti-colonialism, a history of the First, Second and Third Internationals, British politics and much more. That the Indian independence movement was one of the central preoccupations of his political life is undeniable. So too is the fact that his career was marked by an uncritical loyalty to the Soviet Union. In the aftermath of Nikita Khrushchev's secret speech on the excesses of Stalinism, he infamously, and disturbingly, remarked that it merely revealed 'spots on the sun'. It is the latter aspect of his politics, as a representative of 'British Stalinism', that understandably defines his reputation in England (Callaghan 1993). A *Socialist Review* article on the major biography of his life claimed it was 'wearisome to continue an account of the life of this scoundrel. To represent him as a genuine Communist is an insult to the intelligence of . . . readers' (Hallas 1993).

In stark contrast to the tone of reminiscences in Britain was the reaction to his death among Indian Communists. The famous Communist Party of India (CPI) figure, S. A. Dange (1974), wrote that 'to many of us he was in a way an Indian communist in Great Britain . . . RPD could certainly be classified as "one of us'", and his works were 'potent weapons in equipping the revolutionary movements of our time with knowledge and insight'. P. C. Joshi (2014: 314), another CPI leader, spoke of 'RPD' as his generation's 'teacher and guide'. Clearly, the ways in which he was remembered – depending on the context – varied wildly. To a degree, this continues. It is far more common to see Dutt's ideas or works referenced in Indian historiography and on the Indian Left, than in British intellectual life. This means that the consequences of his metropolitan location for his work are relatively understudied.

This chapter will show that revisiting the life and works of Dutt, especially his anti-imperialism, can be a highly generative exercise for thinking through the present conjuncture. His privileging of a 'politically Indian' identity over a narrowly understood cultural affiliation, his highlighting of the intertwined tasks and destinies of working people in both metropole and colony, and his emphasis on anti-colonialism as a task demanding, above all, political *and* economic transformation are incredibly prescient. At a time when debates around authenticity and positionality sometimes produce political paralysis, parochialism and narrow nationalisms run rampant and decolonization risks being emptied of materially transformative potential, there is a great deal of value to be found in returning to the politics and place of Dutt.

Politically Indian?

Despite dedicating virtually all his adult life in the interwar period to thinking, researching and writing about India, Dutt had never been there. It was only in 1946 that he was finally allowed to go, and he recorded his journey in the *Labour Monthly*, a journal he edited for many decades. As R. P. Dutt (1966) put it, as children he and his family could not afford to do so, and by the time they could, he had been banned from colonial territories because of his membership in the CPGB and his strident anti-imperialism. He and his brother Clemens, who was also active in the party, were essentially confined to 'the West' by these restrictions. He was aware he might not fit a narrowly defined idea of what, or who, an 'Indian' was, but did not allow that to deter him from engaging in subcontinental politics. He admitted to feeling a bit strange when he first travelled to India in 1946 – 'I had been kept out for half a century . . . on the one hand I was regarded as an authority on India, and on the other hand in all practical matters I was an absolute greenhorn to whom everything was new' (Dutt, R. P. 1971: 31–2). Nonetheless, worrying about his identity took a backseat to his conviction that the British Empire needed to be overthrown and his determination to play a role in giving it a push. And he did indeed have an impact. R. P. Dutt (1971: 31–2) said that when he met Gandhi on that same 1946 trip, 'the first thing he [Gandhi] said to me was: "So you are the man of whom the whole British Empire was afraid"'.

R. P. Dutt and his siblings had a very 'English' upbringing in some ways, and both he and his brother Clemens went on to study at Cambridge where they became politicized. However, they also had an Indian political education of sorts. R. P. Dutt (1940) dedicated what is considered his 1940 magnum opus – *India To-Day* – to his father for 'teaching him to love the Indian people'. He recalled a vague 'atmosphere' of Indian-ness in his childhood with his father studying Sanskrit, reading Bengali literature and believing in Vedanta philosophy (R. P. Dutt and Muggeridge 1966). Yet, it was the *political* content of his upbringing that was most formative. Some of the visitors his father received in their home were famed figures in the nascent nationalist movement; Nehru, Gokhale, B. C. Pal, Lajpat Rai and his uncle the famed economist Romesh Chander Dutt (Callaghan 1993: 12–13). He heard their discussions, saw photos of famine victims, and his family hosted the first Asian Students' Society in their home; 'all these things mixed together' to shape the Dutts' political trajectory (R. P. Dutt 1966). They were rooted in this milieu from a very young age. So, when asked in a 1966 interview if he thought of himself as an Indian, R. P. Dutt (1966) responded with a striking phrase: '*politically* speaking, yes' (italics added).

Dutt also could not occupy an untroubled place in 'Britishness'. He was keenly aware of his racialization and recalled noticing at a young age that his father suffered from discrimination in their hometown of Cambridge (Callaghan 1993: 9). One of his first political acts was a legal challenge he made in 1916 to his exemption, on racial grounds, from conscription in the First World War. He won his case, promptly refused to be drafted and was jailed for six months (Beckett 1995: 30). And yet, in a 1966 interview, he called himself 'a typical Englishman . . . a mongrel, [but] born in England', and recalled he often joked with Harry Pollitt, another major leader of the CPGB, that they were the only 'real Englishmen' on the Party Central Committee (R. P. Dutt 1966). He may have thought so, but it is unclear whether others did. After all, an interviewer, Malcolm Muggeridge, opened their discussion with 'you're not English, at all, are you?' (R. P. Dutt 1966). Dutt conceded, 'there was not a drop of English blood in me', but went on to say England 'is my country. I like the people'. Still, he was quite aware that he lived in what he called 'the centre of world reaction' (R. P. Dutt 1936).

Yet, of course, for a staunch Marxist like Dutt, there was no question of reducing his politics, or even his identity, to nationalism. All of his political energies were directed towards the ultimate horizon of *world* socialist revolution. It was precisely that internationalism that led to his preoccupation with overcoming the barriers to global working-class solidarity. This perspective was instilled in him from a very young age. In a striking recollection, he remembered how with the onset of the Boer War,

> suddenly wild jingo demonstrations broke out in the streets. I was only four years old at the time, but saw how in the street itself where we lived many of the ordinary decent working people we knew were seized with this wild violent frenzy. I knew nothing except that it was clear that there was some evil spirit that seized the people and I was certain *that I would fight it with everything that I had got in me*.... Then I joined this with the picture of famine in India and the people's struggle, so that in a sense *I was first anti-imperialist, and developed from that to a deeper class understanding of socialism as combining the struggle all over the world*. (R. P. Dutt 1971: 26–7: italics added)

Dutt was of a people subjugated by the British Empire, and even if his connections to India were not as direct as someone born there, as his biographer John Callaghan (1993: 278–9) put it, his 'capacity for detachment from national politics was unusual, if not unique, in the British Party as was its corollary – his unswerving "internationalism"'. However, there was nothing 'unusual' about Dutt's detachment from purely national concerns – he was an interstitial thinker and a racialized subject in the imperial core and, therefore, thought about questions of empire and colonialism in distinctive ways.

The specific consciousness that Dutt, and others like him, derived from their racialization can be understood as what Satnam Virdee has termed the 'second sight' of 'racialized outsiders'. This second sight is 'a form of epistemological standpoint that helped ... play a catalytic role in building solidarity between the different ethnic stratum within the imperialist core and beyond' (Virdee 2017: 3). This tendency in the socialist movement was the result of 'the combination of collective memories of colonial subjugation combined with their own racialized experiences in the imperialist core' (Virdee 2017: 3). Such figures were aware that their 'ancestral nation remain[ed] under the iron heel of the British state [but] they also found themselves excluded from popular conceptions of British national identification' (Virdee 2017: 9). Communism could provide a potential way out of that dual subjugation as well as a programme for mobilizing across ethnic lines for revolutionary politics, but this programme required the intervention of these very same 'racialized outsiders' in order to take precedence over more parochial mindsets. Dutt and others like him were critical voices that urged a greater internationalist and anti-imperialist consciousness from within the British Communist movement.

There was nothing inevitable to Dutt's radicalism and his identification with the struggles of working people in Britain. There are multiple choices open to the colonized when they confront the colonizer. The famed Indian nationalist Subhas Chandra Bose wrote, upon visiting England, 'nothing gives me as much pleasure as seeing the white-skins shine my shoes' (Gordon 1990 cited in Sen 2015: 31). This sense of 'racial humiliation and need for revenge' bred what historian Satadru Sen called decolonization 'in pursuit of a never-ending shoeshine' (Gordon 1990 cited in Sen 2015: 31). Elitist striving, driven perhaps by a sense of resentment, often finds satisfaction in the reversal of roles between exploiter and exploited rather than in the questioning of the edifice upon which exploitation is built. Dutt, on the other hand, was determined to overthrow class society, to fulfil the promise of *worldwide* liberation which the October Revolution seemed to have opened. As he put it, for him the root of Indian problems was 'economic-political, and the cultural problem depends on this' (R. P. Dutt 1940: 60–1).

Amidst alienation and discrimination, there can be a resilient clinging to a sense of 'culture', which in itself often becomes divorced from the changing realities of an ancestral homeland. Vijay Prashad (2000: 289–90) wrote insightfully of the Indian American diaspora's oscillation between a desire to 'assimilate in a one-dimensional way', and a reverse movement which sends some people on a 'cultural mission' to 'rediscover their roots' in a drive towards a vaguely defined sense of 'authenticity [which may be] nothing but a paranoid reaction to the "naturalness" of dominant groups'. It is here that what exactly it means to be 'Indian' becomes fraught with problems. Family elders can position themselves as arbiters of what is and is not 'our culture' in a way that is unchanging, ahistorical and riven with patriarchy or caste prejudice. That does not mean cultural domination, and opposition to it, is not an important part of anti-imperialism. But we need to be attuned to the fact that even the colonized have their own hierarchies, classes, castes and myriad oppressions. Thus, not only is it impossible to identify a unified and homogenous culture but, even if one were able to, such a culture would 'hardly be posited as a unified, transparent site of anti-imperialist resistance' (Ahmad 2008: 8).

Distance from an ancestral homeland sometimes creates its own problems:

> Those desis [South Asian diaspora] who reside outside the territory of the subcontinental states are rendered somewhat incapable of fully experiencing a shared destiny . . . with those who live under the daily rule of the states. Their national culture will not be culture as the lives of the people but as something of a fantasy culture, a nostalgia of distance, without the creative contradictions that provide the lively cultural forms negotiated by the peoples still on the subcontinent. (Prashad 2000: 295–6)

At its worst, this opens the way to a dynamic where a relatively 'rich and powerful diaspora looks at India with an even more Orientalist gaze than the West', as the reporter Vidya Krishnan (2022) recently put it. It becomes little more than an elegant backdrop to Bollywood films, 'an organized marriage market, shopping and street food', with little cognizance of the living political forces and struggles that struggle to remake it for good or ill every day (Krishnan 2022). Yet there are other options, other visions to latch onto. The *Ghadar* movement, largely made up of immigrant Punjabis on the West Coast of North America, consisted of 'people who struggled to make a better world, and for that they turned to their "homeland" for inspiration. Rather than making them chauvinistic, their turn to the "homeland" was geared toward making them all the more concerned about social and political justice globally' (Prashad 2000: 297). I believe Dutt's engagement with India can be placed in a similar register; if he was interested in his ancestral 'homeland', it was for political reasons – the destruction of the Empire and the opening up of a path to worldwide socialist revolution. In a blatant rejection of Orientalism and essentialism, he wrote that those who went to 'visit the immemorial East in India' either in search of 'Oriental spiritual higher thought' or with pretensions to condescend about the 'innate backwardness' of the people were 'visiting only a museum of mediaeval lumber, and [are] blind to the living forces of the Indian people' (R. P. Dutt 1940: 500).

The question of diasporic identity, then, becomes one of selective appropriation and identification rather than an importation of a coherent whole across borders. Yet a worry that one is 'inauthentic' or not 'really Indian' can lead to an impasse too. Does one have to live in the subcontinent to speak about its politics? Should there be a hierarchy of who gets to represent a place like India abroad based on a nebulous cultural authenticity? Not only is 'India' overburdened as an analytic category – with all its regional cultures, languages, religions, traditions, castes – it is also a living reality, constantly changing. To get into debates about authenticity is to fall into a trap, to get into a terrain on which the Left cannot win. Those clad in saffron, extolling the virtues of an imagined pre-colonial golden age and the unique 'genius of India', will always be more 'authentic' than even the most radically decolonial scholar. During the independence movement, the definition of 'India' – as state, territory and people – was in flux. Now, in the face of an increasingly narrow and communal Indian nationalism and alongside new calls to decolonize in the imperial core, there is value for the diaspora in looking back to a time when thinking of oneself as an 'Indian' could entail a radical political identification as much as an ethnic, geographical or religious one.

Jailers and jailed

R. P. Dutt had comrades in the CPGB, like his older brother Clemens or Shapurji Saklatvala, who also worked on tackling what they saw as 'Empire consciousness' in Britain (Gupta 2006: 42). The latter two men focused on fostering trade union solidarity across borders, organizing Indian workers in Britain, developing international connections with groups like the League Against Imperialism, and Saklatvala also used his platform as a Member of Parliament to publicly lambast the Empire.[1] Dutt, as the party's chief theoretician, was a writer before he was an organizer. His work was primarily intellectual. The most thorough and well regarded of Dutt's works on India is certainly his 1940 book, *India To-Day*. In this book, Dutt attempts to survey Indian history, the outcomes of British rule and the political future of the subcontinent. This forms the vast majority of the book. At the same time, however, he also repeatedly emphasizes the importance of India to world politics as well as its relevance to the domestic struggles of the British working class. This was simultaneously an attempt to rhetorically enlist India in the world movement towards Communism and to warn the British Left about the dangers of not taking questions of empire seriously. To do so, however, Dutt had to combat misconceptions and prejudices about India's history and its present. While *India To-Day* is Dutt's most significant attempt to do this, the book encapsulated and reiterated themes and ideas that are a constant presence throughout all of his writings. This involved a form of intellectual work that can broadly be called anti-imperial refutation – combatting ostensibly erroneous ideas about a colonized people as part of a broader case for militant anti-colonialism. It is here that his location in the metropole and as a member of the CPGB determines much of the trajectory of his work on India.

Dutt was convinced that imperialism, racism and Orientalism had distorted British views of India. The requirements of imperial rule had called for the creation of 'a barbed-wire entanglement ... between India and the outer world to hamper any adequate serious interchange of information and opinion', while, on the other hand, 'a riot of imperialist propaganda, from school textbooks to broadcast reports, builds up in the mind of the British public a mythical picture of the real situation in India and the British role in India' (R. P. Dutt 1940: 36). Censorship, therefore, was supplemented by the creation of certain cultural attitudes and narratives of imperial benevolence. R. P. Dutt (1940: 32) felt that 'serious historical analysis is commonly replaced in the Press or on the platform by a schoolboy-Kiplingesque romance'. In a 1923 article for *Labour Monthly*, R. P. Dutt (1923) had decried the 'artificial cult' of empire, which helped to obscure the fact that colonialism had a 'severely material basis woven into the lives of everyone ... holding them by ties not always seen'. It was because of this cult that he warned 'English readers, in approaching Indian questions, to be vigilantly on their guard against facile preconceptions or unconscious assumptions of superiority, which are in fact only a mental reflection of a temporary relationship of domination' (R. P. Dutt 1940: 36–7). By emphasizing the material realities of imperialism, R. P. Dutt (1923) felt that he could expose 'its results in working-class division and corruption, racial separation, tyranny and militarism, and the destruction of working-class internationalism'. Until this was taken seriously, the British Left would remain a largely 'White Labour aristocracy', which, though it might express *moralistic* opposition to the abuses of the Empire, would never truly understand how much it distorted all politics (R. P. Dutt 1923).

The situation called for a comprehensive understanding of what the Empire really was as a *material* force. Moralistic opposition to domination as such, or to specific crimes like the Amritsar Massacre of 1919, was insufficient. R. P. Dutt (1923) wanted anti-imperialism to become a central preoccupation of the Left: they needed to attack 'the real material basis of the Empire ... by making clear the inevitable break-up and destruction of its material structure' and by turning the 'White Labour aristocracy ... to the leaders of a working-class revolt of all the exploited and subject forces against the real seat of power of British capitalism'. That could only be done through 'a very patient and widespread explanation of the real position of the British working class, of the plans of the imperialists, and of the future prospects awaiting the workers'. R. P. Dutt (1923) bemoaned the fact that 'Socialist propaganda in this country is still almost exclusively national in character ("Britain for the British") with an added dose of "internationalism" ... and is thus wholly unsuited to modern conditions'. For much of his career, Dutt would be the one doing the aforementioned 'patient and widespread explanation'.

It is quite clear, then, that for Dutt a critique of colonial discourse was more important, insofar as it challenged attitudes which undermined practical solidarity and radical consciousness in political movements, than a remaking of curriculums or canons. As a leading member of the British Communist movement, he sought to correct misconceptions his erstwhile comrades might have about the colonial world. Furthermore, mere sympathy was not enough: resolutions needed to be passed, funds needed to be collected by unions to support strikes abroad, solidarity funds and campaigns for political prisoners had to be set up, and Labour Party leaders who defended the Empire needed to be tossed aside. All of these tasks were taken up with dedication, but they were often driven only by a small core of supporters.[2] R. P. Dutt's efforts to forge a substantive anti-imperialist consciousness in British Communists earned him the title, of 'evangelist of inter-racial cooperation' from a well-wisher on *Labour Monthly*'s twenty-fifth anniversary (Callaghan 1993: 226).

In his 1927 book, *Modern India*, Dutt argued that imperialism had entered a new phase in India and that industrial development there was changing the material basis of the Empire at home and abroad. Previously, 'the subjection and poverty of the Indian masses was one of the concealed bases of the higher standards of the British workers. To-day an opposite process is developing', and as Indian workers – whose wages were considerably lower than those in the metropole – began to become direct competitors of British proletarians, the wages of both were endlessly lowered (R. P. Dutt 1927: 10). This argument, centred on the competition between cheap labour in India and the workers of Britain and, thus, tying the working conditions of the two together, was a central tenet in the CPGB's anti-imperialism. There was no point of thinking of the Empire in the abstract. The situation in India was not a question of 'a single British "nation" of rulers and a single Indian "nation" of ruled' (R. P. Dutt 1927: 170). Consider, R. P. Dutt (1927: 170–1) wrote, the imagery of a penniless British worker 'touting for a copper before the car of some rich Indian prince or merchant, in front of the Savoy Hotel', and ask 'which is the "ruler" and which is the "ruled"'. Modern imperialism was based 'on the subjection of two social forces', namely the workers in the metropole and the masses in the colonies, and it was only natural that they should join forces in a common struggle (R. P. Dutt 1927: 164).

However, R. P. Dutt (1923) spoke despairingly of how sections of the British workers continued to believe they held, alongside the bourgeoisie, 'a tutelary guardianship of the "subject", "native" or "non-adult" races'. This was a false conception. The reality, in his view, was that the Empire had only

> jailers and jailed. There are only palace slaves and plantation slaves. *And the palace slaves play unconsciously into their masters' hands by looking down upon the plantation slaves as inferior beings, and discuss gravely in their masters' language whether it is 'safe' to give to them the freedom that they, the palace slaves, enjoy.* That is the epitome of the Empire and of the situation of the British workers in the International. (R. P. Dutt 1923: italics added)

Essentially, British workers had to pick a side. Up until now, they had been siding with their class enemies. In a typical expression of his belief in the inevitable victory of Marxism, R. P. Dutt (1923) seems to have believed that this was merely a *temporary arrangement* caused by a particular historical moment, which would soon give way to the 'advancing tide of . . . world revolution'. Unfortunately, it is a testament to the intractability of this problem that Dutt would spend the rest of his life writing about it.

Interdependent revolutions

As a thinker living and operating in the imperial core, Dutt occupied a relatively privileged political space. His works could circulate freely in Europe but were speedily banned in the colonies by the vast censorship apparatus of the British Empire. A common refrain in solidarity work by British leftists, when referring to India and other colonies, was the jarring differences in notions of freedom and justice at home and abroad. Indian trade unionists and leftists would be arrested en masse, as they were in the 1929 Meerut Conspiracy Case, for example, for the same activities that English unions carried out openly. The British Empire's powers of coercion and repression were geographically uneven – the metropole offered an atmosphere of political freedom compared to the colonies, and diasporic radicals took advantage of this fact. They had, as Priyamvada Gopal (2020: 216) put it, 'a dual but intertwined representational responsibility'. In addressing British audiences, anti-colonial thinkers sought to emphasize just how inseparable the destinies of revolutionary movements *within* imperial formations were. When, in 1929, the CPGB's Tenth Congress adopted a resolution declaring 'the overthrow of the capitalist class in Great Britain and the victory of the social revolution are only possible with the co-operation of the oppressed masses in the colonies', they essentially adopted a 'theory of interdependent metropolitan and colonial revolutions' (CPGB 1929 cited in Williams 2022: 44).

From a contemporary perspective, giving prominence to the West in the arc of liberation for the colonized world might well chafe against one's decolonial sensibilities. Yet this was not so much Eurocentrism as a recognition of the material forces that the imperialist countries could, and would, bring to bear on any nascent liberation movement. The countless massacres perpetrated by the West in the semi-colonial and colonial world – in the interwar period and during the Cold War especially – are a stark reminder of the responsibilities and obligations of anti-imperialists in the metropole.[3] At the Second Comintern Congress, Avetis Sultanzade, drawing on the recent experiences of imperialist interventions in his native Iran and in China, asked, in the event of a communist revolution in India 'will the workers of that country be able to withstand the attack by the bourgeoisie of the entire world without the help of a big revolutionary movement in Britain and Europe? Of course not' (Riddell, Prashad and Mollah 2019: 58–9). The Trinidadian revolutionary C. L. R. James also claimed that he and some of his Pan-Africanist comrades knew 'armed rebellion [in the colonies] was sure to be crushed unless the imperialist powers were impotent, and this could only be the result of revolutions within the metropolitan powers themselves' (James as cited in Williams 2022: 132). The terror unleashed by European governments against uprisings in the colonies – in the British case, by the Labour Party and the Tories alike – and the immense disparities in armed strength between the advanced capitalist powers and anti-colonial movements were serious obstacles. The potentialities for liberation were intimately bound up with world events and thus could not be reduced to purely local contexts. As James (2012: 103: italics added) put it, in a stirring phrase, 'should *World events give these people a chance*, they will destroy what has them by the throat'.

In a lecture titled 'Delay of the Socialist Revolution in the West', delivered at Moscow University in 1962, Dutt explored the centrality of the other side of the equation: the importance of the colonial revolution to the metropole. He returned to Marx and Engels's views on 'the Irish question' and its relevance to

British working-class politics. He explored Marx's changing views on Ireland, his understanding of the Indian Mutiny of 1857 and his resolution in the First International that claimed 'a people which enslaves another people forges its own chains' (R. P. Dutt 1963: 85). R. P. Dutt (1963: 86: italics added) concluded that, over time and with the development of anti-colonial struggles, Marx came to view the 'national liberation of the subject peoples of the empire [as] the decisive *prior factor*, "the lever", which would compel social change in Britain and thus open the way to the victory of socialism in Britain'. 'In this sense', he wrote, 'the first stage of the battle for the victory of socialism in Britain would be fought in the countries of the Empire' (R. P. Dutt 1963: 86). Lenin is seen to have developed this understanding further by realizing that the 'national and colonial sphere [was] the decisive next phase of the world revolution' (R. P. Dutt 1963: 92). The centrality of imperialist exploitation to capitalism – the super-profits it provided which allowed the 'bribing' of certain strata of workers in the metropole, its tendency towards war, the stability captive markets gave to the system – meant that anti-colonial movements could indeed be simultaneous strikes against the rule of capital, a position cemented as policy at the Second Congress of the Comintern in 1920 (Seth 1995: 46–7).

This did not mean that workers in the 'advanced' nations needed to simply wait until the colonies achieved independence before pursuing a revolution of their own. Even though, by the time Dutt gave this lecture in 1962, 'the majority of former colonial peoples have won political independence, the economic exploitation by imperialism still continues and even develops in new forms' (R. P. Dutt 1963: 96). The fight continued, and it took on a more clearly economic dimension. Independence *had never been the end goal*, but only a first step towards a more substantive economic and political transformation. When Dutt gave his lecture, the centre of radicalism in the world still seemed to be in Asia and Africa, countries which despite material scarcity and economic underdevelopment, were 'speeding forward' in terms of political struggle. On the contrary, the 'advanced Western countries are rapidly becoming what may be called politically under-developed countries of the world' (R. P. Dutt 1963: 97). However, he believed that, as the forces of anti-imperialism developed further and the effects of losing the colonies set in, there might be a renewed radicalism in the West. Citing Marx, he ended on an optimistic note:

> How soon the English workers will free themselves from their apparent bourgeois infection one must wait and see.... In developments of such magnitude twenty

years are no more than a day – though later on days may come again in which twenty years are embodied. (Marx: Letters to Engels, 9 April 1863)

With the accelerating speed of world development at the present time, we may hope that also in the countries of the West we may soon see the arrival of 'days in which twenty years are embodied'. (R. P. Dutt 1963: 97)

Some of Dutt's favourite themes were the inevitability of capitalism's destruction and the decay of the British Empire, the need for British workers to recognize on which side they ought to be, a point which, when Dutt made it, seems to be a warning of sorts to get on the right side of history before it is too late, reaffirming the need for worldwide socialist fraternity. It is a call for British workers to realize that the system which provides them with the spoils of the Empire is not only limited, but doomed. It made little sense to fear the loss of the Empire when any benefit they derived from it came from the exploitation of their fellow workers and their isolation from the tides of world revolution, all in service of a dying system. In a 1937 speech on 'The Colonial Struggle for Liberation', R. P. Dutt (1937) had made similar points: British workers must realize that 'imperialism was disintegrating and unless the workers were prepared to make sacrifices for the cause of socialism, in the long run conditions must inevitably become much worse'. Communicating a sense of capitalism's *imminent* demise if it was subjected to assault through the concerted efforts of workers around the world is a constant refrain in Dutt's works. Capitalism is yet to collapse, true, but the need to take the long-term view and to realize that temporary benefits from a system built on environmental destruction and human misery are unsustainable remains.

Unfortunately, the record of the British labour movement was a mixed one. There are laudable cases of working-class solidarity with anti-colonial movements. Alongside the myriad resolutions passed by trade unions in solidarity with the anti-colonial struggle and funds sent to striking workers in Bombay, is the striking example of the three white, British Leftists Ben Bradley, Philip Spratt and Lester Hutchinson, who were arrested in the 1929 Meerut Conspiracy Case for their activities in the burgeoning Indian labour movement.[3] British historian Raphael Samuel also wrote about how his childhood in the CPGB was marked by a distinctly internationalist consciousness (Samuel 2017: 48). However, things were quite different in the upper echelons of the Labour movement, especially in the Labour Party itself – whose record of colonial repression when in office led Indian nationalist Ranga Iyer to remark that they made 'British Socialism stink in the nostrils of the Indian people . . . [they] are only imperialists masquerading as Socialists' (R.P. Dutt 1928). This labour aristocracy and their reactionary attitudes, R. P. Dutt (1940: 483) wrote, represented a 'cancer, which holds back the British working class from freedom, [and] still runs in the veins of the dominant sections of the Labour movement'. As he saw it, it was because of the imperial tendencies of this aristocracy, which did in fact enjoy the 'fruits of Empire', that the British working class had lost key battles: 'thus Chartism fell, socialism fell, Labour fell' (R.P. Dutt 1940: 482). It is hard to overstate just how central this question was to R. P. Dutt's (1940: 482) reading of British history: the 'influence of empire holds the main responsibility for the perversion and distortion of the British Labour movement'. Translating anti-imperialist analysis into substantive action, then, required tackling questions of ideology and consciousness.

Of course, India was also important in its own right even aside from the impact its liberation might have on Britain. By virtue of the sheer scale of Indian politics, developments there impacted the fates of hundreds of millions of people. In world politics too, the fact that the 'ideas of socialism are spreading in India . . . herald[ed] a great accession of strength to the forces of the peoples all over the world against the tide of reaction' (R. P. Dutt 1940: 22). In our own time, as India is both more powerful and very much on the side of the tide of reaction, we cannot ignore its importance and weight on the global stage. In a passage that has aged well, Dutt described India as existing in a 'situation packed at every turn with social dynamite' and representing a microcosm of the problems of world politics:

> Every stage of civilization and culture within class-society, from the most primitive to the most advanced, exists in India. The widest range of social, economic, political and cultural problems thus find their sharpest expression in Indian conditions. The problems of the relations and co-existence of differing races and religions; the battle against old superstitions and decaying social forms and traditions; the fight for education; the fight for the liberation of women; the question of the reorganization of agriculture and of the development of industry, and of the relationship of town and country; the issues of class conflict in the most manifold and acute forms; the problems of the relationship of nationalism and socialism: all these varied issues of the modern world press forward with especial sharpness and urgency. . . . *The solution of the problems of India means the solution of the most typical and sharpest problems, in their most complicated form, that confront in common the peoples of the world. . . . The national and social*

liberation of the Indian people will bring great new wealth to humanity. (R. P. Dutt 1940: 23–4: italics added)

Decolonization: Then and now

It is precisely because revolutionary figures of the interwar period sought a horizon *beyond* the postcolonial nation state that their thought remains vital. As Edward Said put it, anti-colonial and anti-imperialist thought was never reducible merely to nationalism or nativism. There was always 'the possibility of a more generous and pluralistic vision of the world', which recognizes that 'imperialism courses on, as it were . . . but the opportunities for liberation are open' – a substantive, material and social liberation is the horizon of the politics of a Marxist anti-colonialism, not merely political independence (Said 1994: 294–5).[4] Yet since formal 'decolonization' and the waning of the anti-colonial liberatory energies, which reached their zenith in the mid-twentieth century, critical scholarship has increasingly turned to critiques of colonial discourses and Western 'power-knowledge', albeit in a quite different way than that of Dutt. In these narratives, as the famed Indian historian Sumit Sarkar (1997: 84) put it, '"Enlightenment rationalism" thus becomes the central polemical target, and Marxism stands condemned as one more variety of Eurocentrism'. This led projects like *Subaltern Studies* to be dismissive of their intellectual predecessors, and Sarkar (1997: 86) points out that Dutt, specifically, had already made some of the same critiques these scholars later made of the nationalist leadership's restraining influence on mass radicalism in India. In a turn away from interwar Marxist understandings of colonialism and nationalism, we risk losing touch with an intellectual tradition that, for all its flaws, dreamt of a future beyond our current postcolonial nightmare.[5]

Still, it would be foolhardy to ignore some of the incredibly valuable contributions made by decolonial and postcolonial scholarship. Works like David Scott's *Conscripts of Modernity* explore how Western capitalist modernity has conditioned the very possibilities of thought of all that live in its temporal snare, and his meditations on the 'tragic' employment of colonial enlightenment and the antimonies of anti-colonial struggle are striking and quite convincing. Sudipta Kaviraj's (2009: 172–200) essay on 'Marxism in Translation' is also a revealing insight into some of the challenges – like a nuanced understanding of caste exploitation or the universalization of concepts contained in Marx's oeuvre – that Indian Communists struggle to meet. Throughout their writings – in the interwar and beyond – there is an expectation that capitalism will flatten difference, and that caste, religious and regional divides will give way to a unified class-consciousness. Behind such confidence, optimism and portents of future proletarian revolt lies a certain underestimation of the weight of history, the stubborn persistence of supposed 'feudal relics' in a society riven by hierarchy, and capitalism's tendency to weaponize and even entrench difference. Many Indian Communists believed in modernity's 'flattening' power and its ability to create an undifferentiated proletariat. Marx himself had believed that capitalism 'would destroy the "peculiarities" of the East' (Seth 1995: 28). In hindsight, the first Indian Communists did not always adequately 'stretch' Marxism to suit their surroundings. The project to create a Marxism for India is an ongoing one, which generations of activists, workers, peasants and intellectuals have contributed to and will continue to do so. Decolonial thinking can help instil a suspicion of unilinear modes of development, challenge Eurocentric understandings of resistance and create a socialist theory and praxis firmly rooted in Indian *and global* conditions.

At the same time, however, an understandable frustration with some of the limitations of economistic Marxism and a suspicion of Western intellectual domination can easily turn into a cultural reductionism of its own. The temptation to romanticize the pre-colonial is omnipresent and has 'stimulated forms of indigenism' that have taken a dark turn in contemporary South Asia (Sarkar 1993: 165). If we construct a flawed binary between the authentic and the Westernized, we struggle to pursue 'sensitive studies of movements for women's rights, or of lower-caste protest: for quite often such initiatives did try and utilize aspects of colonial administration and ideas as resources' (Sarkar 1997: 106). Pre-colonial Indian society was not a monolith, and thus the experience of colonialism was differentiated and uneven. It is also important to comprehend how even supposedly 'indigenous' or 'authentic' spheres of life and culture were themselves fundamentally reconstituted by 'colonial and capitalist transformations' (Goswami 2005: 208). A 'suspicion-cum-contempt for anything 'economic' can blind us to the transformative impact of capitalism and its inextricability from the experience of colonization (Sarkar 1994: 209). The refutation of Eurocentrism, teleological understandings of development and progress, and unpacking the intellectual legacies of colonialism are crucial. Yet, they 'need not sink us into the paradoxical predicament of excising the socio-economic coordinates of colonialism' (Goswami 2005: 209). Furthermore, the latent tendencies towards a kind of indigenism in critiques of the West and colonial discourses are increasingly weaponized by the right. The terrain of 'alterity' is one that Hindu Nationalists, for example, have happily sought to occupy with their incredibly flawed and distorted views of history. R. P. Dutt (1940) wrote about how those who react against imperialist propaganda by depicting a pre-colonial 'golden age' sought to 'slur over the evils of the rotting social system' that existed before the British and glorified 'those reactionary survivals of India's past which hamper progress, weigh down the consciousness of the people and prevent unity'. Those who 'sought to turn the fight against imperialism into a fight against "Western civilisation" in general . . . turn their gaze backwards, not forwards' (R. P. Dutt 1940: 38).

To better understand the polysemic nature of the very *term* decolonization, we can benefit from a brief historicization. 'Decolonization' had very different purchase in interwar Marxist circles than it does today. In Comintern circles, it initially referred to a very specific theory that imperialism would inadvertently develop the productive forces in the colonies and thus might lead to a gradual end to the Empire. However, this understanding was eventually abandoned in the late 1920s. In *India To-Day,* R. P. Dutt (1940: 268–9) referred to the theory of decolonization as a conception held by *defenders* of the Empire that put forth 'the theory of imperialism as a beneficent civilising system for [gradually] helping forward and training backward peoples into national consciousness and eventual self-government'. The idea that untold millions around the world were colonized just so they could eventually be 'freed' – once they had demonstrated their worthiness in their oppressor's eyes – sadly still has some purchase among the Empire apologists. Later, decolonization began to take on a new life in the metropole with the heady days of Third Worldism, which arguably reached its zenith in the 1960s. While it did tend to idealize the 'Third World' 'with all its classes singularized into an oppositionality', it also saw admirable movements in solidarity with liberation struggles in places like Vietnam (Ahmad 2008: 33). As these movements stagnated, and conditions in the Eastern Bloc deteriorated, unfulfilled expectations turned to disillusionment; Third World nationalism and socialism were largely abandoned, to be replaced by a suspicion of 'grand narratives' of liberation, critiques of modernity and 'reason', an inordinate focus on discourses, non-Western alterity and so on (Ahmad 2008: 34–6). Manu Goswami (2005) presciently distinguishes between claims of indigenous 'autonomy' put forth by anti-colonial activists in a particular political conjuncture and as part of an *active political project* that sought to maintain and 'actualize' autonomy through anti-colonial *mobilization* on the one hand and that of recent Subalternist or postcolonial scholars on the other. Despite rhetorical similarities, the latter group is 'unmoored from a concretely political project' and, therefore, relies on 'ontological claim[s] about the presumed underdetermination of indigenous subjectivities' instead (Goswami 2005: 204). The shortcomings of imagining a perceived 'outside' to the influences of global capital have already been mentioned and need not detain us further. Suffice to say that the relative isolation of intellectual work from active political movements is a sobering reality of contemporary academia and impacts both its tone and content.

Consequently, with our struggle to imagine alternative political futures, there is a natural temptation to return to the generation of thinkers, activists and radicals who first waged war on the Empire as part of active political movements. As the chapters in this collection show, this can indeed be an incredibly fruitful intellectual endeavour – thought produced as a companion to praxis often has a vitality beyond its specific conjuncture. In turning to the past, to more expansive visions of what independence could have meant, historians can fan 'the spark of hope in the past' (Benjamin 1969: 255).

To spark the imagination, to begin thinking of the way things might be different, we might start by, as Walter Benjamin put it, 'brushing history against the grain', seeking those moments where an alternative history, and thus an alternative present and future, 'flares up briefly' (Benjamin 1969: 255–6). Recovering the voices of anti-imperialist *revolution* and international solidarity and keeping the memory of their movements alive is vital work. Yet we must be sensitive to the massive shifts in politics, economy and culture since the heyday of European Empires. What can we learn from returning to anti-colonial thought and revisiting questions of empire? Dutt was quite clear on why he chose to study history, and his attitude is one suited to our present:

> Nothing is to be gained by dwelling on the past or centering national propaganda on the recital of past injustices of grievances. Oppressors and oppressed of the past are alike long dead. . . . *The burning question of to-day is the present oppression and the path of liberation.* We are only concerned with the past in order to bring to light the dynamic forces which still live in the present. (R. P. Dutt 1940: 92: italics added)

How, then, can we understand 'the present oppression and the path of liberation'? To a large degree, the international system continues to be defined by imperialism and a continued coloniality. The refusal of the advanced capitalist nations to waive patents on vaccines during the recent Covid pandemic, their shirking of responsibility for the climate crisis and the malign influence of the IMF, World Bank and 'structural adjustment' programmes are all stark reminders that the West has resolutely clung to its power and will continue to do so. The unending litany of coups, foreign interventions and sanctions against the Global South are also indications of the immense coercive power concentrated in Western capitals. Colonialism 'left in place not a series of objects, but a live ecosystem in constant and transformative interaction with other institutions and forces in the present', the most important of which is global capitalism (Linstrum et al. 2022: 299). These very real, *material* and *political* aspects of continued coloniality must be at the forefront of our analysis.

At the same time, Europe and America are not the only centres of capitalism, imperialism and state violence. An anti-imperialist consciousness in the twenty-first century must be attuned to the fact that, for example, Indian capitalists have been engaged in unbelievably violent projects of dispossession, class warfare and exploitation since independence. In light of the Indian state's continued use of repressive colonial-era legislation to stifle dissent, scholars like Priyamvada Gopal rightfully ask, 'power may have been transferred but did the colonial state ever leave?' (Linstrum et al. 2022: 303). As recently as April 2023, the Indian state has engaged in aerial attacks on *Adivasi* (indigenous) peoples in the state of Chhattisgarh as part of its years-long assault on communities who live on mineral-rich land that corporations are eager to exploit (Countercurrents .org 2023). The occupation of Kashmir, continued assaults against Indian Muslims, the persistence of caste and patriarchal oppression and the existence of overwhelming hunger and grinding poverty in a country where the top 1 per cent of the population owns 40.6 per cent of the wealth are the sobering realities of the day (Oxfam India 2023). This is the situation in India, but there are similar harrowing stories from around the world. The 1960s enthusiasm for the Third World Nationalism of the national bourgeoisie and the nation states that movements inspired by it culminated in cannot return. There are far too many instances of those very same states engaging in violent projects of exclusion and forcible inclusion, new regimes of expropriation, violent capital accumulation, exploitation and oppression.

Even now, it is worth recognizing that the diaspora often operates in a highly privileged political space in comparison to those who criticize, for example, the Indian government and big business at home. There are too many stories to count of the intimidation of activists, arrests of protesters and the use of colonial-era laws to stifle dissent. While there has always been a repressive streak to the postcolonial state in India, the Modi government's authoritarianism represents a significant escalation. On the other hand, the diaspora are relatively more free to speak their mind, to write and express themselves without the fear of immediate repression. This is precisely why there have been attempts by the state to encroach on this political space. For example, in the UK, the BJP actively campaigned against Jeremy Corbyn's Labour Party due to the latter's willingness to speak out about human rights abuses in Kashmir (Siddique 2019). Following the assassination of a Sikh–Canadian activist in 2023, which the Canadian government claims was carried out by India, *The Intercept* revealed the likely existence of an international assassination programme that the state uses to target Sikh and Kashmiri activists (Grim and Hussain 2023). The government's attempts at repression are often aided by a servile political and media class in the West which happily turns a blind eye to their crimes and abuses in the pursuit of self-interest and ill-conceived geopolitical strategy (Mishra 2023).

It is also worth pointing out that for all of the South Asian diaspora's rich history of radicalism, there is another strain. Whether it is the fact that the Hindu Right receives huge amounts of funding from abroad (Sud 2008: 50–65), the right-wing extremism of high-profile diaspora members of the Conservative Party of the UK, or the communal clashes of 2022 in Leicester, South Asian migrants' history of solidarity, activism and *radicalism* threatens to be overtaken by a militancy of the right (Chandan 2022). Racialized communities can also be tempted, by their experiences of marginalization and discrimination, into a form of defensive nativism. This nativism, incredibly sensitive to perceived slights and willing to misuse the language of anti-imperialism, is increasingly on display on the world stage and characteristic of contemporary Indian nationalism. It is disconcerting to see ostensibly 'liberal' journalists dressing up Indian hostility to justified criticism from abroad as a 'reflexive anti-imperial instinct' (B. Dutt 2023).

The legacy of colonialism cannot be allowed to stand in the way of international solidarity; British radicals need not engage in handwringing over whether they have the right to speak against injustices in places like India. Dutt's CPGB comrades, white or otherwise, were often just as hostile to the Indian bourgeoisie as their own. With the internationalization of global finance capital and the common, albeit unevenly experienced, calamity that is upon us with climate change, an oppositional socialist consciousness should not stop at one's own borders. The impact of the onset of fascism in India will not be contained purely within the country.⁶ It is crucial to treat the formerly colonized as peoples with their own coherent histories, classes, struggles and politics. There is nothing automatically progressive about 'brown faces in high places', or about 'non-Western' ways of being or knowing. South Asians, like all other peoples, have their own hierarchies, their own pasts and presents to struggle against.

We are desperately in need of a new kind of politics – a socialism that is conscious of its history, willing and able to learn from the successes and shortcomings of past movements and attuned to the problems and challenges of the moment. As the Marxist historian Jairus Banaji put it in a recent interview:

> if the new politics is going to be viable, it has to be totalizing as well as intersectional. It has to be able to think about gender, race, class, caste, etc. as if it was trying to solve a simultaneous equation. And think about the central question of where or what is the working class? *It's all over the world today.* No society in history has had a wider spread of wage labor – of wage domination, waged employment – than contemporary society. (In this sense at least, capitalism has never been stronger.)
>
> To have a viable left politics today, one with imagination, we have to have the ability to contest capitalism on all these levels. (Banaji 2021: italics added)

If the working class is spread around the world, so too are its enemies. History can be an incredibly useful tool in shaping the new politics that is required to confront capitalism in the twenty-first century. Decolonization, in our epoch's understanding, might be related to Dutt's attempts to get English audiences to 'unlearn' what they thought they knew about the Empire and its colonies as a prerequisite to effective action. The latter trajectory of work was specifically aimed at ensuring that metropolitan radicals might be able to exercise an influence on developments abroad through their position in the centres of imperialist power. It *also* sought to impress upon its audiences the inextricability of seemingly disparate struggles around the world. It is in this sense and in a recognition that empire's afterlives are still all too tangible that we can profit from decolonizing knowledge today. If we are more keenly aware of the role our states play on the world stage, on the pressing realities of international politics in an age of accelerated climate breakdown, of an emboldened Far Right and sharpening geopolitical tensions, we must be able to see with clear minds our own histories and positions in structures of power and domination. This also entails, however, viewing the formerly colonized world on its own terms as a place with a living history *before* and *after* colonization – a trajectory irrevocably shaped by its experience of imperialism but not entirely reducible to it, especially not now. It also means rejecting parochial and limiting conceptions of identity or culture which are emptied of their political content. If we return to the past, let it be to grasp that there were dreams of horizons beyond purely formal decolonization, that such horizons have yet to be reached and that it is a collective endeavour towards liberation that must impel us now.

Notes

1. For more on Saklatvala, see Gopal 2020, Chapters 5 and 6. For more on Clemens Palme Dutt, see C. P. Dutt (2016).
2. The solidarity campaign around the Meerut Conspiracy Case, however, was an incredibly striking exemplar of this internationalist project in action. For more, see Gopal (2020).
3. For example, see Bevins (2020).
4. Due to the nature of this chapter, I will focus more on the trajectory of postcolonial scholarship in the Indian context. Of course, I am well aware that umbrella terms such as 'decolonial' and 'post-colonial' refer to vast bodies of work with their own internal differentiations but what follows are some observations on broad academic trends.
5. On how the anti-colonial utopias of the twentieth century 'have gradually withered into post-colonial nightmares', see Scott (2004). However, I am not convinced they have lost all of their disruptive potential.
6. For example, see Dhillon (2023).

References

Ahmad, Aijaz (2008), *In Theory: Classes, Nations, Literatures*, London: Verso.

Banaji, Jairus (2021), 'Where is the Working Class? It's All Over the World Today Part 2', interviewed by Sheetal Chhabria and Andrew Liu, *Borderlines*. Available at https://borderlines-cssaame.org/posts/2021/1/18/part-ii-where-is-the-working-class-its-all-over-the-world-today (Accessed: 3 January 2024).

Beckett, Francis (1995), *Enemy Within: The Rise and Fall of the British Communist Party*, London: Merlin Press.

Benjamin, Walter (1969), 'Theses on the Philosophy of History', in *Illuminations*, 253–65, New York: Shocken Books.

Bevins, Vincent (2020), *The Jakarta Method: Washington's Anticommunist Crusade & the Mass Murder Program That Shaped Our World*, New York, NY: PublicAffairs, Hatchette Book Group.

Callaghan, John (1993), *Rajani Palme Dutt: A Study in British Stalinism*, London: Lawrence and Wishart.

Chandan, Sukant (2022), 'How Decades of South Asian Unity Unravelled in Leicester', *The Caravan*. Available at https://caravanmagazine.in/politics/leicester-violence-south-asian-diaspora-muslim-hindu-swayamsevak-sangh-partition (Accessed: 3 January 2024).

CounterCurrents.org (2023), 'Fourth Drone Bomb Attack on Indigenous People in Bastar, Chhattisgarh! Stop this State Terror Now!' https://countercurrents.org/2023/04/fourth-drone-bomb-attack-on-indigenous-people-in-bastar-chhattisgarh-stop-this-state-terror-now/ (Accessed: 3 January 2024).

Dange, S. A. (1974), 'RPD Is No More', *New Age*, P.C. Joshi Archives on Contemporary History, Biography File 16A, New Delhi: Jawaharlal Nehru University.

Dhillon, Amardeep Singh (2023), 'White and Hindu Supremacists are a Match Made in Heaven', *Novara Media*. https://novaramedia.com/2023/02/23/white-and-hindu-supremacists-are-a-match-made-in-heaven (Accessed: 3 January 2024).

Dutt, Barkha (2023), 'Opinion | The Best Way to Strengthen India's Democracy? Leave it to the Indians', *Washington Post*. Available at https://www.washingtonpost.com/opinions/2023/04/20/india-democracy-indians-strengthen (Accessed: 3 January 2024).

Dutt, Clemens Palme (2016), *On India: Articles and Book Reviews*, Kolkata: R B Enterprises.

Dutt, Rajani Palme (1923), 'The British Empire', *The Labour Monthly*. Available at https://www.marxists.org/archive/dutt/articles/1923/british_empire.htm (Accessed: 3 January 2024).

Dutt, Rajani Palme (1927), *Modern India,* London: The Dorrit Press, Ltd.

Dutt, Rajani Palme (1928), 'Indian Awakening', *The Labour Monthly*. Available at https://www.marxists.org/archive/dutt/1928/06/x01.htm (Accessed: 3 January 2024).

Dutt, Rajani Palme (1936), *World Politics: 1918–1936*, London: Victor Gollancz.

Dutt, Rajani Palme (1937), 'Lecture by Rajani Palme Dutt: 2.12.37', India Office Records (IOR): L/P&J/12/30: P&J 1185 (British Library).

Dutt, Rajani Palme (1940), *India To-Day*, London: Victor Gollancz.

Dutt, Rajani Palme (1963), *Problems of Contemporary History*, London: Lawrence and Wishart.

Dutt, Rajani Palme (1966), 'Looking Backwards', Interviewed by Malcom Muggeridge, *Stephen Peet Recordings*, 1 November and 2 November, Golders Green, London, England, UK. (Recordings on tapes available on request at British Library, shelfmark: C1184/03).

Dutt, Rajani Palme (1971), Interviewed by Shri B.R. Nanda, Oral History Project, 31–2, Nehru Memorial Museum & Library.

Gopal, Priyamvada (2020), Chapters 5 and 6 in *Insurgent Empire: Anticolonial Resistance and British Dissent*, London: Verso.

Goswami, Manu (2005), 'Autonomy and Comparability: Notes on the Anticolonial and the Postcolonial', *Boundary 2*, 32 (2): 201–25. https://doi.org/10.1215/01903659-32-2-201.

Grim, Ryan and Hussain, Murtaza (2023), 'Secret Intelligence Documents Show Global Reach of India's Death Squads', *The Intercept*: https://theintercept.com/2023/11/21/india-assassinations-sikh-pakistan (Accessed: 3 January 2024).

Gupta, Sobhanlal Datta (2006), *Comintern and the Destiny of Communism in India: 1919–1943: Dialectics of Real and a Possible History*, Calcutta: Seribaan.

Hallas, Duncan (1993), 'The Shyster Lawyer', *Socialist Review*, 167. Available at https://www.marxists.org/archive/hallas/works/1993/09/dutt.htm (Accessed: 3 January 2024).

James, C. L. R. (2012), *A History of Pan-African Revolt*, Chicago: Charles H. Kerr Publishing Company.

Joshi, P. C. (2014), 'R.P. Dutt and Indian Communists', in Gargi Chakravarty (ed.), *People's 'Warrior': Words and Worlds of P.C. Joshi*, 313–29. New Delhi: Tulika Books.

Kaviraj, Sudipta (2009), 'Marxism in Translation: Critical Reflections on Indian Radical Thought', in Raymond Geuss and Richard Bourke (eds), in *Political Judgement: Essays for John Dunn*, 172–200. Cambridge: Cambridge University Press. Available at https://doi.org/10.1017/CBO9780511605468.007 (Accessed: 3 January 2024).

Krishnan, Vidya (2022), 'The Hypocrisy of the Indian Diaspora is Overwhelming', *The Caravan*. Available at https://caravanmagazine.in/communities/hypocrisy-indian-diaspora-overwhelming (Accessed: 3 January 2024).

Linstrum, Erik, Ward, Stuart, Ogle, Vanessa, Nasar, Saima and Gopal, Priyamvada (2022), 'Decolonizing Britain: An Exchange', *Twentieth Century British History*, 33 (2): 274–303. Available at https://doi.org/10.1093/tcbh/hwac018 (Accessed: 3 January 2024).

Mishra, Pankaj (2023), 'The Big Con', *London Review of Books*. Available at https://www.lrb.co.uk/the-paper/v45/n08/pankaj-mishra/the-big-con (Accessed: 3 January 2024).

Oxfam India (2023), 'Survival of the Richest: The India Story'. https://d1ns4ht6ytuzzo.cloudfront.net/oxfamdata/oxfamdatapublic/2023-01/India%20Supplement%202023_digital.pdf?kz3wav0jbhJdvkJ.fK1rj1k1_5ap9FhQ (Accessed: 3 January 2024).

Prashad, Vijay (2000), *The Karma of Brown Folk*, Minneapolis: University of Minnesota Press.

Riddell, John, Prashad, Vijay and Mollah, Nazeef, eds. (2019), 'Second World Congress Debate on Anti-Colonial Revolution', in Riddell, Prashad and Mollah, *Liberate the Colonies! Communism and Colonial Freedom 1917–1924*, 38–102, New Delhi: Left Word Books.

Said, Edward (1994), *Culture and Imperialism*, London: Vintage.

Samuel, Raphael (2017), *The Lost World of British Communism*, London: Verso.

Sarkar, Sumit (1993), 'The Fascism of the Sangh Parivar', *Economic and Political Weekly*, 28 (5): 165.

Sarkar, Sumit (1994), 'Orientalism Revisited: Saidian Frameworks in the Writing of Modern Indian History', *Oxford Literary Review*, 16 (1/2): 205–24.

Sarkar, Sumit (1997), 'The Decline of the Subaltern in *Subaltern Studies*', in *Writing Social History*, 82–108, Delhi: Oxford University Press.

Scott, David (2004), *Conscripts of Modernity: The Tragedy of Colonial Enlightenment*, Durham: Duke University Press, 2004.

Sen, Satadru (2015), *Benoy Kumar Sarkar: Restoring the Nation to the World*, New Delhi: Routledge.

Seth, Sanjay (1995), *Marxist Theory and Nationalist Politics: The Case of Colonial India*, New Delhi: Sage Publications.

Siddique, Haroon (2019), 'British Indians Warn Hindu Nationalist Party Not to Meddle in UK Elections', *The Guardian*, sec. Politics. Available at https://www.theguardian.com/politics/2019/nov/11/british-indians-warn-hindu-party-not-to-meddle-in-uk-elections (Accessed: 3 January 2024).

Sud, Nikita (2008), 'Tracing the Links between Hindu Nationalism and the Indian Diaspora', *St Antony's International Review*, 3 (2): 50–65.

Virdee, Satnam (2017), 'The Second Sight of Racialised Outsiders in the Imperialist Core', *Third World Quarterly*, 38 (11): 2396–410.

Williams, Theo (2022), *Making the Revolution Global: Black Radicalism and the British Socialist Movement before Decolonisation*, London: Verso.

8

Labour super-exploitation, Black liberation and communist thought

Andrew Higginbottom

The concept of labour super-exploitation is associated with Marxist dependency theory from Latin America and, in particular, the groundbreaking contribution of Ruy Mauro Marini. The translation into English of Marini's principal work has sparked renewed interest and debate. This is for good reason. In *Dialéctica de la Dependencia* and other works, Marini developed a full concept, placing super-exploitation in an overall theoretical framework that explained the capitalist underdevelopment of an entire continent. Marini (2022) brought together the dimensions of national subordination and harsh working-class exploitation. Avoiding both eclecticism and dogmatism, he achieved a crucial step forward in revolutionary thought. The current debates reviving and interpreting Marini in Latin America and, increasingly, beyond are thus to be welcomed.

One point that has been debated in recent literature is regarding the extent to which the idea of labour super-exploitation was already present in Marx's *Capital* (Higginbotttom 2023). The current chapter relates to this discussion while also filling a gap and, hopefully, providing a fresh angle. In this chapter, I take a step back from Marini and trace the genealogy of labour super-exploitation as an idea, a notion, a concept. We will find that the enquiry provides some interesting results, not only historically but also politically. The influence of the idea has been episodic, but it crystallized earlier in the communist movement to explain the connection between racial oppression and capitalism and was used more widely than perhaps even Marini supposed. Marini's student and collaborator Jaime Osorio (2013: 25) traces the idea back to a 1965 article critiquing capitalist colonialism by the Italian Marxist Paolo Santi. But this still leaves something missing.

What was the story of this concept before Santi? Between Lenin (who it is often supposed is the author of labour super-exploitation as an idea) and Santi, what currents were working with this powerful way of thinking?

In fact, it was the Black liberation struggle that originally prompted the development of the concept in communist thought. The earliest identified expression of super-exploitation came from the African Americans' dialogue with the Communist International (Comintern) in the 1920s, especially Claude McKay, James W. Ford and Harry Haywood, as well as the until recently overlooked Grace P. Campbell (Lindsey 2019). Their purpose was to theorize the specific combination of exploitation and racial oppression that capitalism imposes on Black workers, both internally in the United States and, in parallel fashion, externally by the imperial powers on their colonial possessions. Santi's use of the concept thus has a correlated application to explain racism particularly in the United States and, at least potentially and more generally, other forms of oppression.

Black liberation and anti-imperialism in the Communist International

The earliest expression of the term 'labour super-exploitation' came from the engagement of African Americans with the Comintern in the late 1920s. To set the scene we need to consider two intersecting paths: the leap forward of the international communist movement inspired by the Russian Revolution and the national political dynamics within the United States. This interaction turned out to be highly fluid and complex. We will summarize the zig-zags of this turbulent milieu in order to focus on the emergence of labour super-exploitation as a concept related to Black workers' oppression. Solomon (1998) gives a detailed and perceptive reading of the discussion as it unfolded in a Comintern increasingly factionalized between Stalin and Trotsky. The histories by Adi (2013) and Puryear (2023) narrate one-sidedly from the Stalin camp, whereas Zumoff (2014) is more inclined to Trotksy's version. I am more concerned to get past the factionalism to uncover the emergence of labour super-exploitation as an idea.

Anti-colonial framing

The main contours of the Comintern position on national liberation were established at its first two congresses in 1919 and 1920. The Bolsheviks, primarily Lenin, saw the revolutionary fight against colonialism as a strategic development for the world revolution (Comintern [1921] 1977b). The Second Congress' 'Theses on the national and colonial question' urged support for 'the revolutionary liberation movements' of the colonized nations (Comintern [1921] 1977b). It is probably due to Russia's location that the earliest extensive connections were with 'the peoples of the East' – comrades from many parts of Asia brought together at the Baku Congress in 1920 (Riddel 2020). Congress chair Zinoviev declared at its conclusion (the record states to tumultuous applause and singing of 'The Internationale'): 'Karl Marx, the teacher of us all, issued 70 years ago the call: "Workers of all lands, unite!" We, Karl Marx's pupils, the continuators of his work, can expand this formulation, supplementing and broadening it, and say: "Workers of all lands *and oppressed peoples of the whole world, unite!*"' (Comintern [1920] 1977a). Connections between the Moscow-centred Comintern and Latin America, the Caribbean and Africa took longer. They were initially fleeting and then consolidated in the late 1920s, by which time they became further complicated by the cleavages in the Russian party that carried over into the International.

In the meantime, there had been a prolonged struggle by revolutionary African Americans to get the Communist Party of the United States of America (CPUSA) to take the 'Negro Question' seriously. From its formation in 1919 up to 1928, the white leadership of the CPUSA took a 'race blind' approach, which subsumed race to class in theory and overlooked segregationist racism in practice. For example, even at party events, whites socialized completely separately from Blacks. Those African Americans attracted to communism and the Comintern worked together to convince, then bypass and finally overcome the CPUSA's white reluctant revolutionaries. The pressure went through phases, but only came to a point of real change after the Comintern's Sixth Congress in 1928. This must be read carefully in the overlapping context of developments in Soviet Russia and Stalin's fight for supremacy against Trotsky and, later, Bukharin. Stalin's emergence as victor in these internal struggles certainly had a bearing on the CPUSA, as argued by Zumoff (2014), but it was not the whole story.

There was a problem that had to be solved: 'the party did not have at hand a substantive Marxist theory to cope specifically with the situation of Black Americans' (Foner and Allen 1987: vii). The Baku formulation was of an alliance between two distinct forces – the proletariat of the rich countries and the liberation movements of the colonized peoples, based mostly on the peasantry. Within this framing, how do we locate the specificity of the 'Negro Question' as part of both the worldwide anti-colonial struggle and of the racially divisive class relations of the United States?

McKay's contribution

Jamaican-born Claude McKay, who moved to the United States to study and work, witnessed the racist pogroms against African Americans in the so-called 'Red Summer' of 1919. He wrote the classic poem 'If We Must Die' calling for resistance (McKay 1919). Determined to make contact with the new International, McKay worked his passage and spent some time in London, where he joined Sylvia Pankhurst's *Workers Dreadnought*, the most left-wing strand of the nascent British Communist Party. He travelled on to the Comintern's fourth congress in 1922, where his and Otto Huiswoud's speeches attracted much attention (Riddell 2018; Chapman 2021).

With Trotsky's encouragement, McKay extended his speech into a book, published in Russian but not translated into English until sixty years later (Zumoff 2014: 309). McKay ([1924] 1979: 12) wrote that the 1914–18 war had engendered significant changes in the situation of Africans in America: 'who do the lowest and most exhausting work came to the North from southern states or emigrated from the West Indies, escaping from the unbearable social inequality and contemporary agricultural serfdom'. McKay ([1924] 1979: 23) criticized the refusal of white labour to see the greater exploitation of their Black counterparts and its lack of solidarity with them: 'Labor, tragically, is divided against itself. It conducts a shameful, half-hearted struggle against capitalism, since it does not extend a fraternal hand to the Black working force, historically the most exploited class in American life.' McKay (1922: 2) had not come to the Comintern through the CPUSA, and he was highly critical of their economistic stance that failed to tackle the problem. He noted that in its forty-eight-page pamphlet on the revolutionary movement, 'Negroes' (using the language of the time) were never even mentioned (McKay [1924] 1979: 41).

McKay had a fine sense of the social tensions that arose between the races. In the chapter 'Sex and Economics', he confronted the attitude 'The white man must not allow the white woman to have relations with Negroes' (McKay [1924] 1979: 76), which was often the immediate trigger for lynching. McKay's subtle historical analysis explained how extreme sexual taboo was a way that the ruling class maintained an ideological hold over poor whites in the South. In strikingly modern terms, Mckay ([1924] 1979: 77) argued that 'The Negro question is inseparably connected with the question of woman's liberation'. McKay reported that white communists in the North refused to fight for social equality both programmatically and in their daily practice. In 1924, McKay,

Otto Huiswoud and Rose Pastor Stokes participated in the Comintern's Fourth Congress, proposing a motion that connected the Black struggle in the United States with oppressed peoples fighting colonialism round the world (Solomon 1998: 40–2; Riddell 2011). The revolutionary African Americans who were deeply disappointed by the practice of white communists in the United States were nonetheless drawn to the Comintern and sought direct contact with the Bolsheviks. The Comintern then was the setting in which they grappled with the theoretical challenge of analysing race and class.

The debates around the Comintern Sixth Congress, 1928

Before we delve into the detail, it is vital to recognize that there were three distinct positions on Black liberation in the early CPUSA of the 1920s. The majority leadership defended white privilege; it held to the economistic view that did not want to address racism as a central issue. All the African Americans who had been attracted to communism and were in or close to the CPUSA were, at the same time, in degrees of contradiction with it. In time, two positions emerged within their group. One section of the African Americans saw 'Negroes' as an *oppressed race* and emphasized the fight for equality; and another section saw themselves as an *oppressed nation* and wanted the communist programme to support the right of 'Negroes' to national self-determination. The existing literature on this topic tends to emphasize the difference between the two positions, which was real enough in terms of discussions at the Comintern and efforts to reorient its party in the United States. But looking at the question from this perspective underplays the significant commonality that both sections of African American communists held against the complacency and even racism of the CPUSA: their insistence on the distinct *oppression* of 'Negroes' in the United States and, crucially for present purposes, the articulation of this idea through the new expression in Marxist terminology of labour super-exploitation. Concentrating on the factional debate is understandable, given its immediate repercussions, but it has occluded the genesis of the labour super-exploitation thesis that emerged as a fresh idea from the encounter between African Americans and communism.

As we have seen, much of the idea of labour super-exploitation, insofar as it concerned Black workers, was outlined by McKay. These themes were advanced by Surinam born Otto Huiswoud (1928: 772), who wrote: 'Turning their backs to the oppressive social conditions of the (US) south, with its intense exploitation, low wages, long hours and espionage system, the migrants flocked into the steel mills, coal mines, cement factories, automobile factories, railroads and many other industries.' This corresponds closely to the three elements of the concept formulated by Marini (2022: 161) – intense exploitation leading to exhaustion, low wages and long hours.

The term itself crystallized in the commissions of the Comintern's sixth congress debating the 'Negro Question'. Notwithstanding their common critique of the indifference of the US communists, the African American delegates fell into two camps when it came to the political strategy the party should adopt. One camp framed the 'Negroes' in America as a racial minority, stressing the need to fight for full equality. The other camp framed the 'Negroes' as an oppressed nation and stressed their need for national self-determination. At this juncture, the intersection between the splits in the CPUSA and in the Comintern interacted in a concrete way. The argument that won out in the sixth congress debate was the national self-determination line advanced by Harry Haywood. It was assimilated into the Stalin–Bukharin hegemonic perspective that stressed the separateness of the democratic revolution from the socialist revolution at the sixth congress. However, those African Americans working with the Comintern were not just its pawns. Their chiding of the US party was sharper than ever before, and they were given fresh backing from the Comintern in 1929 and 1930, by which time Stalin had ejected Bukharin and was pushing for a sharp left turn by the communist movement.

The two lines within the African American delegates found support with like minds among the Comintern cadre with an interest in the question. Of the two lines in the debate, Shiek, Ford and Patterson argued for the 'racial minority' concept, while Haywood and Nassanoff took the 'Negro' self-determination stand. Shiek (1928) argued against the cultural nationalist position saying that 'the Negro bourgeois is not averse to having a monopoly in the super-exploitation of the millions of toilers of his own race. It is the colored bourgeoisie who invent all sorts of legends about a "special Negro culture," the "brotherhood of the whole African race" and similar nonsense' (Shiek 1928: 165). Ford and Patterson (1928: 167) argued similarly: 'For the party the organization of the Negro for the revolutionary struggle is easier and can be more successful than the organization of the white worker who suffers much less under the yoke of capital than the super-exploited Negro worker.' Arguing a more pro-revolutionary nationalist perspective, Harry Haywood (1978: 221) also picked up the term from his discussions with Nassanoff at around the same time. Nassanoff, also spelt Nazanov, had visited the United States as a representative of the Young Communist International in 1926, where he and Haywood first met. What became known as the Haywood–Nassanoff thesis stressed the right of 'Negroes' in the United States to national self-determination. Haywood (1978: 230) believed that Marcus Garvey's Universal Negro Improvement Association (UNIA) was a mass movement that expressed an authentic Black nationalism, 'an indigenous product, arising from the soil of Black super-exploitation and oppression in the United States. It expressed the yearnings of millions of Blacks for a nation of their own'. These references show that it is hard, and perhaps unnecessary, to firmly identify one individual as originator of the term; rather, it was the outcome of intense collaboration. Labour super-exploitation seems by 1928 to have become a shared underpinning, part of a developing conceptual lingua franca, a collective effort to analyse and tackle the challenge of Black liberation from white racism.

The Sixth Comintern Congress made the call 'For Complete Emancipation of Oppressed Negro Race' and for 'the right of Negroes to national self-determination in the southern states where the Negroes form a majority of the population' (Foner and Allen 1987: 191–2). The congress resolution admonished 'white chauvinism evidenced in the American Party' (Foner and Allen 1987: 193). The course of the debate during and after the congress is detailed by Adi and Zumoff. Both authors point out that the adoption of the thesis for the United States was strongly influenced by the even more compelling case of South Africa. Concerning South Africa, the preponderantly white and openly racist Communist Party was sharply rebuked by the Comintern, who directed it to adopt a programme for an 'independent black South African Republic' (Zumoff 2014: 345–6) and demand a 'Native Republic' (Adi 2013: 72–6).

After extensive preparatory exchanges, the CPUSA was now effectively directed by the Comintern to take a left turn, which in the United States also meant organizing in the rural South. Under Haywood's hands-on leadership, the CPUSA at last adopted a far more energetic and principled fight against 'white chauvinism' (racism) and for Black liberation in the 1930s than it had in the 1920s. In this period, the party made a real contribution to movement building and involved itself with Black struggles against the deeply racist institutions of Jim Crow segregation, lynching and the Klu Klux Klan. Haywood co-authored a communist pamphlet that asked what the real causes and the real purpose of lynching were:

Every lynching, every degradation, every social persecution and proscription, every Jim Crow humiliation, which the Negro masses suffer in this country is the result of the fact that the Negro millions are in the position of an oppressed nationality. They are subjected to a more intense, a fiercer exploitation on the land and in the factories. While the white workers are miserably exploited by the capitalist robbers, the Negro workers are especially exploited and persecuted. They are super-exploited. They are given the dirtiest jobs, the longest hours, and the least pay. They are the last to be hired and the first to be fired. They must work under the foulest conditions. It is an absolutely undeniable fact that today, nearly 70 years after they were supposed to be 'freed', the Negro masses are in slavery, providing super-profits for their capitalist landlords and bosses. (Haywood and Howard 1932: 5–6)

Debate remains however about whether the party's turn to mass campaigning and grassroots organizing was because of or despite the new national self-determination line. Adi (2013) and Zumoff (2014) provide pro-Stalin and pro-Trotsky interpretations of this turn of the CPUSA, respectively; however, neither account gives visibility to the emergence of labour super-exploitation as an idea. In this section, I have stressed that the drastic reorientation of US communists because of the debate in the Comintern between the two wings of African Americans, a debate that pushed the party to recognize the realities of Black oppression. The theoretical expression of this was the concept of labour super-exploitation. From this fresh starting point, and after a wealth of experiences of struggle in the US South and North, another step in the development of the concept was soon to be taken.

African American women theorize their triple oppression and exploitation

Claudia Jones

Claudia Jones was born in Trinidad and grew up in the United States, where she joined the Communist Party in the 1930s (Lynn 2020: 40). Her mother was a garment worker who died young. Jones was imprisoned four times and then deported from the United States in 1955 for being a communist. She emigrated to England where she played a pivotal role in initiating cultural and political resistance to racism (Boyce Davies 2008).

Jones is buried to the left of Karl Marx in Highgate cemetery in London; this is taken by her biographer as a metaphor for her ideological positioning as well (Boyce Davies 2008: 2). While still in the United States and as a Black feminist leader in the CPUSA, Jones wrote a pamphlet in 1949 *An End to the Neglect of the Problems of Negro Women* that spoke to their triple oppression as women, as Black and as workers. Jones (1949: 5) urgently drew attention to their economic hardships: 'The low scale of earnings of the Negro woman is directly related to her almost complete exclusion from virtually all fields of work except the most menial and underpaid, namely, domestic service.' She conceptualized this discrimination as super-exploitation: 'The super-exploitation of the Negro woman worker is thus revealed not only in that she receives, as woman, less than equal pay for equal work with men, but in that the majority of Negro women get less than half the pay of white women' (Jones 1949: 5). Jones saw that white women, including those in the Communist Party, employing Black women as domestic servants were prone to chauvinism towards them. She argued that this needed to be overcome: 'Chauvinism on the part of progressive white women is often expressed in their failure to have close ties of friendship with Negro women and to realize that this fight for equality of Negro women is in their own self-interest, inasmuch as the super-exploitation and oppression of Negro women tends to depress the standards of all women' (Jones 1949: 12).

This position was before the concept of white privilege became more fully elaborated in the US context, at a time when communists were reluctant to admit that 'The Negro question in the United States is *prior* to, not equal to, the woman question . . . the Negro woman who combines in her status the worker, the Negro, and the woman, is the vital link to this heightened political consciousness' (Jones 1949: 15).

Jones made her observations from within the Communist Party, but she was critical of its practices; she saw the neglect as that of official Marxism. Although Jones did not argue this, Carol Boyce Davies points out that Jones's position had theoretical implications.

> Claudia Jones's position on the 'super exploitation of the black woman,' Marxist–Leninist in its formation, offered, for its time, the clearest analysis of the location of black women – not in essentialized, romantic, or homogenizing terms but practically, as located in U.S. and world economic hierarchies. It thereby advanced Marxist–Leninist positions beyond their apparent limitations. To develop her argument, Jones contended that if all workers are exploited because of the usurping of the surplus value of their labor, then black women – bereft

of any kind of institutional mechanism to conquer this exploitation, and often assumed to have to work uncountable hours without recompense – live a life of superexploitation beyond what Marx had identified as the workers' lot. (Boyce Davies 2008: 2)

Coming back to the positional metaphor, Jones is buried immediately next to Marx as well as to his left. Boyce Davies (2008: 3) rightly argues that the advance beyond Marx to take fuller account of oppression should be considered as a logical extension of his theory, such as the concept of surplus value, rather than its invalidation.

Angela Davis

Moving on to the next generation, young Angela Davis was an African American communist philosophy lecturer closely aligned with the Black Panthers. In 1970, she was detained on trumped up charges; the real reason for the detention was that she befriended prisoner George Jackson and defended the Panthers politically. In a book of essays and prison interviews edited by Davis, we find the thread from Claudia Jones once again articulated in the context of a new chapter of revolutionary struggle. Davis develops the position concretely in relation to the position of imprisoned Black people, that is, those experiencing, with the most brutal immediacy, the realities of US state repression.

The preface of the volume identifies the most exploited with the most politically conscious. Davis (1971: xiv–xv) argues that 'it is essential to view fascist tendencies in terms of their specific challenge to working people; and in the United States, their specific challenge in the first place to the most exploited and at the same time most radical and politically conscious section of the working class – the Black, Puerto Rican and Chicano communities'. Davis (1971: 91) identifies super-exploitation as the foundation of many of the complexities of racism, as here in the case of sacked car worker James Johnson: 'The complex realities of American racism emanate from the basic fact of the over-exploitation of Black workers at the point of production. Capitalists not only reap enormous super profits from underpaid Black labor but use racism as a divisive factor to stave off a united, revolutionary working-class movement'.

In the extended interview, when still imprisoned, Davis treats the connection with political strategy in a dialectical manner, considering the issue both structurally and with respect to agency. Davis was asked whether Black–white unity was possible. There are two sides to her response that brought the objective condition of the greater exploitation of Black working people into play politically. Davis (1971: 193) begins with the following observation: 'starting with the assumption that we African men and women, super-exploited over the centuries in all and sundry forms, want total liberation from capitalism, we must inevitably draw the conclusion that our thrust toward liberation must be organically bound up with the movement involving large numbers of white people who through a socialist revolution will liberate themselves.' So, it should be possible to involve or ally with at least a section of white people who are also exploited.

The other side of the question, however, is on what terms could such an alliance be constructed. Here, Davis (1971: 194) draws attention to the effects of the qualitative difference in exploitation with the additional dimension of racial inequality, the super or extra of super-exploitation: 'Black-white unity with Black people in the forefront – because the phenomenon of racism and super-exploitation under capitalism has not only placed Black people at the very lowest plane of the social order but it has also paralyzed the ability of whites to struggle in a radical fashion.'

Whether or not whites would overcome the paralysis of their ability to struggle is of course open to experience that have been many and varied since then: some hopeful, but far too many not. Recognition of super-exploitation as a condition of the specific oppression of Black working people was here seen as an important step towards overcoming divisions; Davis linked it to the right of Black and other oppressed workers to lead the united struggle. This then is quite a rounded, integrated position on Black liberation that uses the concept of super-exploitation in a structural analysis that grounded a revolutionary political strategy.

In a later work, *Women, Race and Class*, Davis started from the position of Black women under slavery, pointing out the absence of attention to this in the literature. She outlined as major pointers that Black women were workers, and their reproductive capacity was appropriated for profit. Moreover, enslaved women, 'were inherently vulnerable to all forms of sexual coercion. . . . Rape, in fact, was an uncamouflaged expression of the slaveholder's economic mastery and the overseer's control over Black women as workers' (Davis 1994: 7).

What emerges here is the continuing significance of the legacy of enslavement for the condition of Black people in the United States; that US imperialism continues to rely in a structural manner on super-exploitation at home as well as abroad. The analysis of greater oppression of Black people as cheap labour units is structurally endemic to US capitalism. This goes further than institutional racism; it is fundamental to the system. In terms of agency, the political strategy for Black liberation depends in part on what white workers are willing or not willing to do about it: will they come to recognize the gulf of super-exploitation and actively support Black people fighting oppression, or will they repeat the general pattern of collaboration in racism? The question of trust remains open and remains a central issue.

The other side to this point looks at the ways in which African Americans have made common cause with anti-imperialist and national liberation struggles overseas. This strategic Black internationalism was a marked characteristic of the Black Panthers and has been carried forward into the next generation by Angela Davis's consistent solidarity with and highlighting of the Palestinian freedom struggle.

We should add that the applicability of the labour super-exploitation thesis to the racist oppression of African Americans is contested. For example, Cornell West (1993: 229–35) considers it one of three simplistic Marxist accounts that have in common an overemphasis on the economic and insufficient attention to culture within the totality of social relations. Against this objection, there is every reason for the recognition of labour super-exploitation to be located within a holistic methodology that includes culture and, most of all, cultures of resistance. For example, the combination of race, gender and class oppression examined by Jones and Davis provides a positive pathway to connect Marxist thought with contemporary intersectional approaches (for a review, see Carbado et al. 2013 and the section on 'Recent developments' in this chapter.)

African liberation and the fight against neocolonialism

As we have seen, the Comintern sought to position the struggle for Black liberation in the United States in the context of the worldwide struggle against colonial imperialism. That struggle for national liberation continued throughout the twentieth century, and we pick up this second thread in the genealogy of the concept once again in the struggles of African peoples for independence in their own continent.

Fanon, Lumumba, Sartre and African freedom

We start with the Algerians' national movement for liberation from French colonialism. In 1956, Jean-Paul Sartre gave a speech condemning the French occupation of Algeria, emphasizing it operated as a colonial system of exploitation. Sartre explains how the French state and its white settler colonists, by then 10 per cent of the population, had violently seized two-thirds of the land and used it for export production. The colonists received manufactured goods and luxury items from France in exchange for the foodstuffs they exported. Meanwhile the remaining one-third of the land, of poorer quality, was worked by the Algerians for their own subsistence. The labour on the occupied lands was provided by 'the former owners' who were 'exploited at starvation rates'. The effect of limited mechanization in the commercial agriculture sector was to expel workers who ended up as a 'sub-proletariat' in the cities; some of these travelled to France as migrant workers. 'For 90% of Algerians, colonial exploitation is methodical and rigorous: expelled from their lands, confined to unproductive soils, forced to work for derisory wages, the fear of unemployment discourages their revolts' (Sartre 1956).

Sartre pointed out that the social attitude of the white settlers was completely contrary to liberal democratic ideals and France's universalist claims of equality. Their condition led to a specific and deeply racist mentality: 'the colonist, whose interests are directly contrary to those of the Algerians and who can only base his super-exploitation on pure and simple oppression, can only admit these rights for himself and to enjoy them in France, among the French' (Sartre 1956). As Sartre predicted, it was the nationally oppressed and super-exploited Algerians, organized through the Front de Liberation Nationale (FLN), who fought and achieved their liberation. What then was the character of the transition and the nature of the post-independence society? Franz Fanon famously posed this question in his *Wretched of the Earth*, first published in 1961. Fanon's warning was well founded on the immediate experience of other African peoples who dared face up to the imperialist powers at the crucial moment of their independence. Would the outcome be a full independence or a disguised new (neo)colonial form of continuing exploitation and wealth extraction?

In context, the assassination of Congolese leader Patrice Lumumba that same year was a crucial event that continues to cast its shadow over Africa even to this day. Lumumba exemplified the African nationalism that refused to submit to European colonial power. His was the first of several assassinations of revolutionary African leaders, one of many dirty methods that imperialism has deployed to decapitate and defeat militant Pan-Africanism, which were similarly applied in Asia and Latin America to install neocolonial regimes. The most dramatic moment was Lumumba's Independence Day speech as the incoming prime minister on 30 June 1960, captured in the excellent film *Lumumba* by

Raul Peck. Lumumba took the podium in response to a patronizing address by King Baudouin of Belgium, who claimed that colonialism had brought civilization to the Congo and an obsequious response by President Joseph Kasa-Vubu accepting the narrative. It was then Lumumba's turn. He began by praising the liberation fighters, making clear that Congo's independence had to be fought for and was not given willingly. Lumumba summarized what colonialism meant for the Africans:

> We have experienced forced labour in exchange for pay that did not allow us to satisfy our hunger, to clothe ourselves, to have decent lodgings or to bring up our children as dearly loved ones.
>
> Morning, noon and night we were subjected to jeers, insults and blows because we were 'Negroes'. Who will ever forget that the black was addressed as 'tu', not because he was a friend, but because the polite 'vous' was reserved for the white man.
>
> We have seen our lands seized in the name of ostensibly just laws, which gave recognition only to the right of might.
>
> We have not forgotten that the law was never the same for the white and the black, that it was lenient to the ones, and cruel and inhuman to the others. (Lumumba 1960)

Lumumba signalled that the Congo's independence must be more than nominal, he wanted real change.

> Brothers, let us commence together a new struggle, a sublime struggle that will lead our country to peace, prosperity and greatness.
>
> Together we shall establish social justice and ensure for every man a fair remuneration for his labour.
>
> We shall show the world what the black man can do when working in liberty, and we shall make the Congo the pride of Africa.
>
> We shall see to it that the lands of our native country truly benefit its children (Lumumba 1960).

'A fair remuneration for his labour' was not Marxist in the literal sense, but it was an urgent demand of the oppressed African masses, and a demand that imperialism would not tolerate. Such defiance interfered with the plans for a seamless transition securing Western investment, their extensive mining interests. This could not be allowed in the heart of Africa. The United States, the United Kingdom and Belgium (with UN connivance) instigated a military coup that overthrew Lumumba, captured him and then assassinated him. The detailed account by De Witte (2001: 177–80) suggests that the United States and imperial powers were at that moment particularly concerned to avoid the mistake they made in Cuba of letting in a real revolution.

Pulling what he could from the awful wreckage of hopes brutally destroyed, the effects of which are still with Africa to this day, Sartre's essay *La pensée politique de Patrice Emery Lumumba* was first published in French as a preface to a book of Lumumba's speeches. Sartre seeks to build on the themes that Lumumba had set in motion. Sartre's language steps away from Lumumba's popular and idiomatic to the expressions of Marxist concepts, but the essential thought is kept. Unfortunately, the currently published English translation of Sartre's essay usually renders '*super-exploitation*' as just 'exploitation', thereby diminishing the crucial distinction that is being made; so I use my translation of the original French.

Sartre (1963: viii) observed that in the countryside, the African experiences 'misfortune and malnutrition, and the truth of the colonies, which was super-exploitation'. But, he argued, it was only if they got to the city and encountered Europeans would the African be confronted by their racism and the segregation in everyday life. Sartre (1963: viii) concluded from this duality that 'the exhausted, underpaid proletariat suffers much more from super-exploitation than from the racist discrimination that is its consequence'.

Sartre (1963: viii) saw in Lumumba's determination to overcome the effects of colonialism a consistent humanism that refused to accept subhuman status: 'this humanism which, in others, masks the particularity of class interests, he has made his personal passion; he devotes himself entirely to it, he wants to give the sub-humans of colonial super-exploitation their native humanity'. The foreign powers and domestic elites that collaborated to murder Lumumba had made a pact that became widely known as neocolonialism (Nkrumah 1963). Sartre (1963: xxxviii) highlighted Lumumba's rigorous rejection of the neocolonial solution, and he positioned super-exploitation as the basis of a double appropriation, with the profits shared between the two main parties: 'In this perspective, the national army, a symbol in the naive eyes of sovereignty, becomes the instrument of a double exploitation: that of the working classes by the "elite" and, through it, that of the Blacks by Western capitalism".

Sartre saw Lumumba's clear and principled stand as dispelling much of the confusion spread by the machinations and competing factions of other newly independent African states. The weakness of Lumumba's situation, his premiership only lasted three months, was matched by the clarity of his revelations. 'In fact, African nations were discovering their own destiny, the destiny of Africa in that of the Congo; neocolonial countries were deciphering the mystification which had released them from all their chains except super-exploitation' (Sartre 1963: xliii) Inspired by Lumumba's steadfast resistance and despite the terrible outcome of imperialist intervention, Sartre drew out a major point: the purpose of the imposed neocolonial settlement was to secure continued super-exploitation of the African masses. Tragically, this has without doubt continued in the Congo.

Even within Africa, the scope, form and degree of labour super-exploitation would vary from country to country.

Jaffe on South Africa as an example of the worldwide split in workers experience

Hosea Jaffe grew up in Cape Town, South Africa, where he joined the radical Non-European Unity Movement before being forced into exile in 1960. In his extensive body of writings, we encounter several parallels with Marini's contributions. The analyses are not identical, but they have a strong convergence, dealing with similar issues in the 1960s and 1970s, albeit starting from different locations.

There has been a broad ranging discussion in the literature on how to conceptualize the acutely racist system in South Africa. Certainly, the foundations of the unitary state were colonial, dating back to the seventeenth century. Then at the end of the nineteenth century, British imperialism went to war to defeat the earlier farming mode of the Dutch Boers to restructure the state and society around the requirements of the burgeoning mining industry. The outcome was a white settler deal with big business, with British interests dominating but including the Boers as junior partner, sharing in the privileges of European conquest. In 1910, the British engineered a constitution of supposed 'self-government', but South Africa was a semi-colony, a dominion within the British Empire. The terms of the deal were reset in 1948 when the Dutch descendant Boers recaptured political power, which they used to advance their sectional interests and intensify racism against the African majority even further. The uniqueness of the apartheid system of segregation, horrific as it was, is nonetheless often overstated by liberal opinion at the expense of recognizing that the principal contours of a modern racial capitalism were actually set in place by British imperialism (Terreblanche 2002: 3–21). Apartheid was an adjustment within the white minority; the core economic power remained with Anglo American corporation and connected mining houses and their financiers and was, in fact, boosted by an influx of investment from the UK and other Western countries (Higginbottom 2019).

Again, we encounter national oppression, extreme and violent, connected with abysmal pay and working conditions for the Africans. Jaffe theorized this as an acute case of labour super-exploitation. He found empirically that in the mines white 'workers', in fact foremen, were paid sixteen times more than African miners, who received just £1 a week. Jaffe (1964: 26–7) estimated that the white overseers produced no surplus value at all, that they were, in fact, receiving a portion of the surplus value produced by the African workers under their control. Jaffe (1964: 27–8) considered South Africa as a microcosm of the world capitalist system, and he gave three other examples: Chilean copper miners functioned at the same level of productivity as their US counterparts, but were paid only one-fifth of the wages; African workers constructing the Kariba dam in Zambia were paid twenty times less than Italians on the same project; the average income of Black households in the United States was one half of that of white households. Jaffe (1964: 28) concluded: 'These four illustrations are typical of the general relation between *cheap* semi-colonial labor (i.e., *super-exploitation*) and *super-profits*.'

Forced into exile, Jaffe continued to elaborate on this theme, mostly writing in Italian. In 1978, he published in Spanish *La Plusvalía Oculta: Como funciona el imperialismo* (*Hidden Surplus Value: How Imperialism Functions*), which explains how the two departments of commodity production (means of production and means of consumption) that Marx introduced in the last part of Volume 2 of *Das Kapital* are configured distinctly between the imperialist countries and the subordinated semi-colonies. In terms that mirror Marini, Jaffe found that the latter region typically produced raw materials and foodstuffs for export and imported the higher technology means of production, plus items of luxury consumption for the rich. For Jaffe, the secret of the unequal exchange between these sets of commodities on the world market was the surplus value hidden in the low prices of the exports from countries in the subordinated region (see Latimer's chapter in this volume). We thus find here again, as in Marini's contribution, a systemic analysis that remains crucially significant for today.

In a later work, Jaffe (1985: 140) pointed to the profound differences in the experiences of capitalism depending on one's location: 'The capitalist system in Africa is not the same as that in Europe: it is the hell below the European heaven.' He saw these distinct realities as fundamentally, that is, materially shaping the proletariat in the two regions, with ideological consequences for the character of Marxism. 'European Marxism . . . self-interestedly undervalued imperialism and explained world surplus value more through "productivity" in the "metropoles" than through colonial super-exploitation' (Jaffe 1985: 141). The concept of labour super-exploitation that first arose to explain the combined oppressions and especially harsh exploitation of African Americans had leapt across continents and found resonance in Southern Africa as well as Latin America.

Recent developments

This chapter has traced the connections between capitalist labour super-exploitation, colonialism and racism as they emerged and developed in twentieth-century communist thought. Now it is time to turn to the present and future, in support of the new generation of Black scholars' intent on recovering and rethinking the structural relations between racism and capitalism as well as the agency between African liberation and communism (Cha-Jua 2010; Wood 2022; Burden-Stelly 2023; Okoth 2023). I can only give a brief indication of the vitality and depth of this important contemporary literature.

Sundiata Keita Cha-Jua emphasizes the durability of '*black racial oppression*' in the United States that has persisted through three transformations in the dominant mode of racism, from slavery to sharecropping to industrialization. He notes: 'By the late 1970s, with the transformation toward global capitalism, African Americans' dominant role in the U.S. economy as a super-exploited industrial proletariat was ending. Deindustrialization, deproletarianization and their reconscription into non-unionized low paying menial jobs would come to symbolize African Americans' dominant experience in the restructured global capitalist economy' (Cha-Jua 2010: 55).

Cha-Jua identifies a 'new nadir' in the racialization of Black people from Reagan on. The neoliberal period has seen a resegregation of Black residences, state repression through huge growth in the incarceration of young Black men and, at the same time, the consolidation of a small middle-class elite. The new nadir is characterized by a race–class dynamic of incorporation on the one hand and political destabilization on the other.

These themes are picked up and developed by Augustus Wood (2022). Wood (2022: 462) conceptualizes the African American working class as a 'subproletariat: a subsection of the working class generally restricted to unstable, unskilled, low-wage, non-union, and "dirty" labor'. Building on key contributions of earlier authors, he proposes that for 'understanding the complexities of contemporary forms of anti-Black racial oppression' (Wood 2022: 462), we need to start from the conditions of Black labour. Wood argues that the neoliberal shift out of manufacturing to service jobs did not mean an end to the super-exploitation of Black workers, rather that the dual labour market structure identified by Harold Baron (1971) had shifted the terrain in which it operates. Moreover, the 'steady increase in underemployment over the last three decades' (Wood 2022: 467) has accentuated the crisis in Black communities. At the level of theory, Wood (2022: 470-7) applies the proletarianization thesis advanced by Joe Trotter (2007) and argues for a critical extension of Marx's discussion on the reserve army of labour to take racism more directly into account.

As the subtitle of her latest book *Black Scare / Red Scare* states, Charisse Burden-Stelly takes the theorization of capitalist racism in the United States seriously. It is hard to do justice to the depth and range of this comprehensive study that has the idea of violent, racialized super-exploitation and social subordination at its core. Burden-Stelly (2023: 21) frames the United States around three perspectives: US Capitalist Racist Society and Wall Street Imperialism conjoin to determine 'the Structural Location of Blackness'.

> The simultaneous reliance on the immense value extracted from Blacks and the denial of their indispensability engenders 'a sense of worthlessness and unwantedness' among Blacks and an unwarranted attitude of superiority among whites – an attitude whose material consequences emanate from a sense of white entitlement to Black production and productivity. As a result, oppression is mischaracterized as inferiority. (Burden-Stelly 2023: 22)

Blackness is an ontological political reality, in which any expression of Black radicalism is immediately sensed by the US ruling class as an existential challenge that has to be stamped out, eliminated. Burden-Stelly (2023: 160) shows that the Black Lives Matter movement against repeated police killings and the repressive narrative defining resistance as criminal is a total confrontation of the state and 'the genocidal logic of capitalist racism'.

While the recently revived extensive discussion of 'racial capitalism' lies outside the scope of this chapter, we have identified an authentic theoretical perspective that both predates and offers a different take on its significance. I broadly agree with Kevin Ochieng Okoth's insightful evaluation of Cedric Robinson's *Black Marxism*, leading to the conclusion that the racism of capitalism is both inherently connected with its colonizing and enslaving past and to its continuing imperialist character (Okoth 2023; Robinson 2000). Robinson (2000: 200) concluded from his study of Du Bois's classic *Black Reconstruction* that focused on the specifically racialized exploitation of Black labour, that 'American slavery was a *subsystem* of world capitalism'. Okoth builds on this: he assesses the 'afterlives of slavery', and he seeks to recover the legacy of African Marxists committed to national liberation struggles, which he calls 'Red Africa'. Okoth explains their negative assessment of the emptiness of neocolonialism, anticipating regimes that today preponderate in the continent. This outcome is not by accident, but the product of repeated, targeted violence by the imperialist powers. For Okoth (2023: 101–3), the return to Africa is a political call that should embrace Africa's legacy of revolutionary Black politics, recovering the footsteps of Lumumba, Fanon, Cabral, Rodney, Ngũgĩ and lesser-known African women exemplified by Maryse Condé.

This brings us to another line of discussion – that of the external movement. It is widely documented that, in the current phase of neoliberal globalization, many aspects of manufacturing production have shifted from the imperialist countries to export processing zones, to the *maquiladoras,* to China and other parts of the 'global South'. A new generation of works is now employing the concept of labour super-exploitation to explain the shifting dynamics in the world system. The contributions of Smith (2016) and Cope (2019) stand out as significant analyses in their own right and critiques of the continuing inadequacy of Eurocentric Marxism to explain, let alone confront, the new reality.

The story of the recognition of labour super-exploitation by Black and African communists has developed quite apart from Latin Americans critiquing the decline and stagnation of Eurocentric Marxism. Application of the concept of labour super-exploitation has proceeded along parallel lines without much interchange between them. In broad terms, the two strands focus on the internal and external modes of imperialism respectively. While each is necessary, there is still a need to bring them together in constructive dialogue – as links in the chain of resistance, reviving the spirit of the Comintern in contemporary conditions.

Summary and reflections

In this chapter, I have sought to recover some of the history of an idea whose genealogy had been rather unclear. We have identified some instances in the articulation of the concept that help throw new light on how it might be regarded. The survey is incomplete; even so the research has revealed some interesting political results and has also suggested a theoretical direction.

The genealogy of labour super-exploitation is the story of a prolonged battle within Marxism for the ontological recognition of the extra surplus labour produced by racism as it bears upon especially oppressed workers. The notion arose from the encounter between oppressed groups of workers and Marxist thought. Strong connections have been made between super-exploitation and the way capitalism oppresses certain groups, identified thus far by race and gender. This emphasizes that, whatever the claims of liberalism and their echo in Eurocentric Marxism, capitalism does not treat workers equally. On the contrary, as Black theorists have argued at least since W. E. B. Du Bois (1903) onwards, capitalism systematically reproduces oppressive inequalities within the working class, both within nations and across international borders. While the oppressions of race and gender are specific in their social relations, they overlap, and both have the aspect that these groups are paid less for their labour power and are correspondingly exploited more harshly through qualitatively distinct social processes and state institutions. In general, oppressed workers are paid significantly less than the established norm, that is, they receive less remuneration in exchange for their labour power. Oppressions are used to justify greater exploitation, a means of increasing surplus value (Higginbottom 2023).

The issue of labour super-exploitation had been raised from the left of the mainstream communist parties' overall trajectory. It implies a critique of narrow and overly literal interpretations of Marx that do not develop communist thought to address the reality of persistent inequalities within the working class produced by capitalism and especially by imperialism (see Latimer's chapter in this volume).

This survey suggests that the character of labour super-exploitation is more than the particularity of any one social formation; it is a general condition of the world system that can be found in different ways in all capitalist societies. Labour super-exploitation is both the strongly characteristic condition of the majority of workers in the subordinated, underdeveloped regions of the 'global South' and of oppressed sections or layers of the working class that suffer real social inequalities in the United States and other imperialist countries. Where racial or gender inequality within a society occur, the conditions of the oppressed section of workers are subject to immediate comparison with more privileged sections. Where the inequality is built into the world system through the international differences perpetuated by imperialism, the comparison is indirect, in that it is mediated through the prices of production of the commodities produced. While there are distinctions between these two broad conditions, there is nonetheless an underlying connection. Labour super-exploitation is a *relational* concept that involves the harsher exploitation of some sections of workers than the exploitation of others, not because they are less skilled or less productive but because the capitalist mode of production systemically perpetuates especially oppressive conditions against them. Labour super-exploitation is not only reproduced by imperialism but is of the essence of capitalism (Higginbottom 2020).

We have found repeated examples to show how the concept of super-exploitation is connected with the fight for liberation. The concept of the super-exploitation of oppressed workers brings their liberation struggles into the centre of Marxist theory. We need to integrate theoretically with this concept the perspective of women's oppression through unpaid or 'low paid' domestic labour as the necessary, permanent underpinning of the production of surplus value and, hence, of all capitalist social relations.

I hope that the interchange of these ideas will contribute to the rebirth of internationalism for the twenty-first century. Marini strongly theorized the capitalist international division of labour as a system based on labour super-exploitation as its fundamental condition and result. His work and that of the Latin American Marxist dependency school is not diminished by these prior expressions and rediscovered theoretical connections, rather their contribution is enhanced through moments of resonance and amplification. Beyond the scope of this chapter, there will have been similar reflections in Marxist theory of the experiences of oppressed working people across Asia. The concept of labour super-exploitation reflects on the strategic basis of a new unity between oppressed working people and their allies against the racism of capitalist imperialism in all its forms.

References

Adi, Hakim (2013), *Pan-Africanism and Communism: The Communist International, Africa and the Diaspora, 1919–1939*, London/others: Africa World Press.

Baron, Harold (1971), 'The Demand for Black Labor: Historical Notes on the Political Economy of Racism', *Radical America*, 5 (2): 1–2.

Boyce Davies, Carole (2008), *Left of Karl Marx: The Political Life of Black Communist Claudia Jones*, Durham, NC/London: Duke University Press.

Burden-Stelly, Charisse (2023), *Black Scare / Red Scare: Theorizing Capitalist Racism in the United States*, Chicago/ London: The University of Chicago Press.

Carbado, Devon, Crenshaw, Kimberlé, Mays, Vickie and Tomlinson, Barbara (2013), 'Intersectionality: Mapping the Movements of a Theory', *Du Bois Review: Social Science Research on Race*, 10 (2): 303–12. https://doi.org/10.1017/S1742058X13000349

Chapman, Frank (2021), *Marxist-Leninist Perspectives on Black Liberation and Socialism*, Minneapolis, MN: Freedom Road Socialist Organization.

Cha-Jua, Sundiata Keita (2010), 'The New Nadir: The Contemporary Black Racial Formation', *The Black Scholar*, 40 (1): 38–58.

Comintern ([1920] 1977a), *Congress of the Peoples of the East Baku, September 1920 Stenographic Report*, London: New Park. Available at https://www.marxists.org/history/international/comintern/baku/cpe-baku-pearce.pdf (Accessed: 25 March 2024).

Comintern ([1921] 1977b), 'Theses on the National and Colonial Question', in *Second Congress of the Communist International, Minutes of the Proceedings, Volume One and Two*, London: New Park. Available at https://www.marxists.org/history/international/comintern/2nd-congress/ch05.htm#v1-p177 (Accessed: 25 March 2024).

Comintern ([1928] 1987), 'The Communist International Resolution on the Negro Question', in Philip S. Foner and James S. Allen (eds), *American Communism and Black Americans: A Documentary History, 1919–1929*, 189–96, Philadelphia: Temple University Press.

Cope, Zac (2019), *The Wealth of (Some) Nations: Imperialism and the Mechanics of Value Transfer*, London: Pluto Press.

Davis, Angela (1971), 'Political Prisoners', in Davis, Angela (ed.), ([1971] 2016), *If they Come in the Morning: Voices of Resistance*, London/New York: Verso.

Davis, Angela ([1981] 1994), *Women, Race and Class*, London: The Women's Press.

De Witte, Ludo (2001), *The Assassination of Lumumba*, London/New York: Verso.

Du Bois, W.E.B. ([1903] 1996), *The Souls of Black Folk: Essays and Sketches*, New York: Dover Thrift Publications.

Foner, Philip S. and Allen, James S. (eds.) (1987), 'Introduction', in *American Communism and Black Americans: A Documentary History, 1919–1929*, vii–xvi, Philadelphia: Temple University Press.

Ford, James and Patterson, William ([1928] 1987), 'On the Question of the Work of the American Communist Party Among Negroes', in Philip S. Foner and James S. Allen (eds), *American Communism and Black Americans: A Documentary History, 1919–1929*, 166–72, Philadelphia: Temple University Press.

Haywood, Harry (1978), *Black Bolshevik: Autobiography of an Afro-American Communist*, Chicago, IL: Liberator Press.

Haywood, Harry and Howard, Milton (1932), *Lynching: A Weapon of National Oppression*, New York: International Pamphlets. Available at https://www.marxists.org/archive/haywood/1932/Lynching_H_Haywood-M_Howard-1932.pdf (Accessed: 25 March 2024).

Higginbottom, Andrew (2019), 'Anti-apartheid, Anti-capitalism, and Anti-imperialism: Liberation in South Africa', in Immanuel Ness and Zac Cope (eds), *The Palgrave Encyclopedia of Imperialism and Anti-Imperialism*, Cham: Palgrave Macmillan.

Higginbottom, Andrew (2020), 'Marx's "Capital", Labour Super-exploitation and a Fresh Take on the "Transformation Problem"'. Available at https://rdln.wordpress.com/2020/12/28/capital-vol-3-the-andy-higginbottom-lectures-series/ (Accessed: 25 March 2024).

Higginbottom, Andrew (2023), 'Superexploitation and the Imperialist Drive of Capitalism: How Marini's Dialectics of Dependency goes beyond Marx's Capital', *Monthly Review*, April: 29–53.

Huiswoud, Otto (1928), 'The Negro and the Trade Unions',*The Communist VII*, (2): 770–5.

Jaffe, Hosea (1964), *Colonialism Today*, London: Mimeo.

Jaffe, Hosea (1978), *La Plusvalía Oculta: Como Funciona el Imperialismo*, Bilbao: Zero S.A.

Jaffe, Hosea ([1985] 2017), *A History of Africa*, London: Zed Books.

Jones, Claudia (1949), *An End to the Neglect of the Problems of Negro Women*, New York: New Century Publishers. Available at https://palmm.digital.flvc.org/islandora/object/ucf%3A4865 (Accessed: 25 March 2024).

Lindsey, Lydia (2019), 'Black Lives Matter: Grace P. Campbell and Claudia Jones—An Analysis of the Negro Question, Self-Determination, Black Belt Thesis', *Africology: The Journal of Pan African Studies*, 12 (10): 110–45.

Lynn, Denise (2020), 'Deporting Black Radicalism: Claudia Jones' Deportation and Policing Blackness in the Cold War', *Twentieth Century Communism*, 18: 39–63.

Lumumba, Patrice (1960), *Speech at the Ceremony of the Proclamation of the Congo's Independence*. Available at https://www.marxists.org/subject/africa/lumumba/1960/06/independence.htm (Accessed: 25 March 2024).

Marini, Ruy Mauro (2022), *The Dialectics of Dependency*, New York: Monthly Review Press.
McKay, Claude (1919), *If We Must Die*. Available at https://www.poetryfoundation.org/poems/44694/if-we-must-die (Accessed: 25 March 2024).
McKay, Claude (1922), *Speech to the 4th Congress of the Comintern, Nov. 1922*. Available at http://www.marxisthistory.org/history/usa/groups/abb/1922/1100-mckay-cominternspeech.pdf (Accessed: 25 March 2024).
McKay, Claude ([1924] 1979), *The Negroes in America*, Port Washington / London: Kennikat Press.
Nkrumah, Kwame ([1963] 1970), *Neocolonialism: The Last Stage of Imperialism*, London: Panaf.
Okoth, Kevin Ochieng (2023), *Red Africa: Reclaiming Revolutionary Black Politics*, London/New York: Verso/Salvage.
Osorio, Jaime (2013), 'Fundamentos de la Superexplotación', *Razón y Revolución* (25): 9–34.
Puryear, Eugene (2023), 'Introduction', in 'The Black Belt Thesis Study Group' (ed.), *The Black Belt Thesis: A Reader*, xix–xxxiv, New York: 1824 Books.
Riddell, John (2011), *Black Liberation and the Communist International*. Available at https://johnriddell.com/2011/09/11/black-liberation-and-the-communist-international/ (Accessed: 25 March 2024)
Riddell, John (2018), *The Comintern's 1922 Initiative for Global Black Liberation*. Available at https://johnriddell.com/2018/05/08/the-comintens-1922-initiative-for-global-black-liberation/ (Accessed: 25 March 2024)
Riddell, John (2020), *The Baku Congress of 1920 Sounded the Call for the End of Empire*. Available at https://www.jacobinmag.com/2020/09/baku-congress-azerbaijan-1920 (Accessed: 25 March 2024)
Robinson, Cedric (2000), *Black Marxism: The Making of the Black Radical Tradition*, Second edn, Chapel Hill, NC: University of North Carolina Press.
Sartre, Jean Paul (1956), *Le Colonialisme est un Système*. Available at https://nonaumuseefasciste.wordpress.com/2013/08/08/le-colonialisme-est-un-systeme-de-jean-paul-sartre/ (Accessed: 25 March 2024).
Sartre, Jean Paul (1963), 'La Pensée Politique de Patrice Emery Lumumba', in Patrice Lumumba (ed.), *Discours de Lumumba*, iv–xlv, Bruxelles: Présence Africain.
Shiek, Andre (1928), 'The Comintern Program and the Racial Problem', in Philip S. Foner and James S. Allen (eds), (1987) *American Communism and Black Americans: A Documentary History, 1919–1929*, 164–6. Philadelphia: Temple University Press.
Smith, John (2016), *Imperialism in the Twenty First Century*, New York: Monthly Review Press.
Solomon, Mark (1998), *The Cry Was Unity: Communists and African Americans, 1917–1936*, Jackson, MS: University Press of Mississippi.

Terreblanche, Sampie (2002), *A History of Inequality in South Africa 1642–2002*, Pietermaritzberg: University of Natal Press.

Trotter, Joe W. (2007), *Black Milwaukee: The Making of an Industrial Proletariat, 1915–1945*, Urbana and Chicago: University of Illinois Press.

West, Cornel ([1993] 2009), *Keeping Faith: Philosophy and Race in America*, New York / London: Routledge.

Wood, Augustus C. (2022), 'Toward a Theory of Super-Exploitation: The Subproletariat, Harold "Hal" Baron, and the Crisis of the Political Economy of Black Labor', *Labor Studies Journal*, 47 (4): 462–87.

Zumoff, Jacob (2014), *The Communist International and US Communism, 1919–1929*, Leiden: Brill.

9

Before intersectionality

Difference, exploitation and emancipation in Ruy Mauro Marini, Walter Rodney and Andaiye[1]

Amanda Latimer

Introduction

For more than two generations, the disunity of the global working class has been one of the key factors behind the weakening of class-based politics. While in the neoliberal period, the structural roots of disunity (e.g. multiple tiers of pay, rights and security) intersect at times with vectors of oppression based on gender, race, ethnicity and nation, the embedding and leveraging of divisions within the working class has been central to strategies of capital accumulation in all moments of imperialism. In fact, during the mid-twentieth century, anti-capitalist and anti-imperialist thinkers in the Americas worked to build movements of working people that moved deliberately across the lines that had been surgically implemented in divide-and-rule policies.[2] In their theoretical work, they connected these divisions to the exploitation and super-exploitation of workers and insisted that these forms of exploitation were not deviations from the way capitalism normally develops but rather core features of the world economy. In this discussion, the periphery spoke back to the core, telling us something about the development and underdevelopment of our world from a different and particular angle.

However, the political projects that contextualized these works did not leave the particular behind. Decolonial projects in this period also begin to recover from the subjective damage left in the wake of the colonial denial of self, of full lifecycles, family and collective life outside the requirements of capital and to give what was recovered robust, life-giving political expression. These projects did not simply dwell on a race-first, class-first or even gender-first line of thought which so appeals today. What some might call 'identity politics' was not a dead end for class-based projects of liberation; rather, affirmations of the particular were necessary and generative starts to the practice of unity. While these experiments all ended in some form of defeat, the effort to give such insights political form led to some of the most exciting and innovative ways of organizing of the era.

For this reason, it is fitting to revisit a series of exceptional writers and organizers who addressed this issue during the last generation of anti-imperialist class struggle. This chapter examines the treatment of difference and division in the working class in the works of Ruy Mauro Marini (1932–97), Walter Rodney (1942–80) and Andaiye (1942–2019). A Brazilian Marxist who would pass twenty years of his adult life in exile, Ruy Mauro Marini's political life intersected with revolutionary processes in Brazil, Chile and Mexico. His theoretical work would form a major pillar of Marxist dependency theory, itself the product of intensified class struggle and a break from traditional Marxist accounts of capitalist development that emerged in the late 1960s. In *The Dialectics of Dependency*, Marini ([1973], 2022) established the contours of the specifically 'dependent' form of capitalism that arose in Latin America following independence, spurred by the very insertion of the region in the world system. Here, I draw lightly upon Marini's analysis of the ways that the international division of labour of the nineteenth century fostered disparate forms of exploitation across the global working class, which were connected through the impersonal trade relations of this period: of enhanced labour productivity in England on the one hand and of labour super-exploitation in Latin America on the other.

In June 2020, we passed the fortieth anniversary of the assassination of Guyana's 'guerrilla intellectual', Walter Rodney. The act, for which no one has been held responsible to this day, marked the abrupt start of the unwinding of the Caribbean radical tradition. Better known for works like *How Europe Underdeveloped Africa* ([1972] 2018) and *The Groundings with My Brothers* ([1969] 2019), Rodney's work as a historian of his native country challenged the notion that the racial animosity between African and Indian sections of the working class were timeless and inevitable. It did so by exposing the particular and imbricated histories of class formation of each community from a markedly Pan-Africanist and Marxist perspective. Even prior to his return to Guyana, this approach was given political expression in the Working People's Alliance (WPA), a multiracial alliance launched in 1974 to oppose the dictatorship of

Forbes Burnham. It would be another WPA leader, the radical thinker and feminist organizer Andaiye, who would take this praxis even further with Red Thread, an organization that mobilized women across racial lines against dictatorship, the effects of structural adjustment on women's waged and unwaged labour and against domestic and sexual violence. Andaiye's (Andaiye and Trotz 2020) reflections on her role in Guyanese, regional and international feminist movements have only recently become publicly available in *The Point Is to Change the World: Selected Writings of Andaiye*, edited with long-time member of Red Thread, Alissa Trotz.

While the selection of these authors may appear random, their work epitomizes the effort of the generation of 1968 to ground Marxism in the characteristics and contradictions of their particular social formations and to build a praxis of liberation on that basis. This chapter first examines the segmented formation of the working class in two nineteenth-century divisions of labour, one regional and one national, in the works of Marini and Rodney. Turning specifically to Guyana, it then explores the way that workers organized within and across difference to reach a strategic unity, as discussed by Rodney and Andaiye. In contrast to often-clumsy and disingenuous statements around identity politics by some Marxists today, these experiences indicate how difference in the (international) division of labour can become, not an obstacle to working-class unity, but the basis of solidarity in an effective fight against the race to the bottom.

Working-class formation in the imperialist division of labour

Without reducing their legacies to any one thing, Marini, Rodney and Andaiye were all engaged in attempts to make sense of their particular realities in the setting of intensified class conflict in the 1960s (Westmaas 2009; Andaiye 2020d: 247–8). Their work represented a break with the orthodox Marxist–Leninist tendencies of the day, particularly represented by communist parties, whether on the issue of class formation and exploitation or of the precise character that a socialist revolution would need to take in each setting.

In the works under discussion, both Marini and Rodney examined the tactics used to leverage greater rates of exploitation (and so, of profits) in the international division of labour at moments of systemic transition.[3] Marini's essays examine the structural drivers of super-exploitation in Brazil and Chile following the end of formal empire, whereas Rodney's work examines the same in the transition from a slave-based plantation economy to one based on wage labour and, to the extent allowed, smallholder production. It would be Andaiye whose political work and writing would add the dimension of gender to the exploration of race and class in Guyana; intersectionality in all but name, with a firm grounding in class relations.

Marini and super-exploitation in the imperialist division of labour

Marini (1973, 2022) begins his analysis of underdevelopment with the insertion of Latin America into the imperialist division of labour of the nineteenth century. He then turns to the effects of this insertion on the development of the productive apparatus in Brazil and Chile, and more particularly, the generation of a sui generis form of capitalism which he characterizes as dependent. For the author, dependency is 'understood as a relationship of subordination between formally independent nations, in which the relations of production of subordinate nations are modified or recreated to ensure the expanded reproduction of dependency' and, essentially, of value transfers to the dominant nations or metropole (Marini 2022: 117).

This characteristic emerges at a moment of transition at two nodal points in the world system. Between 1821 and 1824, Brazil transitioned from its colonial status to a form of political sovereignty, albeit one still based on oligarchical control of a racialized plantation economy powered by enslaved African labour and the export of primary goods. Industrial production in England, on the other hand, underwent a qualitative shift in the 1840s with the passage of the Factory Acts, which limited the working day to 10 hours, making it no longer legal to increase surplus value solely on the basis of a prolonged working day (i.e. by increasing absolute surplus value). For this reason, capitalism in England resorted to higher productivity in an intensified and increasingly mechanized labour process (i.e. relative surplus value). For Marx, however, this transition holds the threat of crisis, with the rate of profit tending to fall due to the relative reduction of living labour compared to the total capital advanced (1991: 317–8). In fact, Latin America's exports to England would help to mitigate this tendency in two main ways: with the provision of cheap raw materials to feed accelerating production and of cheap foodstuffs to lower the wage bill for a burgeoning industrial working class (Marini 2022: 62).

However, the trade in these commodities would have a contradictory effect on the periphery. Industrializing economies producing manufactured goods were able to 'sell [their] products at prices higher than their value, thus creating an unequal exchange' to the detriment of economies producing primary goods (Marini 2022: 128). As such, the agrarian and mercantile bourgeoisies of the latter see a drain or transfer of surplus value to their counterparts in the metropole. To offset this loss and to meet the heightened demand for its exports, Latin American bourgeoisies took recourse, not to enhancing labour productivity (mirroring their counterparts in the metropole), but to harsher exploitation. Marini conceptualizes this as super-exploitation, involving two things. First, the intensive and extensive use of labour power in a way that allows the capitalist to extract extra surplus value, rather than through the development of the worker's productive capacity as such. Second, it involves the reduction of wages to the point where they fall below the level necessary to reproduce the worker's labour power in a given time and place, even to the extent of putting the worker's longevity or lifeforce in jeopardy; something made possible in dependent export economies, where workers are not expected to act as consumers of the use values they produce (Marini 2022: 130).

This marks the beginning of a structural divergence between the English and Brazilian working class within the international division of labour. In dependent economies, super-exploitation hinders the transition to a state where the production of relative surplus value becomes generalized as it did in the metropole. For Marini, this composite mode of exploitation marked those economies based on cheap labour rather than capital investment; this is, those centred around extractive activities and plantation agriculture. He does not address the interplay of social difference within the workforce and exploitation directly,[4] but it is interesting to note the contradictions in Britain's trade relations that arise from his analysis in this moment: where, having rid itself of slave labour and entered into wage relations with racialized labour in its own colonies following Abolition in 1838, British industry nonetheless benefits and is able to advance from the proceeds of super-exploited and still-enslaved African labour in Brazil.[5]

Rodney on labour segmentation in colonial Guyana

In his final major work *A History of the Guyanese Working People, 1881-1905*,[6] Walter Rodney (1981) charts the creation of a segmented working class, beginning from the key transition cited above: the abolition of slavery as an institution in British colonial possessions, including in the former Dutch colonies of Essequibo, Berbice and Demerara, which were consolidated into the single colony of British Guiana in 1831. Rodney (1981: 96–7, 174, 187) begins by examining the constraints placed on the (enslaved) African working class, who laboured to tame the colony's beautiful but unyielding coastlands, the main setting of the colonial economy from which Indigenous peoples were programmatically displaced, other than those hired as trackers to return runaway slaves. Like Marini ([1973], 2022), Rodney (1981: 19, 217) begins by briefly considering the effects of circulation on the Caribbean's 'dependent integration into the world capitalist system' before turning to the organization of production.

Over the course of the 1820s, the planter class of British Guiana faced 'endemic slave revolts' that forced them to accept 'that slavery as a form of control over labor was proving uneconomical and unstable' (Rodney 1981: 31). Slavery was abolished in 1834 in letter alone; it was extended in practice for a further four years through the system of 'apprenticeship', which kept former slaves tied to the estates for a nominal wage. Crucially, former slaves (including women and children) began to organize against the reluctance of the planter class to accept the wage system immediately following the end of apprenticeship in 1838. Their demands for an increase to apprenticeship wages for general field and factory (i.e. sugar mills) hands were backed by work stoppages, which culminated in a strike wave among sugar workers lasting twelve to thirteen weeks in 1842 and in 1848. Rodney (1981: 33) suggests that 'less than three years after being emancipated from slavery, the new wage-earning class was acting in certain respects like a modern proletariat; and the first recorded strike in the history of the Guyanese working class was a success'.[7]

But the unfolding class struggle also took on a spatial dimension. Against the powerful opposition and machinations of the colonial legislator and planter, African 'Creoles' (enslaved Africans born in Guyana) managed to collectively secure parcels of land over the following decade, often near the estates that continued to rely on their labour – a mid-nineteenth-century undertaking to realize the self-determination, peaceful communal life and at least a partial alternative to impoverished wage labour promised by Emancipation that came to be called the 'Free Village Movement' (Rodney 1981: 42–4, 46). In this setting, Africans organized themselves into democratic village councils and task gangs in an attempt to negotiate terms for the sale of their labour power. In response, the planter class fought to maintain profits by making minimal concessions, whether in terms of productivity demands made of, or the wages paid to, people they still viewed as slaves. They used a variety of strategies to make the village economy unviable, forcing African workers to return, time and again, to the plantations: from reducing wages to reducing the legal workday, increasing the price of land and land tax rates, and limiting the medical services those taxes would pay for, and by preventing squatting, hunting and fishing on Crown lands (Rodney 1981: 31–59; Mintz 1982: 215).

It is in this very context that the first experiments in workers bound to a contract of indenture (*girmit*) took place, where workers were imported mainly from India but also intermittently from Madeira, China, Africa and elsewhere from the West Indies (Rodney 1981: 33). The first experiment with indentured 'coolie labour' was undertaken by John Gladstone, a sugar estate and slave-owner in Jamaica and Demerara (and father of British prime minister William Ewart Gladstone), financed in part by compensation he received for lost human property following Abolition ('John Gladstone' n.d.). What is important to note, however, is the year in which the experiment began: 1838, precisely the year of Emancipation. And as illustrated above, this occurred at a moment in which there was no labour shortage in the colony (Rodney 1981: 47). Rather, Indian workers were brought to aid the efforts of colonial capitalism to scupper the conscious and organized resistance of African Creoles and their efforts to exact a living wage for their labour power (Rodney 1979: 43). Despite the added costs it entailed, indentureship was also attractive to the extent that it allowed the planter class to retain control over the entire labour process (Rodney 1981: 39).[8]

What followed was the construction of a racialized division of labour between the skilled labour of the African villages and the (for now) unskilled labour of the Indian newcomers, bound to a given plantation on a five-year contract, at a statutory rate of pay of 1 shilling/day.[9] Work on the estates for both groups was divvied up and paid for by 'task': weeding, manuring, forking and more specialized skilled tasks such as reaping or cane cutting, punt-loading, 'shovel work', trench digging and dam construction. Beyond having the power to regulate the deployment of workers and their working and living conditions, it was the ability of the planter class to define the parameters of a given task, by quota or time, and the number of tasks that would be offered or withdrawn that was the source of its control over the labour process and which thus became the site of struggle with 'free' labourers. This struggle was made more difficult by the ability of indentured workers to supplement their meagre daily wage rate (described by one immigration agent as 'insufficient to support life' and even less were the worker in question a woman) with recourse to additional tasks (Rodney 1981: 33–58).

The segmented nature of the workforce allowed the planter class to work one group off against the other to the point of super-exploitation (Rodney 1981: 42–6, 58, particularly 188). Quite independent of Marini, Rodney approximates the concept of super-exploitation in his discussion of socially necessary labour time in the determination of wage rates, a calculation still informed by the echo of slavery. 'The inference is clear: planters and African villagers had conflicting appraisals of what constituted a "decent" living wage – a concept that must be based on minimum objective standards of physiological subsistence but which in the final analysis is socially, culturally, and historically determined' (Rodney 1981: 43).[10]

This tendency to push the pay or keep of both groups downwards was particularly clear to Rodney (1981: 36–7, 49) when the colony faced falling prices for its main export, sugar, in the last quarter of the nineteenth century during which planters attempted to sustain the rate of profit by driving both sections of the working class to 'the abyss of desperation'. Wage and task rates would not recover to their levels prior to the international depression once it ended in 1896 (Rodney 1981: 59).

Both Marini and Rodney attest to the inherently perverse rationality of dependent capitalism, which forgoes investment in greater labour productivity in favour of super-exploitation. For Marini ([1973] 2022), the ample supply of labour power in Latin America and the fact that workers' consumption was not required for capital realization in its export economies informed the tendency towards super-exploitation. In Guyana, African wage earners made the case for a 'more rational political economy', using the existing 'free' workforce, which would be cheaper than the import and maintenance of bonded workers (Rodney 1981: 175). In keeping with this line of argument, a more rational system might also involve investment in modern technology, with which some plantation owners did indeed experiment. Here, too, the existence of a sizeable reserve army mitigated in the other direction, towards the reproduction of cheap, super-exploited labour.

> The alternative response of mechanized agriculture (with a stable and better-paid workforce) . . . was never seriously pursued in the colony as a whole. Although factory modernization continued where possible, technological stagnation characterized the field routines – resting as they did on the basis of cheap indentured and time-expired resident immigrant gangs . . . the availability of subsidized external sources of labor simultaneously guaranteed the persistence

of backward hand-husbandry and of heavily supervised work routines associated with the plantation as a unit of production. (Rodney 1981: 59)

The political importance of *A History of the Guyanese Working People* at the time of its publication cannot be overstated. In reconstructing the dialectical history of the composition of the working class as a whole, Rodney challenged the hegemonic view that the antipathy between Guyana's two largest ethnic groups was primordial, based in deep-seated cultural differences brought by enslaved Africans and Indian *girmitiya* from their places of origin (Gutzmore 1998). Crucially, Rodney (1981: 46–7) exposes the source of openly racist beliefs regarding African labour in the reactions of the planter class to the former's efforts to exact a '"decent" or "fair" living wage', by withdrawing the supply of their labour from time-sensitive tasks (e.g. reaping at harvest) and contesting the length of the workweek or '[c]onscious of the specter of slave labor, [refusing] tasks when the conditions were particularly unpleasant'. Returning to the myth that the import of indentured workers was necessary to address a labour shortage, Rodney writes:

> Planters and their spokesmen continually asserted that Africans were unwilling to work more than two or three days per week. . . . Villagers alleged that they were perfectly willing to hire themselves throughout the week but planters refused to give them more than two or three days work. . . . Village labor could and did work steadily on the estates when the terms of work were acceptable. [However, planters] in their own class interests determined that African labor was in short supply, since it was not forthcoming on conditions judged essential for the realization of surplus value. (Rodney 1981: 46)

Rodney (1981: 151) likewise challenges the assumed docility of the Indian working population by highlighting its own struggles from 1884 to 1903, noting that 'Each day in the life of a member of the working population was a day on which there was both struggle and accommodation'.

In other words, the degree to which communal thinking became internalized by Guyana's working people was a product of bourgeois self-interest and divide-and-rule tactics.[11] By way of contrast, 'Taken in its broadest sense, the "culture" of the racial fractions of the working people included their work environment and their responses to capital at the point of production. In these critical areas, Africans and free Indians were on common ground' (Rodney 1981: 58, 179). Rodney (981: 58, 179) soberly notes that such common ground would be 'insufficiently developed to contribute decisively to solidarity' among what were essentially 'two semiautonomous sets of working class struggles against the domination of capital'. However, only rarely did this lack of unity spill into open communal violence; all the more remarkable, given the insistence on the myth of 'primordially conflict-driven' violence (Gutzmore 1998) on the basis of 'acute and absolute cultural differences coincident with race' (Rodney 1981: 58, 179).

'Yuh'all does produce surplus value': Sounding out working people on the move

This would change in the struggle for independence. In a story at once notorious for people from the Caribbean and more generally unknown, in 1953 the British government invaded the colony, suspended its new constitution and, under the cover of 'keeping the communists out', overthrew a newly-elected government following the country's first free election (Curtis 2004). Over the next decade, imperialist powers with large investments or strategic interests in the region, including Britain, the United States and Canada, would actively foster the rupture of the anti-colonial movement along ethnic lines: with the deposed Progressive People's Party (PPP), originally a multiracial party under the socialist Cheddi Jagan, coming to represent the Indian population; and the People's National Congress (PNC), a breakaway party of mainly African Guyanese, led by the co-founder of the PPP, Forbes Linden Burnham. It was only when this division had been reinforced by a system of proportional representation, described by Curtis (2004) as a constitutional coup, did Britain reinstate the constitution and allow independence to take place in 1966.

The period that followed witnessed the reification of racial politics in which the two main parties came to act as 'bases of racial self-defence' (Andaiye and Trotz 2020: 59). Two generations later, the women's collective Red Thread conducted an oral history project with survivors of the spectacular racialized and gendered violence of the era. Despite common experiences of sexual violence and displacement by women in each community, for members of that generation, the crisis continues to raise rancour and division. However, Andaiye (2020b) also recounts the formation of a new politics meant to meet this challenge in a series of organizations that provided a backbone to the ongoing mass struggle, which would go on to form a Working People's Alliance in 1974 (Westmaas 2009).

The first key formation was the African Society for Cultural Relations with Independent Africa (ASCRIA). Initially an ally of the PNC, the aims of ASCRIA 'were the defense of Africans globally, the restoration of their cultural pride, and their economic and social transformation . . . although always with a focus on the working people of the race' (Andaiye 2020b: 77). While the organization and its leadership (namely, Eusi Kwayana, a former PPP leader who briefly served as the general secretary of the PNC) sought to connect ASCRIA with the global movement for African emancipation, it also aimed to, as Kwayana said, 'defend Africans in Guyana against what it saw as a threat of "Indian domination"' (as quoted in Andaiye 2020b: 79). In the capital of Georgetown, the group led political education which made the case for 'a collectivist revolution based on African traditions and the Guyana post-1838 village movement, while in the rural interior, it established a series of autonomous cooperative settlements' (Kwayana as quoted in Andaiye 2020b: 80–1). However, ASCRIA's relationship with the Burnham regime would reach its breaking point in 1970, when the government cracked down on a strike of African mine workers at the Demerara Bauxite Company, a subsidiary of the Canadian bauxite giant ALCAN (Westmaas 2009: 117–18). In a moment in which 'Black Power became synonymous with Black workers' control' (Kwayana 2012), ASCRIA declared its break with the PNC: '*They have . . . made themselves into a class and must be attacked as a class*' (as quoted in Andaiye 2020b: 82; italics in the original).

In an exchange with Andaiye, Kwayana recalls an internal debate in which members debated 'whether the enemy of the Africans in Guyana was the European or the Indian presence' and reached the conclusion that 'a revolution of one race was not possible' (as quoted in Andaiye 2020b: 84). The group pivoted to a new tact, forcefully expressed in a call for a 'land rebellion' in 1973, one made to workers and peasants of all races. ASCRIA 'called upon African and East Indian workers and peasants to rebel against feudal-capitalism, the system by which Foreign Sugar Companies, notably [the British firm] Bookers, control the best lands of the coast, 200,000 acres, almost exactly as they did during African slavery and Indian indenture' (as quoted in Andaiye 2020b: 84). Pointing out that 'racial competition between Africans and Indians was the deliberate design of the Sugar Plantations', the organization 'demanded that to begin solving this contradiction the African and Indian workers and peasants must make a joint assault on imperialist property, beginning with unused sugar lands' (Kwayana as quoted in Andaiye 2020b: 84–5).

The response to the call was 'overwhelming', and several organizations came together to form a popular campaign around it. In addition to ASCRIA, this included Ratoon (a radical anti-imperialist group providing support for labour struggles based at the University of Guyana, of which Andaiye was herself a member), the Indian Political Revolutionary Associates (IPRA) and the Working People's Vanguard Party (WPVP) (Westmaas 2009: 112). The campaign issued a set of guidelines to help workers work through potential conflicts during the seizure of land and to help villagers establish democratic people's committees once land had been occupied (Kwayana 2012: 168–9; Andaiye 2020b: 85–6). In the end, this 'insurrection of the "landless across race"' saw some 2,000 people involved and 245 acres of land occupied (Westmaas 2009: 118). While broken up by a 'frightened state' after five weeks, the event ultimately forced the industry federation of sugar producers to turn over its unused land, not to the landless as such, but to the government.

IPRA, another key organization, was launched in 1973 to fill the need for an Indian organization independent of the PPP, which increasingly 'laboured only to harvest ethnic votes', according to founder Moses Bhagwan (as quoted in Andaiye 2020b: 87). The group also aimed to address feelings of marginalization under a government and civil service dominated by Afro-Guyanese, although this sentiment had 'to be seen too in the context of shared poverty, colonial control, the plantation system and the exploitation that dominated social existence' (Bhagwan as quoted in Andaiye 2020b: 87). Inspired by ASCRIA's cultural work, IPRA committed to working with Indo-Guyanese to instil an understanding of their own history in Guyana and to build confidence through popular education so that Indians could meet their African neighbours 'without fear or sense of inferiority or hostility' and work towards a system of shared power (Bhagwan as quoted in Andaiye 2020b: 88).

The work of ASCRIA, IPRA and others included creating vital space for each community to speak to its particular experience of the racialized violence of the early 1960s, rather than trying to bury the trauma in a premature call to unity. A popular and joint Race Commission was set up in 1972, which allowed each group to hold 'bottom-house meetings in both Indian and African villages, seeking the people's views on race relations and the possibility of non-race politics' (Westmaas 2009: 120; Andaiye 2020b: 89). Andaiye would later argue that this commission, as well as the individual organizations that it comprised, should have been maintained, particularly in light of subsequent violence in the late 1990s and early 2000s (Andaiye 2020b: 91–3).

Finally, in November 1974, the Working People's Alliance (WPA) was formed out of 'the moral and organizational strands consecrating the vision of the new politics in Guyana' (Westmaas 2009: 120). In its founding document, the WPA committed to 'teach and fight to bring about the unity of the working people – workers, employees, farmers, landless peasants, the unemployed, housewives, students, progressive professionals, working producers, small traders, craftsmen, and self-employed toilers' (WPA as quoted in Westmaas 2009: 121). It would work 'to [cross] the race divide between the Indian and African working people', while making a concerted effort to end 'the historical exclusion of Amerindians from the political process' (Andaiye 2020b: 89, 91).[12] Projecting this work into the regional sphere, the WPA committed to 'strengthen the unity of the Caribbean masses', to 'the destruction of imperialism and its neocolonial systems and for the revolutionary unity of all subject and liberated peoples' (WPA as quoted in Westmaas 2009: 106).

Andaiye returned from a period in the United States and joined the WPA Executive in January 1978 (Andaiye 2020b: 90). She notes the impact that Walter Rodney's writings and reputation had on the new politics even prior to his return home (Andaiye 2020a: 48), but it is clear that this politics was being fashioned in practice prior to his arrival. In fact, Andaiye herself argues that it was this collective work that facilitated Rodney's return to Guyana (Andaiye 2020b: 96). This trajectory also continued with the formation of the women's collective Red Thread in 1986.

Kwayana suggests that, upon his arrival, Rodney took time to sound out working people to gauge whether they were in fact ready to engage in cross-racial politics (as quoted in Andaiye 2020b: 92). According to Andaiye, Rodney's analysis changes over time.[13] Mindful that the racialized violence of the 1960s was still raw and that it had sparked 'a tremendous amount of ill-will and suspicion, on both sides', Rodney saw the need for separate organizations in this period, echoing Andaiye's assessment above (as quoted in Andaiye 2020b: 92). But '[n]either [Rodney] nor ASCRIA and IPRA were being separatist; for all of them, a major aim of separate organizing of Indians and Africans was to build mutual understanding and respect and a shared project . . . which also included Indigenous peoples' (Andaiye 2020b: 91–2). Having said that, Rodney also joined the WPA in 1974, aware 'that racial unity and effective resistance were product and producer of each other' (Andaiye 2020d: 251).

The WPA's trajectory also responded to the authoritarianism of the Burnham regime, producing results that would have been unthinkable a generation earlier. In 1973, the country witnessed a rigged election backed by the Guyanese military. A year later, attempting to build its socialist bona fides by strengthening ties to Third World socialist countries, the regime declared the 'paramountcy of the party', subjugating the state to the PNC and to the figure of Burnham (Westmaas 2009: 118–19). In response and in the very year of its creation, the WPA challenged the current state of Guyanese democracy, not by entering the electoral sphere, but by creating grassroot participatory spaces that stood in stark contrast to the centralized power of the regime. It 'offered forms of struggle against, not only the Westminster system but also the manipulation of the system', endorsing a collective approach to leadership (Westmaas 2009: 123).

In parallel, a series of new trade unions which broke from the 'weight of the racialized partisan politics' (Westmaas 2009: 117) were created, and the WPA attempted to explore the 'possibility of multiracialness' with striking workers in the bauxite sector (mainly African Guyanese in the PNC-stronghold of Linden) and sugar workers (mainly Indian Guyanese) (Andaiye 2020c: 47). However, a key moment was the campaign to defend Arnold Rampersaud, a PPP activist charged with the murder of an Afro-Guyanese policeman, John Henry (Andaiye 2020c: 45, 2020d: 247). Rodney, Kwayana and Bhagwan joined the committee and worked to mobilize a mainly Afro-Guyanese base, arguing that Rampersaud had been framed by the PNC due to his PPP membership. In one of his most important street-corner speeches,[14] Rodney argued that Afro-Guyanese people should not allow themselves to be used to further the divide-and-rule politics of the PNC government and that it was in their very self-interest not to (Andaiye 2020d; Andaiye and Trotz 2020).[15]

> I'm not rebelling just as an abstract citizen. I'm rebelling as a Guyanese with this particular heritage – as an Afro-Guyanese.... [It] is insulting to be sitting down and seeing ordinary working class or peasant black people being reduced to the level of being made toys and puppets of people who do not have their interests at heart. Whatever else we have been in our history in this country, we have been a people with dignity.... No ordinary Afro-Guyanese, no ordinary Indo-Guyanese can *today* afford to be misled by the myth of race. Time and time again it has been our undoing. Does it have anything to do with race that the cost of living far outstrips the increase in wages? (Rodney 1982: 7–8)

A father to three children of his own, Rodney's popular work as a historian also looked to influence the next generation. He began work on a series of children's books (initially, radio programmes), each of which charted the cultural heritage and journey of a given group to Guyana 'so that the children, at least, might better understand themselves and each other' (as quoted in Andaiye 2020d: 251).

Andaiye (2020d: 252) recalls that it was a project that Rodney hoped to carry out collectively and which he was determined to complete despite the 'difficult and dangerous times' in which they all lived. Two would be published posthumously by Andaiye and other members of the WPA – *Kofi Baadu Out of Africa* (1980b) and *Lakshmi Out of India* (2000) – although an additional three books were planned on the Chinese, Dutch and Portuguese journeys, in addition to a book on Indigenous history.

Repression of the WPA began in earnest during a civil uprising in 1979, whose energy met and matched state repression that started a year earlier. It is clear from Andaiye's (2020a) writing that it was this effort to organize across the forcefully hewn fragments of the working class, and not the purported intention to form a political party and contest the Burnham regime in the electoral sphere,[16] which made the WPA a perceived threat, as unity had been a threat to British and US imperialism a generation before (2020a). Two WPA activists, Oheme Koama and Edward Dublin, would be killed by security forces, and its supporters regularly dismissed, arrested, beaten and jailed (Andaiye 2020: 54–5; 2020b: 93). Rodney and two other members of the WPA Executive (Omowale and Rupert Roopnaraine) were accused of setting fire to key PNC buildings during the uprising in July; a charge of which they were later acquitted. The process would culminate in the assassination of Walter Rodney on 13 June 1980 by an operative of the Burnham regime; a fact confirmed by a Commission of Inquiry in 2016.[17] While the work of the WPA continued following Rodney's murder, the act brought to a close this period of racial unity (Andaiye 2000: 60).

Picking up the threads: Andaiye, Red Thread and cross-racial feminist praxis

Despite these blows, the early 1980s sees a new dynamism in the regional women's movement (Andaiye 2020d: 247; Westmaas 2009: 123). Previous women's organizations had formed mostly as side projects of political parties or trade unions. However, Red Thread, an organization that Andaiye would co-found with six other WPA organizers in 1986, took its start in a series of concrete projects aimed at addressing women's need for food and income. Following the start of the Third World debt crisis in 1982, the Burnham regime placed an abrupt ban on the import of staple foods. This provoked a rebellion consisting of mass protests and the eruption of petty commodity trading (now illegal), both of which were led by housewives (Andaiye 2000: 55). In response, Andaiye and other WPA women took the decision to organize with women outside of the party, and again across racial lines, forming a 'Sugar and Bauxite Workers Unity Committee' which would give shape to the rebellion from 1982 to 1983.

In its early years, Red Thread focused on income generation in rural villages and semi-urban communities. The group conducted popular education with working-class women who were openly fed up with Guyana's party politics and involved a deliberate effort to bring their leadership to the fore. It conducted participatory forms of research designed to help women cope with the fallout of structural adjustment policies and a collapsing economy (Kempadoo 2013). The group's experience resonated with organizations elsewhere in the region which found 'no space for gender in the party's preoccupation of "class", race sometimes – and in Guyana's case, always, but not gender' (Andaiye 2000: 56). Similar to the WPA, Red Thread organized deliberately across racial lines, connecting with local organizers throughout the country, including Indigenous women in the interior (Kempadoo 2013: 2). Andaiye poignantly notes that, with the scattering of families to more ethnically homogeneous communities for self-protection following the violence of the 1960s, women from a given ethnicity were no longer familiar with how the other lived as people had been when she was growing up (Kempadoo 2013: 6). Projects that aimed to help working women meet their daily needs also became opportunities for them to 'tell the stories of their work and culture . . . the why of your experience – the overwork, the violence, the no money, the family stress and conflict' (Kempadoo 2013: 2–3) – to women experiencing the same thing in nearby communities. From 1982 onwards, Red Thread joined the International Campaign for Wages for Housework (and subsequently, Global Women's Strike), whose approach to 'counting' and valuing women's particularly unpaid labour also shaped their grassroots work. Andaiye said:

> What happened first with Red Thread was that when I told the working-class women – I used the phrase that came from [Selma] James – that housework was the production and reproduction of labour power, I was about to explain what that meant when their faces lit up. And the thing that came to my mind was Walter Rodney once telling me that over and over again he had taught students at university level the Marxist principle that workers produce surplus value, and they would take one month, two months, three months, four to understand this. Then he went to Linden [the bauxite mining town in Guyana] and he said basically, 'Yuh'all does produce surplus value' and he said the response was 'Yes, right. Next' – meaning that what he had done was to uncover a fundamental

truth about their lives, which they therefore 'knew' at some deep level – and that's the response I got from Red Thread when I said that they produced and reproduced labour power. They really understood it. (as quoted in Kempadoo 2013: 4)

The thread of praxis that Red Thread would recover from the experience both of the WPA and of its constituent entities was a trust in working people and their understanding of their economic condition and role. Nonetheless, despite their successes, Andaiye's (2020c) writing is also critical of the power dynamics that would come to characterize Red Thread (and more broadly, regional feminist organizations) in the 1990s, with the dying down of grassroots women's mobilization, the neoliberal capture of the feminist movement through NGO-ization, the turn towards service provision and the preference for middle class, urban women as interlocutors by the state and aid agencies.

Conclusion

From where I write in the Global North, the connections between decolonizing projects today (largely limited to academic settings and to questions of the equitable representation of racialized and gendered minorities, among others, in hiring and curriculum)[18] and the kind of struggles under discussion are vague, and perhaps posing questions of difference and working-class unity to the contemporary discussion is unfair. However, it is fair to ask after the class and material content of current projects, particularly in the metropolitan and still-imperialist centres of the world system. Decolonial efforts in the metropole often rely on a notion of intersectionality from the 'post' moment of the 1990s, which may or may not recognize class as a key vector or, to be more demanding still, class reckoned and reproduced across national boundaries. The relationships of the decolonizing university to the material conditions of everyday people, and to internationalism as a material strategy, are also missing. The very question of anti-capitalism seems to be a non-starter in a discourse captured by neoliberal nihilism, despite regular economic crises and the increasing precarity of the planet's life-sustaining processes. With all this in mind, it might be more fitting to declare this to be the second coming of the postcolonial moment of the 1980s, which also dwelled on unpacking colonial ways of producing knowledge, subjectivities and representation while maintaining a tenuous relationship to anti-systemic movements. Meanwhile, the relationship between the debate on university campuses and movements actively combatting the colonial afterlife of dispossession and land theft, gender-based violence, femicide and violence against gender-non-conforming folk, racialized state violence, the outsourcing of emissions and dirty industries, and – my particular interest here – the race to the bottom between workers has yet to be defined.

Reflecting on the works discussed in this chapter, I argue that theoretical framings of the race to the bottom[19] and histories of struggle to combat the phenomenon radiating from the periphery offer general lessons for class-based organizing in a decolonial and anti-capitalist way. These authors drew attention to the division and ordering of workers in international, racialized and gendered divisions of labour to exert greater rates of exploitation; and particularly so at moments of systemic transition, be it Abolition and the shift to a waged but still racialized workforce, or independence and the shift to neocolonial and dependent relations.

In Guyana, this process led to a new pattern of racial conflict, in which 'cultural differences were easily transformed into hostilities at some times, in a situation almost designed to make possible the pitting of groups against each other under conditions of genuine want and suffering. The success of the planters in dividing the Guyanese people lives on' (Mintz 1982: 222–3). The strength (and legacy) of *A History of the Guyanese Working People* is how Rodney captured the dialectic between 'the class nature of Guyanese resistance to the plantation system' and the particular material bases of race in the same setting; in the very first instance, for example, the system of Indian indenture could not and cannot be equated with the African experience of chattel slavery and its afterlife (cf. Rodney 1981: 39).

And yet, Rodney was also at pains to show that 'in the worst of times there is resistance, even when hidden. . . . Much of his digging into old documents in archives and in people's homes was aimed at finding the invisible makers of history' (Andaiye 2020d: 250). This formative tension in Guyana's dependent economy, in turn, gave rise to a new politics to meet the challenge: autonomous organizations, particularly of the Afro-Guyanese working class, but also tactical alliances between sections of the class to oppose exploitation, dictatorship, neocolonialism and, into the 1980s, gendered exploitation and super-exploitation. Rather than an ideological obstruction to class unity, the race–class–gender nexus here was structural, something to be worked through strategically by working people. Arguably, it was the promise of the new politics that led to the repression of the WPA as a movement and the assassination of Walter Rodney.

Turning back to Marini, while little of his theoretical work speaks directly to the implications of labour segmentation for organizing, one of his final essays notes the generalization of labour super-exploitation the world over under neoliberal globalization, in which the law of value itself has become globalized (Marini 1997). He highlights the recourse to technological innovation to increase productivity and to super-exploitation through the intensification of labour in global production chains, both in service of the hunt for permanent sources of extraordinary surplus value and profit. Without using the phrase, he argues that this process will only intensify a race to the bottom within the global working class; one that can only be challenged through the unification of workers' struggles across the boundary of those in work and those unemployed, as well as across national boundaries, across national boundaries, 'putting in march a radical democratic revolution' (Marini 1997: 268).

The charge may be that the politics discussed here is an older approach that, with the neoliberal counterrevolution, simply failed. However, the degree to which the world has changed from the period in which Marini, Rodney and Andaiye were writing has been overstated, in my view, by a decolonial politics fitted to a lower political horizon which simply elides issues of division, the crisis of labour, social reproduction and planetary stability in favour of relatively easier issues that do not threaten to upset the balance. We could do worse than to return to a generation that faced these issues head on.

Notes

1 A preliminary version of this chapter was delivered at the *Ninth Annual Historical Materialism Conference*, London, on 8 November 2012, as part of the Marxism and the Challenges of the Third World panel, organized by Radha D'Souza. I thank Radha for her patience, then and now. I'm also deeply grateful to Matthew Quest, Peter Hallward, Cecil Gutzmore, Ruben Martins and Andy Higginbottom for their insights on the draft.
2 The same problematic was being worked through in the struggles and writings of Indigenous and Black (and often Marxist) feminists generations before in North America and the UK (Bhandar and Ziadah 2020; see also Higginbottom's chapter in this volume).

3 Rodney's analysis of Guyana clearly builds on his earlier works on capitalist exploitation using slavery, colonialism and neocolonialism, which illustrate the super-exploitation of African labour, whether or not the term is explicitly used (1971, 1980a, 2012). Thanks to Cecil Gutzmore for raising this point.
4 Marini elides gendered exploitation in the context of both waged and unwaged work, which should be a major theme in the analysis of social reproduction where wages are paid below their value, adding pressure to the tasks of social reproduction in the non-waged sphere. However, this line would be developed by his colleague, Vânia Bambirra (Bambirra 1972).
5 This is only one vector of trade, production and dependency in a complex international division of labour centred around the British Empire that has yet to be mapped in its entirety. Such a research agenda would need to overcome characterizations of the British Empire as having developed in a haphazard, disconnected way (e.g. 'respond[ing] to diverse motives and interests') which treats formal empire (such as in the Caribbean) separately from informal (such as Britain's relations with a variety of new sovereign states of Latin America) in the nineteenth century (Knight 1999: 124). A good place to begin might be an effort to re-examine dynamics between the systems of trade, finance, productive investment, labour control and exploitation in colonies like Guyana and dependent economies like Brazil, as captured by Marini (1973, 2022) and Rodney (1981).
6 Published through the efforts of Andaiye following his assassination in 1981.
7 In an otherwise glowing review, Sidney Mintz (1982) challenges Rodney's thesis that the formerly enslaved became a 'rural proletariat' immediately following Abolition; a position that mirrors that of C. L. R. James (Cecil Gutzmore, *personal comment*, 22 September 2023). Mintz cites the efforts of planters to destroy the conditions for an autonomous village economy, all the while relying on the village production of 'ground provisions' to subsidize social reproduction, and, instead, suggests that Africans pursued a variety of 'contrastive adaptations' better characterized as an overlap between wage labour and smallholder (peasant) production (1982: 216).
8 Mintz astutely observes that, from the moment of Abolition, the colony's 'entrenched planter class faced the future concerned above all with labor – or, better said, with the price of labor. Such preoccupations have never ended in Guiana . . . a delusion that the availability of labor should not be related to its cost' (Mintz 1982: 211).
9 Eventually, a third grouping of time-expired immigrants developed, of former indentured workers who created their own 'independent task gangs' in the late nineteenth century and, when inevitably faced with the same discrimination and

exploitation as African villagers, escalated their resistance (Rodney 1981: 34, 51–3, 178).

10 It is also worth noting the observations of Chief Justice Joseph Beaumont with respect to the backbreaking labour – and systemic underpayment – of the African shovelmen of the colony; in other words, their super-exploitation. 'We have [in England] no excavating work so heavy as trench digging in Demerara and if the reader were to see a stalwart negro. . . . I venture to think he would not only wonder at but admire . . . the "lazy nigger"' (1871, in Mintz 1982). Mintz continues, 'Beaumont estimated that the work done by a Guyanese shovelman in one day paid one-fourth what it would have earned an English laborer – and "the best English laborer" would have needed two to three days to complete the job the Guyanese did in one' (Mintz 1982: 210–11).

11 Note, I'm referring to specific discourses regarding the relative compliance and productivity of each group that served to naturalize competition between them and which averted attention away from the group that this competition ultimately served, rather than the considerable work of cultural self-recovery, healing and community building that decolonization meant for each, epitomized by revolutionary Pan-Africanism and feminism, embodied by Rodney and Andaiye's praxis, respectively.

12 While calls to support Amerindian communities in their struggles against capitalist depredations predate 1974, it is not clear whether an autonomous and oppositional organization *of* Indigenous peoples existed along the lines of ASCRIA and IPRA. However, the intention to include Indigenous communities in the new politics is clear. In 1976, the WPA broadsheet *Dayclean* called out the seizure of Akawaio land for the construction of a hydroelectric dam by the PNC government.

> If we accept the flooding and dispossession of the Akawaio, we will become accomplices to Genocide. . . . For us, it is not simply a question of helping others. It is our own self-interest. In the first place, the Amerindians are part of the working population of this country; and in the second place, we must combat dictatorship and socially negative politics so as to lay down a firm, principled line for future socialist reconstruction. ('PNC-State vs Amerindians' 1976)

13 In a broader context, this topic flows through Rodney's work on Black Power in the Caribbean in *The Groundings with My Brothers* (1969, reissued by Verso in 2019), which maintains a dialectical tension between African identity and revolutionary Pan-Africanism, and, second, 'Black' as an oppositional category in a tactical sense, which included Indian and African sections of the working class in their joint confrontation with neocolonial capital in this period (Andaiye 2020b: 77–9;

Andaiye 2020d: 246). In Guyana, this position was represented by Ratoon and underscored a tense exchange between its members and Kwame Ture during his visit to the University of Guyana in the late 1960s (Andaiye 2020b: 78, 95; Westmaas 2009: 112–13).

14. Email communication, Alissa Trotz, 6 December 2020. See also Andaiye 2020d.
15. Matthew Quest argues that the pamphlet is also significant insofar as it marks the first time that Rodney clearly advocates for workers' self-emancipation and self-management in Guyana, where the 'power of workers beyond just producing surplus value' becomes clear in his thought (personal communication, 11 October 2021).
16. They would only do so in 1979, with the issue of the programme *Towards a Revolutionary Socialist Guyana*. Even then, the group always 'functioned more like a movement' (Andaiye as quoted in Kempadoo 2013: 16).
17. See Walter Rodney Foundation, 'Report: The Commission of Inquiry on the Death of Walter Rodney' (2016).
18. A point made by Adrija Dey during the online workshop, Decolonising Then and Now, 30 April 2021.
19. Captured in Marx's chapter on the general law of accumulation (Marx 1976).

References

Andaiye (2000), 'The Red Thread Story', in Suzanne Francis Brown (ed.), *Spitting in the Wind: Lessons in Empowerment from the Caribbean*, 51–98, Kingston: Ian Randle.

Andaiye (2020a), 'Conversations about Organizing: Revised Excerpts from an Interview with Andaiye by David Scott [2004]', in Alissa Trotz (ed.), *The Point is to Change the World*, 47–57, London: Pluto.

Andaiye (2020b), 'Organizing within and against Race Divides: Lessons from Guyana's African Society for Cultural Relations with Independent Africa, Indian Political Revolutionary Associates, and the Early Working People's Alliance [2008, 2017/2018]', in Alissa Trotz (ed.), *The Point Is to Change the World*, 77–97, London: Pluto.

Andaiye (2020c), 'The Grenada Revolution, the Caribbean Left, and the Regional Women's Movement: Preliminary Notes on One Journey [2010]', in Alissa Trotz (ed.), *The Point is to Change the World*, 37–46, London: Pluto.

Andaiye (2020d), 'Last Word: Walter Rodney's Last Writing on and for the Guyanese Working People [2010]', in Alissa Trotz (ed.), *The Point is to Change the World*, 246–53, London: Pluto.

Andaiye and Trotz, Alissa (2020), '1964: The Rupture of Neighborliness and its Legacy for Indian/African Relations [2008; 2018]', in A. Trotz (ed.), *The Point is to Change the World*, 58–76, London: Pluto.

Bambirra, Vânia (1972), 'Women's Liberation and Class Struggle', Translated by Krebs, Leslie and Bayer, Barbara, *Review of Radical Political Economics,* 4 (3): 75–84.

Bhandar, Brenna and Ziadah, Rafeef, eds. (2020), *Revolutionary Feminisms,* London: Verso.

Curtis, Mark (2004), 'The intervention in British Guiana, 1953', in *Unpeople: Britain's Secret Human Rights Abuses,* London: Vintage.

Gutzmore, Cecil (1998), 'Of Nile and Ganges, Thames and Berbice: On Walter Rodney's Explanation of Violent Conflict in the Encounter between Africa's and Asia's Diasporas', in *International Conference, African Diaspora Studies: on the Eve of the 21st Century,* 30 April–2 May, University of California at Berkeley. Unpublished.

'John Gladstone' (n.d.), *Legacies of British Slavery Database,* UCL History Department. http://wwwdepts-live.ucl.ac.uk/lbs/person/view/8961 (Accessed: 26 August 2021).

Kempadoo, Kamala (2013), 'Red Thread's Research: An Interview with Andaiye', *Caribbean Review of Gender Studies,* 7: 1–17.

Knight, Alan (1999), 'Britain and Latin America', in A. Porter (ed.), *The Oxford History of the British Empire Volume 3, The Nineteenth Century,* 122–45, Oxford: Oxford University Press.

Kwayana, Eusi (2012), *The Bauxite Strike and the Old Politics,* ed. Matthew Quest, Atlanta: On Our Own Authority!

Marini, Ruy Mauro (1973), *Dialéctica de la dependencia,* Mexico City, DF: Ediciones Era.

Marini, Ruy Mauro (1997), 'Proceso y tendencias de la globalización capitalista', in Carlos Eduardo Martins (ed.), *América Latina, dependencia y globalización. Fundamentos conceptuales Ruy Mauro Marini. 2ª edición,* 247–71, Bogotá, Colombia: CLACSO y Siglo del Hombre Editores.

Marini, Ruy Mauro (2022), *The Dialectics of Dependency,* ed. Amanda Latimer and Jaime Osorio, trans. Amanda Latimer, New York: Monthly Review Press.

Marx, Karl (1976), *Capital Volume I,* London: Penguin.

Marx, Karl (1991), *Capital Volume III,* London: Penguin.

Mintz, Sidney (1982), 'Descrying the Peasantry', *Review* (Fernand Braudel Center), 6 (2): 209–25.

'PNC-State vs Amerindians' (1976), *Caribbean Dialogue,* 2 (2): 6–7.

Report: Commission of Inquiry on the Death of Walter Rodney (2016), Available at https://www.walterrodneyfoundation.org/coi/report-the-commission-of-inquiry-on-the-death-of-walter-rodney-february-2016 (Accessed: 24 May 2024).

Rodney, Walter (1971), 'Some Implications of the Question of Disengagement from Imperialism', in Issa G. Shivji (ed.), *The Silent Class Struggle,* 61–9, Dar es Salaam: Tanzania Publishing House.

Rodney, Walter (1979), *People's Power, No Dictator,* Georgetown: Working People's Alliance.

Rodney, Walter (1980a), 'Class Contradictions in Tanzania', in Haroub Othman (ed.), *The State in Tanzania: A Selection of Articles*, 18–41, Dar es Salaam: Dar es Salaam University Press.

Rodney, Walter (1980b), *Kofi Baadu – Out of Africa*, Georgetown: Guyana National Lithographic Co.

Rodney, Walter (1981), *A History of the Guyanese Working People, 1881–1905*, London: Johns Hopkins University Press.

Rodney, Walter (1982), 'In Defence of Arnold Rampersaud', Georgetown: Working People's Alliance [Pamphlet].

Rodney, Walter (2000), *Lakshmi – Out of India*, Georgetown: Guyana Book Foundation.

Rodney, Walter ([1972] 2018), *How Europe Underdeveloped Africa*, London: Verso.

Rodney, Walter ([1969] 2019), *The Groundings with My Brothers*, London: Verso.

Westmaas, Nigel (2009), '1968 and the Social and Political Foundations and Impact of the "New Politics" in Guyana', *Caribbean Studies*, 37 (2): 105–32.

10

From statehood to democratic confederalism

Decolonization and Abdullah Öcalan's solution to the Kurdish question

Behnam Amini

Introduction

The Kurdish question is widely known, inside and outside Kurdistan, to signify the national oppression of the Kurds as a nation (Chaliand 1980; Olson 1989; Hassanpour 1992; McDowall 1992). This perception took on a new dimension in the 1970s when the founders of Partîya Karkerên Kurdistanê (the PKK: the Kurdistan Workers Party) explained the Kurdish question as a case of colonization (PKK 1978). Since then, the PKK and its leader, Abdullah Öcalan, have maintained this interpretation of the Kurdish question. However, their views on decolonization have changed dramatically. Öcalan's new conception of liberation is built upon the understanding that hierarchy and domination are the root causes of oppression and inequality; therefore, liberation is realized through establishing non-hierarchical and democratic structures and relations in human societies. Thus, Öcalan's theory of democratic confederalism explains liberation, that is, decolonization, of the Kurds and other oppressed nations in terms of gradual disappearance of capitalist modernity and the nation state as well as decolonizing the concept of the nation. The novelty of Öcalan's democratic confederalism is most evident in his attempt at redefining the nation and presenting the idea of the democratic nation. In fact, Öcalan's notion of the democratic nation offers a decolonized conception of the nation that dissociates the nation from political identification with ethnicity or any other cultural and ideological entities and, instead, argues for a nation that weaves people together through forming democratic and autonomous social and political institutions. In other words, people in the democratic nation become a nation because of their association with autonomous self-organization as opposed to the nation state where a nation is defined in terms of ethnic and/or religious identifications. This is different from, and in some ways in contrast with, the position of the PKK leadership and Öcalan before the 2000s when they had defined decolonization as forming a national and independent Kurdish state.

In what follows, I begin by briefly elucidating the concept of colonialism, followed by a discussion of the historical events and actors shaping the colonization of Kurdistan. This is followed by a discussion of Öcalan's account of colonialism in Kurdistan. Then Öcalan's earlier and recent conceptions of decolonization are compared and the reasons for the changes in Öcalan's thoughts on liberation and decolonization are discussed. And finally, I contextualize the notions of democratic confederalism and democratic nation in the recent debates on decolonization as well as on the nation state and its relationship with colonialism. This section will also include a critical assessment of theoretical and practical limitations of Öcalan's theory.

Colonialism: A conceptual clarification

Colonialism in Kurdistan, or the land of the Kurds, has been marked by a double colonization, signifying the role of both Western and regional powers in colonizing the Kurdish people. The recognition of Western as well as non-Western colonizers indicates a certain understanding of colonialism that differs qualitatively from culturalist approaches to the question of colonialism. For culturalist scholars of postcolonial studies (Said 1979; Mohanty 1984), it is not certain socio-economic conditions and social relations but rather the agents that primarily define colonialism. This agent is not referred to as a specific social class or group, for example, bourgeoisie, but a dematerialized and ideological entity called the 'West'. This implies that colonization intrinsically belongs to Western thought and practice and renders colonial agency ontologically exclusive to white Western people (Lazarus 2004: 54–8). The materialist approach, however, views colonialism as a certain type of social and political relations. This means that it is colonial relations rather than geographical or national qualities of the agents that define colonialism.

Thus, adopting a materialist approach, colonialism can be defined as a relation of domination which is exploitative by nature and denies self-rule to the colonized. Colonialism in effect creates hierarchical relations that put the colonized, their belongings and resources, and generally their existence, at the service of colonizers. In other words, colonies and the colonized people are after all nothing but instruments for the material prosperity and political superiority of the colonizers. Also, racism functions as the cultural foundation of colonialism as it asserts the superiority of colonizers over the colonized by establishing essentialized and normatively hierarchized differences between them. Defined in these terms, it applies to the modern or post-Renaissance practices of colonialism that differ qualitatively from pre-modern instances where some earlier empires and civilizations had colonies that were perceived inferior to the metropoles (Ashcroft, Griffiths and Tiffin 2007: 40). One crucial factor in distinguishing modern colonialism is its decisive and systematic role in the creation and development of capitalism, particularly by providing raw materials, slaves and indentured labor for the expansion of industries in Europe, as well as creating external markets for the sale of goods made in the colonial metropoles (Loomba 2005: 9).

Colonization of Kurdistan

The first partition of Kurdistan took place long before the First World War when in 1514 it was divided between the Ottoman Empire and Iranian Safavid dynasty. Until late nineteenth century when centralizing and Westernizing policies were put in practice, Kurds enjoyed a significant level of autonomy in both Iranian and Ottoman empires. Several Kurdish emirates and principalities ran the affairs of Kurdish areas, and the Kurdish local rulers had immense control over the territories they ruled (Yadirgi 2017: 94). The years immediately following the First World War witnessed the disintegration of the Ottoman Empire and the division of its colonies. This division was planned by the Allied powers throughout the course of the First World War and afterwards, and stipulated in several agreements and treaties, most notably the Sykes–Picot agreement in 1916. According to this agreement, which was signed by the British diplomat Mark Sykes and the French diplomat François Georges-Picot, the Ottoman Empire was divided as spheres of influence and control between Britain, France, Tsarist Russia, Greece and Italy (McDowell 2007: 115). After the war, Britain and France promised the Kurds an autonomous and eventually independent Kurdistan as per Articles 62 to 64 of the Treaty of Sèvres in 1920 (McDowell 2007: 137). However, hopes for an independent Kurdistan were dashed as Britain and France reneged on their promise during the Lausanne conference in 1923 to appease Turkey, whose troops were progressively advancing towards the frontiers of British and French spheres of influence in the region. It is important to note that the British grand strategy in the region aimed at isolating Bolshevik Russia and, thus, made cooperation with Turkey through conceding Northern Kurdistan indispensable. Turkey was keen on reclaiming the whole Ottoman Kurdistan, but Southern and Western Kurdistan were put under British and French mandates, respectively, since a powerful Turkey could inflame anti-British sentiments among Muslim populations of the region (Ali 1997: 523). Therefore, in the years after the First World War, Kurdistan was once again partitioned, and the lands of the Kurds, once under the sovereignty of the Ottoman Empire, were eventually split among the newly established nation states of Turkey, Iraq and Syria while Iran kept its part (Ghassemlou 1980). The political and social status of the Kurds changed drastically thereafter, and, unlike their situation under the Ottoman Empire and various Iranian dynasties, the Kurds were not only stripped of their local autonomy, hence having their natural and human resources exploited and instrumentalized by the centre, but also subjected to cultural racism and forced assimilation (Yildiz 2005; Vali 2011; Yadirgi 2017).

Initial reactions of the Kurds to the new political order of things were mixed but altogether marked by the lack of unity, tribal rivalries and religious sectarianism (McDowall 2007). A number of rebellions against the mandates transpired, including the revolt of Sheikh Mahmoud Barzanji against the British mandate in Southern Kurdistan during the 1920s and the Murud movement (1933–40) against the French mandate in Western Kurdistan (Yildiz 2005; Tejel 2009). Nevertheless, refusing Arab rule and calling for local autonomy, many Kurdish leaders in Western and Southern Kurdistan (Syria and Iraq) embraced French and British mandates, respectively. In Northern Kurdistan (Turkey), the pan-Islamic propaganda of Turkish nationalists had attracted the majority of Kurds in wars of independence (1919–23) against Greek and Armenian non-Muslims, but national chauvinistic policies and practices of the Kemalist state following the establishment of the Republic of Turkey provoked several Kurdish uprisings in the interwar period, most prominently Sheikh Said's revolt in 1925 and the Ararat rebellion (1927–31). Eastern Kurdistan (Iran) was not affected by the designs of the Sykes–Picot agreement and the post-war developments, but even there the centralizing and national chauvinistic efforts of Reza Shah's government faced opposition from some Kurdish tribal chiefs among whom Ismail Agha Simko was the fiercest (McDowall 2007).

Since the interwar period, Kurdish movements and struggles for self-rule have often articulated their demands in nationalist terms, fighting for Kurdish statehood or Kurdish autonomy. In other words, the Kurdish question or the oppression of the Kurds within the four modern nation states of Iran, Iraq, Syria and Turkey has largely been framed as a political issue of denying a nation or national minority of its right to form its own state. Prior to 1970s, this formulation was inspired by and in line with national liberation struggles in other parts of the world. In the 1970s Turkey, a group of Kurdish and Turkish leftists called Kurdistan Revolutionaries, who later formed the PKK, began to see Kurdish oppression as a case of colonialism. This understanding of the Kurdish question dramatically impacted the ways in which the oppression of the Kurds was conceptualized within the Kurdish movements: it pivoted from an issue of political oppression to colonization of Kurdistan. Although there are a few other writings and analyses of colonization of Kurdistan (Kivilcimli 1979; Ghassemlou 1996; Beşikçi 2015), Öcalan and the PKK are the main representatives in this pivot.

Young Öcalan and colonization of Kurdistan

Öcalan's account of colonization of Kurdistan first appeared in *Kürdistan Devriminin Yolu* (The Road to the Kurdistan Revolution or *The PKK's Manifesto*), one of the founding documents of the PKK. This manifesto contains Öcalan's and the PKK's analysis of Kurdish oppression and details how to overthrow it. *The PKK's Manifesto* was also a reaction to the Turkish Left's dogmatic position on the Kurdish question. As late as the 1970s, the Turkish Left considered the national oppression of Kurds and Armenians as secondary to the fight against Western imperialism. In that light, they viewed the Turkish bourgeoisie and Kemalism as anti-imperialist cornerstones. While recognizing the Kurdish people as oppressed, this oppression was construed not in national and racial terms but in class terms. Therefore, Kurds were oppressed as peasants and workers just like their Turkish counterparts. Apart from Hikmet Kivilcimli (1979), a prominent Turkish communist, the Turkish Left at that time generally refused to acknowledge the colonial character of the Kurdish question since they associated colonialism exclusively with outside imperialist forces. For the Left, Turkey was a semi-colony of larger global capitalist forces and as such could not be a colonizer itself (Jongerden and Akkaya 2012: 7).

In *The PKK's Manifesto*, Öcalan explicitly defines the situation of Kurdistan as a colonial situation and refers to Kurdistan as a divided colony. Öcalan states that 'The history of Kurdistan from its division into four parts until today is characterized by occupation, massacre and plunder on each part. It is nothing but the history of colonialism carried out' (PKK 1978: 29). Öcalan recognizes that the Kurds have been subjugated by different forces throughout history: the Persian and Roman empires in antiquity as well as the Arab Muslims to maintain other slave and feudal social formations. But he is primarily concerned with the current form of subjugation which, contrary to its historical predecessors, takes on an 'imperialist-colonial' form maintained by modern capitalist structures (PKK 1978: 49).

Öcalan traces the roots of Kurdish colonization within the Ottoman Empire and, more notably, in the early efforts among the Turkish bureaucratic bourgeoisie and intellectuals to assert Turkish national independence in the late nineteenth century. As these classes witnessed the Empire's compounding military defeats and successive losses of land, they anticipated its inevitable decline and took the opportunity to formulate the earliest ideas of Turkish independence by defining a Turkish homeland and drawing up its potential boundaries. Therefore, the Committee of Union and Progress (CUP), backed by the Turkish bourgeoisie, in its attempts to define and form a Turkish nation in the remaining lands of the empire, began to formulate a racist and chauvinist Turkish nationalism inspired by the idea of Turanism – the notion of ethnic unity of Ural–Altaic peoples mostly populating Central Asia. After the First World War and during the disintegration of the Ottoman Empire, under the leadership of Mustafa Kemal Ataturk and with a Kemalist nationalist ideology, the political programme of CUP was pursued with greater vigor. With resistance against a decaying Ottoman Empire and the wars against Greeks and the British, Kemalists portrayed themselves as part of a greater Turkish nationalist movement (PKK 1978: 29). But as Öcalan points out, Kemalism showed its true colours after the Ottomans lost in the First World War and the Republic of Turkey was founded in 1923.

> Under the republican regime, every measure was taken for the progress of the Turkish bourgeoisie. The trade carried out by the Armenian and Greek minorities was seized. All the demands of the workers and peasants were forcibly suppressed. The chauvinistic character of the new regime clearly showed that any just demand that expressed the interests of both minority peoples and Kurds would be suppressed by force. (PKK 1978: 30)

When the dust settled, Kemalism as the state ideology of the modern Turkish Republic became a tool to justify the political and economic domination of the Turkish nation over the rest of its national minorities, so much so that the Kemalists did not shy away from depicting the occupation and colonization of Kurdistan as part of a civilizing mission aimed at Kurdish 'savages' (PKK 1978: 30).

Öcalan notes that the Republic of Turkey, due to its weak economic infrastructure, consolidated colonial relations in Kurdistan by military occupation during a process that lasted from 1925 to 1940 (PKK 1978: 30). Another reason for this long-term military phase, according to Öcalan, stemmed from the Turkish bourgeoisie's awareness of the fact that the complete political, economic and cultural colonization of Kurdistan would not be possible without stabilizing the military occupation and subjugation of Kurdistan. The military phase of colonizing Kurdistan in modern Turkey was followed, according to Öcalan, 'by a period of assimilation, symbolized in boarding schools, which were used for the Turkish state enculturation of the Kurdish youth, and then, from the 1960s onwards, a period of economic colonization, symbolized by (state-led) agricultural modernization which functioned to break up the traditional (tribal-based) structures of Kurdish society' (Jongerden and Akkaya 2012: 11).

It is important to note that for Öcalan, the colonization of Kurdistan in Turkey and elsewhere was not merely the work of Turkey's ruling class. Global imperialist forces were also actively involved in the colonization and collaborated with regional colonizers to help them in their aims. Partition and colonization of Kurdistan, Öcalan notes, was part of the grand plans of the winning bloc of the First World War, that is, the Allied Forces to reshape and reorganize the world order according to their interests. He succinctly presents the main reason for the partition and colonization of Kurdistan, which satisfies the interests of both imperialists and regional dominant classes, in the following terms:

> Independent Kurdistan, which is incompatible with the interests of feudal and comprador classes, and therefore inevitably gaining a democratic structure, is the greatest danger for imperialism's entire Middle East policy. A fragmented Kurdistan, which can at times be used as a trump card to extract more concessions from its collaborators and turn them into their pawns, is the most ideal for the interests of imperialism. (PKK 1978: 32)

Since the early days of the republic in Turkey, Öcalan argues, Turkish bourgeoisie chose to side with imperialism in fear of the October Revolution and the struggles of workers and peasants. This pro-imperialist stance was even further aggravated after the Second World War when, in the US-led world order, Turkey was subject to the US neocolonialism. However, Öcalan emphasizes that US neocolonialism and 'development of classical colonialism in Kurdistan by the Turkish bourgeoisie do not contradict each other; on the contrary, they complement each other. In this period, strong economies develop neocolonialism, while economies dependent on imperialism can only sustain classical colonialism' (PKK 1978: 31). In other words, the United States did not need to directly colonize Turkey and other so-called developing countries to protect its economic and geopolitical interests in the region. Instead, given the economic and military superiority of the United States, it used and supported the Turkish bourgeoisie and the Turkish military for their own interests. Therefore, Turkey acted as a bulwark against the influence of the Soviet Union during the Cold War. Due to a weak economy and dependence on US imperialism, the Turkish bourgeoisie was unable to establish neocolonial relations with any other country, but US support helped Turkey in maintaining the colonization of northern Kurdistan within the territory of Turkey.

Öcalan challenges the false anti-imperialist roots of Kemalism adopted by many Turkish Leftists. Kemalists presented their movement as anti-imperialist especially during and after Turkey's wars of independence when they fought against British, French, Greek and Armenian forces. This view was also shared widely by the Turkish Left, although some sections of the young leftist generation of the 1970s challenged this understanding and only considered the pre–Second World War Kemalism as anti-imperialist (Korkmaz 2021: 2672). By highlighting the double colonization of Kurdistan and the conditions of colonization endured by the Kurds, Öcalan demonstrates that when in power – since 1923 – Kemalism has been working with rather than against Western imperialism. Similar double colonization took place in other parts of Kurdistan. Öcalan contends that with the support of British, and subsequently American, imperialism, an ethnicized hierarchy of power was established soon after the First World War in Iran, where a privileged Persian nation dominated and subjugated other nationalities and ethnicities in the country, particularly colonizing Kurdish, Baloch, Arab and Azeri-Turkish territories in Iran (PKK 1978: 32). During the British mandate of Iraq (1920–32) and the French mandate of Syria (1920–46), the Kurds of Iraq and Syria were in effect ruled by Western as well as local Arab rulers. After the independence in each country and under Arab nationalist rule, according to Öcalan, Kurds were subjected to colonial policies and practices such as forced assimilation and Arabization, forced displacements and creation of Arab belts, that is, encircling and controlling Kurdish territories with settler Arab communities (PKK 1978: 33). Outlining the subjugation of Kurds in four countries to similar, if not entirely the same, dynamics of colonial rule allows the young Öcalan to argue for a Kurdish national liberation movement that aims at forming an independent Kurdish state.

Young Öcalan and decolonization in older national liberation movements

The final section of the founding PKK Manifesto discusses the party's vision and plan for the liberation of Kurdistan. Given the Marxist–Leninist ideology of the PKK at the time, Öcalan's and the PKK's solution for ending the colonization of Kurdistan was informed by Lenin's understanding of the right of nations to self-determination. Lenin believed in and acted on a general principle that the working class must be freed from both class and national oppression (Davis 1978: 65), hence arguing that 'Victorious socialism must achieve complete democracy and, consequently, not only bring about the complete equality of nations, but also give effect to the right of oppressed nations to self-determination, i.e., the right to free political secession' (Lenin 1916: 19). In that vein, working-class unity and international solidarity of workers entailed the recognition of the right of colonies and oppressed nations to be free from colonization and the yoke of national oppression.

Inspired by Maoist ideas popular among the radical Left in Turkey and elsewhere in the 1970s, Öcalan, in the manifesto, argues that the national democratic revolution, which aimed to create an independent and democratic Kurdistan, was the PKK's agenda for decolonization and liberation of the Kurds and Kurdistan. Since national oppression is the main reason for stalling the development of productive forces and cultural capacities and resources of the Kurds, according to Öcalan, the main contradiction in Kurdistan is national oppression, whose resolution is a precondition for settling all other contradictions and issues. Therefore, 'creating an independent Kurdistan is possible by eliminating the economic colonialism over Kurdistan's underground and surface resources, labor, agriculture, trade, finance and industry, [as well as] cultural and political colonialism that hinder development of language, history, culture, and social and political areas' (PKK 1978: 46).

Since for young Öcalan 'national and class' or 'national and feudal' contradictions are intertwined, the independence phase of the revolution must be accompanied by a democratic phase, that is, 'the elimination of heavy feudal-comprador pressures on the social structure of Kurdistan' (PKK 1978: 46). In fact, by offering the national democratic revolution as a decolonizing project, Öcalan kills two birds with one stone; he rejects both orthodox Turkish Leftist and Kurdish nationalist politics that are oblivious to the particularities of the colonial situation in Kurdistan, including the intersection of class and national oppressions, and their implications for the emancipation and political struggles of the Kurds. He also rules out alternatives to national independence such as 'regional autonomy', 'federal unity' and 'language and cultural autonomy' (PKK 1978: 49) due to their reformist and reactionary nature and, instead, advocates an independent state as the only legitimate substantiation of the right of nations to self-determination. Öcalan envisions a socialist transition after the anti-colonial national democratic revolution in Kurdistan accomplishes its mission. But as young Öcalan ambitiously claims, the Kurdistan Revolution itself, due to its geopolitical position and its influence over neighbouring countries, will be decisive in driving out imperialism from the region just as the Vietnamese Revolution did in Indochina (PKK 1978: 51).

It is understandable that forming an independent state in a historical context where colonial ideologies framed the colonized people as incapable of ruling themselves and being sovereign was a political achievement. However, this does not obviate the need for a critical stance on the role that the state plays in cementing and perpetuating hierarchies of power and status in society. It is more important to do so in post-independence contexts where states play an even greater role in addressing the damages inflicted on society by the former colonizers. Öcalan's later version of decolonization deals specifically with the categories of nation and the state.

The later Öcalan and decolonization: Democratic confederalism and the end of the nation state

More than two decades later, Öcalan offers an alternative programme of decolonization which, I shall argue, builds upon a new conception of liberation and a rejection of his earlier statist understanding of decolonization. Contrary to popular belief, the shift in Öcalan's thinking did not occur during his imprisonment, nor was it merely shaped by his acquaintance with Murray

Bookchin's ideas (Hussain 2015; Leverink 2015). Already in the 1990s and before his abduction in 1999, Öcalan was frustrated with what he called 'fetishization of the state' in socialism (Akkaya 2020: 10). Ironically enough, it was in prison and in solitary confinement that Öcalan's critiques of really existing socialism and the state evolved into a systematic account of liberation and decolonization. In his prison writings, Öcalan proposes a new roadmap for decolonization which retains certain elements of his earlier anti-colonial stance while providing a radically new critique of the nation state now seen as a countervailing force to liberation. There is no doubt that Bookchin's ideas had a direct impact on how Öcalan articulated his critique of the state, but Öcalan's creative encounter with Bookchin's insights must not be downplayed, particularly the ways in which he builds on Bookchin's thoughts to develop theoretical and political frameworks for the specific contexts he addresses in his writings.

In his prison writings, Öcalan agrees with Bookchin's idea that hierarchy and domination are the historical root causes of the misery of human societies and that true emancipation lies in putting an end to hierarchy and domination. Like Bookchin, Öcalan contends that the creation of hierarchy and domination made nature an object of exploitation by humankind and, consequently, destroyed the equilibrium that existed between human communities and the environment. Excessive urbanization driven by profit-oriented essence of civilization has led to an ecological crisis which has reached its peak in capitalism (Öcalan 2020: 300–1).

Furthermore, Öcalan deals strategically with Bookchin's theory to articulate a political programme best suited for not only the liberation of the Kurds but also the realization of a free and egalitarian social and political system in the Middle East. Notable among his efforts to tailor Bookchin's theory to his political agenda was to foreground the social and political role of women in forming a liberated society. But just like his mode of analysis regarding the Kurdish nation, Öcalan's essentialist conceptualization of identities is also at play in his theorization of women's subjugation and liberation. Öcalan maintains that women were controlling and distributing the limited surplus product of the natural societies or 'primordial socialism' of the Neolithic era before the rise of statist civilization (Öcalan 2017b: 61). This status of women stemmed from their natural power of giving birth and nurturing other members of society, and for this reason, they were closer than men to nature. The woman–mother figure's administration of natural societies in pre-Sumerian Mesopotamia, according to Öcalan (2013:

14–15), was based on the principles of sharing and solidarity as opposed to ownership and force. Therefore, it was key for the establishment of hierarchical societies to subjugate and exploit women; a structural issue that has continued in modern liberal and illiberal nation states. This makes liberation of women so central to any emancipatory politics to the point that Öcalan believes that

> Freedom and equality cannot be realized without the achievement of gender equality. The most permanent and comprehensive component of democratization is woman's freedom. The societal system is most vulnerable because of the unresolved question of woman; woman who was first turned into property and who today is a commodity; completely, body and soul. The role the working class have once played, must now be taken over by the sisterhood of women. (Öcalan 2013: 52)

On the face of it, Öcalan's account suggests the primacy of gender over class in analysing social relations of domination, but his overall approach advocates the co-constitutive relationship between the two as he contends that 'class and sexual oppression develop together' (Öcalan 2013: 51) or 'the ruling class character is formed concurrently with the dominant male character' (Öcalan 2013: 49). To dismantle patriarchy, or to 'kill the dominant male' (Öcalan 2013: 49), as Öcalan puts it, a new approach to women is required. While acknowledging the progressive role of feminism and its achievements for women, Öcalan maintains that feminism has not accomplished its mission due to lack of 'a strong organizational base; inability to develop its philosophy to the full; and difficulties relating to a militant women's movement' (Öcalan 2013: 55). Jineology is what Öcalan offers as a new discourse of women's freedom, a social science whose fundamental assumptions are shaped by Öcalan's thoughts on women and produces knowledge about women for the purpose of their liberation. It must be noted that Öcalan too deals with feminism as a singular body bereft of philosophical, ideological and political plurality. There is little evidence of engagement with feminist schools of thought in Öcalan's prison writings, and this reality stems partly from the fact that these writings were penned under strict state surveillance with very limited access to sources. Its essentializing features notwithstanding, jineology was instrumental in providing Kurdish women activists with 'ideological and political tools' to fight the dominant masculine power relations within the Kurdish movement (Al-Ali and Kaser 2020: 4). Moreover, it should be emphasized that the Kurdish women movement played a key role in challenging male dominance within the PKK both discursively and politically, and in fact, jineology grew out of 'continuous discussions among women cadres in the political and armed structures of the Kurdish Freedom Movement' (Al-Ali and Kaser 2020: 8).

Identifying Mesopotamia as the birthplace of civilization, Öcalan (2007: 8) calls Sumer the first state in history, which was formed following the agricultural revolution, creation of class society and the establishment of gender hierarchies. The formation of the Sumerian state signalled the institutionalization of hierarchical relations of political power. Öcalan is of the opinion that all states, despite real differences in the forms of governance, consolidate and perpetuate domination and inequality. With the arrival of capitalism and industrialization in history, these repressive characteristics are even further accentuated in the modern state. According to Öcalan, the nation state is the specific political form of capitalist modernity which 'is the most developed unity of monopolies such as trade, industry, finance and power. One should also think of ideological monopoly as an indivisible part of the power monopoly' (Öcalan 2017b: 32). Moreover, the nation state is 'the most developed organization of violence in social history', and the main reason, Öcalan (2011: 15) argues, for the unbridled and systematic violence in the modern nation state is 'the capitalist system's tendency' for uninterrupted accumulation of capital and maximization of profit.

In his conceptual framework for decolonization and liberation, Öcalan envisions the transition from capitalist modernity represented politically by the nation state to democratic modernity whose political form is democratic confederalism. Öcalan (2017a: 62) defines democracy 'as the self-governance of a non-state society. Democracy is governance that is not state; it is the power of communities to govern themselves without the state'. Democratic confederalism as an interrelated network of communes, people's councils and grassroot organizations is that system of non-state self-governance that replaces the state. However, this replacement is not realized through toppling the state, but rather it is a process through which the extent and scope of the state's power and functions are restricted to the point where the state becomes redundant (Öcalan 2017a: 63). The state will become irrelevant and will disappear 'when democratic confederalism has proved its problem-solving capacities with a view to social issues' (Öcalan 2011: 32). A society organized as such will be an ecological society as well since the formation of alternative, non-hierarchical mechanisms and institutions facilitates the harmony between communities and environment that was lost in human history with the emergence of hierarchies.

A democratic nation, in turn, represents a society deliberately organized in accordance with democratic confederalism. Unlike nations formed and created by modern states and nationalist doctrines, a democratic nation, as Öcalan (2017a: 21) understands it, is built by the will of free and equal individuals and communities that are unified through autonomous institutions run by the people. It is not predicated on the kind of homogenization that rigid borders or a single culture and language imply. 'It is a new type of nation that encompasses all cultural entities, from ethnicity to religion, from urban, local and regional to national communities formed through democratic autonomous political formations and its main political form: democratic confederalist implementations' (Öcalan 2017a: 64). The principle of democratic autonomy which guarantees the self-governance of communities and institutions further distinguishes the democratic nation from current nation states (Öcalan 2017a: 30). While it is understood that all segments of society need to coordinate with one another, this coordination is not used as an excuse to remove people's ability to manage the specifics of their own affairs. Individuals in a democratic nation, Öcalan (2017a: 33–4) argues, see their freedom in 'the communality of society' and 'the more functional life of small communities', whereas in capitalist societies individuals are 'bound to the sovereignty of money' and manipulated by 'the wage system', even though liberal individualism boasts of free individuals and denies the existence of society. Although Öcalan does not specifically discuss the question of sovereignty, drawing on the contrast he establishes here between 'the sovereignty of money' in capitalist political formations and the communal form of political life in democratic confederalism, one may deduce that, in the latter society, sovereignty lies in people or, more specifically, in people's communes.

Nevertheless, while it is rather obvious and predictable that a radical project of decolonization provokes adversity on the side of colonizing states, not to mention global superpowers, Öcalan's democratic confederalism offers very little to tackle such adversities except for general recommendations on the necessity of preparing self-defence whether militarily or by extending confederate structures. Put simply, democratic confederalism lacks 'a practicable concept of state building in periods of violent antagonism' (Oveisy 2019). Perhaps this problem was most conspicuous in the war situation of recent years in Rojava where 'the territorial logic of war on ISIS' and 'the battlefield of counterrevolution' intensified the centralization of decision-making and hierarchies of power (Oveisy 2019).

Democratic confederalism, democratic nation and democratic autonomy constitute the political pillars of democratic modernity, which is a free and egalitarian type of modernity. For Öcalan (2017a: 17), in this type of modernity, which he proposes to replace capitalist modernity, 'an economy free of monopolism, an ecology that signifies harmony with the environment, and a technology that is friendly to nature and humanity are the institutional bases of democratic modernity and thus the democratic nation'.

Against this backdrop, one can conclude from Öcalan's analysis that forming a Kurdish state as a solution for the national oppression of the Kurds, a political agenda that Öcalan and the PKK fought for over two decades, is neither viable nor desired as it elicits enormous opposition from multiple states. An independent Kurdish state is likely to, in Kurdistan also, reproduce the repressive qualities of the nation state such as hierarchy of nationalities/ethnicities, patriarchy and class society. Therefore, Öcalan states,

> Without opposition against the capitalist modernity there will be no place for the liberation of the peoples. This is why the founding of a Kurdish nation-state is not an option for me. The call for a separate nation-state results from the interests of the ruling class or the interests of the bourgeoisie but does not reflect the interests of the people since another state would only be the creation of additional injustice and would curtail the right to freedom even more. The solution to the Kurdish question, therefore, needs to be found in an approach that weakens the capitalist modernity or pushes it back. (Öcalan 2011: 19)

Decolonization and the nation state: Öcalan's contributions

Decolonizing the nation, reflected in the concept of the democratic nation, is a key defining aspect of Öcalan's new decolonization. The idea of decolonizing the nation is not unique to Öcalan as interrogating the concept of the nation or introducing alternative conceptions of the nation (Ashcroft 2009) are very contemporary to Öcalan. Yet the novelty of Öcalan's contribution lies in the fact that in his capacity as a political leader, he comes up with a new conception of the nation as an integral component of the whole process of a true decolonization. For colonization is not merely a matter of establishing exploitative relations and apparatuses, but it also involves defining the colonized and ruling them (Mamdani 2012). Therefore, a decolonizing project must include concepts and definitions that problematize and replace the colonial discursive constructions of the colonized. Thus, he puts forth an alternative conception of the nation in contrast to what the nation state stands for: 'While the state's nation pursues homogenised society, the democratic nation mainly consists of different collectivities. It sees diversity as richness. Life itself is only possible through diversity' (Öcalan 2017a: 25). It is a known fact now that in their colonial enterprises European colonizers defined and created nations in their colonies by politicizing ethnicities and even tribes (Mamdani 2020). However, Öcalan's democratic nation is, in fact, framed through reversing and undoing the colonial conceptualization of the nation and, hence, decoupling the nation from the nation state. A democratic nation is not identified with a single ethnicity or cultural entity but the free coalescing of 'different collectivities' which are bound together by autonomously formed political and social institutions (Öcalan 2017a: 25). Therefore, while nation of the nation state and that of the democratic nation are both politically constructed entities, the former is woven together by cultural elements such as ethnicity, language, or religion, whereas the latter is threaded by a political mechanism. As Öcalan (2017a: 24–5) puts it: 'the democratic nation is not content with a common mindset and culture – it is a nation that unifies and governs all its members in democratic autonomous institutions. This is its defining quality.'

What remains unclear about Öcalan's thoughts on the concept of nation is that while the inclusive character of the democratic nation suggests an alternative to, or a negation of, the exclusive understanding of the nation – centred on common culture and ethnicity – he still sticks with a primordial conception of the nation when he refers to the Kurds and their supposedly centuries-old history as a nation. This paradox in Öcalan's thoughts is further aggravated by the imprecise contours of the democratic nation. In other words, how can an exclusive entity like nation become so inclusive even while it maintains its nationness? For this reason, a term like 'democratic society' seems more appropriate as the alternative that Öcalan has in mind for the nation of the nation state. Further, Öcalan's account is silent on the fate of national entities, including the Kurdish nation, within the frameworks of the democratic nation and democratic confederalism and on whether they will wither away eventually.

Decolonizing the nation, in Öcalan's (2011, 2017a, 2020) formulation, must be accompanied by a gradual weakening and disappearance of the state about which he has written extensively. Unlike anti-colonial positions that are critical of the nation state but are content with a state without a nation (Mamdani 2020), for Öcalan, a truly emancipatory and democratic solution requires withering away of the state. Mamdani's (2020: 18) analysis sheds light on the role of the nation state in creating colonial relations by building a nation or a majority and 'the making of permanent minorities and their maintenance through the politicization of identity'. However, his suggested alternative of 'replacing the nation-state with the mere state' (Mamdani 2020: 330) or decoupling the state from the nation limits the gruesome reality of colonialism to mere 'politicization of identities' (Mamdani 2020: 18) and overlooks the role of the state in bolstering and perpetuating hierarchical relations as well as facilitating economic exploitation and the rule of capital. By facilitating the free movement of capital while establishing strict regimes of border and immigration controls, the nation states, of post–Second World War in particular, have produced enormous violence, including forced displacements, land grabs, massacres and genocides (Sharma 2020). Arguing from a similar position, Öcalan (2017a: 15) tends to see the relationship between capital and the nation state as more structural. 'Without an organisation of violence like the nation-state, the laws of capitalist accumulation could not operate and industrialism could not be maintained.'

It is fair to argue that in the later Öcalan, decolonization or liberation becomes synonymous with democracy, hence his insistence on the democratic qualifier in categories and concepts such as democratic modernity, democratic confederalism, democratic nation and democratic autonomy, signifying non-hierarchical social formations and relations. The idea of decolonization as putting an end to domination and hierarchies is reminiscent of how decolonization from coloniality of power is envisioned, after all, as 'the process of social liberation from all power organized as inequality, discrimination, exploitation, and as domination' (Quijano 2010: 32). In fact, coloniality of power in the sense of power creating social discriminations and hierarchies is also implied in Öcalan's civilizational narrative. However, whereas coloniality of power in the decoloniality school is an exclusively modern phenomenon emerging since 1492, for Öcalan, that power has a much longer history, dating back to the emergence of statist civilization in Mesopotamia and becoming only more developed and complex with the arrival of capitalist modernity.

Öcalan's project of decolonization and his critique of the nation state would be much richer if he had included a detailed discussion of the relationship between race, class and nationalism, given the central role of racialization in the construction of the Kurds as colonized people. Öcalan's project of decolonization, and this is also the case with his earlier version expressed in the PKK's Manifesto, suffers from the absence of an account of deep-seated and institutional anti-Kurdish racism and how specifically decolonization intends to address it. Also, for an explicitly anti-capitalist social and political formation, Öcalan offers little outline of what the mode of production in democratic confederalism looks like. In fact, he seems increasingly uninterested in discussing alternative economic structures and doubts that such discussions are even meaningful (De Jong 2016). Öcalan prescribes a cooperative economy, but it is unclear how this economy manages to survive within a global capitalist system in an age of hegemonic neoliberalism. The failure of Öcalan's project to provide compelling answers smacks of a wider theoretical blindness to the effects of 'the international' on the actual workings of democratic confederalism. Put differently, Öcalan fails to address the ways in which 'international and geopolitical factors' impact the character and practice of the political and social formations that he discusses (Matin 2019).

Conclusion

From classical national liberation movements of the twentieth century to the anti-colonial struggles and discourses that came later, particularly in the twenty-first century, decolonization has been imagined in different, and at times contrasting, terms. While for the former, decolonization more or less meant a national, independent state, for the latter it largely signified questioning the nation state and seeking more radical conceptions of decolonization. Young Öcalan and the later Öcalan embody and represent these two periods of decolonizing thought and practice in the Kurdish context. Identifying hierarchy and domination as the root causes of inequalities, discrimination and oppression, the later Öcalan has developed a new understanding of decolonization which centres on non-hierarchical and democratic structures and social relations. Like with many other anti-colonial leaders and thinkers, the failure of so-called postcolonial states as well as Communist states of the twentieth century in ending various forms of political subjugation, economic exploitation and social discrimination was key in leading Öcalan to seek a broader understanding of decolonization.

The later Öcalan's conception of liberation and decolonization builds on the rejection of capitalist modernity and its political form, that is, the nation state, due to the role that the nation state plays in reinforcing and reproducing patriarchal, capitalist and national/ethnic hierarchies. As an alternative to capitalist modernity, Öcalan calls for a transition to democratic modernity whose political form is democratic confederalism, a stateless, eco-friendly form of bottom-up democracy committed to women liberation. Moreover, the democratic nation is another key component of Öcalan's alternative to the nation state that redefines the nation and relieves it from its colonial construction, forming an inclusive and just society. It is no exaggeration that Öcalan's thorough critique of the nation state, which argues for fizzling out the state, reconstructing the nation and replacing the nation state with democratic confederalism, contributes significantly to the growing literature on the oppressive and colonial features of the nation state. Yet, Öcalan's account of liberation suffers from some flaws and ambiguities. His account lacks an analysis of racism and its integral role in colonialism as well as strategies to deal with racism in a decolonizing project. Furthermore, Öcalan offers so little in terms of the mode of production in democratic confederalism, and except for a recommendation to expand confederate networks, there is little explanation as to how democratic confederalism can survive the reactions of external forces, most notably other nation states. This latter point is particularly important in the Kurdish context, given the multiple states confronting the formation of democratic confederalism in Kurdistan. Despite its shortcomings, the later Öcalan's programme of liberation is a call for reimagining decolonization through the transformation and destruction of oppressive structures and relations. It draws our attention to relations of domination and subjugation instead of focusing exclusively on the identity of oppressors. Learning from the failure of national liberation movements of the twentieth century, Öcalan's project aims at changing the colonial relations rather than changing the colonizers.

References

Akkaya, Ahmet Hamdi (2020), 'The PKK's Ideological Odyssey', *Journal of Balkan and Near Eastern Studies*, 22 (6): 730–45. https://doi.org/10.1080/19448953.2020.1801241.

Al-Ali, Nadje and Käser, Isabel (2020), 'Beyond Feminism? Jineolojî and the Kurdish Women's Freedom Movement', *Politics & Gender*, 18 (1): 1–32. https://doi.org/10.1017/S1743923X20000501.

Ali, Othman (1997), 'The Kurds and the Lausanne Peace Negotiations, 1922–23', *Middle Eastern Studies*, 33 (3): 521–34. https://doi.org/10.1080/00263209708701167.

Ashcroft, Bill (2009), 'Beyond the Nation: Post-Colonial Hope', *The Journal of the European Association on Australia*, 1 (1): 12–22

Ashcroft, Bill, Griffiths, Gareth and Tiffin, Helen (2007), *Post-Colonial Studies: The Key Concepts*, 2nd edn., Milton Park, Oxfordshire: Routledge.

Beşikçi, İsmail (2015), *International Colony Kurdistan*, London: Parvana.

Chaliand, Gérard (1980), *A People without a Country: The Kurds and Kurdistan*, London: Zed Books.

Davis, H. B. (1978), *Toward a Marxist Theory of Nationalism*, New York: Monthly Review Press.

De Jong, Alex (2016), 'The New-Old PKK', *Jacobin*, 18 March. Available at https://www.jacobinmag.com/2016/03/pkk-ocalan-kurdistan-isis-murray-bookchin/ (Accessed: 29 April 2019).

Ghassemlou, Abdul Rahman (1980), 'Kurdistan in Iran', in Gérard Chaliand (ed.), *A People without a Country: The Kurds and Kurdistan*, 107–34, London: Zed Books.

Ghassemlou, Abdul Rahman ([1965] 1996), *Kurdistan and the Kurds*, Stockholm: Apec Publishing.

Hassanpour, Amir (1992), *Nationalism and language in Kurdistan 1918–1985*, San Francisco: Mellen Research University Press.

Hussain, Sophia (2015), 'Murray Bookchin and the Öcalan Connection: The *New York Times* Profiles the Students of PKK Rojava'. Available at https://www.versobooks.com/blogs/2368-murray-bookchin-and-the-ocalan-connection-the-new-york-times-profiles-the-students-of-pkk-rojava (Accessed: 16 December 2022).

Jongerden, Joost and Akkaya, Ahmet Hamdi (2012), 'The Kurdistan Workers Party and a New Left in Turkey: Analysis of the Revolutionary Movement in Turkey through the PKK's Memorial Text on Haki Karer', *European Journal of Turkish Studies*, 14 (14): 17.

Kıvılcımlı, Hikmet (1979), *İhtiyat Kuvvet: Milliyet (Şark)*, Yol: 6, İstanbul: Kitap, Yol Yayınları.

Korkmaz, Emre Eren (2021), 'Turkish Left and Anti-imperialism in the 1970s', in Immanuel Ness and Zac Cope (eds), *The Palgrave Encyclopedia of Imperialism and Anti-Imperialism*, 2nd edn., 2665–73, Cham: Palgrave Macmillan.

Lazarus, Neil (2004), 'The Fetish of "the West" in Postcolonial Theory', in Crystal Bartolovich and Neil Lazarus (eds), *Marxism, Modernity and Postcolonial Studies*, 43–64, Cambridge: Cambridge University Press.

Lenin, Vladimir Ilych (1916), 'The Socialist Revolution and the Right of Nations to Self-Determination', *Lenin Collected Works*, 22: 143–56. Available at https://www.marxists.org/archive/lenin/works/1916/jan/x01.htm (Accessed: 29 June 2021)

Leverink, Joris (2015), 'Murray Bookchin and the Kurdish Resistance', *Roar*, 9 August. Available at https://roarmag.org/essays/bookchin-kurdish-struggle-ocalan-rojava/ (Accessed: 16 December 2022).

Loomba, Ania (2005), *Colonialism/Postcolonialism*, London: Routledge.

Mamdani, Mahmood (2012), *Define and Rule: Native as Political Identity*, Cambridge MA: Harvard University Press.

Mamdani, Mahmood (2020), *Neither Settler nor Native: The Making and Unmaking of Permanent Minorities*, Cambridge MA: The Belknap Press of Harvard University Press.

Matin, Kamran (2019), 'Democratic Confederalism and Societal Multiplicity: A Sympathetic Critique of Abdullah Öcalan's State Theory', *Geopolitics*, 26 (4): 1–20. https://doi.org/10.1080/14650045.2019.1688785.

McDowall, David (1992), *The Kurds, a Nation Denied*, London: Minority Rights Group.

McDowall, David (2007), *A Modern History of the Kurds*, London: I.B. Tauris.

Mohanty, Chandra Talpade (1984), 'Under Western Eyes: Feminist Scholarship and Colonial Discourses', *Boundary 2*, 12 (13): 333–58. https://doi.org/10.2307/302821.

Öcalan, Abdullah (2007), *Prison Writing: The Roots of Civilization*, London: Pluto Press.

Öcalan, Abdullah (2011), *Democratic Confederalism*, London: Transmedia Publishing.

Öcalan, Abdullah (2013), *Liberating Life: Women's Revolution*, Cologne: International Initiative Edition/Neuss: Mesopotamian Publishers.

Öcalan, Abdullah (2017a), *Democratic Nation*, Cologne: International Initiative Edition/Neuss: Mesopotamian Publishers.

Öcalan, Abdullah (2017b), *The Political Thought of Abdullah Öcalan: Kurdistan, Women's Revolution and Democratic Confederalism*, International Initiative Edition, London: Pluto Press.

Öcalan, Abdullah (2020), *Manifesto for a Democratic Civilization: Volume Three, The Sociology of Freedom*, Oakland: PM Press.

Olson, Robert W. (1989), *The Emergence of Kurdish Nationalism and the Sheikh Said Rebellion, 1880–1925*, 1st edn, Austin: University of Texas Press.

Oveisy, Fouad (2019), 'Revolution and Counterrevolution in Rojava', *The Bullet*, 27 October. Available at https://socialistproject.ca/2019/10/revolution-and-counterrevolution-in-rojava/ (Accessed: 28 June 2021)

PKK (1978), *Kürdistan Devriminin Yolu*, Köln: Wesanen Serxwêbun. Available at https://birinsanbirkitap.files.wordpress.com/2014/08/kurdistan-devriminin-yolu-pkk-manifestosu.pdf (Accessed: 11 June 2021)

Quijano, Aníbal (2010), 'Coloniality and Modernity/Rationality', in Walter Mignolo and Arturo Escobar (eds), *Globalization and the Decolonial Option*, 22–32, London: Routledge. https://doi.org/10.4324/9781315868448.

Said, Edward W. (1979), *Orientalism*, New York: Vintage Books.

Sharma, Nandita (2020), *Home Rule: National Sovereignty and the Separation of Natives and Migrants*, Durham NC: Duke University Press.

Tejel, Jordi (2009), *Syria's Kurds: History, Politics and Society*, London: Routledge.

Vali, Abbas (2011), *Kurds and the State in Iran: The Making of Kurdish Identity*, London: I.B. Tauris.

Yadirgi, Veli (2017), *The Political Economy of the Kurds of Turkey: From the Ottoman Empire to the Turkish Republic*, Cambridge: Cambridge University Press.

Yildiz, Kerim (2005), *The Kurds in Syria: The Forgotten People*, London: Pluto Press in association with Kurdish Human Rights Project.

11

Reflecting on coloniality of power, colonial violence and decolonization through the University of Rojava

Jan Yasin Sunca

It was early in the morning when a colleague and friend, with whom we have been working on founding the Faculty of Political Science at the University of Rojava (UoR),[1] called me to inform me that we would have to postpone the interviews, which we initially aimed to conduct for student selection. The night before, we had been discussing the possibility of starting the academic year on time: it had been hindered in previous years due to the conditions created by military aggressions. That very night, Turkey had launched yet another campaign of bombardment, shelling and armed drones, rendering everyday life impossible, as it mainly targeted the civilian infrastructure of Rojava. The students and teachers at the university, just like the rest of the people of Rojava, were immediately impacted by this aggression of the second largest army of NATO. We were obliged to postpone the interviews for safety reasons. Some of our students were supposed to travel from Shehba, a region where a good majority of the people of Afrin had migrated after the invasion of Turkey in 2018, to Qamishlo, where the UoR is located. Many other students, teachers and all other workers of the university from different cities and towns were supposed to come to the building for it to be functional. The UoR has been built, enlarged and become an institution of the Revolution under these conditions, and this day was not an isolated case of emergency, but rather an everyday insecurity of the people.

There were several layers of colonialism at play in this very short story of not holding the interviews for admissions. Turkey's, Syria's and the United States's differentiated colonial practices were hindering educational activities in Rojava. Notwithstanding this, several other issues, as diverse as the legacy of the Ba'ath regime and the place of the English language in university education, also result directly from the global coloniality of power. All in all, UoR operates within several layers of colonialism, a structure against which the university has to carry out decolonial educational activities while simultaneously resisting ongoing colonial aggressions. To be sure, despite the fact that the majority in the West has gradually become disinterested in Rojava, the anti-colonial struggle continues as a fundamental obligation. The experience of Rojava University, as I illustrate in this chapter, is an inseparable part of the overall struggle for liberation. While the role the university plays is much larger, I limit the focus of this chapter to three issues that are representative of colonialism, coloniality and decolonization: geopolitical violence, pedagogy of resistance and the debate on and around language.

In what follows, I first reflect on how the layers of colonialism in Kurdistan inform the experiences and struggles in Rojava. Second, I briefly focus on the idea of democratic confederalism that underpins the Rojava revolution. Then, I differentiate between struggles for emancipation and struggles for building free life, which informs the place of Rojava University in the overall struggle. Third, I elaborate the meaning and practice of decolonization through the experience of the UoR, focusing on the Faculty of Political Science in particular. I conclude with some connecting points on the place of the university in the overall anti-colonial struggle for liberation.

Layers of colonialism in Kurdistan and Rojava

The university system in Rojava materialized under the conditions of what I call layered colonialism. A broad definition of colonialism is the rejection of the right to self-determination of one polity by another, a rejection that not only affects governance structures, law and economy but also gradually imposes ways of being, knowing and doing (Maldonado-Torres 2016; Mignolo and Walsh 2018). If one takes this definition, there exist at least three forms of colonial domination in Kurdistan – colonial nationalism, geopolitical domination and double coloniality of power – each one holding specific meanings, appearances and modes of functioning in and on Rojava.

Colonial nationalism

Colonial nationalism involves the rejection of the Kurdish identity and their right to self-rule by the nation states formed on the territory historically inhabited by the Kurds: Turkey, Iran, Iraq and Syria. These nation states have historically tried to assimilate Kurds into their national unity in differentiated ways, and when Kurds have sought some form of self-determination, whether as a nation state or cultural/democratic rights, they have been punished by the centralized structures of the nation states (Bozarslan 1997; Sunca 2022). Internally, heavy nationalist propaganda and, externally, the sovereignty discourse have been used to justify the domination of Kurds. It is true that all four states were either under the direct colonial rule of Western powers or carried out a war of independence against Western attempts at domination. However, once they joined the so-called family of independent nations, they reproduced the colonial practices within their territorial exclusivity (Sunca 2023b).

Colonial nationalism has two different replications in Rojava: Turkish and Syrian Arab nationalisms. The Turkish aggressions are colonial because it denies the Kurds their right to self-determination, ranging from legal measures of punishment due to Kurdish identity to various forms of military domination in response to Kurdish political demands. It is nationalist because every period of state violence against the Kurds has been justified in the name of the Turkish nation and the 'indivisible integrity' of the Turkish state. The main reason Turkey carries out these bombardments is rather straightforward. In Rojava, the Kurds leading the revolution have followed the ideological leadership of Abdullah Öcalan, the imprisoned leader of the Kurdistan Workers' Party (PKK, *Partîya Karkerên Kurdistanê*), an organization formed by Kurds whom the Turkish state was unable to assimilate/exterminate. This organization has been engaged in an anti-colonial struggle for liberation since the late 1970s (Akkaya and Jongerden 2010; Ünlü 2018). Although the PKK has been engaged in some form of direct or mediated talks/dialogue with successive Turkish governments since the early 1990s, the conflict continued. One of the primary reasons is the colonial origins of the Kurdish question, which pushed Turkey into a zero-sum game with the PKK-led Kurdish movement: the denial of the historical Kurdish question makes the Kurds the ontological other. Any development favouring the Kurds is automatically seen as destructive to the indivisible Turkish unity. The latest example of this was the peace talks between 2013 and 2015. It ended, among other reasons, due to the global appreciation of the Rojava revolution, which was perceived as a threat to Turkey's unity and position in regional security dynamics (Sunca 2016; Jongerden 2018; Çandar 2020). The colonial nationalism of the Turkish state is one layer of colonialism in Rojava.

Another form of colonial nationalism is that of the Syrian Arab Republic. The Rojava revolution added another dimension to the pre-existing colonial Arab nationalism that rejects the Kurds and their rights since the independence of the Syrian state. In Rojava, years of preparation and mobilization by the Rojava people resulted in an unusual power shift. The Assad regime withdrew from the northern regions to fortify Damascus and Aleppo, allowing the People's and Women's Defence Units (respectively, YPG and YPJ, *Yekîneyên Parastina Gel and Yekîneyên Parastina Jin*) to gain military control in July 2012 (ICG 2014; Sunca 2021). Ever since, the regime of Bashar al-Assad operates under an unresolvable contradiction that is essentially colonial. On the one hand, it refuses to negotiate any form of autonomy or greater rights for the people living in Syria, including the Kurds, based on the 'indivisible integrity' discourse. The de facto Autonomous Administration of North and East Syria has made countless appeals and engaged in talks with the Syrian state in an effort to gain de jure recognition. However, these efforts have remained inconclusive, largely due to the American presence in Syria. On the other hand, when it comes to defending the 'indivisible integrity' of Syria against Turkey, the Syrian regime shows reluctance to defend a part of its territory, aiming to punish the Kurds for their collaboration with the United States (I reflect on the question of 'collaboration with the US' in the following paragraph). It should be emphasized that the Rojava revolution never sought to separate a part of Syria and form a Kurdish state; rather, it aimed to be part of a truly democratic Syria. This policy of the Syrian regime is a second layer of colonialism because it demands either total submission of the Kurds to the regime or else, their extermination by the Turkish state. (Tejel 2009; Knapp, Flach and Ayboga 2016)

Geopolitical domination

A second form of colonialism in Kurdistan is Western geopolitical domination. The region as a whole is under the control of external forces in various ways. For instance, Israel would not exist without unconditional US support, and the Syrian regime would not survive without Russia's support. Similar dynamics occurs in Kurdistan, sometimes against Kurdish rights and at other times in favour of Kurdish autonomy but always in the service of Western interests. The United States has supported the gradual emergence of the Kurdistan region of Iraq since the early 1990s and has played a significant role in the formation of the Kurdistan Regional Government (KRG) after the invasion of Iraq. This support seems inconsistent with the United States orchestrating the delivery of Abdullah Öcalan to Turkey in 1999, a move that pushed the PKK, representing the Northern Kurds (Turkey), into a deep crisis. However, from the US perspective, these actions are compatible as they punish its enemies in Iraq and appease its Turkish allies. In both cases, however, Kurds and their aspirations have been instrumentalized. Thus, managing the contradictions in the region is a method by which the West continues its historical colonial domination. It is intrinsically related to the integration of the regional-level Kurdish question into the colonial world order (Matin 2020; Sunca 2022). No polity is free from this domination, whether it is a state, a stateless people or a political/guerrilla movement. This, however, is by no means a justification for collaboration with imperialism but highlights the fact that Western domination in the region is a form of colonialism that no one can escape. It is a condition imposed against the will of the region's peoples, which makes it essentially colonial.

These original colonial conditions have obvious and inherently contradictory reflections on Rojava's anti-colonial struggle due to its anti-ISIS collaboration with the United States. US support for Rojava first took place against the Islamic State in 2014, when ISIS besieged the city of Kobanê, the last line of defence against the jihadist masculinity of ISIS. Western media's coverage of the fight led by Kurdish women, in combination with strong mobilization, protests and demonstrations in Western capitals, forced the United States to intervene. The battle was won by the YPG and YPJ forces, marking the beginning of the territorial decline of ISIS. However, the international consciousness was primarily formed by fear of ISIS attacks in Western capitals, rather than the values of the Rojava revolution, such as women's liberation, ecological awareness and cooperative economy; the fundamental rights of the people of Rojava were even lesser a concern. As a result, once the threat of jihadism diminished from Western media headlines, international support for the Rojava Revolution gradually waned, leaving only those who embraced its values supportive of the project. The official US policy has been limited to anti-ISIS military cooperation with the Syrian Democratic Forces, which justifies US' presence in Syria. These geopolitical dynamics compels Rojava to act in certain ways in exchange for limited military protection against Turkish and Syrian threats. However, this position has thus far hindered political recognition of the Autonomous Administration, and allowed constant threats and bombardments from the Turkish state, and the actual invasion of part of Rojava territory in Serê Kaniyê in 2019, with the United States's green light. Given the colonial nationalism of

Turkish and Syrian regimes, the limited protection provided by the United States has been crucial for the geopolitical survival of Rojava while creating a deep contradiction in terms of its anti-colonial position.[2] However, the overall US position is colonial because the primary concern of the US administration has been to maintain its hegemonic continuity in the region, often at the expense of the will and determination of the people of Rojava for liberation.

Double coloniality of power

A third form of colonial domination is the coloniality of being, doing and knowing. Colonialism cannot be reduced to only extractivism, enslavement and domination of one people by another militarily and economically superior power. It has perpetuated conditions of permanent domination extending well beyond the immediate period of colonialism: imposing criteria of being, knowing and doing, in other words the acceptable forms of existence, knowledge and action (Law 2011; Mignolo and Walsh 2018: 17–20). The ways in which the colonized identify themselves, their ancestral ways of understanding or their historical methods of producing knowledge in service of their society, and how they act, such as building relationships, constructing homes or educating future generations, are all undermined by the very presence of colonial forces and their enforcement of the ways of the colonizer. Colonial domination reproduces ambiguity regarding the identity of the colonized that is hateful towards its kind while admiring the colonizer; it enforces a system of knowledge that associates the knowledge of local people with backwardness and gives an unquestionable superiority to the colonizer's form of knowledge and identifies the colonizer's ways of action as correct. It is imperative to understand that the colonizer's power is normalized, accepted and recognized by the colonized as the correct path of development. Linear developmentalism, prescribed as the sole path to progress in modernity, relegates those diverging from this path to the exteriority of modernity, deeming them archaic and ultimately subhuman (Dussel 1994; Escobar 2004).

In Kurdistan, these forms of colonial domination have been applied in two ways, which I name the double coloniality of power. First, there is the overarching structure of colonial hierarchies of modernity, atop which is placed the white Western male. The entire region, the Kurds included, is placed within this global colonial hierarchy. Second, there is the reinforcement of nationalist colonial power over the Kurds, placing them in an inferior position within the global racial hierarchy of colonial modernity. In other words, the four nation states (Turkey, Iran, Iraq and Syria) have imposed their particular colonial ways of being, knowing and doing on to the Kurds. The most detrimental aspect is that the Kurds have historically acclimated to this colonial structure to varying degrees (Zeydanlıoğlu 2008; Goner 2023; Sunca 2023c).

The movements that carried out anti-colonial struggles against colonizers ultimately reproduced colonial conditions in the lands that were formally decolonized. The processes of formal decolonization partially ended direct colonial rule. However, due particularly to the conditions of colonial continuities, postcolonial administrations were reproducing the coloniality of power within the former colonies. This reproduction extended from unrepresentative governance to hierarchical reorganization of postcolonial society and capitalist developmentalism to exclusions based on ethnic discrimination (Getachew 2019; Mamdani 2020; Sunca 2023c). Moreover, the majority of postcolonial societies have been far from addressing questions of gender-based domination and the reproduction of cultural essentialism, which relies on religion, sectarianism or pre-colonial tribal rules.

In Rojava, these pitfalls of formal decolonization were observable on at least three layers: the global coloniality of power, the colonial nationalism of postcolonial regimes and ostensibly anti-colonial Kurdish nationalism. The conditions under which the non-West operated were the same for all peoples: development would be assured if a people managed to form national unity through a nation state and, in this way, join the state-based world order, build industries, control nature and grow its economy. To achieve all these, the education of its people was tailored to enable collective progress towards a harmonious and prosperous nation embodying 'liberty, equality, and fraternity'. However, this romanticism was limited by the power accumulated within the structures of capitalism and the nation state, where societies were entrapped within internally unrepresentative but externally legitimate governance in the great majority of the world, in the service of global capitalism. Nonetheless, the romantic notion of a prosperous nation of liberty, equality and fraternity remained as a hegemonic direction for the rest of the world (Maldonado-Torres 2008; Sanjinés 2010; Bhambra 2018). After the revolution in Rojava, this structure was, and perhaps still is, intact. Western material superiority is an incontestable fact; however, the recognition of Westerners as superior poses a deeper problem because the ways of being, knowing and doing in Rojava were historically devalued against colonial modernity.

The colonial nationalism in Rojava, enforced by the Syrian state, has resulted in various forms of state violence. What matters in terms of being, knowing and doing is the enforcement of Arabization and the imposition of standards aligned with the regime characterized by nepotism and kleptocracy in Syria. Arabization policies have been evident in practices such as the establishment of Arab belts and the stripping of Kurds' citizenship in Rojava, exemplifying forced population displacement and the marginalization of indigenous Kurds in the region (Tejel 2009). The Syrian regime sought to exert control over the entire Syrian population, including Kurds, through a system of nepotism and kleptocracy, gradually established since 1963, to ensure the domination of the Assad family (Daher 2019). This had coerced society to adapt to new ways of being, knowing and doing for basic survival in a dictatorship. The dominance of the Assad regime has instilled enduring customs in Syria, almost becoming second nature, like the routine practice of bribing civil servants or seeking influential individuals to resolve their daily issues, which typically are government responsibilities. Addressing this fundamental problem became essential for the institutions established after the Rojava revolution.

The prescribed solution of colonialism was, for a long-time, state-seeking Kurdish nationalism. Its failure to establish a Kurdish state since the late nineteenth century presents two dilemmas. First, the fight to form a Kurdish state means not only confronting four major states that have colonized Kurdistan but also challenging an entire regional and global system of state-based order, which makes the goal of statehood very difficult, if not impossible. Second, the strict control over South Kurdistan by two families and how they have obliged the people of Kurdistan to submit to their corrupt family system illustrate that the mother tongue of the dominant might have changed, but the structure of domination remains the same. In Rojava, Kurdish nationalism is present in the everyday consciousness of the people as a major challenge against the anti-nationalist stand of the revolution (Sunca 2020).

Ultimately, the layered colonialism in Kurdistan brings about the necessity of not only emancipation from geopolitical domination but also the struggle for living a free life beyond coloniality of power and knowledge.

Democratic confederalism as an anti-colonial struggle

The idea of democratic confederalism, underlying the revolution in Rojava, is a political–practical and moral–philosophical response to this layered colonialism, suggesting original and imaginative solutions that emerge from Öcalan's synthesis of the PKK's struggle, the history of resistance and domination in the broader Middle East and reflections of Western and Eastern thinkers and philosophers (Üstündağ 2016: 198; D'Souza 2020). While it may not be the right place for a detailed account of its emergence, it is nevertheless important to reflect on some constituents of democratic confederalism as it forms the basis of the revolution in Rojava, including the university system. Democratic confederalism can be described as the ideology of anti-colonial struggle for liberation by the PKK through radical and direct democracy. It not only seeks the emancipation of the Kurdish people from colonial domination but also aims to overcome all forms of domination, including those of gender, racism, capitalism and nationalism, over time through struggle with the aim of forming a free society. It is constituted of *democratic autonomy*, which refers to the direct democratic self-rule of people through a bottom-up system of neighbourhood or village communes and regional assemblies; *democratic confederalism* as an umbrella organization of all democratic autonomous structures across borders that aims to gradually render state borders meaningless through everyday struggle; and *democratic nation*, which means the radical democratic coexistence of society with all its different colours, identities, orientations and values and which struggles for the recognition of this radical multiplicity of societies by existing states (Öcalan 2013a; Jongerden 2019; Sunca 2020).

Democratic confederalism is not the end goal of a struggle but the struggle itself, that is defined in two fields, broadly speaking. The first one can be named in the field of emancipation, which relates to *freedom from* direct domination as the etymological origins of the word *mancipium* suggest – release from enslavement. The second one is defined in the field of actually living freedom with full rights, that is, *freedom to* build the conditions of a free life.[3] As highlighted, formal decolonization has perhaps ended direct colonial rule, but it is far from ensuring freedoms; rather, it has reproduced old and new hierarchies. In the formulation of the struggle for democratic confederalism, emancipation and freedom are not in confrontation, nor are they in continuum but rather coexistent. The combination of both refers to prefigurative politics advanced by the PKK-led Kurdish movement (Jongerden 2013).

The emancipation in the vocabulary of democratic confederalism presents a pragmatic solution to the nation state-based world and regional order. The formula that democratic confederalism uses is that the more the space of radical and direct democratic structures, the less the centralized structures of the state. Forcing sovereign nation states by military means to withdraw from Kurdistan would mean a continuous armed conflict against four states. And yet, the feasibility of emancipation and compatibility of a Kurdish state with a free life are highly questionable, as the history of Kurdish nationalism shows. It therefore does not aim to bring down existing states but rather seeks to create a democratic space in which the structures of democratic autonomy and their active self-defence can gradually be built. Living freedom, as the second field of struggles, counters the entrapment of postcolonial states in nationalist, religious and patriarchal hierarchies. As discussed earlier, postcolonial states reproduce originally colonial exclusions based on national and religious identities that are safeguarded by the state and almost invariably perpetuate violent gender hierarchies. Democratic confederalism struggles for radical democratic coexistence of all identities through their internal autonomous self-rule on the one hand and their direct democratic interactions with all other identities on the other.

The revolution in Rojava has been built upon these principles. A revolution is usually defined as a radical transition of (political) power to a new group based on a popular mobilization which is followed by substantive and radical politico-social change. The revolutionary core of Rojava is the form of self-rule that has been materializing on the ground as much as its successful military defence. In other words, it is a revolution not merely because of power transition but mainly due to the values it materialized, such as women's liberation, radical democratic self-rule, exclusion of nationalism and ecological awareness.

The revolution in Rojava is a process of transition from the enforced truth of layered colonialism towards an imaginative solution where the historically conceivable truth of the colonized can enact liberation. The struggle for emancipation from direct colonial rule in the form of geopolitical dominations and the struggle for building a free life against all forms of social hierarchies encoded in the society are the two building blocks of democratic confederalism. It is essential to highlight that for the revolution to continue, Rojava should on the one hand continue to defend itself and on the other hand continue building what it stands for as an anti-colonial radical politico-social project. Although the transition has taken place, it is still far from being perfect as represented in several criticisms (Leezenberg 2016; Hammy and Miley 2022; Sunca 2023a), and it is this imperfection that is an undisputable precondition for the advancement of its revolutionary claims, which otherwise loses its impetus to continue radical transition. The remainder of this chapter will reflect upon the role of the UoR, particularly its Faculty of Political Science, in the struggles for emancipation and freedom.

The University of Rojava and decolonization

In the Western context, decolonizing university often means the decolonization of individual disciplines, curricula, modernist and colonial knowledge structures or hierarchy-driven teaching methods. Similarly, efforts related to Equity, Diversity, and Inclusion (EDI) practices, such as diversifying faculty and student profiles, have been acknowledged to some extent as primary concerns. These endeavours undoubtedly expose not only the established knowledge structures in the West but also the institutional practices that have fortified and perpetuated them. In this sense, efforts and practices aimed at decolonizing universities are intertwined with the global anti-colonial struggle. These efforts, however, can only be a part of the overall struggle for decolonization. The knowledge structures of colonized peoples are divided between two alternative truths: one that is oppressive and internationally legitimized and another that is historically resistant. Colonized peoples must reflect upon and consciously make sense of their colonization in order to overcome it. UoR aims to fill this gap by articulating the truth of colonized subjectivity as part of the overall anti-colonial struggle.

The first university established after the Revolution was Afrin University in 2015, which had to halt its activities in 2018 due to the Turkish invasion. The UoR was established in 2016, followed by Kobanê University in 2017 and the University of Al-Sharq in Raqqa in 2021. Each university is autonomous and coordinated by a Coordination Committee. The autonomous governance of the universities is ensured through councils and committees, such as the Women's Council or Student Council, where student representatives from each department are involved and sit together with university administration and professors to participate in decision-making processes (Rojava Information Center 2022).

The UoR currently has fourteen faculties, operating 31 departments with a total of 1,950 students. The majority of students receive their high school degrees from the schools of the Autonomous Administration which, by 2019, was running 70 per cent of primary, secondary and high schools according to their own curriculum. More than 65 per cent of students are women, reflecting the reality of ongoing war and economic conditions. The education system does not impose any age barrier for student admissions, allowing many who never had formal education before the Revolution to study and obtain diplomas right up to the university degree. Several students from other parts of Kurdistan study in Rojava. A prominent example are the students from *Mexmur* (Makhmur) refugee camp,[4] who study in different departments.[5]

For the great majority of Kurdish students, access to higher education was out of reach before the revolution. Only those with means were able to study in Aleppo or Damascus if they had citizenship. The establishment of the university system following the revolution was itself a foundational anti-colonial act, in the sense that the people of Rojava would be able to train not only their future generations but also produce the knowledge of the people of Rojava. Moreover, given the conditions of war, people with higher education diplomas in Rojava sought to escape Syria due to unemployment. The establishment of the university system in Rojava has played a crucial role against brain drain, as it provided employment in the university.

A fundamental philosophy of the Universities in Rojava is that knowledge and knowledge production are organic parts of society and therefore should be in service to empower it, rather than in service to power, capital or elites to reproduce their superiority. For reducing knowledge and knowledge production to vocational or professional training of technicians is the ultimate result of the neoliberalization of universities in service of neoliberal capitalism. Similarly, particularly in the Middle East but also in other parts of the world, universities are often established to reproduce the power positions of certain elites or serve as instruments of control over the population, not only through the type of education offered but also by controlling prestigious positions in higher education. A particular example for the university system in Rojava at its inception was the experience of universities of the KRG in Iraq, where each university belonged to a particular member of one of the ruling families. Maintaining the university as an autonomous locus of critical thinking, integrated as an organic part of society in service of that society, diverges from the pitfalls encountered in other experiences where universities submit to power. However, this path is not unchallenged.

Geopolitics of higher education

Building a university system from scratch under conditions of ongoing war, aggressions and bombardments makes higher education an immediate part of the anti-colonial struggle. The geopolitical aspect of colonial domination is perhaps the clearest example of this, consisting of several distinct forms of violence, while also reproducing its solutions from within. The near-constant bombardments have various impacts on education. They directly threaten the safety of students, professors and other university workers, given that the distance between the UoR and the Turkish border is approximately 3 kilometres. Moreover, low-altitude flights by warplanes and shellings make it impossible to continue classes. Another aspect of geopolitical limitations is the triple embargo by Turkey, Syria and the KRG, resulting in a lack of educational materials. This situation forces the university to rely on smugglers to bring in educational materials, such as books, and other necessary items. The recognition of students' diplomas by the Syrian state and internationally presents a real challenge. Before the revolution, diplomas could be obtained through bribery or with the help of influential people connected to the regime, rendering Syrian diplomas almost worthless. The non-recognition of diplomas is related to political motivations rather than the quality of education. This situation compels students to study in other universities, such as al-Furat University, a public university of the regime, or for students with means, a private university in Qamishlo. Internet connection is fundamental in Rojava, particularly for the Institute of Social Sciences and the Faculty of Political Science, mainly because these bodies carry out daily activities primarily through online participation of Kurdish-speaking professors from outside Rojava, mostly from Europe and North America, who are convinced of the values of the revolution. However, internet connection often poses a significant problem due to the lack of infrastructure.

Given the challenging conditions of war, which significantly impede the conduct of higher education, the UoR has primarily relied on international solidarity as a main form of struggle. The UoR has numerous collaborations with universities in the region and the West, including institutions like Bremen University. Additionally, many renowned public intellectuals such as Slavoj Žižek[6] and Noam Chomsky have delivered guest lectures, which have been instrumental in amplifying the voice and highlighting the issues faced by UoR. The Institute of Social Sciences plays a significant role in establishing connections with various universities worldwide. For the past two years, the institute has organized summer schools that attract scholars and researchers from around the globe. These research-intensive summer schools focused on topics like everyday practices of decolonization, indigenous struggles or abolitionism with participation from both Rojava and across the world.[7] Furthermore, there is a Centre for Solidarity with the Universities of North and East Syria, based in Paris, which is an association of scholars abroad engaged in solidarity work with Rojava.[8] They organize conferences, publish informational documents and, more importantly, are in constant engagement with various universities and civic organizations in support of the universities in Rojava. The UoR has established many connections with different communities, grassroot organizations and universities across the world, from Colombia to Thailand. One prominent example is that the university is a member of the Peace and Justice Network.[9]

Although the actual contribution of UoR to struggles for decolonization is much larger than can be covered here, these examples help in understanding it to some degree. It is important to differentiate between what is tactical and aims at emancipation from geopolitical domination and what is strategic and aims at freedom. For example, Zizek and Chomsky are not necessarily known for their anti-colonial positions, nor is Bremen University an actor for decolonization. However, first, through the visibility that such activities bring, the university system endeavours to organize solidarity, aiming to mitigate the impact of the ongoing war by exerting pressure on political actors in the West to contribute to the diplomatic recognition of Rojava and the academic recognition of its universities. Second, organizing together with other structures across the globe, such as the Peace and Justice Network, goes beyond the limited context of 'learning from each other'. This is strategic and contributes directly to living freedom by developing a common resistance to the imposed knowledge of colonial modernity.

Pedagogical practices

Before the revolution, the student agency was largely removed from the sphere of higher education resulting in the continuation of the originally colonial hierarchies. One major issue frequently observed with our students is their tendency to limit their participation to merely being physically present and listening to the instructor. Preparing for classes, actively engaging in discussions and undertaking additional work after classes to better understand the subject matter have rarely been prioritized. The focus has been predominantly on listening to the instructor and memorizing instructions for exams, with the goal of passing. This model has been fully embraced and internalized by some of our university professors as well, as it relieves them of further responsibilities and confines the process solely to instruction. There has been little emphasis on foregrounding the subjectivity of students and involving them in discussions. As a result, this instructional model establishes a hierarchical environment in the classroom, where students may not necessarily have the opportunity to engage in debates even if they desire to do so. The origins of this model can be traced back to the Ba'ath regime's imperative, particularly in social scientific disciplines, to instil unquestionable obedience and indoctrinate students, ensuring they do not pose any political challenges, both during their student life and as future critical thinkers. Many of us have observed, particularly in the Faculty of Political Sciences, that although the revolution has brought about numerous changes, this instructional model persists to a significant extent.

Similarly, when we began preparing for the establishment of the Faculty of Political Science, we encountered two major problems in organizing the curriculum and course content. The previous models were evidently what the Ba'ath regime's rule heavily relied on for fostering obedience by suppressing the subjectivity of students, similar to the educational model adopted in South Kurdistan. Meanwhile, neoliberal Western universities predominantly reproduced colonial superiority, with some notable exceptions found in professors who incorporate anti-colonial pedagogy into their courses rather than rely solely on institutional countermeasures. This was particularly apparent in the disciplines of political science and international relations (IR). Neither of these models aligned with our initial goal of forming critical thinkers equipped with values rooted in anti-colonial emancipation and sociopolitical liberation.

These two major issues, however, were not unexpected. Our experienced colleagues at the UoR enlightened our path through prior discussions. From the initial discussions until the present, the Faculty of Political Science has been striving for two main goals: disrupting obedience and fostering critical thinking against the layered colonial structure. We have succeeded in building an educational model primarily based on research, enabling our students to develop independent thinking before, during and after classes. Independent thinking here defines a delinking from the coloniality of knowledge rather than an independence from its social reality, as the positivist subject/object distinction alludes to. This approach ensures that the knowledge acquired through their courses extends well beyond the course period. Our primary aim is to teach them research methods to allow them to make their own learning rather than relying solely on teacher instruction. With few exceptions, we have eliminated traditional assessment methods such as exams.

To further cultivate critical thinking in our students, we have instituted a critical counter-reading of every course or module. For instance, in the course I teach, IR, I have implemented a double critical examination of the mainstream IR curriculum. In the first semester, we cover the ways in which IR is traditionally taught in the West, while in the second semester we engage with more critical approaches that challenge the omissions, acceptances and assumptions perpetuated by Western-centric practices in IR. Moreover, within each subject matter, we counter the Western-centric narrative with perspectives from non-Western, decolonial and/or feminist viewpoints. For example, when discussing genocides, while students are familiar with the Nazi genocide against the Jewish people and its international recognition, we also reflect on other genocides, such as the Belgian genocide in Congo, which are equally foundational to the constitution of the existing international order but have been overlooked in mainstream IR courses. Similar methods are employed across all our courses. These experiences demonstrate our efforts not only to decolonize teaching methods that objectify students and reinforce obedience but also to challenge the colonial construction and reproduction of truth.

As mentioned, the anti-colonial ideology underlying Rojava, democratic confederalism, aims to dismantle and potentially eradicate all forms of hierarchical power structures, including patriarchy. Therefore, fighting sexism throughout Rojava is an irrevocable priority for the university. The Department of Jineology (*Jineolojî*) holds particular significance in terms of reflecting on and ultimately dismantling masculinity and the domination of women. Jineology has evolved within the ideology and practice of the Kurdish movement as the science of women, with extensive reflections, work and exchanges dating back to the 1990s (Jineoloji Komitee Europa 2021). The transformation of society under this leadership has also been integrated into the university system. Jineology is not only a department and an academic field that trains young women to take the role of leading society but also a mandatory course for all students at the UoR. After completing Jineology courses, students at UoR gain a deeper understanding of the relationship between the construction of patriarchal power and cultural, traditional and religious beliefs regarding the place of women in society. Such a transformation is an essential part of decolonization, for decolonization is beyond ending direct colonial rule to overcome every kind of dominations that shape societies.

All in all, the pedagogical approach at UoR aims to disrupt internalized obedience to both colonial modernity, where the truth of the oppressed is distorted by various power structures, and the reproduction of this truth primarily benefits the same structures. These efforts go beyond the simple 'modernization' of a university in an 'underdeveloped' region. Modernization would suggest establishing Western mode of being, doing and knowing, while the primary duty of the underdeveloped would be to 'catch up with' the developed. However, the pedagogical practices at UoR challenge the very obedient personality that structures of power, such as colonial modernity, colonial nationalisms and gendered hierarchical dominations have created in the people of Rojava. These pedagogical practices are probably far from sufficient for genuine decolonization. But their continuation under the very conditions of war and their challenge to the functioning of power, is a direct contribution to the struggle for a free life. The layered colonialism is as real as falling bombs, and the UoR is responsible for producing knowledge of this reality. The brutal realness of colonization here underpins the knowledge of decolonization at the university system level, which in turn is identified within, and not outside, the overall anti-colonial struggle.

Language

One major contribution of the UoR, along with the University of Kobane, to the anti-colonial struggle has been higher education in Kurdish. Before the revolution, Kurdish was primarily confined to the private sphere, and its use in the public sphere was forbidden. According to the colonial nationalist mindset, Kurdish was not considered developed enough to enable an entire education, a statement of colonial superiority often used to justify the prohibition of the Kurdish language. Similarly, the fact that Kurdish is not standardized creates challenges for effective communication according to some Kurdish nationalists. Additionally, due to years of domination and prohibition of the Kurdish language, there is a significant lack of written materials, translations, books and articles indispensable for effective teaching. This is a primary concern for many professors at UoR. In some cases, it is even used as an excuse by some professors to continue traditional instructional methods that were customary before the revolution.

However, the fact that the UoR and the University of Kobane primarily conduct teaching in Kurdish deconstructs colonial nationalist discourse and revalues the Kurdish language as a language of education and reshapes the perceptions of younger generations in Rojava. It is particularly impactful when Kurds from Western countries converse in Kurdish with our students, allowing a greater appreciation for the language, although it reinforces the higher power position of professors from the West and the perceived superiority of Western education.

As far as the question of standardization of the language is concerned, it has always been highly questionable given that standardization is a direct opposite of multiplicity and a practice that subordinates the cultural and historical richness of the language to its functionality. In the Faculty of Political Science, after thorough discussions, we have acknowledged standardization as a colonial practice that erodes the cultural and historical depth of language. Despite the diversity of dialects among our students and professors, mutual comprehension has never been an issue. Any existing misunderstandings are resolved through discussion.

The scarcity of materials, such as books and articles, remains a persistent issue. However, we have established two alternatives to address this challenge. First, the Institute of Social Sciences sponsors translations of major works into Kurdish, which are then published by the recently established Rojava University Press. A notable example is the translation of Fanon's *The Wretched of the Earth*, titled *Cihêlîyên Cîhanê*, symbolizing the importance of anti-colonial thinking at UoR. Second, at the Faculty of Political Science, we teach English to our students in their first year as a year-long preparation course. This equips them with the ability to read many books and articles in English, alongside Kurdish and Arabic.

However, the importance accorded to English language at the Faculty of Political Science sparked a heated debate regarding its colonial status. The essence of the debate was twofold: on the one hand, the perpetuation of colonial superiority of English and its speakers within a political and social context striving for liberation and on the other hand, the undeniable necessity of learning English for the nature of work that graduates of our faculty would undertake. Important questions emerged in this context and continue to be relevant: the potential impact of an advanced English language curriculum on the status and perception of Kurdish, the challenges of teaching English due to the shortage of English teachers and the emergence of an 'elitism gap' between speakers and non-speakers of English. However, the Faculty of Political Science was primarily established to train future diplomats and political practitioners, who would predominantly operate in English. This fact reflects the global conditions of the domination of the West and the related status of the English language. The Rojava revolution emerged and will continue to exist under these circumstances, and it has to deal with it in one way or another.

This debate, which at times appears almost like a point of friction, teaches us about the colonial reality. Decolonization does not emerge in vain; rather, it operates against a violent sociopolitical reality of colonialism. Speaking English is essential for those who are trained to be the practitioners of emancipation from colonial geopolitics. Advancing the status of Kurdish, on the other hand, is intimately related to the struggle for building a free life. This duality makes Rojava University part of the overall anti-colonial struggle. It involves the principles of removing all forms of domination and the means to that end, which can only be omnipresent. In other words, it is not about either the predominance of the principles of a free life or emancipation from colonial realities. Such aspects of 'decolonizing universities' are probably less visible in the West, if they exist at all, given that the great majority of intellectual debate is already taking place in colonial languages, mainly among Black and Brown intellectuals.

Conclusion

Colonialism is a reality constructed over time through various forms of violence. A significant aspect of decolonization involves deconstructing this colonial reality. The experience of the UoR has emerged in such a spirit, not merely limiting itself to emancipation from direct colonial rule but actively undoing coloniality of power and knowledge. While discussions on decoloniality were part of its alternative university system, being face to face with the actual work of decolonizing the university, knowledge production and educational practices posed numerous challenges and dilemmas, exposing the reality of a colonized people. This chapter has touched upon only some of these issues. Nevertheless, the conclusions drawn from these experiences are crucial for any debate on decolonizing the university.

First of all, colonial ways of being, knowing and doing are primarily perpetuated and enforced through colonial violence. Acculturation into these structures and the normalization and mainstreaming of coloniality are direct outcomes of prolonged colonial violence. The struggle in Rojava is primarily against various forms of internalization of coloniality. The university system in Rojava actively participates in resistance through its global networks, curriculum, teaching methods and epistemological frameworks, some aspects of which I have highlighted in this chapter.

Second, the overall dynamics and overarching direction of decolonization also determine its methods. In Rojava, democratic confederalism has been the guiding principle underpinning the practice of decolonization, which has equally influenced the practices within the university system. Understanding democratic confederalism not as the endpoint of a revolutionary process or a completed project of emancipation, but rather as an ongoing struggle at various levels to build a free life, has enabled Rojava to continue the sociopolitical transformation it has promised. Without the concept of democratic confederalism, our focus might have been solely on the emancipation of Kurds in Rojava, without considering questions such as women's liberation, nationalism or the enforced superiority of the West. The history of the region, combined with the structural challenges within the specific conditions of Kurdistan, has facilitated such reflection, translating into actual struggles for liberation. In this regard, the role of Jineology in shaping the way decolonization is conceptualized provides invaluable insights into what went wrong in previous attempts at formal decolonization. The university system in Rojava is responsible for producing this knowledge of colonialism and decolonization.

Finally, decolonization is a whole and the university is part of it, and not vice versa. As the experience of the UoR shows, while the entirety of society is under unceasing colonial domination, and the violence is affecting every single aspect of the politico-social life, the debate on decolonization of the university cannot and should not remain indifferent. We cannot keep this debate at the level of intellectuals. In this continuum, one important aspect of it is to establish and nurture relations with the universities that struggle, on the one hand, against the geopolitical violence and, on the other hand, against global coloniality of power. Solidarity with the universities in Rojava can be seen in this context. Organizing together with the members of this alternative university system; understanding the Rojava revolution and its institutions, the universities included, on its own terms and not in pre-existing frames; reflecting on the ways the diploma recognition can be ensured; and denouncing the ongoing military aggression are just some practical ways of actually decolonizing university.

Notes

1 Rojava means 'west' in Kurdish and stands for West Kurdistan. It broadly refers to the territory run by the Democratic Autonomous Administration of North and East Syria.
2 It is essential to highlight that the representatives of Rojava particularly, and the Kurdish political movement following Öcalan's ideology in general, have continuously mentioned that they are very well aware of both the US position and pursuit of interests in the region, as well as its overall short- and long-term perils, not only for Rojava but also for the overall region. The ways in which the US–Rojava collaboration is represented in the Western mass media does not consider at all how it is being debated within and monitored by the movement. The difference they make is between the tactical handling of immediate situations and strategic alignment with global forces of resistance against capitalist modernity. For an assessment on the question of anti-imperialism, see the interview with Riza Altun, an executive member of the Kurdistan Communities Union: https://anfturkce.net/dunya/altun-anti-amerikancilik-anti-emperyalizm-degildir-98797
3 It should be emphasized here that living a free life refers to 'azadî', a collective form of 'being free' which requires continuous reflexivity for its reproduction in everyday life through struggle against any kind of domination. The freedom here is not individual freedoms but rather defined in inextricable connectivity with community (Öcalan 2013b: 285–6). In this sense, it is far from the Western liberal appropriation of the 'freedom' and its ideological reproduction in the service of capitalism (Öcalan 2013b: 320–5). The former defines an indispensable combination of liberated beings, doings and knowings, while the latter is the exploitation of freedom by capitalist modernity in the reproduction of an individualized, egocentric distortion of humanity.
4 *Mexmur* is a camp formed in the early 1990s by those who fled Turkish state atrocities. Established in Iraq and officially recognized by the UNHCR, the camp does not have access to developed educational facilities.
5 This data was provided by the Coordination Committee of the universities in Rojava.
6 See Zizek's address: https://www.youtube.com/watch?v=gTSta58iIl8
7 See the details of summer school in 2022: https://csua-paris.org/summer-school-2022-1
8 The centre's website gives detailed information on its activities: https://csua-paris.org/
9 See the network's website: https://www.peacewithjustice.org/

References

Akkaya, Ahmet Hamdi and Jongerden, Joost (2010), 'The PKK in the 2000s. Continuity through Breaks?' in Marlies Casier and Joost Jongerden (eds), *Nationalisms and Politics in Turkey: Political Islam, Kemalism and the Kurdish Issue*, 143–62, London: Routledge.

Akkaya, Ahmed Hamdi and Jongerden, Joost (2013), 'Confederalism and Autonomy in Turkey: The Kurdistan Workers' Party and the Reinvention of Democracy' in Gunes, Cengiz and Zeydanlıoğlu, Welat (eds.) *The Kurdish Question in Turkey: New Perspectives on Violence, Representation, and Reconciliation*, 186–204, London and New York: Routledge.

Bhambra, Gurminder K. (2018), 'The State. Postcolonial Histories of the Concept'. in Olivia U. Rutazibwa and Robbie Shilliam (eds), *Routledge Handbook of Postcolonial Politics*, 1st edn, 200–9, London: Routledge. https://doi.org/10.4324/9781315671192.

Bozarslan, Hamit (1997), *La Question Kurde: États et Minorités Au Moyen-Orient*, Paris: Presses de Sciences Po.

Çandar, Cengiz (2020), *Turkey's Mission Impossible: War and Peace with the Kurds*, London: Lexington Books.

Daher, Joseph (2019), *Syria After the Uprisings: The Political Economy of State Resilience*, London: Pluto Press.

D'Souza, Radha (2020), 'Reading Öcalan as a South Asian Woman', in International Initiative "Freedom for Abdullah Öcalan—Peace in Kurdistan" (ed.), *Building Free Life: Dialogues with Öcalan*, 103–18, Oakland: PM Press.

Dussel, Enrique D. (1994), *El Encubrimiento del otro: hacia el origen del mito de la modernidad*, Quito: Abya-Yala.

Escobar, Arturo (2004), 'Beyond the Third World: Imperial Globality, Global Coloniality and Anti-Globalisation Social Movements', *Third World Quarterly*, 25 (1): 207–30. https://doi.org/10.1080/0143659042000185417.

Getachew, Adom (2019), *Worldmaking After Empire. The Rise and Fall of Self-Determination*, Princeton: Princeton University Press.

Goner, Ozlem (2023), 'Rightful Recognition of Kurdistan as a Colony and De-Colonizing Knowledge Production', *The Commentaries*, 3 (1): 165–96. https://doi.org/10.33182/tc.v3i1.3147.

Hammy, Cihad and Miley, Thomas Jeffrey (2022), 'Lessons From Rojava for the Paradigm of Social Ecology', *Frontiers in Political Science*, 3 (January): 815338. https://doi.org/10.3389/fpos.2021.815338.

ICG (2014), 'Flight of Icarus? The PYD's Precarious Rise in Syria', *International Crisis Group*. Middle East report. https://www.crisisgroup.org/middle-east-north-africa/eastern-mediterranean/syria/flight-icarus-pyd-s-precarious-rise-syria (Accessed: 17 May 2024).

Jineoloji Komitee Europa, ed. (2021), *Weaving Another Future: Jineolojî – Readings in Womens Science*, Montreal: Black Rose.

Jongerden, Joost (2018), 'From Containment and Rollback to Escalation: Turkey's Kurdish Issue under the AKP', *Europa Ethnica* 75 (1/2): 40–48.

Jongerden, Joost (2019), 'Learning from Defeat: Development and Contestation of the "New Paradigm" within Kurdistan Workers' Party (PKK)', *Kurdish Studies*, 7 (1): 72–92.

Knapp, Michael, Flach, Anja and Ayboga, Ercan (2016), *Revolution in Rojava: Democratic Autonomy and Women's Liberation in Syrian Kurdistan*, London: Pluto Press.

Law, John (2011), 'What's Wrong with a One-World World', *Heterogeneities* (19): 14.

Leezenberg, Michiel (2016), 'The Ambiguities of Democratic Autonomy: The Kurdish Movement in Turkey and Rojava', *Southeast European and Black Sea Studies*, 16 (4): 671–90.

Maldonado-Torres, Nelson (2008), *Against War. Views from the Underside of Modernity*, Durham: Duke University Press.

Maldonado-Torres, Nelson (2016), 'Colonialism, Neocolonial, Internal Colonialism, the Postcolonial, Coloniality, and Decoloniality', in Yolanda Martínez-San Miguel, Ben Sifuentes-Jáuregui and Marisa Belausteguigoitia (eds), *Critical Terms in Caribbean and Latin American Thought*, 67–78, New York: Palgrave Macmillan.

Mamdani, Mahmood (2020), *Neither Settler nor Native: The Making and Unmaking of Permanent Minorities*, Cambridge, MA: The Belknap Press of Harvard University Press.

Matin, Kamran (2020), 'Liminal Lineages of the "Kurdish Question"', *Middle East Report* (295) (Summer). Available at https://merip.org/2020/08/liminal-lineages-of-the-kurdish-question/?fbclid=IwAR1JH_8eatYQUTQFBhj9nh2BYZBGKkQKnbr71EkGNhYMlRsd8Qur9W3-Lfk (Accessed: 17 May 2024).

Mignolo, Walter and Walsh, Catherine E. (2018), *On Decoloniality: Concepts, Analytics, Praxis*, Durham: Duke University Press.

Öcalan, Abdullah (2013a), *Demokratik Uygarlık Manifestosu III. Kitap: Özgürlük Sosyolojisi Üzerine Deneme*, Abdullah Öcalan Sosyal Bilimler Akademisi Yayınları.

Öcalan, Abdullah (2013b), *Demokratik Uygarlık Manifestosu IV. Kitap: Ortadoğu'da Uygarlık Krizi ve Demokratik Uygarlık Çözümü*. Abdullah Öcalan Sosyal Bilimler Akademisi Yayınları.

Rojava Information Center (2022), 'Young and Promising: An Introduction to the NES University System', Rojava Information Center report. https://rojavainformationcenter.org/2022/09/young-and-promising-an-introduction-to-the-nes-university-system/ (Accessed 17 May 2024).

Sanjinés, Javier (2010), 'The Nation: An Imagined Community?' in Walter D. Mignolo and Arturo Escobar (eds), *Globalization and the Decolonial Option*, 149–62, London and New York: Routledge.

Sunca, Jan Yasin (2016), *Infrastructures for Peace in Turkey. A Mapping Study*, Berlin: Berghof Foundation.

Sunca, Jan Yasin (2020), 'The Bifurcated Trajectory of Nation Formation in Kurdistan: Democratic Confederalism, Nationalism, and the Crisis of Capitalist Modernity', *Nations and Nationalism*, 26 (4): 979–93. https://doi.org/10.1111/nana.12609.

Sunca, Jan Yasin (2021), 'The Revolution in Rojava and the International', in Sandra Holtgreve, Karlson Preuss and Mathias Albert (eds), *Envisioning the World: Mapping and Making the Global*, 105–26, Bielefeld: Transcript.

Sunca, Jan Yasin (2022), *The Regional Kurdish Question in a Global World: Mentalities, Policies and Geopolitical Dynamics*, Istanbul: Truth Justice Memory Center.

Sunca, Jan Yasin (2023a), 'Colonial Continuities in the Kurdish Liberation', *The Commentaries*, 3 (1): 71–89. https://doi.org/10.33182/tc.v3i1.2915.

Sunca, Jan Yasin (2023b), 'Decolonial Politics: State, Statelessness, and Coexistence in Peace', *Journal of Intervention and Statebuilding*, June: 1–17. https://doi.org/10.1080/17502977.2023.2212992.

Sunca, Jan Yasin (2023c), 'Unpacking Inter-Subaltern Hierarchies: Gramsci, Postcolonial Nationalism, and the Kurdish Third Way', *Ethnopolitics*, October: 1–20. https://doi.org/10.1080/17449057.2023.2265636.

Tejel, Jordi (2009), *Syria's Kurds. History, Politics and Society,* London and New York: Routledge.

Ünlü, Barış (2018), *Türklük Sözleşmesi: Oluşumu, İşleyişi ve Krizi*, Ankara: Dipnot Yayınları.

Üstündağ, Nazan (2016), 'Self-Defense as a Revolutionary Practice in Rojava, or How to Unmake the State', *South Atlantic Quarterly*, 115 (1). https://doi.org/10.1215/00382876-3425024.

Zeydanlıoğlu, Welat (2008), '"The White Turkish Man's Burden": Orientalism, Kemalism and the Kurds in Turkey', in Guido Rings and Anne Ife (eds), *Neo-Colonial Mentalities in Contemporary Europe? Language and Discourse in the Construction of Identities*, 155–74, Newcastle: Cambridge Scholars Publishing.

Index

#RhodesMustFall 1

activism
  of Algerian women 64, 75
  Chomsky's political 37
  South Asian migrants' history of 156
Afghanistan 8, 55, 56, 69
Afghan women. *See* collateral damage
  dehumanization of 55
  feminist politics and 67–70
  the veil and 69–70, 74
African American/s
  bottom of the social order 86
  formation of racial categories 97 n.3
  racial minority *vs* 'negro' self-determination 168
  vs racism of CPUSA 167
  women and triple oppression 170–2
African continent
  cultures 126
  diaspora 126
  elite/elites 129
  emancipation/liberation 127
  ethnic groups 131
  leaders/ruling class/rulers 26, 127, 129, 130, 132
  politicians 125
  politics 125, 126
  slave labour/labour 131
African liberation literature
  Cha-Jua's '*black racial oppression*' 180–1
  Du Bois' *Black Reconstruction* 182
  Okoth's 'afterlives of slavery' 182
  Robinson's *Black Marxism* 182
  Wood's working class as proletariat 181
African Society for Cultural Relations with Independent Africa (ASCRIA)
  for defense of Africans globally 199
  IPRA and Moses Bhagwan 200
  'land rebellion' in 1973 199–200
  racial competition (*see* design of Sugar Plantations)
  Ratoon and Andaiye 200
  relation with Burnham's regime 199
  vs threat of Indian domination 199
aims of democratic confederalism
  coexistence of society 243
  emancipation from colonial rule 244
  freedom from social hierarchies 244
  radical direct democratic structures 243–4
Akkaya, Ahmet Hamdi 217, 219, 223, 237
Al-Ali, Nadje 224, 225
Algeria
  Algerians' national movement 174–5
  Front de Liberation Nationale (FLN) 175
Algerian women
  defiance of Islamist laws 67
  and dynamism of the veil 76 n.4, 77
  veiling and unveiling 58–62, 67, 76 n.2
Algeria Unveiled. See Fanon, Frantz; feminists responses to *Algeria Unveiled*
al-Saji, Alia 70
alterity 153
American Anthropological Association 90
Andaiye
  exchange with Kwayana 199
  as executive of WPA in 1978 201
  new dynamism in women's movements 203
  The Point is to Change the World: Selected Writings of Andaiye 191
  Red Thread organisation, co-founder of 201, 203

annihilation
    cultural suppression and   101
    epistemic   116
    of millions, Nazi regime   44
anthropology
    disciplinary forms for Indigenous
        peoples   84
    of the Iroquois   86–7
    The League of the Haudenosaunee   87
    political currents, critiques and
        philosophical trends   83
    voice of the colonized   81
anti-Bolsonarism   111
anti-colonial
    Algerian women's movement   56
    Fanon's *Algeria Unveiled*
        framework   64
    movements across European
        empires   42
    Öcalan's socialist transition from   222
    struggles   230, 236
    studies and politics   57, 75
anti-colonial framing   164–5
anti-colonialism
    demanding political and economic
        transformation   138
    Fanon's intellectual-political
        approach   63
    Marxist   151
    militant   144
    R. P. Dutt's work on   137
anti-hegemonic movements   105
anti-imperialism
    anti-imperialist consciousness   141,
        145, 155
    anti-imperialist resistance   142
    anti-imperial refutation   143
    and Black liberation   164–70 (*see also*
        Black liberation)
    Comintern Sixth Congress (*see*
        Comintern Sixth Congress)
    and the Left   144
    McKay's contribution   166–7
    and renewed radicalism in the
        West   148
anti-racism
    'anti-racism racism'   115
    anti-racist manifestations   118

Black Lives Matter (*see* Black Lives
    Matter)
Djonga (*see* Djonga)
hip-hop musical expression   110
Racionais (*see* Racionais)
anti-racist movements
    Black Panther Party   3
    North American Civil Rights
        Movement   107
    Black Lives Matter   12, 105
    Feminists' refusal to recognize
        activism of colonized women   75
apartheid
    decolonizing the mind against   15, 16
    and racial capitalism   179
art
    artistic manifestations   110, 118
    Black art   112
    Black literature and   105
    Djonga's   113
    subverting the tradition   109, 113
    visual art   107
ASCRIA. *See* African Society for Cultural
    Relations with Independent
    Africa
Ashcroft, Bill   215, 227
Asian Students' Society   139
authoritarianism
    Bolsonarism   109, 118, 119
    Burnham regime in Guyana   201
    'far right' or 'ultra-conservative right'
        movements   102
    significant escalation in India   156
Autonomous Administration of North
    and East Syria   238
Azikiwe, Namdi   126, 127

Bacon, Francis   33, 35
Baker, Lee   86, 97 n.3
Baku Congress   165
Balanta/s   130, 131
Balkan. *See* uranium
Bantu Education Act of 1953   1
barbarism/barbarity. *See* veil
    anti-Islam discourses   56, 69, 74
    Gaza War against purported Islamic
        barbarity   71
    of Islamic culture   75

Belo Horizonte 112, 118
BET Hip Hop Awards 2020 112
Bhabha, Homi 57, 90
Bhambra, Gurminder K. 13, 14, 48, 241
Bial, Pedro 112, 116, 117
Bill C-31
  blood quantum code 89
  Indian women, reinstatement in federal registry 88–9
  legacy in Kanhawake 94
Black/Algerian male 66
Black Arts movement 107
The Black Jacobins, Toussaint L'Ouverture and the San Domingo Revolution 130
Black liberation
  Black struggle 167, 169
  Black workers 164, 167, 172
  internationalism 174, 184
  labour super-exploitation 164, 167, 169, 170
  nationalism 169, 175
Black Lives Matter
  anti-Black racism 12
  anti-racism movement 12, 105
  George Floyd's cry 2
  North American Civil Rights Movement 107
  police repression 181
Black Lives Matter movement 181
Blackness, construction of 14
Black Orpheus (Sartre, Jean Paul) 115
Black Panther Party/Black Panthers 3, 172, 174
Black Power Movement(s) 107, 108
Black(s)
  Black Lives Matter 181
  Black Power Movement 107, 108
  Harlem Renaissance 105–8
  literature 105, 115
  Négritude movement (*see under* Négritude)
  North American Civil Rights Movement 107
  pride 101, 110
  struggle 104, 105, 107, 118
  victimisation of 115, 119

Black Scare / Red Scare (Burden-Stelly, Charisse) 181
Black Skin, White Masks 57. *See also* Fanon, Frantz
Black–white unity 173
Blyden, Edward Wilmot. *See* Pan-Africanists
Boers, Dutch 178
Boer War 140
Bolsheviks 164, 167
Bolsonarism 109, 118, 119
Bolsonaro, Jair 109, 110, 113, 119, 121 n.9
Born, Max 36, 38, 41, 43, 44
bourgeoisie
  British workers and the 146–8, 156
  divide-and-rule tactics of Guyana's 197
  Latin American bourgeoisie 193
  and the separate nation state 155, 218, 227
  'special Negro culture' and the coloured 168
  Turkish Left's view of the Turkish 217
  and US imperialism, Öcalan on Turkish 219, 220
British Guyana 127
British invasion of Guyana 1953 198
British Labour movement 149, 150
British rule 139, 143
Bukharin 165, 168
Burnham, Forbes
  assassination of Rodney 203
  dictatorship of 190–1
  'paramountcy of the party' 202
  relationship with ASCRIA, breaking point 199
  WPA, a perceived threat 203
  WPA's commitment to destruction of imperialism 201

Cabral, Amilcar
  analytical contributions 132–3
  on Guinea-Bissau under Portuguese rule 128
  on privileges of the ruling class 132
  on social structures of African ethnic groups 131–2

two faces of colonialism 20
Callaghan, John 2, 137, 139, 140, 145
Canada
  empowered political forms 84
  ethnographies of Native North
    America 86
  federal registry reinstation 88
  The Indian Act 88–91
  Riel Rebellion 92
  strategic interests in Guyana 198
Canadian government
  assassination of Sikh-Canadian
    activist 156
  gender bias in the Indian Act 89
capitalism
  in Africa *vs* in Europe 183
  class struggle and 130
  and imperialism 8
  racial 12, 16, 18, 179, 182
  racial capitalism 12, 16, 18, 179, 182
  racial oppression and 163, 164
  slave labour and global 130–3
  structural relations with racism 180
  and Third World neocolonialism 10
  Western capitalism 177
capitalist modernity
  Conscripts of Modernity 151
  crucial factor of modern
    colonialism 215
  developed and complex power 229
  economy free of monopolism to
    replace 227
  exploitation of freedom by 255 n.3
  global forces of resistance
    against 255 n.2
  gradual disappearance of 213
  institutional conditions for 28
  modernist knowledge systems 10
  nation-state, specific political form
    of 225
  rejection of 230
  transition to democratic
    modernity 225
Caribbean
  conception of Africa 127–8
  nationalism 128
  political-intellectuals 125, 128
  rehabilitation 127

Caribbean New Left 128
caste
  capitalism and 152
  and contemporary society 157
  exploitation 151
  oppression 155
censorship
  apparatus of British Empire 146
  of artistic manifestations 118
  as imperial benevolence 144
Centre for Contemporary Cultural Studies,
  Birmingham University 3
Césaire, Aimé
  anti-colonial sentiments in
    poetry 20, 102
  Discourse on Colonialism 114–15
  Discours sur l'art africain ('Discourse
    on African Art') 115
  Djonga and the poetry of 20
  on Hitler 114–15
  Miraculous Weapons 105
  Négritude movement 12, 106, 108–9,
    115–17, 127
  ontological suppression and epistemic
    annihilation 116
Chartism 150
chauvinism 169
Chhattisgarh 155
Choice MC 118
Chomsky, Noam 37–9
Ciep Operário Vicente Mariano
  elementary school 118
*Citizen and Subject: Contemporary Africa
  and the Legacy of Colonialism*
  (Mamdani, Mahmood) 132
citizenship
  colonial 81
  import for larger questions 83
  membership in Kahnawake
    community, and 88, 93–4
  nationhood, and 86
civilization, Iroquois. *See* Iroquois
civilization. *See* Iroquois
  to the Congo 176
  dualisms of Western 176
  in India 150–1
  Mesopotamian 225, 229
  semiology of 34

Index

class-based organisation
   decolonial and anti-capitalist
      way 206
   racialized and gendered division of
      labour 205
class warfare 155
climate crisis 155–7
collateral damage 70
collective memories 140
colonial
   accounting 93
   citizenship 81
   contact 83
   encounter 83
   impositions 89
   possibilities 84
   residues and reminders 91
   situations 82, 91
colonial domination
   colonial nationalism 236, 238, 239, 241
   double coloniality of power 236, 240–2
   geopolitical domination 236, 238–40, 242, 248
colonial enlightenment 151
colonialism. *See* Fanon, Frantz
   anti-colonial thinkers 9–11, 15, 21, 147
   coloniality of power 101
   colonial subjugation 66, 140, 218
   concept of 214
   distinct forms of violence 247
   French 174
   materialist approach 214
   Negritude movement against 117
   political–practical, moral–philosophical response 242
   racism and super-exploitation 180
   Rojava revolution (*see* Rojava revolution)
coloniality
   explanation of 12
   of power 101–4, 229
colonial nationalism
   Arabization 242
   rejection of Kurdish identity and self-rule 236
   Syrian Arab nationalism 237
   of Turkey, Iran, Iraq and Syria 237, 241
   Turkish nationalism 218
colonial rule
   ending of 4, 5, 75
   and imperialist domination 12
colonization and slavery 128
colonization of Kurdistan
   CUP's formulation of Turkish nationalism 218
   first partition in 1514 215
   global imperialist forces 219
   'imperialist colonial' form, Öcalan's view 218
   Kemalism, as Turkey's ideology 219, 220
   military phase of colonizing 219
   northern Kurdistan, colonization by Turkey 220
   PKK's manifesto 220
   Sykes–Picot agreement of 1916 216
   Treaty of Sèvres, promise of independence 215
   US neocolonialism in Turkey 220
colonizer/s
   brutalized to a point of savagery 114
   and the colonized elite 133, 141
   imperialist forces and regional 217, 219
   language as weapon 109, 116
   organization of violence 225
   'politicization of identities' 229
   superiority of 215, 240
Comintern
   Fourth Congress 166, 167
   reviving the spirit of 183
   role in Black liberation 174
   Second Congress 164
   Sixth Congress (*see* Comintern Sixth Congress)
Comintern Congress 147, 169
Comintern Sixth Congress
   call for complete emancipation 169
   emergence of labour super-exploitation idea 170
   labour super-exploitation, McKay on 167–8

national self-determination,
    Haywood 168
oppressed race and oppressed
    nation 167, 168
point of real change in CPUSA 165
Shiek, Ford and Patterson 168
Universal Negro Improvement
    Association (UNIA) 169
communism
  and African liberation 165, 167, 180
  British Communist
    movement 141, 145
  communist revolution in India 147
  global working-class solidarity 140
  the Indian Left 138
  and policies to combat 6
Communist International. *See* Comintern
Communist Party of Great Britain
    (CPGB)
  Dutt, R. P., member of 137, 138, 144
  hostile to Indian bourgeoisie 156
  tackling 'Empire consciousness' 143
  Tenth Congress 1929 147
Communist Party of India
    (CPI) 137, 138
Communist Party of the United States of
    America (CPUSA)
  Black liberation, three positions 167
  Claudia Jones, Black feminist leader
    in 171
  directed to a left turn by the
    Comintern 169, 170
  McKay's criticism of 166
  the 'Negro Question' 165
  the splits and their intersection 168
  Stalin's victory over Trotsky, impact
    on 165
Communists, white 166–7
confederalism. *See* democratic
    confederalism
Congo, Congolese 175, 176, 178
Consciência Black (1988) 110
conscientização or conscientization
  art for 105 (*see also* hip-hop)
  Freirean dialogue 103–5
consciousness
  anti-imperialist 141, 150, 155
  'Empire consciousness' 143

historical 11
internationalist 149, 239
post-colonial 90
revolutionary 16, 56, 57
Conscripts of Modernity (Scott,
    David) 151
Conservative Party 1, 156
Cook, Captain 84, 85
coups, military 6, 125, 155
Covid-19 112, 113, 155
CPGB. *See* Communist Party of Great
    Britain
CPI. *See* Communist Party of India
CPUSA. *See* Communist Party of the
    United States of America
Criminal Code 1940 117
Crow, Jim 169, 170
cultural suppression 101
culture
  anthropological concept 97 n.1
  complexities of 125–34
  difference, and 81–2, 85–6, 96
  dualisms in European 29–31
  foreign 93
  Indian 86
  Iroquois 87
  parochial conceptions of 141, 158
  'special Negro' 168
cybernetics 37, 38

Damas, Léon 106, 127
da Silva, Gustavo Pereira. *See* Djonga
da Silva, Marcos Vinicius 118
Davis, Angela
  activist-scholar 16
  Black internationalism 174
  Black people as cheap labour 173–4
  on Black-white unity as exploited
    people 172–3
  over-exploitation of Black
    workers 172
  Women, Race and Class 173
Decker, Liam 67
decolonial educational activities
  fundamental philosophy of UoR 246
  truth of colonized subjectivity 245
decoloniality 11, 12, 18, 229
decolonial pedagogy 113

decolonization. *See* national liberation
		struggles/movements
	colonizer's politicization of
		ethnicities 229
	concept of nation, new 228
	decolonial scholar 143
	liberation movements to anti-colonial
		struggles 230
	Öcalan's broader understanding 230
	Then and now (history of) 151
	and Third Worldism 2, 153
decolonization of the university
	challenges and dilemmas 253
	deconstructing the colonial
		reality 253
	pitfalls of formal decolonization 240
	practical ways of 254
decolonizing projects   205, 206
decolonizing science education   47-9
dehumanization. *See* fetishization of
		the veil
	of Afghan/Muslim women 55, 73
	backlash to lyrical anger against 115
	of colonized people 15
	of Palestinians 55, 58, 72
	of Palestinian women 3, 73, 75
deindustrialization and
		deproletarianization 180
democracy
	Enlightenment 31
	liberal 36
	Öcalan on 225-31
	promotion of 7
Democratic Autonomous Administration
		of North and East
		Syria 255 n.1
democratic confederalism
	aims of 242-3
	building blocks of 244
	definition of 243
	democratic nation, idea of 231
	democratic nation 226
	'different collectivities' 228
	disappearance of capitalist
		modernity 213
	and entrapment of postcolonial
		states 244
	flaws in Öcalan's liberation ideas 231

living freedom with full
		rights 255 n.3
	non-state society 225
	Öcalan's synthesis 243
	political pillar of democratic
		modernity 227
	roadmap for decolonization 223
democratic modernity
	economy free of monopolism 227
	institutional bases of 227
	non-hierarchical social
		formations 229
	political form of democratic
		confederalism 225, 230
democratic nation
	democratic autonomous
		institutions 228
	free and equal individuals and
		communities 226
dependency   108 n.5, 192
dependency theory/ies
	Marini's 190, 192, 208 n.5
	Marxist 21, 163, 184
deracialization   4, 8
design of Sugar Plantations   199-200
development, industrial   145
The Dialectics of Dependency (Marini, Ruy
		Mauro) 190
dialogue
	of African Americans and
		Comintern 164
	PKK and Turkish governments, failure
		of 237
	rap and 109, 110
	via conscientization 103-5, 107
	word as the essence of 108
diaspora
	African 106, 126, 134
	cultural mission 141
	desis (South Asian diaspora) 142
	diasporic identity 142
	diasporic radicals 146
	Indian American 141, 143
	privileged political space 155
	question of 'authenticity' 20
	South Asian 142, 156
difference
	culture and 81-2, 85-7, 96

describing the 95
    as unit of analysis 83
difference and division in working class
    Andaiye 190, 198–200
    Marini, Ruy Mauro 190, 192–3
    Rodney, Walter 190, 193–8
Discours sur l'art Africain (Discourse
    on African Art), Césaire,
    Aimé 115
discrimination
    alienation and 141
    of Black people 106
    a form of defensive nativism 156
    and hierarchies 229
    and oppression 230
    resistance of indentured
        workers 208 n.9
    as super-exploitation 171, 177
dispossession
    of the Akawaio 209 n.12
    colonial 62
    combatting the colonial afterlife
        of 206
    families' survival in conditions of 71
    and genocide of the Indigenous 16
    justification of 85
    violent projects of 155
dissent, colonial-era legislation to
        stifle 155–6
divide-and-rule tactics
    in Guyana 189
    of Guyana's bourgeoisie 197
    of the PNC government 202
DJ Kld 110
Djola/s 130, 131
Djonga
    on becoming 'the king of rap' 112
    BET Awards nomination 112
    Césaire's poetry, reminiscent of 20
    collective call for concern 119
    creative work 112–19
    Favela Vive 3 (Favela Lives 3) 118
    'fire on the racists!' (*fogo nos
        racistas!*) 111
    highlight of the North American
        Billboard 121 n.10
    Histórias da Minha Área (Stories From
        my Area) 112

international celebrity status 113
Junho de 1994 (June of 1994) 116
negative reactions to lyrical
        rage 117–18
Olho de Tigre (Tiger Eye) 113–14
poetry as incitation of
        violence 116–17
'reverse racism' accusation 113
domination of Kurds 237
Dossa, Parin 69, 70
double coloniality of power 240–1
double colonization of Kurdistan 214
D'Souza, Radha
    decolonization of education 5, 8–9
    democracy promotion by imperial
        powers 7–8
    emergence of NIS as a political
        force 4–5
    identitarian theoretical
        frameworks 6–7
    neocolonialism 5–6
    seeds of racial, religious and national
        discord 4
    'Third World, in Theory' reading
        group 9
dualism. *See* non-dualist approach/es
    civilized/uncivilized 32
    cosmological dualism 30, 31, 40
    epistemological dualism 29–31
    nature/culture divide 38, 39, 47
    ontological dualism 30, 31, 40
    power/culture 31
    spiritual/material 46
    'West *vs* the Rest' critique 32–3, 35,
        47, 48
dualist structure/s
    in European thought/
        modernity 28, 31–4
    Newton's theory of optics 35
Du Bois, William 14, 15, 103, 106, 183
duopoly of knowledge 31, 32
Dutt, Rajani Palme
    anti-imperialist revolution 154–5
    conscription case, First World
        War 139
    critique of colonial discourse 145
    decolonization, pluralistic vision of the
        world 151–2

'Delay of the Socialist Revolution in
    the West' 147–9
early years 137, 139
'Empire consciousness' 143
Indian liberation's impact on
    Britain 150–1
Indian state's repressive colonial-era
    legislation 155–6
India To-Day 139, 142–3, 153
inevitability of capitalism's
    destruction 149
interdependent revolutions 146–7
'jailers and jailed' 146
Labour Monthly article 144
militancy of the right 156–8
Modern India 145
overthrow of class society, aim to
    141
political interest in the
    'homeland' 142–3
reputation in England 137
romanticization of the pre-
    colonial 152–3
Sandhu on 20
'The Colonial Struggle for
    Liberation' 149
Third Worldism 153–4
The Eastern Door 92

Edgerton, David 36, 38, 40, 42
Edi Rock 110
education
    decolonizing science education
        47–9
    in neocolonial contexts 2, 19
    neoliberalization of 1, 2
    as soft power 6, 19
    steps to recolonize 6
Einstein, Albert 36, 38
emancipation, African 199
Emicida 102, 105
Empire. *See* US Empire
    anthropological relationship to 95
    colonial situations 81–2
    Indigenous scholars and 96
    settler societies 83, 96
Empire consciousness 143
endo-cannibalistic events 29

*An End to the Neglect of the Problems
    of Negro Women* (Claudia
    Jones) 171
English as preparation course
    need for the language 252
    perpetuation of colonial
        superiority 252–3
English audiences 157
English political scene 129
English readers 144
English translation 163, 166, 177
English unions 146
English workers 148
Enlightenment rationalism 151
Enlightenment thinkers 33
epistemological dualism/s 29, 30, 31
Equal Rights for Indian Women 89
essentialization
    of Afghan women 58
    of Islamic culture 75
    of Muslim women 75
    of 'nativism' 16
ethics
    and European modernity 38
    and knowledge workers in the
        humanities 39–40
    science, humanities and 3
    and scientists (*see* scientists)
    and sociology 43–4
ethnic cleansing 71
ethnicity. *See* race; racism
ethnographic analysis 83
ethnographic refusal
    as alternative to 'recognition'
        politics 20, 86, 87, 96
    to the authority of the state,
        Kanawake:non 90
    example of 93–5
ethnography
    documentary, *The League of the
        Haudenosaunee* 87
    in the familiar 92–5
    Mohawk nationhood, of 86
ethnological comparison 81
Eurocentric epistemologies 104
Eurocentric Marxism 182, 183
Eurocentric psycho-analytic
    tradition 63, 67

Eurocentric social theory   13
Eurocentrism
　anti-colonial critiques of   14, 15
　deepening the university's whiteness
　　and   17
　Marxism as a variety of   151
　refutation of   152
　theory of interdependent
　　revolutions   147
　Uberoi's critique of European
　　modernity   32
　'West vs Rest' argumentation   33
European modernity. See European
　　underground
　adapted to Indian conditions   45–6
　destructiveness of   16, 28, 31–4,
　　39–40, 48
　explained   29–31
　non-dualist critique of   32–5
　and states and corporations   40–4, 46, 49
　Uberoi's critique   28–35
Europeans   34, 129, 130, 177
European underground   34, 35
exo-cannibalistic events   29
exploitation, disparate forms of   190

Fanon, Frantz
　Algerian revolution, politics of   56
　on Algerian women and the veil
　　59–64, 75
　Algeria Unveiled   56, 58–9, 174, 175,
　　182, 252 (*see also* feminists'
　　responses to *Algeria Unveiled*)
　anti-colonial framework/
　　revolution   58, 61, 63
　biography   57
　Black Skin, White Masks   57
　critique of Eurocentric
　　psychoanalysis   63–4
　cultural essentialization of
　　nativism   16
　on culture during conflict   104–5,
　　109, 110, 119
　dynamics of racial–gender
　　politics   56, 57
　fetishization of the veil   57, 60
　on historical subjectivity   104–5, 109,
　　110, 119
　iconic anti-colonial revolutionary   19
　transformation of Algerian
　　society   62–3
　understanding of Algerian women   64
　women's relation to un/veiling   56,
　　59–62, 76 n.4
　The Wretched of the Earth   11, 57,
　　104–5, 175, 252
fascism   36, 101, 118, 119, 137, 156
Faulkner, Rita   65
Favela Vive 3 (Favela Lives 3)   118
Feminists' responses to *Algeria Unveiled*
　Cornell's favourable view   68
　Decker's contention   67
　Faulkner's argument   65
　Helie-Lucas' response   64–5
　Lazreg's analysis   64
　McClintok's nuanced approach   65–7
　Sharpley-Whiting's receptive
　　reading   67–9
fetishization of the state   223
fetishization of the veil
　and colonial policies in Algeria   56–7
　feminist   19
　and the racial–gender politics   75
　as reflection of Algerian agency   58
　symbol of Islamic terror/
　　barbarism   55, 58, 69, 74
　Western   76 n.1
Fim de Semana No Parque (Weekend at
　　the Park)   111
fire on the racists   101, 102, 103, 110,
　　111, 112, 113, 114, 116, 119
First World War   36, 37, 40, 42
FLN. *See* Front de Liberation Nationale
fogo nos racistas. See fire on the racists
formation of Kurdish state   237, 242
four class alliance of China   5, 7
Freire, Paulo   103, 108
Front de Liberation Nationale (FLN)   175
Fula   131, 132

Garvey, Marcus (Pan-Africanist)   126,
　　127, 169
Gaza War. *See* War on Terror
　'open air prison'   71
　racial–gender politics and the   72–4
　silence on the veil in the   55, 71

gaze and reverse-gaze   10, 33
genocide
   feminist complicity in   75
   gendered dimension in Gaza   58
   racial–gender politics in Gaza   72–4
geopolitical domination
   control of external forces   238
   international support for Rojava, waning of   239
   Rojava *vs* the Islamic State   239
   US policy, inconsistency of   239–40
   Western domination   239
geopolitics of higher education in Rojava   247–8, 253
Getachew, Adom   14, 16, 18, 241
Ghadar movement   142
Ghana (Gold Coast)   127, 128
Ghassemlou, Abdul Rahman   216, 217
global South   155, 182, 184
global working class
   decolonial projects   189–90
   difference and division in, treatment of (*see* difference and division in working class)
   exploitation, disparate forms of   190
   labour super-exploitation, generalization of   207
   structural roots of disunity   189
Goethe's non-dualistic theory of optics   35
Gold Coast. *See* Ghana
Gonzalez, Lelia   102, 103
Group for Research and Initiative for the Liberation of Africa (GRILA)   126
Grundrisse (Marx, Karl)   32
Guinea-Bissau   128, 131, 133
Gulf War Syndrome. *See* uranium
Gutzmore, Cecil   197, 198, 207 n.1, 208 n.3, 208 n.7
Guyana's independence in 1966
   divide-and-rule policy in Guyana   189
   Red Thread's oral history project   198
   reification of racial politics   198
   Working People's Alliance, formation of   200–1

Half-breeds in Kahnawake   92
Hamas
   attack on 7 October 2023   71
   construct as barbaric   55, 71–74
   dehumanization of Palestinian women   3, 73, 75
Gaza War   71
Harlem Renaissance   105–8
Haywood, Harry
   'Negro' self-determination stand   168–70
   super-exploitation notion   164
Haywood–Nassanoff thesis   169
hegemony   101
Helie-Lucas, Marie   58, 64–5, 69
hierarchization   102, 116
hindering educational activities in Rojava
   BA'ath regime, legacy of   249
   differentiated colonial practices   235
   English language, place of   252–3
   military agressions   235
   Turkey's, Iraq's and US colonial practices   235
Hindu Nationalists   153
Hindu Right   156
Hip-hop movement
   Brazilian   110
   culture   107, 108
   generation   107, 119
   movement   105, 107, 108, 112
   and rap   108–10, 113
Hiroshima–Nagasaki bombings
   and the compartmentalization of the brain   37
   and the Holocaust   29, 36, 46
Histórias da Minha Área   112
historical memory   116
historical subjectivity   104, 119
histories, Eurocentric   5
history
   of colonialism   83
   in the familiar   92–6
   and Iroquois studies   87
   living histories   85
   of the Mohawks   94–5
   political   86
A History of the Guyanese Working People 1881-1905

assumed docility of Indian workers 197
communal thinking, product of
    bourgeois self-interest 197–8
labour shortage, myth of 197
segmented working class, creation
    of 193
strength (and legacy) of 206
*A History of the Upper Guinea
    Coast* 128, 129
Hitler, Adolf 114–16
Holocaust
    absence of sociological studies 43
    and Hiroshima-Nagasaki
        bombings 26, 29, 46
    and organization of
        corporations 42, 49
How Europe Underdeveloped Africa
    (Rodney, Walter) 131, 190
Huiswoud, Otto 167–8
humanization of Israeli women 73
human rights 7, 70, 88, 115, 156
Hussain, Sophia 156, 223

Ice Blue 110
identitarian theories/politics
    colonialism and 5–6
    neocolonialism and 4
ideology
    anti-colonial 106
    fascist 109
    political 109
imperialism
    colonial, British 178, 179
    feminist theory and 69, 76
    imperialist countries 147, 179,
        182, 184
    and the spread of European
        modernity 33
    Wall-Street 181
imperialist division of labour 191
indentured (girmitya) from
    India 195, 197
India
    independence movement 137, 143
    Indian-ness 139
    Indian society 152
Indian Act in Canada
    interview of citizen of Kanhawake 93–5
    modification to the 88–9
    rules of recognition in 91–3
Indian Mutiny of 1857 148
Indian Political Revolutionary Associates
    (IPRA) 200
Indian Wars 92
Indian women, status of. *See* Bill C-31
India's 'unity in diversity' 5, 7
India To-Day (Dutt, Rajini Palme) 139
indigeneity
    colonialism and anthropology 81
    historical and legal effacements
        of 83, 85
indigenism 88, 152, 153
indigenous
    as a category 83
    contexts 82 (*see also* indigeneity)
    occupation 85
    'radical indigenism' 88
    scholars and the Empire 96
    SettlerState relations 88
indigenous critique. *See* West *vs* Rest
Indigenous peoples
    ancestral territories, legal title to 85
    empower and disempower 84
    of Guyana 194, 201, 209 n.12
    of India *(Adivasi)* 155
    of North America 96, 97
    and self-governance 4
Indonesia. *See Pancasila*
industrial revolution, second 41
injustice, epistemic 47
The Intercept 156
The Internationale 165
internationalist consciousness 149
Internationals, First, Second and
    Third 137
intersectional approaches 174
intragender power 68
IPRA. *See* Indian Political Revolutionary
    Associates
Iran
    imperialist interventions in 147
    oppression of Kurds in 217, 220,
        236–7, 241
    partition of Kurdisthan 215
    status of Kurds post First World War
        in 216

Iroquois
  citizenships 91
  confederacy 86–7, 97 n.2
  peoples 90, 96
  studies 87
Islamic 'terror'. *See* barbarism/barbarity
Islamist laws, defiance of. *See*
    Algerian women
Islamophobia. *See* orientalism
  women and Islamic terror 58
Islamophobic racialized discrimination.
    See Palestinian women
Israel
  Israeli occupation of Gaza (*see*
    Gaza War)
  Israeli propaganda 72
  Israeli sexual fixation 73

Jaffe, Hosea
  acute case of labour super-
    exploitation 179
  apartheid 179
  labour super-exploitation 179–80
  *La Plusvalía Oculta: Como funciona el
    imperialismo* (Hidden Surplus
    Value: How Imperialism
    Functions) 179
  Non-European Unity Movement
    178
  racist system in South Africa 178–9
jailers and jailed 143–6
James, C. L. R.
  on abolition and the rural
    proletariat 208 n.7
  on armed rebellion 147
  association with Walter Rodney 129
  *The Black Jacobins: Toussaint
    L'Ouverture and the San
    Domingo Revolution* 130–1
  Haitian Revolution, classic work
    on 128
  idealized perception of Africa 127
  literacy campaign in African
    societies 125–6
  Lo's response to 126
  role as an exiled intellectual 134 n.1
  slave labour and global
    capitalism 130, 131
  social and political state in
    Africa 125
  writing from the outside 126
James, Selma 129, 204
jazz 106, 109
Jineoloji Komitee Europa 250
Jones, Claudia
  analysis of the location of black
    women 171–2
  cultural and political resistance
    170
  discrimination as super-
    exploitation 171
  *An End to the Neglect of the Problems of
    Negro Women* 171
  white privilege 171
Jongerden, Joost 217, 219, 237, 243
Jornal Nacional 112
Junho de 1994 116. *See also* Djonga
justice
  decolonization for 11, 15, 19
  epistemic 47
  global 37
  social 45

Kahnawake
  blood quantum code in 89
  The Eastern Door 92
  half-breeds in 92
  and the Indian Act 89–91
  membership in reservation community
    of 88–90
  Mohawk Council of 92
  Mohawks of 82, 97 n.2
  non-Indians in 92–5
Kahnawakero:non 90
Kenyatta, Jomo 126, 127
knowing
  anthropological limits of 96
  methods and modalities 81
  ways of 83–6
knowledges
  adapt, modify and change 19
  adaption of Western 46
  'diversity and inclusion' of 47, 48
  hierarchization of 102
  violence of the fragmented
    disciplinary 27, 36, 41

Kofi Baadu Out of Africa (Rodney, Walter)   203
Kurdish language in higher education   252
Kurdish question
  democratic confederalism (*see* democratic confederalism)
  independent Kurdish state   213
  new dimension   213
  Öcalan's ideas, early and later years (*see* Öcalan's ideas)
  roadmap for decolonization   223
Kurdistan Workers' Party (PKK)
  anti-colonial struggle for liberation   237, 243
  economies dependent on imperialism   220
  'imperialist colonial' form   218
  Kurdish movement   21, 243
  Kurdish question   213–14
  Marxist–Leninist ideology   220, 221
  national independence   222
  national oppression of the Kurds   213
  Öcalan, founder of   21
  Öcalan' arrest   243
  The PKK's Manifesto   217
  US–Rojava collaboration   239–40, 255 n.2
  Women's movement   224–5
Kwayana, Eusi
  ASCRIA and global emancipation movement   199
  campaign to defend Rampersaud   202
  on Rodney's arrival in Guyana   201

Labour Monthly   138, 144, 145
Labour Party   145, 147, 149, 156
labour super-exploitation. *See* workers
  and Black liberation struggles   164
  of Black women   171–3
  of Black workers in the US   167–70, 172, 181
  and capitalism   183–5, 189
  cheap labour in Guyana   193
  concept of   163, 164, 167, 193
  and divide-and-rule policy   189
  in the global South   184
  and imperialism   184, 185
  in Latin America   190
  Marini's concept   168, 184
  Marxist theory and liberation struggles   184
  by Negro bourgeoisie   168
  ontological recognition of surplus labour   183
  perverse rationality of dependent capitalism   196
Lakshmi Out of India (Rodney)   203
language in higher education in Rojava
  English as preparation course   252–3
  lack of materials in Kurdish   251
  teaching in Kurdish in UoR   252
La pensée politique de Patrice Emery Lumumba (Sartre, Jean Paul)   177
La Plusvalía Oculta: Como funciona el imperialismo (Hidden Surplus Value: How Imperialism Functions), Jaffe, Hosea   179
Latin America   163, 165, 175, 180, 190
Lazreg, Marnia   60–2, 64
League Against Imperialism   143
The League of the Haudenosaunee   87
legacy of slavery   127
Lenin   125, 148, 163, 164, 221
L'Étudiant Noir (The Black Student), Césaire, Aimé   106
liberation, worldwide   141, 147, 153, 154
Locke, John   33, 35, 85
Lokayata   46
Lorde, Audre   104, 114
Lumumba, Patrice
  African nationalism, exemplified by   175
  assassination of   175–7
  Congo's independence, significance of   176
  Congo the pride of Africa   176
  Independence Day speech   176
  Lumumba by Raul Peck   175–6
  Okoth in the footsteps of   182
lynching   106, 166, 169–70

Mabo decision   84
machine learning   38

Makonnen, Ras   127
Maldonado-Torres, Nelson   12, 236, 241
Mamdani, Mahmood
   analysis of the nation state   228–9
   Citizen and Subject: Contemporary Africa and the Legacy of Colonialism   132
   Colonization's implications   227–8
   global war consequences   12
   'minority–majority' categorization   2
   reproducing coloniality of power   241
Mano Brown   110
Marini, Ruy Mauro
   Brazil's transition to political sovereignty   192
   on capitalist/imperialist division of labour   184, 191
   capitalist international division of labour   184
   Dialéctica de la Dependencia (The Dialectics of Dependency)   163, 190
   The Dialectics of Dependency   190
   exhaustion, low wages and long hours   168
   expanded reproduction of dependency   191
   and Jaffe's works   178–80
   labour super-exploitation   190–1, 207
   political life   190
   production of relative surplus value   193
   racial oppression and capitalism   163–4
Marini's analysis of super exploitation
   benefits from super-exploited slave labour   193, 208 n.5
   Brazil's political sovereignty   192, 193, 208 n.5
   Factory Acts of 1840 in England   192
   industrializing economies and labour exploitation   192–3
   intensive and extensive use of labour   192
   sui generis form of capitalism   192
Martinique   57, 106, 127
Marx, Karl
   and Claudia Jones   171–2
   Das Kapital, Volume 2, 179
   dualisms in capitalist societies   32
   Dutt on Marx's optimism   148–9
   and Engel's views on Ireland   147–8
   general law of accumulation   210 n.19
   on the general law of accumulation   210 n.19
   Grundisse   32
   and Indian Communists   151
   on Ireland   148
   on the Irish question   147–8
   from Letters to Engels   148–9
   logical extension of his theory   172
   means of production and consumption   179
   narrow and literal interpretations of Marxism   183
   on transition to mechanized labour   192
   way to socialism in Britain   148
   workers' class-consciousness   131
   Workers of all lands, unite   165
Marxism
   economistic   152
   Eurocentric   182
   as Eurocentrism   151
   for India   152
   Marxist anti-colonialism   151
Marxist–Leninist positions   171, 191, 221
materialist approach to colonialism
   creation and development of capitalism   215
   double colonization (*see* double colonization of Kurdistan)
   relation of domination by the colonizer   214
   social and political relations, type of   214–15
Matin, Kamran   230, 239
McClintock, Anne   65–7
McDowall, David   213, 216
McKay, Claude
   idea of labour super-exploitation   167
   'If We Must Die'   166
   'Negroes'   166
   participation in Comintern's Fourth Congress   166–7

'Sex and Economics' 166
Meerut Conspiracy Case
   trade unionists' arrest 146, 149
   trade unions' solidarity 158 n.2
Mignolo, Walter 10, 12, 236, 240
military industrial complex 13
Mintz, Sidney 195, 206, 208 n.7, 208 n.8, 208 n.10
miraculous weapons. *See* Césaire, Aimé
   Brazilian rap as 102
   spoken words as 105–12
Modern India (Dutt, Rajini Palme) 145
Modernist knowledge. *See* European modernity
Mohawk(s)
   Council of Kahnawake 92
   history 92
   of Kahnawake 82
   language 83
   member nation 86
   nationhood 86, 88, 90
   single nation 97 n.2
   valley 92
Montreal Congress of Black Writers 128
Morgan, Lewis Henry 86–7
Mudimbe, V. Y. 126, 127
Muggeridge, Malcolm 139
multilayered colonialism
   colonial nationalism in Rojava 241, 251
   double coloniality of power in Kurdistan (*see* double coloniality of power)
   geopolitical domination in Kurdistan (*see* geopolitical domination)
   hindering education in Rojava (*see* hindering educational activities in Rojava)
Muslim woman/women
   Afghan women 55, 67–70, 74
   Algerian women 58–62, 67, 76 n.2, 76 n.4, 77
   Palestinian women 3, 71–5 (*see also* Palestinian women)

Nagasaki. *See* Hiroshima–Nagasaki bombings
nation, new concept of
   autonomous social and political institutions 213
   cooperative economy 230
   emancipatory and democratic solution 228
   homogenised society *vs* different collectives 228
   imprecise contours of democratic nation 228
   threaded by political mechanism 228
national liberation struggles/movements
   African Americans' common cause with 174
   classical to present 230
   decolonization as trigger for 4
   legacy of African Marxists 182
   in line with other parts of the world 217
   Öcalan's aim to change colonial relations 231
nationhood and citizenship 86
Native Women's Association of Canada 89
nativism
   anti-colonial and anti-imperial thought 151
   defensive 156
   essentialization of 16
nature/culture divide 38, 39, 47
Négritude
   anti-racism racism 115
   Fanon's critiques of 58
   movement 105–8, 113, 115, 127
   and whiteness 106
Negroes
   and labour super-exploitation 167–9, 176
   as oppressed nation 168, 170
   as oppressed race 167
   plight, McKay's views on 166
   as a 'racial minority' 168
   right to self-determination 168, 169
neocolonialism
   in the early years of decolonization 5–6
   and identitarian politics in the Third World 7
   and its widespread pattern 130

and military intervention 8
and Okoth's assessment of its
  emptiness 174, 177, 182
and recolonizing education 6–7
neoliberal globalization 12, 178,
  182, 207
New International Economic Order
  (NIEO) 4
Newly Independent States (NIS) 4–6
Newton, Isaac 33, 35
New World Order
  emergence of the Newly Independent
    States 4
  events that marked the
    inaugural of 36
  implications for Turkey 219, 220
  and the meaning of
    decolonization 44
NIEO. *See* New International
  Economic Order
Nkrumah, Kwame 5, 126, 127, 177
non-dualism 31, 32
non-dualist approach
  to knowledge, Uberoi's 32–4, 49
  to philosophical traditions 19, 27
non-dualist theory of optics 35
Non-European Unity Movement 178
North American Civil Rights
  Movement 107
nuclear bombing. *See* Hiroshima–
  Nagasaki bombings

Öcalan, Abdullah
  anti-colonial struggle 243
  democratic confederalism (*see*
    democratic confederalism)
  dialogue with Turkish Government,
    failure of 237
  early years (*see* Öcalan, Abdullah, early
    years)
  freedom, individual *vs*
    community 255 n.3
  'imperialist colonial' form 218
  Kurdistan Workers' Party (PKK),
    founder 21, 213
  later years (*see* Öcalan, Abdullah, later
    years)
  new concept of liberation 213

Öcalan, Abdullah, early years
  double colonization of Kurdistan
    (*see* double colonization of
    Kurdistan)
  Kurdish state, formation of 227
  liberation of Kurds 220
  national democratic revolution 221
  PKK's manifesto 221–222
  resolution of national oppression
    222
  roots of Kemalism, challenging 220
Öcalan, Abdullah, later years
  Bookchin's ideas, influence on 223
  capitalist modernity, replacing with
    democratic modernity 227
  democratic nation (*see* democratic
    nation)
  domination and inequality in all
    nation-states 225
  feminism, lack of organizational
    base 224
  hierarchy and domination, cause of
    misery 230
  institutionalization of hierarchical
    relations 225
  Jineology, discourse on women's
    freedom 224
  Kurdish question (*see* Kurdish
    question)
  Middle East, free and egalitarian
    system 223
  Neolithic era, role of women 223
Öcalan's ideas
  democratic confederalism (*see*
    democratic confederalism)
  independent Kurdistan 219, 227
Öcalan's synthesis 243
Of Property (Locke, John) 85
O Homem na Estrada (The Man on the
  Road) 111
Okoth, Kevin Ochieng 182
Olho de Tigre (Tiger Eye), Djonga 101
O Menino Que Queria Ser Deus 116
ontogeny 63
ontological dualism 30, 31, 40
Oppenheimer, Robert 38
oppression
  of African American Women 170–1

of Black workers   164, 169, 170,
    173, 174
caste and patriarchal   155
of 'Negroes'   167
Orientalism
    and the distorted picture of
        India   142, 144
    and Islamophobia   56–7
    and 'West *vs* Rest' critique of European
        modernity   32

Palestinians
    dehumanization of   55, 58, 72
    freedom struggle   174
    Gaza War and ethnic cleansing   71
Palestinian women
    dehumanization of   3, 73, 75
    feminist silence on   74
    relation to the veil   71
    role in resistance to Israel   71–2
    sexualizing 'unveiling' of   73
Pan-African identity   106
Pan-Africanism
    assassinations to defeat militants
        175
    Carribean/West Indian Pan-
        Africanists   126, 127, 129
    dialectical tension between African
        identity and   209 n.13
    Fifth Pan-African Congress   127
Pan-Africanist(s)   126, 127, 129, 147, 190
Pancasila   5, 7
Pânico na Zona Sul (Panic in South São
        Paulo)   110
Pankhurst, Sylvia *(Workers
        Dreadnought)*   166
Party Central Committee   139
pedagogical practices in Rojava University
    Ba'ath regime and neoliberal
        models   249
    critical thinking, fostering of   250
    Department of Jineology   250–1
    domination of women,
        dismantling   250
    independent thinking,
        developing   249
    reproduction of truth, challenging
        colonial construction   250

summer schools, organization of   248,
    255 n.7
Women's Council or Student
    Council   245
pedagogy/pedagogies
    anti-colonial   249
    decolonial   101, 113, 114
    Eurocentric   113
    resistance of   236
People's Defence Units (YPG)   238, 239
People's National Congress (PNC)
    Forbes Linden Burnham, as
        leader   198
    paramountcy of the party   202
Phallocentrism
    in Fanon's *The Wretched of the
        Earth*   57
    in Muslim society   67
phylogeny   63
PineappleStormTV   101, 113, 114, 119
PKK. *See* Kurdistan Workers' Party
PNC. *See* People's National Congress
politics
    African   125, 126
    India and world politics   143
    Indian   150
    intersectional   157
    left   157
    revolutionary   141
    subcontinental   138, 142
    working class   148
    world   150
postcolonial Africa
    Cabral and class differentiation   133
    colonial ways of producing
        knowledge   205
    and decolonial scholarship   151,
        158 n.4
    future beyond the nightmare   151
    and nation states   151, 156, 230, 244
    postcolonial studies   14, 17, 90, 214
    reorganization of society and capitalist
        developmentalism   241
poverty of Indian masses   145, 155
power-knowledge   151
PPP. *See* Progressive People's Party
Présence Africaine   127
privilege, *a priori*   84

Progressive People's Party (PPP)   198
proletarianization theory (Trotter,
   Joe)   181
proletarian revolt   152
proletariat
   the Baku formulation   165
   the enslaved becoming a
      rural   208 n.7
   factories like modern proletariats   131
   proletarian revolution   152
   realities shaping the   180
   suffering of the underpaid   177
   wage-earning class as a modern   197
psychoanalytic tradition, Eurocentric   63
Punjabis   142

Quijano, Aníbal
   analysis of the works of   102
   coloniality, definition   12
   coloniality of power   103
   decolonization from coloniality of
      power   229
   global configuration of power   101
   on structures of modernist
      knowledge   10

Rabaka   107, 108, 111
race–class dynamic   181
race–class–gender nexus   206
Race Commission   200
race/s
   co-existence of different races in
      India   150
   and colonialism, Fanon on   56–7
   critical race theories/studies   15, 16
   identitarian politics in the Third World
      and the structural critique
      of   6–8
   inter-racial cooperation   145
   racial humiliation   141
   racialization   140
   racialized outsiders   140, 141
   scientific conception of   97 n.1
   structural critique of, in Anglo
      American academia   2–3
racial conflict in Guyana
   cultural differences as basis for
      hostilities   206
   new politics to meet the
      challenge   206–7
racial–gender politics. *See* feminists'
   responses to *Algeria Unveiled*
   and colonial violence   56, 57, 63,
      65, 66
   and dehumanization of Afghan
      women   55
   and dehumanization of Palestinian
      women   73, 75
   in the Gaza War   72–74
   veiling and unveiling of Algerian
      women   58–62, 67, 76 n.2
racialization   139, 140, 180, 229
racialized communities   156
racialized division of labour
   skilled Africans *vs* unskilled
      Indians   195
   super-exploitation of the workers   196
Racionais MC's   102, 110, 111, 120 n.2
racism. *See* anti-racism
   anti-Black/Asian   12, 15
   apartheid   15, 16, 179
   Black Panther Party and   3
   in CPUSA   165, 167, 169
   deracialization   4, 8
   Floyd, George   2
   institutional   1–3, 174
   L'Étudiant Noir (The Black
      Student)   106
   Olho de Tigre (Tiger Eye)   101
   relationship with colonialism   180
   reverse racism   113
   in Sao Paulo   111
   in segregation in everyday
      life   177, 178
   structural racism   117
   structural relations with
      capitalism   180–2, 185
   and super-exploitation   172, 173
   white   169
radical indigenism   88
radicalism
   diasporic radicals   146
   mass   151
   South Asian migrants   156
radicals, metropolitan   157
Rai, Lajpat   139

'rainbow constitution' 1
Rainey, Ma 106
Raio X do Brasil (Brazil X-ray) 111
Rampersaud, Anand 202
rap
  acronym for rhythm and poetry 108
  anti-hegemonic 108
  Brazilian rap 102, 10810
  expression of hip-hop 107–9
  Gustavo Pereira da Silva, aka Djonga (*see* Djonga)
  a miraculous weapon 109
  pedagogical power of 102
  Racionais MC's 110
  songs and albums 110, 111, 114, 115, 118, 119
  using word as vehicle for reflection 110
recognition
  colonial rules of 9
  'feeling side' of 96
  forms of 84, 91, 96
  Indian Act and rules of 89
  intra-community 93
  legal 91
  mis-recognition(s) and 84, 95
  political 83, 89, 93
  social identity 103
  statist forms of 96
  traditional Iroquois modalities of 91
  wrongful 92
Red Summer 166
Red Thread organisation
  power dynamics in 1990s, change in 205
  projects to help working women 204
  rural income generation, early focus 204
  valuing women's labour 204–5
reductionism, cultural 152
reification of racial politics 198
repression
  attempts by Indian government 156
  British Empire's 146, 149
revolution
  Algerian 56, 62–6, 68
  anti-colonial 63, 76
  Cromwell's 125
  democratic 168, 207, 221, 222
  French 125
  Grenada 128, 134
  intercontinental revolution 63
  Islamic 76 n.3
  Kurdistan 217, 222
  Russian (October) 129, 141, 164, 219
  second industrial 41
  socialist 140, 142, 147, 168, 173, 191
  Third World (*see* Third World Revolution)
  world socialist 140, 142
revolutionary struggle 67, 168, 172
Riddell, John 147, 166, 167
Riel Rebellion in Canada 92
Rio de Janeiro 112, 118
Rodney, Walter
  anti-imperialist class struggle 190
  assassination of 190, 203, 207
  association with James, C. L. R. 128–9
  assumed docility of Indian workers 198
  books for children to promote cooperation 203
  class struggle and capitalism 130–1, 208 n.3
  Djola and Balanta tribes 130, 131
  Europe's role in the slave trade 130
  'Free Village Movement' 194–5
  The Groundings with My Brothers 190, 209 n.13
  A History of the Guyanese Working People, 1881–1905 193, 197–8, 206
  A History of Upper Guinea Coast 128, 129, 193, 197, 208 n.6
  How Europe Underdeveloped Africa 131, 190
  indentured 'coolie labour' 195
  need for indentured workers, myth of 197
  racialized division of labour 195, 208 n.5
  rational political economy 196–7
  Rodney Riots in Jamaica 128–33
  slave-based economy to wage-based labour 191–2, 208 n.9

Walter Rodney Speaks: The Making of an African Intellectual 128
working-class unity 191
WPA launch 200–1
Rodney in colonial Guyana
  class struggle's spatial dimension 194
  democratic village councils, creation of 194
  endemic slave revolts 194
  Indian workers, import of 195
  racialized division of labour 195
  technological stagnation in fields 196
  village economy, unviable strategies 194–5, 208 n.7
Rodney Riots 128
Rojava Information Center 245
Rojava revolution
  anti-colonial struggle for liberation 236, 237, 251
  decolonization, meaning and practice 241
  democratic confederalism (*see* democratic confederalism)
  principles of 244
  role of UoR 245–6 (*see also* Rojava University)
  US–Rojava collaboration 239–40, 255 n.2
Rojava University (UoR)
  building free life, struggle for 236
  decolonial educational activities (*see* decolonization of the University)
  decolonization, the Western context 245
  emancipation, struggle for 244, 245
  English as preparation course 252–3
  establishment of 243
  faculties, students, administration 245–6
  Faculty of Political Science 235, 236, 245, 247, 249, 252
  geopolitics of higher education (*see* geopolitics of higher education in Rojava)
  hindering education (*see* hindering educational activities in Rojava)

knowledge structures 245
language in higher education 251–3
  (*see also* language in higher education in Rojava)
liberation, struggle for 237, 243
Mexmur refugee camp, students from 246, 255 n.4
pedagogical practices 248–50 (*see also* pedagogical practices in Rojava University)
RPD. *See* Dutt, Rajani Palme

Saha, Meghnad 44, 45
Said, Edward W
  anticolonial struggles, role of James, C. L. R. 134 n.1
  culturalist scholar of postcolonial studies 214
  on orientalism 56, 57, 59
  on Palestine 71
  pluralistic vision of the world 151
  Western fixation with gender 59
Saklatvala, Shapurji 143, 158 n.1
Santi, Paolo 163, 164
Sartre, Jean Paul
  the African's experience, rural *vs* city 177
  Black Orpheus 115
  on French occupation of Algeria 174–5
  La pensée politique de Patrice Emery Lumumba 177
  on Lumumba 175–8
  on Négritude movement 109, 115, 120 n.7
  on social attitude of white settlers 175
  on super-exploitation 177
  weapons of the colonizer 109, 120 n.7
schizophrenic existence 37
Science and Culture 45, 46
science in India
  post-independence 45–6
  at the time of Independence 44–5
Science Technology and Society (STS) studies 39

scientists. *See* Chomsky, Noam; Wiener, Nobert
  and the production of destructive knowledge   36–7
  Union of Concerned Scientists   38, 39, 49
Second Congress of the Comintern   148, 164
semiological theory and bimodal existence   29
semiology of civilization   34–5
Senghor, Léopold Sédar
  on choosing French for Negritude movement   108–9, 120 n.7
  literary-philosophical Negritude movement   127
  Pan-African identity, creation of   106
'Sex and Economics' (Mckay, Claude)   166
Shalhoub-Kevorkian on Palestinian women   71, 72
Sharpley-Whiting, Tracy Denean   67–8
Sikh–Canadian activist, assassination of   156
Six Nations   87, 97 n.2
slavery   128–33
socialism
  Dutt on deeper class understanding of   140
  Marx on socialism in Britain   148
  need for a new kind of   157
  perversion and distortion in British socialism   150
  Third World nationalism and   153
  Workers' sacrifices for the cause of   149
Socialist Review   137
Social Sciences and Humanities Research Council of Canada   90
society, pre-colonial   143, 152, 153
sociogeny   63
South Africa   1, 2, 4, 8
sovereignty/ies
  anthropological portraits of timelessness   82
  central to the lives of people   92
  involving the need to know ethnography   88
  and membership, political recognition and autonomy   93
  to protect, limit and entrench   91
  questions concerning just forms of   83
Stalin, Josef   164, 165, 168
Stalin–Bukharin hegemonic perspective   168
stereotypes
  racial/racist   117, 119
  white man's image   115
The 'Structural Location of Blackness'   181
structural roots of disunity
  common ground, insufficient development of   197
  divide-and-rule politics of PNC   202
  embedding and leveraging of divisions   189
  race to the bottom   191
  strategies of capital accumulation   189
Sunca, Jan Yasin   21, 241–4
super-exploitation. *See* labour super-exploitation
suppression
  beliefs, ideas, images, symbols and knowledge   103
  cultural   101
  ontological   116
Syrian Arab nationalism
  American presence, and the   238
  'indivisible integrity' discourse   237
  replication in Rojava   237
  Rojava revolution (*see* Rojava revolution)
  total submission of Turks, demand for   238

tactics for labour super-exploitation
  Andaiye, and the gender dimension   190
  Marini in Brazil and Chile   191–3
  Rodney in Guyana   196
Tanzania. *See* Ujamaa
Tejel, Jordi   216, 238, 242
territories of the familiar   86–8
Third Worldism   2
Third World nationalism   153, 155

Third World revolution
  Fanon's theorization 56
  intellectual traditions of the anti-colonial thinkers of the 15
  revolutionary spirit of Algerian women and the 75–6
  women's revolutionary consciousness in the 58
Thobani, Sunera
  anti-Islam discourses 56–7
  devastations of Afghan population 70
  Fanon's *Algeria Unveiled* 56
  fixation with the veil and feminist politics 68–9
  racial gendered dehumanization 55
  role of violence in colonial relations 19
Trade unionists 146
trade union solidarity 143, 149
triple oppression of Black women 170–2
Trotz, Alissa 191, 198, 202, 210
Truth
  and reality, dualism of 30, 31, 40
  as socially constructed 40
  and values 44
Turkey, Iran, Iraq and Syria
  assimilation of Kurds into the nation 237
  colonial practices, reproduced 237
Turkey, Iraq and Syria, last partition
  initial reactions of the Kurds 216
  oppression of the Kurds 217
Turkish nationalism against the Kurds 237

Uberoi, Jit Pal S.
  architecture of science knowledge and violence 28
  critique of European modernity 28–35 (*see also* European Modernity)
  The European Modernity: Science, Truth and Method 27
  explanation of European Modernity 29–31
  Indian science, the two roads 44–7
  Indian sociologist 19
  non-dualist critique of European Modernity 32–5
  problem with European Modernity 31–2
  science and scientists, producers of knowledge 36–40
  states and corporations, users of knowledge 28, 40–4
  unity of knowledge, values and action 47–9
Ujamaa 5, 7
Unequal Trade theories 4
UNESCO 4, 46, 47
UNIA. *See* Universal Negro Improvement Association'
Union of Concerned Scientists 38, 39, 49
United Nations 4, 72, 89
Universal Negro Improvement Association' (UNIA) 169
University of Rojava (UoR). *See* Rojava University
unveiling
  of Algerian women, veiling and 58–62, 67, 76 n.2
  Algerian women and dynamism of the veil 76 n.3, 76 n.4, 77
  of Palestinian women, sexualizing 73
UoR. *See* Rojava University
uranium, use of 36, 45
urban-rural dilemma 132
US Capitalist Racist Society 181
US Empire
  colonialism and the 12, 13
  critiques of the 15, 16
  protests against the 18
  racial–colonial violence and the 76
US imperialism and Afghan women 70

veil. *See* fetishization of the veil; Unveiling
  in the Afghan war 69–70, 74
  Algerian women and dynamism of the 76 n.3, 76 n.4, 77
  al-Saji on Western obsession with 70
  de-orientalizing approach to 56
  dynamism of the 76 n.3, 76 n.4
  Fanon on Algerian women and the 59–64, 75

French sexual obsession with
the 59–60
Gaza war and silence on the 55, 71
orientalizing European
approach to 65
Palestinian women's relation to
the 71
use by Iranian women 76 n.3
Western feminists on *Algeria
Unveiled* 64–9
veiled Phallic Mother 67
violence
against Blacks 118, 119
colonial 13, 18, 19, 105, 113
dehumanization as (see
dehumanization)
economic 41, 105
imperialist 3, 69
incitation of 113, 116, 117
police 2, 12
power and 102, 103
racial–colonial 66, 76
racial/racist 106, 114
state 13, 16
and whiteness 114, 116
voice and sovereignty 82
Voz Ativa (Active Voice) 110, 111

Walsh, Catherine E 236, 240
*Walter Rodney Speaks: The Making of an
African Intellectual* 128. See
also Rodney, Walter
warfare. See uranium
and 3C technologies 37–8, 40
chemical and biological 41–3
industrial 40–1
modern 36
total war 40
transformed by technologies 37, 40
war on terror
9/11: attack on Western
civilization 69
attack on Afghanistan 69
consequences for 'decolonization' and
the 'decolonial' 12, 13, 18
Gaza War 71
and gender–racial politics 55
and Islamophobia 55–7

Western Feminists
on Fanon's '*Algeria Unveiled*' 64–9
and representation of Afghan
women 69–70
silence on Palestinian women 74, 75
West Indians 127, 128
Westmaas, Nigel
African mine workers' strike 199
intense class conflicts 191
joint assault on imperialist
property 199–200
Red Thread organization 203
subjugation to PNC and
Burnham 202
WPA, formation of 198, 200–1
West *vs* Rest critique 33, 35, 47–8
white boy 114–16
White Labour aristocracy 144
white man 109, 111, 115
whiteness
lyrical rage against 113
of social sciences 15
university's 17
white privilege 167, 171
Wiener, Nobert 37–8
Williams, Henry Sylvester (Pan-
Africanist) 126
Wilmot, Blyden, Edward (Pan-
Africanist) 126
Women, Race and Class (Davis,
Angela) 173
Women's Defence Units (YPJ) 238, 239
workers. See African Society for Cultural
Relations with Independent
Africa (ASCRIA)
difference in wages in South African
white and Black 179, 183
indentured (girmitiya) from
India 195, 197
racialized division of labour 192,
195, 206
unification of 199, 201, 202, 204, 207
Workers Dreadnought (Pankhurst,
Sylvia) 166
working-class solidarity 140
working conditions 145, 179
Working People's Alliance (WPA)
aim to unite working peoples 201

Burnham's 'democracy' challenge to   203
campaign to defend PPP activist Rampersaud   202
formation in 1974   200–1
Red Thread's formation in 1986   201
Rodney's books for children   202–3
uprising and suppression   202
Working People's Vanguard Party (WPVP)   200

World Bank   7, 155
WPVP. *See* Working People's Vanguard Party
The Wretched of the Earth (Fanon, Frantz)   57, 104, 175, 252

Yadirgi, Veli   215, 216
YPG. *See* People's Defence Units

Zumoff, Jacob   164–6, 169, 170